全国高等院校法律英语专业统编教材
法律英语证书（LEC）全国统一考试指定用书

法律英语
精读教程

上

Legal English
Intensive Reading Course

张法连　主编

北京大学出版社
PEKING UNIVERSITY PRESS

图书在版编目(CIP)数据

法律英语精读教程.上/张法连主编.—北京:北京大学出版社,2016.8
(全国高等院校法律英语专业统编教材)
ISBN 978-7-301-27269-5

Ⅰ.①法… Ⅱ.①张… Ⅲ.①法律—英语—教材 Ⅳ.①H31

中国版本图书馆 CIP 数据核字(2016)第 159117 号

书　　　名	法律英语精读教程(上)
	FALÜ YINGYU JINGDU JIAOCHENG (SHANG)
著作责任者	张法连　主编
策 划 编 辑	郭栋磊
责 任 编 辑	刘　爽
标 准 书 号	ISBN 978-7-301-27269-5
出 版 发 行	北京大学出版社
地　　　址	北京市海淀区成府路 205 号　100871
网　　　址	http://www.pup.cn　新浪微博:@北京大学出版社
电 子 邮 箱	编辑部 pupwaiwen@pup.cn　总编室 zpup@pup.cn
电　　　话	邮购部 62752015　发行部 62750672　编辑部 62759634
印 刷 者	北京溢漾印刷有限公司
经 销 者	新华书店
	787 毫米×1092 毫米　16 开本　26.5 印张　462 千字
	2016 年 8 月第 1 版　2025 年 4 月第 8 次印刷
定　　　价	68.00 元

未经许可,不得以任何方式复制或抄袭本书之部分或全部内容。
版权所有,侵权必究
举报电话:010-62752024　电子邮箱:fd@pup.cn
图书如有印装质量问题,请与出版部联系,电话:010-62756370

前　言

　　法律英语是法律科学与英语语言学有机结合形成的一门实践性很强的交叉学科,是 ESP(English for Specific Purposes)最重要的分支之一。法律英语是以普通英语为基础,在立法和司法等活动中形成和使用的具有法律专业特点的语言,是指表述法律科学概念以及诉讼或非诉讼法律实务时所使用的英语。当今世界的发展日新月异,经济全球化进程突飞猛进,国际交流合作日益加强,涉外法务活动空前频繁。十八届四中全会提出要加强涉外法律工作,运用法律手段维护国家的发展利益。经济全球化过程中我们所面临的很多问题其实都是法律问题,而这些法律问题中的绝大多数又都属于涉外法律的工作范畴,所有这些工作都需要法律工作者通过专业外语完成。国家急需明晰国际法律规则、通晓英语语言的"精英明法"复合型人才,法律英语的重要性日益彰显,掌握专业外语已经成为法律人必备的职业素质。法律英语证书(LEC)全国统一考试的成功推出和中央政法委、教育部"卓越法律人才计划"的顺利启动无疑把法律英语的学习和研究推向了高潮。

　　法律英语是高校英语、法学等专业教学改革的新方向。随着高校英语专业教学改革不断深化,国内许多高校在外语院系开设了法律英语课程,有的院系设置了法律英语方向,有些高校大胆创新,开始尝试设置法律英语专业,收到了良好的社会效果。2013年高等教育出版社出版发行《法律英语专业教学大纲》,标志着法律英语专业的诞生,给高校外语院系设置法律英语专业指明了方向。本套教材正是以该大纲为重要依据编写而成。

　　美国法是英美法系的典型代表,其法律体系完整、内容丰富,既有传统的普通法,又有新兴的成文法;既有统一的联邦法,又有各州的法律。同时,美国法在世界范围内影响深远,学习研究美国法意义重大,这不仅表现为许多国家都在研究美国的法律规则,借鉴其成熟做法,还表现为许多国际公约也参照美国法的理念、原则、规则制定。因此,本书作为法律英语专业的精读教材,主要介绍美国法,希望学生通过学习权威、实用的美国法律知识,掌握地道、纯正的法律英语。一般的语言教材都会系统地讲授语法知识,但本书认为法律英语的学习者应当已经完成了基础阶段的普通英语学习,系统掌握了英语语法等基础知识并具有了一定的词汇量。

本套教材共包括《法律英语精读教程》《法律英语泛读教程》《法律英语写作教程》《法律英语翻译教程》和《法律英语文化教程》，以及配套学习使用的《英美法律术语双解》。

编写本书的过程中，编者参考了大量的美国原版法学书籍，包括美国法学院教材及大量判例，力求实现教材内容的权威性和丰富性。本书引用了许多极具代表性的英文案例。英美法系是判例法系，无论是法官还是律师都特别注重对判例的研究，因此学习美国法不能绕过案例，通过研究案例更有利于掌握标准的法律英语，也更容易掌握美国法的精髓。本书选取了几十个经典案例，以期最大程度地展现美国法原貌。

本书力求内容丰富，可读性强，几乎涉及了法律英语的听、说、读、写、译的各个方面。本书在每部分或各章后面都附有相关的练习题，以期帮助学生检查自己对基础美国法知识和英美法律文化知识以及法律英语读写基本能力的掌握程度。教材在编写上遵循由总述到具体、由浅入深的原则，基本上达到《法律英语专业教学大纲》提出的目标要求。

本书共由两部分组成。第一部分是英美法律文化知识简介。语言是文化的载体，法律文化知识是法律英语学习过程中不可或缺的内容；第二部分分别对美国六个主干部门法（美国宪法、合同法、侵权法、财产法、证据法、刑法/刑事诉讼法）基本内容进行概括介绍并选取典型案例诠释有关知识点。这两部分内容浑然一体，又相互独立。学习本教材不一定要严格按前后编写顺序进行，教师完全可以根据学生的具体情况挑选合适的内容安排教学。

编写本书过程中，我们参考了大量国内外有关资料，在此谨对原作者表示谢忱。参加本书编写工作的还有北京外国语大学郑小军教授、中国石油大学徐文斌副教授、甘肃政法学院唐丽玲教授、河南工业大学杜巧阁副教授、聊城大学胡朝丽副教授等。感谢法律英语证书（LEC）全国统一考试指导委员会将该套教材指定为复习应考 LEC 的参考用书。

各位教师或同学在使用本书的过程中有什么问题，欢迎及时与编者联系：zhangbook16@yahoo.com。

编者
2016 年 3 月于中国政法大学

CONTENTS

≪ Part One Anglo-American Legal Culture

Chapter 1	Historical Development of the Common Law	003
Chapter 2	The Doctrine of Stare Decisis and Ratio Decidendi or Holding of a Case	014
Chapter 3	Federal Courts and What They Do	023
Chapter 4	The Opinions of the Appellate Courts and Precedents	047

≪ Part Two Introduction to American Laws

Constitutional Law   055

Chapter 1	The Judicial Power	057
Chapter 2	Legislative Power	063
Chapter 3	Executive Power	068
Chapter 4	Individual Guarantees Against Governmental or Private Action	072
Chapter 5	Due Process	074
Chapter 6	Equal Protection	077
Chapter 7	Fundamental Rights	082
Chapter 8	The First Amendment	085

Contracts   102

Chapter 1	Basics of Contracts	104
Chapter 2	Contract Formation	108
Chapter 3	Capacity of a Contract	127

Chapter 4	Vitiating Factors	130
Chapter 5	Discharge	145
Chapter 6	Breach of Contract	150
Chapter 7	Remedies for Breach of Contract	153

Torts — 164

Chapter 1	Intentional Torts	166
Chapter 2	Defenses to Intentional Torts	173
Chapter 3	Negligence	177
Chapter 4	Cause in Fact	185
Chapter 5	Proximate Cause	188
Chapter 6	Multiple Tortfeasors	191
Chapter 7	Damages for Personal Injuries	193
Chapter 8	Limited Duties: Special Limitations on the Scope of Duty	198
Chapter 9	Premises Liability: Duties of Owners and Occupiers of Land	203
Chapter 10	Defenses	210
Chapter 11	Vicarious Liability	220
Chapter 12	Products Liability	226
Chapter 13	Defamation	231
Chapter 14	Competitive Torts	234

Property Law — 244

Chapter 1	Acquisition of Property	246
Chapter 2	Possessory Estates	249
Chapter 3	Future Interests	252
Chapter 4	Concurrent Estates	255
Chapter 5	Landlord and Tenant	259
Chapter 6	Fixtures	263
Chapter 7	Rights in the Land of Another—Easements, Profits, Covenants, and Servitudes	265
Chapter 8	Conveyancing	270
Chapter 9	Cooperatives, Condominiums, Zoning and Nuisance	281

Evidence Law — 289

Chapter 1	General Considerations	291
Chapter 2	Relevance and Judicial Notice	294
Chapter 3	Real Evidence	299

Chapter 4	Documentary Evidence	302
Chapter 5	Testimonial Evidence	306
Chapter 6	The Hearsay Rule	322
Chapter 7	Procedural Considerations	331

Criminal Law 342

Chapter 1	Basics of Criminal Law	344
Chapter 2	How Defendants' Mental States Affect Their Responsibility for a Crime	350
Chapter 3	Criminal Offenses	356
Chapter 4	Implications of a Crime's Classification	360

Criminal Procedure 367

Chapter 1	Exclusionary Rule	369
Chapter 2	Fourth Amendment	372
Chapter 3	Confessions	378
Chapter 4	Pre-Trial Procedures	382
Chapter 5	Trial	387
Chapter 6	Guilty Pleas and Plea Bargaining	395
Chapter 7	Constitutional Rights in Relation to Sentence and Punishment	399
Chapter 8	Constitutional Problems on Appeal and Rights During Punishment	403
Chapter 9	Double Jeopardy	406
Chapter 10	Forfeiture Actions	410

References 416

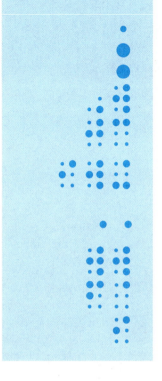

Anglo–American Legal Culture

Part One

Chapter 1

Historical Development of the Common Law

导 读 <<

"普通法"亦称"不成文法"或"案例法",对于大陆法系的法律工作者而言这是一个怪诞的概念:它既不是"普通"的法,又不是"普遍通用"的法(除英语国家外);它虽称"不成文",可又有永远读不完的案例。

当诺曼底人以武力征服英格兰时,他们得到的仅仅是王位和朝廷,在乡下,人们处理实际纠纷时所依据的还是传统的标准,由于交通和信息交流的不便,各地法庭所采取的标准由于历史沿革、民族传统和生活习惯的不同而有很大差别,导致了相同的问题往往会因不同的判断标准产生不同的判决结果。当上诉到"国王的法庭"时,便逐渐产生通过文字记录法官的思考过程以确立统一标准的制度。

其"普通"的意义在于:法是独立于个人感情和情感意识之外的客观标准,不能人为创造而只能发现,不受时间和地域限制而普遍适用的行为准则。

所谓"不成文"是指这些客观原则并非以法条的文字形式公之于众,而是在法官确立原则的推理过程中记录于"法庭意见"。其可取之处在于,这些原则可以在不断变换的客观环境中实时得到完善,错误的判决可以通过上诉得到纠正,经过时间检验的标准可以上升为立法,从而避免了成文法体系中的"法律滞后"问题。

本章还介绍了英美法体系中独特的"衡平"制度对于法律制度的完善和补充作用。

Part One Anglo-American Legal Culture

The common law system came into being, historically, in England largely as the result of the activity of the royal courts of justice after the Norman Conquest. In England, first, there were Germanic laws during the Anglo-Saxon period. Though England was ruled by a single monarch, the law in force was still made up of strictly local customs. With the Norman Conquest, the period of tribal rule was finished and feudalism installed. Gradually, through the **institutionalization**[①] of the royal courts and the extension of their **jurisdiction**[②], a body of laws called the common law applied to the whole country came into being. There is also a dissenting view that common law is also royal law; the basic characteristics of much of the common law can be traced back to royal legislation.

There are four distinct periods:

First, Pre-Norman Period

This is the period when different tribes of Germanic origins(Saxons, Jutes, Danes and Angles) divided up England. These tribes applied local customs for dispute resolution.

Second, Formation of the Common Law (1066—1485): From Writs to Actions on the Case

The Norman Conquest brought about a strong and centralized administrative organization. With it, the period of tribal rules was finished and feudalism installed. The highly organized character of English feudalism prepared the way for the development of the common law. The following are some of the most important developments.

(1) County and Local Courts

The hundred local or country courts that applied local custom were gradually replaced by new feudal courts that still applied the same local customary law. But how could the highly organized character of the feudal

---

① 制度化
② 管辖权

system of government and the establishment of feudal courts help the development of the common law since the new feudal courts applied also local customary law? What was done is that in either case, the applicable law or rule was extended to all the people in the jurisdiction.

(2) Jurisdiction of Royal Courts—Restricted Reach

The creation of the commune ley, an English law truly common to the whole of England, was to be the exclusive work of the royal courts of justice.

At first, the King only exercised "high justice." The Curia Regis, from which the King dispensed justice assisted by his closest officials and highest ranking persons, was a court for only the important personalities and disputes.

Feudal barons resisted the jurisdiction of royal courts. Certain parts of the Curia Regis gradually became autonomous bodies and established their seats at Westminster.

Royal courts had jurisdiction only over Royal finance, ownership and possession of land, and serious crimes.

(3) Extension of Royal Jurisdiction

Reasons for extension included: more cases meant more fees for the kingdom, people viewed the royal courts superior to feudal courts, only royal courts had the means to summon witnesses and to enforce judgments, and only the King, apart from the church, could require the swearing of an oath. Royal courts followed modern procedures and availed of the verdict of a jury.

(4) Writs

Until 1875, the royal courts remained special courts to which the citizen had no automatic access. The person who pressed a claim had first of all to address his request to an important royal official, the Chancellor, asking him to deliver a writ. A writ is simply another term for a court order. The effect of a writ was to enable the royal courts to be seized of the matter upon the payment of fees. It was not automatic that a writ would be issued. The judges had to be convinced to take up the matter complained. Each instance had to be individually examined. The list of established situations where writs were granted automatically was slow to grow.

Nonetheless, the list grew and increased over times. Neither should the extension of royal jurisdiction be measured by such increase nor was caused by the passage of the Statute of Westminster II of 1285. That statute authorized the Chancellor to deliver writs in *consimilicasu* (in instances having great similarity to others for which the delivery of the writ was already established). The reasonable explanation for the extension over times is to accommodate increasing social needs.

(5) Actions on the Case

What is significant and decisive is the appreciation by the royal courts of the significance of the declaration made by the plaintiff explaining the details of the facts of the cases. And this led to the admission by the royal courts of their jurisdiction over new factual situations or instances because of the compelling nature of the moral and justice issues. In time, these admissible actions multiplied and were given special titles in the light of the facts which justified them—actions of **assumpsit**[①], deceit, **trover**[②], negligence, and so on. These actions may be generally classified under three headings: trespass to land, trespass to goods, and trespass to the person. Trover is defined as a common law action to recover the value of personal property illegally converted by another to his or her own use. In old French, trover means find.

Third: Growth of Equity (1485—1832)

(1) Emergence of Equity

The strict compliance with formalist procedure exposed the common law to two dangers: that of not developing with sufficient freedom to meet the needs of the period and that the dangers of becoming paralyzed because of the conservatism of the legal world of the time.

Unfortunately, these shortcomings of the royal courts could not be rectified or corrected by other courts that had general jurisdiction, for these courts were themselves in decline and gradually disappeared from the scene.

The situation led to the eventuality that in a number of cases, no just solution could be found. In seeking another way of obtaining redress, a direct

---

① 约定,允诺;口头合同;违约诉讼
② 追索侵占物诉讼

appeal to the King, the fountain of all justice and favor, was the logical and natural option.

In cases of no solution or shocking solution, people addressed the King asking him to intervene as an act of royal grace to satisfy conscience and as a work of brotherly love. As the King's confessor, the Chancellor had the responsibility of guiding the King's conscience and would, if he thought it appropriate, transmit the request to the King for judgment in his council.

In other countries, the judges themselves could supply the required remedy by prohibiting the abuse of a right or fraud, or by applying the principle of public order and good morals; such remedies were possible on the European continent within the very framework of the legal principles. In England, however, the royal courts did not have the same freedom of action because they had never had the same general jurisdiction and were bound to observe rigid procedures.

This recourse to the royal prerogative, perfectly justifiable and unopposed so long as it remained exceptional, could not fail to give rise to a conflict when it became institutionalized and developed into a system of legal rules set up in opposed to the common law.

Gradually request for intervention by the Chancellor became more frequent; the practice became institutionalized. At the time of the Wars of the Roses (1453—1485), the Chancellor became a more and more autonomous judge deciding alone in the name of King and his council. Decisions were made on the basis of "the equity of the case." Equitable doctrines grew out of the chancellor's decisions. These worked to add to and correct the legal principles applied by the royal courts.

After 1529, the Chancellor no longer served as confessor to the sovereign and was not an ecclesiastic① but examined the petitions addressed to him as a real judge and observed a written procedure inspired by Canon law. The substantive principles he applied were also largely taken from Roman law and Canon law rather than the very often archaic and outmoded common law rules.

A number of legal institutions (the principal one being the trust) and

---

① 神职人员,牧师

concepts such as misrepresentation, undue influence, specific performance, and subrogation were developed in the Chancellor's equitable jurisdiction.

In all of these matters, the intervention of the Chancellor is discretionary. He only intervened if it was considered that the conduct of the defendant was contrary to conscience, and if the plaintiff had no cause for reproaching himself; he, on his side, had to have "clean hands" and must have acted without undue delay in asserting his right.

The English sovereigns favored the chancellors' jurisdiction due to their concern for justice and good administration. The procedure of Chancery was private, written and inquisitorial in nature and also preferred by a monarch of authoritarian disposition.

As the chancellor applied Roman law, this worked to reduce the law to a simple private law and lawyer's work. And all these features helped give a greater scope to royal absolutism and executive discretion.

The risk is that the success of the Chancellor's equitable jurisdiction and the decay of the common law carried potentially the seed of a danger that disputing parties would eventually abandon the common law court.

(2) Conflict and Compromise Between Common Law and Equity

The royal courts and the common law lawyers resisted the encroachment by the Chancellor on their jurisdiction and the Chancery's continuing expansion.

To defend their position and work, and to support them against royal absolution, the Common law courts also found an ally in Parliament. The organization of Chancery, its congestion and venality (that is, association with corruption or bribery) were also used as effective weapons.

A compromise was finally reached and pronounced by James I. The common law courts and the courts of Chancellor worked side by side in a kind of equilibrium of power.

Specifically, no new <u>encroachments</u>① at the expense of the common law courts by the Chancery were allowed. The Chancellor would continue to adjudicate according to its precedents, not morality alone and arbitrary. The king also agreed he would no longer use his prerogative to create new courts

---

① 侵入,侵占,侵害

Chapter 1
Historical Development of the Common Law

independent of the established common law courts. The Chancellor, as a legal or political figure, was no longer seen as judging on the basis of morality alone and tended to act more and more as a true judge. Further, after 1621, the control of the House of Lords over the decision of the Court of Chancery was admitted.

Over the centuries, the rules of Equity became as strict and as legal as the rules of the common law. Today, the body of rules developed in Equity is an integral part of English law. The reasons formerly justifying the intervention of the Chancellor no longer exist; if English law is in need of remedial measures, there is Parliament. The security of legal relations and the supremacy of the law would be threatened if judges were allured to bring the rules of established law back into question under the pretext of equity.

Yet, key distinctions between law and equity remain important today. Among the distinctive features of a suit in equity as opposed to an action at law were:

• The absence of jury—the judge instead of a jury is the exclusive decision-maker in equity;

• Court of equity follows a more flexible procedure;

• It enjoys a wider scope of review on appeal;

• While the law courts were generally restricted to the award of money damages as a relief, equity operated on the person of the defendant (equity acts in personam). The court of equity could, for example, issue an injunction, forbidding a particular breach of promise of an obligation, or it could decree specific performance of obligation. A defendant who disobeyed could be punished by fine or by imprisonment for contempt of court until compliance;

• In the beginning at least, the Chancery was not considered a court, it did not appear to be deciding "in law";

• Even the terminology adopted by the Chancery's court bears witness to the distinction. The procedure before the court is a "suit," not an "action"; one invokes "interests," not "rights"; the Chancery grants a "decree" not a "judgment"; he may award "compensation," not "damages."

Fourth: The Modern Period

(1) Duality Versus Unity in Action: Fusion or Merger of the Common Law and Equity

Before 1873—1875, in any one dispute, it might have been necessary to institute two actions: one before a common law court, the other in Chancery. Such, for example, was the case, if in addition to the specific performance of a contract (a remedy obtained in Equity), damages for the delay in the performance of the contract (a remedy obtained at common law) were also wanted.

The 19th and 20th centuries are periods of fundamental transformation. Legislation brought about reform and modernization. Adjudication is free of formalistic procedural framework of forms of action. Greater attention is devoted to substantive law. Rules of established law are systematic and re-organized.

Judicial organization was greatly changed by the Judicature Acts of 1873—1875, which removed the formal distinction between common law courts and the court of the Chancellor. The Acts did not change the law as it stood before but merely enabled common law and Equity to be administered concurrently by the same courts. By virtue of the Acts, all English courts became empowered to apply the rules of common law as well as those of Equity.

Equity is a body of rules that were given effect by the Chancery to correct English law in the course of history. Today, it is an integral part of English law. In the High Court of Justice, some judges sitting in the Queen's Bench Division decide according to the oral and contradictory procedures of traditional common law, and others sitting in the Chancery Division, decide cases according to the written, inquisitorial procedures derived from the old Equity proceedings.

The same barrister does not plead in both divisions; the tradition of being either a "common lawyer" or an "Equity lawyer" persists.

As to the assigning of subject matters to one or another of the divisions of the High Court, the historical origin of the law to be applied is no longer of any importance. What is decisive is which of these two procedures is most appropriate in the circumstances. Equity now includes that a series of subjects in which it appears appropriate to proceed by way of written procedures; whereas the common law comprises those in which the oral procedures of the past are retained.

Generally speaking, today, in order to know whether one is within the area of the common law or that of Equity, it is more important to know which branch of law is involved rather than what sanction is available. These two branches of law are made up of certain number of subject matters and characterized by the use of a definite procedure and marked by their own juristic attitude. Common law thus comprises criminal law, the law of contract and torts; but the common lawyers apply equally doctrines as misrepresentation, undue influence and estoppel. Equity includes the law of real property, trusts, partnerships, bankruptcy, the interpretation of wills and the winding up of estates.

The United States adopted the dual system of law and equity along with the general principles of the common law system. The courts at both the federal level and the state level perform the dual function of law and equity.

(2) Landmarks in the History of the Development of English Law

13th century was the formative period of the common law;

16th century is the formative period of Equity;

17th and 18th centuries is the period of Harmonization;

18th and half century is the absorption of the law merchant.

(3) Lessons Learned from the Historical Development of the Common Law in England

Many conclusions may be drawn from the study of historical development of the common law in England. The following observations are offered as a starter for further analysis and study.

• The way of the birth and growth of the common law in England appears to reflect the general trend of political development of most societies in the West during that period. This is manifested in the acquisition of a superior and dominant status by the royal courts of the kingdom at the sacrifice of feudal courts and tribal courts as well as a law that is generally and commonly applicable to people throughout the kingdom.

• The system of law as demonstrated in the emerge of the court of equity and its fusion with the common law court into one hierarchical structure and the development of a scheme of procedure and remedies to meet the different and growing needs serve to satisfy the expectations of justice, fairness and equality.

Part One Anglo-American Legal Culture

• We witness the progressive development of the law over time. Both the legal system and the system of laws make themselves more complete and perfect.

Exercises

Please choose the best answer to the following questions:

1. The common law system came into _____, historically, in England largely as the result of the activity of the royal courts of justice after the Norman Conquest.
   A. life   B. name   C. existence   D. been
2. Royal courts had _____ only over Royal finance, ownership and possession of land, and serious crime.
   A. authority   B. autonomy   C. action   D. auspices
3. The effect of a writ was to _____ the royal courts to be seized of the matter upon the payment of fees.
   A. embody   B. ensure   C. entrust   D. empower
4. In other countries, the _____ themselves could supply the required remedy by prohibiting the abuse of a right or fraud, or by applying the principle of public order and good morals.
   A. courts   B. governments   C. parties   D. laws
5. Gradually request for intervention by the Chancellor became more frequent, and the practice became _____.
   A. constitutionalized   B. established
   C. commercialized   D. systemized
6. The Chancellor, as a legal or political figure, was no longer seen as judging on the basis of _____ alone and tended to act more and more as a true judge.
   A. morals   B. mutuality   C. correctness   D. conscience
7. While the law courts were generally restricted to the award of money _____ as a relief, equity operated on the person of the defendant.
   A. injuries   B. compensation   C. payback   D. collection
8. Judicial organization was greatly changed by removing the _____ distinction between common law courts and the court of the Chancellor.

Chapter 1
Historical Development of the Common Law

    A. ceremonial   B. formal   C. significant   D. judicial

9. The United States adopted the _____ system of law and equity along with the general principles of the common law system.

    A. bilateral   B. bidirectional   C. bifurcated   D. bicentennial

10. The way of the birth and growth of the common law in England appears to reflect the general _____ of political development of most societies in the West during that period.

    A. tendency   B. inclination   C. result   D. sentiment

Chapter 2

The Doctrine of Stare Decisis and Ratio Decidendi or Holding of a Case

导 读 《《

普通法的基本原则,如"遵循先例"不仅体现在法官判案的过程中,也体现在立法和行政程序中,这是普通法中的方法论。

在法庭判决意见书中,法官通常会先阐述相关事实,在此基础上,指出诉讼双方的一个或多个争议焦点,并分别提出解决争议所应该依赖的法律原则。如果有成文法依据,法官应首先遵循成文法;如果没有成文法,法官应当遵循相同或相似事实类型的在先判例;如果都没有,法官还可以参照其他法院的判例或权威学者的论述。如果没有任何可依赖的依据,则该案可以被视为"首例"(case of first impression),而法官可以根据任何可以找到的依据(如逻辑推理、其他相关案例、权威著述,等等),从而确立一个新的普通法原则。

因此可以说,一起案件中争议焦点的背景事实是确定法律依据的重要参数;同时,这也决定了判例的适用范围。

Chapter 2
The Doctrine of Stare Decisis and Ratio Decidendi or Holding of a Case

The justifications commonly given for the doctrine may be summarized in four words: equality, predictability, economy, and respect. Equality argues that the applications of the same rule to successive similar cases results in equality of treatment for all coming before the courts. Consistent following of precedents contributes to predictability in future disputes. Economy requires the use of established criteria to settle new cases to save time and energy. Adherence to earlier decisions show due respect for the wisdom and experience of prior generations of judges. Computer storage and retrieval of legal information provides a massive amount of relevant/applicable cases and arms lawyers with a rich base of sources of law in argument and persuasion, which judges must consider and take into account in decision and stipulating ratio decidendi.

The doctrine of stare decisis rests mainly on the assumption that a "case in point" has "binding authority" over the issues in a case to be decided. Binding authority, to which the doctrine of precedent does apply, includes decisions of higher courts of the same jurisdiction and decisions of the same court.

The doctrine of stare decisis closely relates to the concept of the holding of a case or ratio decidendi and whether or not a holding is narrowly or broadly cast in terms of the fact-situation involved in the case.

Transforming Facts into Binding Legal Rules

The holding of a case or **ratio decidendi**① can be further cast in the form of a legal rule.

Judges must in making decision take into account the facts of the case and then generalize from those facts as far as the statement of the court and the circumstances indicate is desirable. Facts permeate the structure of the common law and often accede themselves to the rank of legal rules.

How could a general statement of facts by a judge become a legal rule? Doesn't this mean "what it is" amounts to or counts as "what ought to be?" What is the **alchemy**② in the process of normative transformation? Is judge alchemist?

---

① 〈拉〉法律原则,判决理由
② 魔力,神秘方法

Not just judges transform facts into legal rules. Other branches of the government perform this trick, too. One could also ask: Is the legislature e.g., the United States Congress, or a government agency, or a federal official, an alchemist of legislation essentially formulated on the basis of facts and happenings, past, present and projected? There is a simple answer to this question. Congress is authorized by the Constitution to make laws and the Department of Transportation, for example, is to make rules under the enabling law. H. L. A. Hart offers a theoretical answer by crafting an innovative idea that every legal system has rules of recognition that validate what the law is. In the United States, by virtue of the Supremacy Clause of the Constitution, a valid discretionary act by a single federal administrative official is not only recognized as law, it even prevails over a conflicting provision enshrined in a state constitution.

Other theories have been advanced to justify the transformation of an "is" as an "ought." According to the popular progressive view, any effective power holders (socially allocated) can make law however it is based. Whether or not what is proposed or the "law" as projected is authoritative and effective is another question.

In Search of an Ideal Holding or Ratio Decidendi of a Case

The holding of a case must be determined from an analysis of the material facts, from the decisions, and from the reasoning of the opinion. Even this may be more difficult than would seem to be at least. It is often hard to know how far the process of abstraction should be continued.

There are some problems and difficulties in stating with precision the holding (ratio decidendi) of an appellate court—the core of the opinion that represents the propositions of law that will be binding on lower courts.

Factors compounding the formulation of ratio include:

First, each judge is free to enter a dissenting or different strand of reasoning for the decision.

Second, courts are not supposed to declare authoritative legal generalities in the abstract. Propositions of law must be connected and related to the facts of the dispute that judges are adjudicating, and the holding of a case can lonely be

Chapter 2
The Doctrine of Stare Decisis and Ratio Decidendi or Holding of a Case

stated in term of its essential facts. But what facts are essential or most important is neither **preordained**① nor obvious.

Third, what is more difficult is to decide how broad or how narrow are the propositions of law found in the opinion that can be thought of as necessary for the decision of the case on the basis of the facts found to be essential.

Fourth, the problem is further complicated by the tendency of American courts to write opinions at the considerable length, in which the main issues are revisited, with a variety of pronouncements and the proffering of different lines of reasoning, outcome of which may appear to be much broader than others.

A factual example of possibilities runs as follows:

In a case in which a woman companion had poured most the lemonade liquid into a glass, drunk some of it and discovered decomposed remains of a snail at the bottom of a bottle of lemonade offered by her host.

A fact-specific but intuitively ridiculous approach would formulate the proposition such manufacturers of lemonade in opaque bottles are liable to people who become ill after drinking the beverage and then discovering a decomposed snail in the bottle.

At the highest level of generality, one may postulate that all manufacturers of goods are liable to any person who is injured by defects in the product.

The holding may be further modified to limit its application to food and drink products or to consumers as a class. So the proposition may be refined to read that manufacturers are liable to consumers who are exposed to traps or hidden dangers, and where they are entirely free of negligence in failing to discover the defect.

Ratio decidendi is a proposition of law that decides the case in the light and in the context of the material facts. The ratio is the central core of the meaning of a case. It is the sharpest cutting edge of the case that only is blinding. The greater the number of facts in the ratio, the narrower its scope. Conversely the fewer or the higher the level of abstraction, the broader the reach of the ratio and the more fact situations it covers. The inclusive nature of such broader statement of the ratio would come close to resemble the general rules found in

---

① 预先规定,命中注定

codes of the civilian family.

Doctrine of Stare Decisis in United States Law

The doctrine of stare decisis dictates that like cases should be decided today the same as they were decided in the past. However, the doctrine is not as vigorously applied in the United States as in England. In order to avoid an over-differentiation of the law between states, some suppleness in the rule of precedent is desirable when facing the need for security and stability.

The United States Supreme Court and the supreme courts of the different states are not bound to observe their own decisions and may in fact operate a reversal of previously established judicial practice. In the operation of state courts, lawyers themselves tend to exert pressure to align the law of one state with the dominant current prevailing in other states. At the federal level, the Supreme Court sees the compelling importance and needs to adapt the Constitution to modern social thinking and economic necessities, as the Constitution can only be amended with very great difficulty. Many celebrated examples of how the United States Supreme Court had brought about fundamental changes to the law and about significant social and economic consequences and impacts were made through imaginative and novel interpretation of the Constitution and the technique of distinguishing previous decision. This is because the rule of precedent is a static and constraining factor instead of being an activist and liberating force. The mechanism of interstitial change in the common law through a case-by-case manner simply is not suitable for the instrumentalist demands of the modern age.

In fact there may only be a slight difference between the juridical recognition of this rule and the voluntary adhesion by judges to some rules or doctrines stated by their predecessors on account of arguments based on reason. The whole question is really much more a matter of legal psychology than of law. It may very much lie in the willingness or hesitation of judges to admit that distinctions may be drawn. Whether or not they consider themselves bound by an aging principle, whether they are indeed aware of the need that the law evolves or, whether they are to be guided by progressive or conservative ideas. And the fact that every shade of opinion can find supporting precedents in the

Chapter 2
The Doctrine of Stare Decisis and Ratio Decidendi or Holding of a Case

extreme mass of published judicial reports is another important factor.

No case has a meaning by itself. What counts and gives you lead and sureness is the background of other cases in relation to which you must read the one at hand. The ratio is not fixed but a formula that is capable of adjustment according to the force of later development.

Exercises

Please choose the best answer to the following questions:

1. Consistent following of precedents contributes to predictability in future disputes.
   A. Because of stare decisis, people will be in a better position to know the possible outcome of their cases.
   B. Future cases, unexceptionally, will have to be decided according to previous cases.
   C. Once a case has been decided, it will be faithfully followed in all future ones.
   D. A case has to be consistent with the precedent, or the result will be unpredictable.

2. Facts permeate the structure of the common law and often accede themselves to the rank of legal rules.
   A. All common law rules are fact-specific.
   B. All common law rules are promoted from far-reaching facts.
   C. All common law rules are stated in the form of stories filled with facts.
   D. All common law rules are derived from the facts of specific cases.

3. Not just judges transform facts into legal rules; other branches of the government perform this trick, too.
   A. Turning facts into legal rules is a game of dirty politics.
   B. Deductive reasoning is not only used in judicial process, but also in political process.
   C. The courts and administrative agencies generally follow the same procedures.
   D. The courts have set examples for other branches of government to

Part One Anglo-American Legal Culture

follow.

4. If it is a law that all manufacturers of goods are liable to any person who is injured by defects in the product, then _____
   A. Apple will never be liable for any injury caused by iPhone since Apple is only a "designer" while all the parts are "manufactured" by other companies.
   B. a person still has to show that the product that injured him is defective.
   C. a manufacturer is always liable when its product is found to be defective.
   D. a person injured by a defective product can go directly to the manufacturer for compensation without having to sue.

5. The doctrine of stare decisis dictates that like cases should be decided today the same as they were decided in the past.
   A. The doctrine is like an old feudalistic shackle that all judges would love to get rid of.
   B. To decide a similar case as was decided before is required under the previous case.
   C. A common law judge does not have the power or the right to question how a previous case was decided, but to follow it.
   D. Once a legal rule is found to be the law, a judge is bound to adhere to it in similar future cases.

6. The doctrine of stare decisis is not as vigorously applied in the United States as in England.
   A. Once a legal rule is established in England, it cannot be as easily overcome as in the United States.
   B. The United States does not follow the English legal practice very vigorously.
   C. The United States does not give too much weight to old cases decided many years ago, as England does.
   D. The doctrine of stare decisis is not as vigorous in the United States as in England.

7. The Supreme Court sees the compelling importance and needs to adapt the Constitution to modern social thinking and economic necessities, as the Constitution can only be amended with very great difficulty.

Chapter 2
The Doctrine of Stare Decisis and Ratio Decidendi or Holding of a Case

    A. As time changes, it is important and necessary that the Constitution be interpreted in modern ways because the constitutional text cannot be easily modified.

    B. Since the constitutional text is very difficult to change, the Supreme Court is urged to modify the application of the Constitution.

    C. The Supreme Court has compelled to change the way the Constitution is amended so as to better fit the social and economic needs of society.

    D. Although the Supreme Court is not bound to change the Constitution, it may change its own prior decisions in order to better serve the societal needs.

8. There are some difficulties in stating with precision the holding (ratio decidendi) of an appellate court that represents the propositions of law binding on lower courts.

    A. The law is less binding on lower courts if it is difficult to understand what it exactly is.

    B. The scope of the holding of a decision may be difficult to determine, and if so, it would not carry much of a precedential value.

    C. The precedential value of an appellate decision may not always be stated in plain terms, but it is still binding on lower courts.

    D. If a legal rule is hard to express, it is hard to propose it to lower courts to follow.

9. The greater the number of facts in the ratio decidendi, the narrower its scope.

    A. The more fact-specific, the less far-reaching of a decision.

    B. The more you say, the more likely you will make mistakes.

    C. Facts are irrelevant to abstraction of legal rules, and can weigh down the value of a decision.

    D. Legal rules derived from simple fact stories are generally more powerful.

10. Lawyers tend to exert pressure to align the law of one state with the dominant current prevailing in other states.

    A. Lawyers try to influence the court by putting pressure on it so as to change the state law in line with most other states.

    B. Lawyers are more likely to push their ideas about law in their home states.

C. Lawyers will be able to change the law of a state if they get support from greater authorities such as the president of the United States.

D. It is mostly due to the efforts of lawyers to move the legislature for a change of the law.

Chapter 3

Federal Courts and What They Do

> **导 读** <<
>
> 　　美国的联邦共合体制(Republican Form of Government)决定了美国双重权力的政治构架:各州权力(即主权)来自于向英国宣告独立,而联邦政府的权力(即联邦宪法)来自于由各州代表组成的制宪会议授权。这意味着:州的权力来自于民众授权,因而是无限的,除非宪法予以限制;联邦政府的权力来自于拥有主权的各州,仅限于宪法明确授权,是有限的。在司法体系方面也是如此:各州有自己的法院系统和法律体系,其最高法院为本州法律事务的最终裁定机构,拥有普遍管辖权,除非宪法明确予以排除;而联邦法院的设立、诉讼管辖、上诉管辖、诉讼内容、法官任命和任职期限(包括工资),完全由宪法规定,是权力有限的司法体系。
>
> 　　不论是各州还是联邦法院的司法体系都有详尽而近乎繁琐的诉讼程序,其中最为与众不同的是"证据公开"制度——双方均可向对方索取相关证据——以确保法庭审理的公开、公平、公正,以及避免在庭审中出现突如其来的证据而造成对方无法提供相反证据和反驳理由。换句话说,在庭审之前的调查取证过程中未提出的证据,一般在庭审中不予采纳。
>
> 　　由此可知为什么美国的诉讼耗时费钱,且大多数诉讼以和解告终。这是因为证据的充分、公开使得庭审已没有过多悬念,即使不开庭,胜负也已基本揭晓。
>
> 　　本章着重介绍了美国司法体系、诉讼程序和参诉人员等内容。

Part One Anglo-American Legal Culture

There are both federal courts and state courts in the United States of America. The two kinds of courts are a result of a principle of its Constitution called federalism. Federalism gives some functions to the United States government and leaves other functions to the states. The functions of the U.S.—or federal—government involve the nation as a whole and include regulating commerce between the states and with foreign countries, providing for the national defense, and administering federal lands and other property. State governments perform most of the functions you probably associate with "government," such as running the schools, managing the police departments, and paving the streets.

Federal courts are established by the U.S. Government to decide disputes concerning the federal Constitution and laws passed by Congress, called statutes. State courts are established by a state, or by a county or city within the state. Although state courts must enforce the federal Constitution and laws, most of the cases they decide involve the constitution and laws of the particular state.

Of all the federal courts, the U.S. district courts are the most numerous. Congress has divided the country into ninety-four federal judicial districts, and in each district there is a U.S. district court. The U.S. district courts are the federal trial courts—the places where federal cases are tried, witnesses testify, and juries serve. Within each district is a U.S. bankruptcy court, a part of the district court that administers the bankruptcy laws.

Congress has placed each of the ninety-four districts in one of twelve regional circuits, and each circuit has a court of appeals. If you lose a trial in a district court, you can ask the court of appeals to review the case to see if the judge applied the law correctly. Sometimes courts of appeals are also asked to review decisions of federal administrative agencies, such as the National Labor Relations Board.

The map of the United States shows the geographical boundaries of the ninety-four districts and the twelve regional circuits (eleven numbered circuits and the District of Columbia Circuit). There is also a Federal Circuit, whose court of appeals is based in Washington, D.C., but which hears certain types of cases from all over the country.

The Supreme Court of the United States, in Washington, D.C., is the

Chapter 3
Federal Courts and What They Do

most famous federal court. If you lose a case in the court of appeals (or, sometimes, in a state supreme court), you can ask the Supreme Court to hear your appeal. However, unlike a court of appeals, the Supreme Court doesn't have to hear it. In fact, the Supreme Court hears only a very small percentage of the cases it is asked to review.

Article III of the Constitution establishes a Supreme Court and authorizes whatever other federal courts Congress thinks are necessary. Congress creates the district courts and the courts of appeals, sets the number of judges in each federal court (including the Supreme Court), and determines what kinds of cases they will hear. (Congress has also created courts under Article I of the Constitution, such as military courts and the U. S. Tax Court. But judges of those courts decide only certain kinds of cases and do not have the judicial powers and protections of judges on courts created under Article III.)

What's the Difference Between Civil Cases and Criminal Cases?

Civil cases are different from criminal cases. Civil cases usually involve disputes between persons or organizations while criminal cases involve some criminal action that is considered to be harmful to society as a whole.

Lawyers use the term party or litigant to describe a participant in a civil case. A person who claims that another person has failed to carry out a legal duty or violated his or her right, such as those under the Constitution or other federal law, may ask the court to tell the person who violated the right to stop doing it and make compensation for any harm done. For example, Congress has passed a law saying that people have a right not to be denied employment because of their gender. Suppose an employer refuses to hire women as construction workers. Women who had applied and been qualified for jobs might bring a civil case against the employer—sue the employer—for lost wages and seek an order requiring the company to hire them.

Another legal duty is the duty to honor contracts. If a lumberyard promises to sell a specific amount of wood to a construction company for an agreed-upon price and then fails to deliver the wood, forcing the construction company to buy it elsewhere at a higher price, the construction company might sue the lumberyard for damages.

When a jury (or a judge in cases in which the defendant waived a jury) determines that an individual committed a crime, that person may be fined, sent to prison, or placed under the supervision of a court employee called a U.S. probation officer, or some combination of these three things. The person accused is charged in an indictment or information, which is a formal accusation that the person has committed a crime. The government, on behalf of the people, **prosecution**① the case. It is not the victim's responsibility to bring a criminal case. In fact, there may not always be a specific victim. For example, the federal government prosecutes people accused of violating federal laws against spying because of the danger spying presents to the country as a whole. State governments arrest and prosecute people accused of violating laws against drunk driving because society regards drunk driving as a serious offense that can result in harm to innocent bystanders.

What Kinds of Cases Are Tried in State Courts?

State courts are essential to the administration of justice in the United States because they handle by far the largest number of cases and have the most contact with the public. State courts handle the cases that people are most likely to be involved in, such as robberies, traffic violations, broken contracts, and family disputes.

The state courts have such a heavy caseload because their general, unlimited jurisdiction allows them to decide almost every type of case. Jurisdiction refers to the kinds of cases a court is authorized to hear. In recent years, the annual number of state court cases has been roughly 50 million. By contrast, in the same period, about 2 million cases have been brought each year in the federal courts; approximately 80% of these were bankruptcy filings, 15% were civil cases, and the rest were criminal cases. The number of judges in each system further illustrates the difference: There are some 1,700 judges in the federal courts, but more than 30,000 in the state courts.

---

① 控告,起诉,检举

Chapter 3
Federal Courts and What They Do

What Kinds of Case Are Tried in Federal Courts?

As the preceding numbers suggest, federal courts do not have the same broad jurisdiction that state courts have. Federal court jurisdiction is limited to the specific types of cases listed in the Constitution and specifically provided for by Congress. For the most part, federal courts only hear cases in which the United States is a party, cases involving violations of the Constitution or federal laws, cases between citizens of different states, and some special kinds of cases, such as bankruptcy cases, patent cases, and cases involving maritime law.

Some cases are such that only federal courts have jurisdiction over them. In other cases, the parties can choose whether to go to state court or to federal court. In most cases, however, they can only go to state court.

Although the federal courts hear significantly fewer cases than the state courts, the cases they do hear tend more often to be of national importance, because of the federal laws they enforce and the federal rights they protect.

Most cases in federal courts are civil rather than criminal. As described earlier, one type of federal civil case might involve a claim by a private citizen that a company failed to carry out its duty under the law—for example, that the company refused to hire the person simply because she was a woman. Another kind of federal civil case might be a lawsuit by a private citizen claiming that he is entitled to receive money under a government program, such as benefits from Social Security. A third type of federal civil lawsuit might require the court to decide whether a corporation is violating federal laws by having a monopoly over a certain kind of business.

Appeals for review of actions by federal administrative agencies are also federal civil cases. Suppose, for example, that the Environmental Protection Agency issued a permit to a paper mill to discharge water used in its milling process into the Scenic River, over the objection of area residents. The residents could ask a federal court to review the agency's decision.

There are many more federal civil cases than criminal cases because most crimes concern problems that the Constitution leaves to the states. We all know, for example, that robbery is a crime. But what law says it is a crime? By and large, state laws, not federal laws, make robbery a crime. There are only a few

Part One Anglo-American Legal Culture

federal laws about robbery, such as the law that makes it a federal crime to rob a bank whose deposits are insured by a federal agency. Examples of other federal crimes are sale or possession of illegal drugs and use of the U.S. mails to swindle consumers.

Federal courts also hear bankruptcy matters. Bankruptcy laws enable people or businesses who can no longer pay their creditors as their debts come due to organize their affairs, liquidate their debts or create a plan to pay them off, and get a fresh start. There is a whole code of laws that sets out how the parties involved in a bankruptcy case should proceed: the bankruptcy code. Bankruptcy judges decide matters that arise under the code.

How Does a Case Come into a Federal Court?

Courts can't reach out to decide controversies on their own initiative. They must wait for someone to bring the controversy to them. Moreover, courts only decide legal controversies. They are not intended to decide every disagreement that individuals have with one another, or to give advice.

Civil cases. A federal civil case begins when someone—or more likely, someone's lawyer—files a paper or electronic document with the clerk of the court that states a claim against another person who is believed to have committed a wrongful act. In legal terminology, the plaintiff files a complaint against the defendant. The defendant may then file an answer to the complaint. These written statements of the parties' positions are called pleadings.

Criminal cases. Beginning a federal criminal case is more complicated. A criminal case usually begins when a lawyer for the executive branch of the U.S. government—the U.S. Attorney or an assistant U.S. attorney—tells a federal grand jury about the evidence that, according to the government, indicates a person committed a crime. That person may or may not already have been arrested when the grand jury meets. The U.S. attorney will try to convince the grand jury that there is enough evidence to show that the person probably committed the crime and should be formally accused of it. If the grand jury agrees, it issues a formal accusation, called an **indictment**[①].

---

① （刑事）起诉书

Chapter 3
Federal Courts and What They Do

A grand jury is different from a trial jury, also called a petit jury. A grand jury determines whether the person should be released or held for further proceedings; a petit jury listens to the evidence presented at the trial and determines whether the defendant is guilty of the charge. "Petit" is the French word for "small"; petit juries usually consist of twelve jurors in criminal cases and from six to twelve jurors in civil cases. "Grand" is the French word for "large"; grand juries have from sixteen to twenty-three jurors.

After the grand jury issues the indictment, the accused person (the defendant) is arrested, if not already under arrest. The next step is an **arraignment**①, where the defendant is brought before a judge and asked to plead "guilty" or "not guilty" of the crime. If the plea is "guilty," a time is set for the defendant to return to court to be sentenced. If the defendant pleads "not guilty," a time is set for the trial.

Grand jury indictments are most often used for felonies, which are the more serious crimes, such as bank robberies. Grand jury indictments are not usually necessary to prosecute less serious crimes, called misdemeanors, and are not necessary for all felonies. Instead, the U.S. attorney issues an information, which takes the place of an indictment. Typical misdemeanors are disturbing the peace(a state misdemeanor) and speeding on a highway in a national park(a federal misdemeanor).

Is There a Trial for Every Case?

Although there is an absolute right to trial in both civil and criminal cases, trials are often emotionally and financially costly, and a person may not want to exercise the right to trial. So usually the parties agree to settle the case without going to trial.

Some civil cases are decided by the judge, who may decide based on the facts presented that there is no need to have a trial. Thus, more than nine out of ten civil cases never come to trial, and about eight out of ten defendants in criminal cases plead guilty rather than stand trial. If you watch a trial in progress, remember that what you're seeing is only one part—though a very important part—of the total legal process.

---

① 提审,过堂

Part One Anglo-American Legal Culture

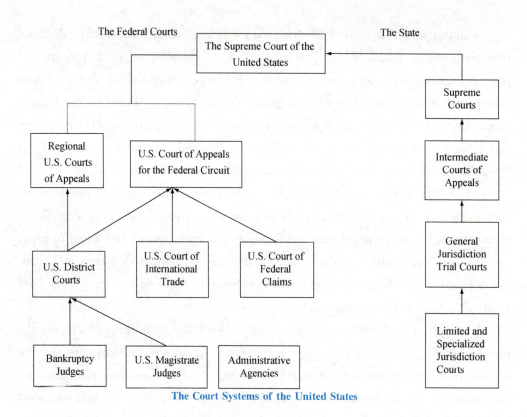

The Court Systems of the United States

What Is the Purpose of the Trial?

Role of judge and jury. If the parties in a civil case can't agree on how to settle the case on their own, or if a defendant in a criminal case pleads not guilty, the court will decide the dispute through a trial. In a civil case, the purpose of a trial is to find out whether the defendant failed to fulfill a legal duty to the plaintiff. In a criminal case, the purpose of a trial is to determine whether the defendant committed the crime charged.

If the parties choose to have a jury trial, determining the facts is the task of the petit jury. If they decide not to have a jury and to leave the fact-finding to the judge, the trial is called a bench trial. In either kind of trial, the judge makes sure the correct legal standards are followed. If there is a jury, the judge tells the jury what the law governing the case is. For example, in a robbery case in which an unloaded gun was used, the judge would tell the jury that using an unloaded gun to rob a store is legally the same as using a gun that is loaded. But the jury would have to decide whether the defendant on trial was actually the

Chapter 3
Federal Courts and What They Do

person who committed the robbery and used the gun.

Adversary process. Courts use the adversary process to help them reach a decision. Through this process, each side in a dispute presents its most persuasive arguments to the fact finder (judge or jury) and emphasizes the facts that support its case. Each side also draws attention to any flaws in its opponent's arguments. The fact finder then decides the case. American judicial tradition holds that the truth will be reached most effectively through this adversary process.

The evidence the jury (or judge, in a bench trial) relies on to decide the case consists of two types: (1) physical evidence, such as documents, photographs, and objects, and (2) the testimony of witnesses who are questioned by the lawyers.

Standards of proof. The courts, through their decisions, and Congress, through statutes, have established standards by which facts must be proven in criminal and civil cases. In criminal cases (federal or state), the defendant may be convicted only if the jury (or judge, in a bench trial) believes that the government has proved the defendant's guilt "beyond a reasonable doubt." Remember that for the grand jury to issue an indictment, it only has to believe that the defendant probably committed the crime. But for the petit jury to find the defendant guilty, it must be certain that the defendant committed the crime; it can have no "reasonable doubt" about it. A jury verdict must be unanimous, meaning that all jurors must vote either "guilty" or "not guilty." If the jurors cannot agree, the judge declares a mistrial, and the prosecutor must then decide whether to ask the court to dismiss the case or have it presented to another jury.

In civil cases, in order to decide for the plaintiff, the jury must determine by a "preponderance of the evidence" that the defendant failed to perform a legal duty and violated the plaintiff's rights. A preponderance of the evidence means that more of the evidence favors the plaintiff's position that favors the defendant's.

Much of the way our court system works can be traced back to developments in England in the seventeenth century, at the time when America was a group of English colonies. During that century, England abolished the hated Court of the Star Chamber, a court that was tied closely to the prosecutor and that brought enemies of the king to trial for treason and other serious crimes, invariably finding them guilty. A century of criminal justice reforms in England resulted in a number of protections for individuals accused of crimes and adoption of the idea that courts should make their judgments free of pressure from prosecutors. American courts inherited these traditions from England and incorporated them into our judicial system.

Who Are the People in the Courtroom?

The judge. The judge presides over the trial from a desk, called a bench, on an elevated platform. The judges have five basic tasks. The first is simply to preside over the proceedings and see that order is maintained. The second is to determine whether any of the evidence that the parties want to use is illegal or improper. Third, before the jury begins its deliberations about the facts in the case, the judge gives the jury instructions about the law that applied to the case and the standards it must use in deciding the case. Fourth, in bench trials, the judge must also determine the facts and decide the case. The fifth is to sentence convicted criminal defendants.

Federal appellate and district judges are appointed to office by the President of the United State, with the approval of the U.S. Senate. Federal judges come from a variety of professional backgrounds. Some were private attorneys before they were appointed. Some were judges in state courts, federal magistrate or bankruptcy judges, or U.S. attorneys. A few were law professors. Once they become judges, they are strictly prohibited from working as lawyers. They must be careful not to do anything that might cause people to think they would favor one side in a case over another. For this reason, they can't give speeches urging votes to pick one candidate over another for public office, or ask people to contribute money to civic organizations.

Under Article III of the Constitution, federal judges serve "during good behavior." Therefore, they may be removed from their jobs only if Congress determines, through a lengthy process called impeachment and conviction, that they are guilty of "treason, bribery, or other high crimes and misdemeanors." Congress has found it necessary to use this process only a few times in the history of our country. From a practical standpoint, almost all federal judges

Chapter 3
Federal Courts and What They Do

hold office for as long as they wish. Article III also prohibits lowering the salaries of federal judges "during their continuance in office."

The Constitution includes both of these protections—life tenure and unreduced salary—so that federal judges will not fear losing their jobs or having their pay cut if they make an unpopular decision. Sometimes the courts decide that a law that has been passed by Congress and signed by the Present, or a law that has been passed by a state, violates the Constitution and should not be enforced. For example, the Supreme Court's decision in *Brown v. Board of Education* in 1954 declared racial segregation in public schools to be unconstitutional. This decision was not popular with large segments of society when it was handed down. Some members of Congress even wanted to replace the judges who made the decision. The Constitution wouldn't let them do so, and today, almost everyone realizes that the decision was right.

The constitutional protection of federal judges that gives them the freedom and independence to make decisions that are politically and socially unpopular is one of the basic elements of our democracy. According to the Declaration of Independence, one reason the American colonies wanted to separate from England was that King George III "made judges dependent on his will alone, for the tenure of their offices, and the amount and payment of their salaries."

Bankruptcy judges and magistrate judges are appointed by the courts they serve. They conduct some of the proceedings held in federal courts. They also assist the district judges. Bankruptcy judges handle almost all bankruptcy matters. Magistrate judges often conduct proceedings before trial to help prepare the district judges' cases for trial. They also may preside over misdemeanor trials and may preside over civil trials when both parties agree to have the case heard by a magistrate judge instead of a district judge. Magistrate judges and bankruptcy judges don't have the same protections as judges appointed under Article III of the Constitution.

The jury. The group of people seated in the boxed-in area on one side of the courtroom is the petit jury or trial jury. You won't be able to observe the grand jury during your visit because its proceedings are always secret.

Juries were first used hundreds of years ago in England. The jury was a factor in the events that led to the Revolutionary War. The Declaration of

Part One Anglo-American Legal Culture

Independence charged that King George III deprived the colonists "in many cases, of the benefits of trial by jury." Thus, our Constitution now guarantees the right to a jury trial to most defendants in criminal cases and to the parties in most civil cases.

In federal criminal cases, there are usually twelve jurors and between one and six alternate jurors. Alternate jurors replace regular jurors who become ill, disqualified, or unable to perform their duties. In federal civil cases there can be from six to twelve jurors. Unlike in criminal cases, there are no alternate jurors. All of the jurors are required to join in the verdict unless the court excuses a juror from service during the trial or deliberations.

The lawyers. The lawyers for each party will either be sitting at the counsel tables facing the bench or be speaking to the judge, a witness, or the jury. Each lawyer's task is to bring out the facts that put his or her client's case in the most favorable light, but to do so using approved legal procedures. In criminal cases, one of the lawyers works for the executive branch of the government, which is the branch that prosecutes cases on behalf of society. In federal criminal cases, that lawyer is the U.S. attorney or an assistant U.S. attorney. A U.S. attorney is chosen by the President, with the approval of the Senate, for each of the ninety-four judicial districts. The U.S. attorney also represents the United States in civil cases in which the U.S. government is a party.

Under the Constitution, as the Supreme Court has interpreted it, persons accused of serious crimes who can't afford to hire a lawyer may have lawyers appointed to represent them. In the federal courts, these lawyers are usually from the federal Defenders Office, a federal agency, or from private defense organizations, or from panels of private lawyers deemed qualified to represent such persons. Although the judge may appointed these lawyers, and they are usually paid with public funds, they don't work for the judge—they work for their client, the defendant.

On relatively rare occasions, defendants in criminal cases or parties in civil cases attempt to present their cases themselves, without using a lawyer. Parties who act on their own behalf are said to act prose, a Latin phrase meaning "on one's own behalf."

The parties. The parties may or may not be present at the counsel tables

Chapter 3
Federal Courts and What They Do

with their lawyers. Defendants in criminal cases have a constitutional right to be present. Specifically, the Sixth Amendment to the Constitution provides that "the accused shall enjoy the right... to be confronted with the witnesses against him." Parties in civil cases may be present if they wish, but are often absent.

The witnesses. Witnesses give testimony about the facts in the case that are in dispute. During their testimony, they sit on the witness stand, facing the courtroom. Because the witnesses are asked to testify by one party or the other, they are often referred to as plaintiff's witnesses, government witnesses, or defense witnesses.

The courtroom deputy or clerk. The courtroom deputy or courtroom clerk, who is usually seated near the judge, administers the oaths to the witnesses, marks the exhibits, and generally helps the judge keep the trial running smoothly. Sometimes the deputy or clerk is away from the courtroom performing other tasks during parts of the trial. The courtroom deputy is employed by the office of the clerk of court. The clerk of court is appointed by all of the judges on the court and works closely with the chief district judge, who is responsible for the court's overall administration.

The court reporter. The court reporter sits near the witness stand and usually types the official record of the trial (everything that is said or introduced into evidence) on a stenographic machine. (In some courts, the official record is taken on an electronic recorder.) Federal law requires that a word-for-word record be made of every trial. The court reporter also produces a written transcript of the proceedings if either party appeals the case or requests a transcript to review.

What Happens During a Trial?

Pretrial activity in civil cases. In most cases, the lawyers and judge agree before trial, often at pretrial conferences, what issues are in dispute and must be decided by the jury and what issues are not in dispute. Both sides reveal whom they intend to call as witnesses and, generally, what evidence they will introduce at trial. However, just because they agree on these matters before the trial doesn't mean that they agree on how the case should be decided. Rather, the judge holds a conference to avoid wasting time during the trial on issues that can be decided before.

During the pretrial discovery process, the lawyers try to learn as much as possible about their opponent's case, as well as build their own case, by asking to inspect documents and talking to people who know something about what happened. If the lawyers have done a thorough job of preparing the case, they shouldn't be surprised by any of the answers the opposing attorney's witnesses give to their questions during trial. One of the basic rules trial lawyers follow is "Don't ask a question if you don't know what the answer will be." The lawyers and witnesses for each side also prepare for the trial by rehearing their questions and answers.

Frequently, all of this pretrial activity in a civil case results in a decision by both parties to settle the case without going through a trial. Settling does not necessarily mean that the parties have reconciled their dispute; they have merely agreed to compromise out of court. Often it means that the plaintiff has agreed to accept an amount for damages that is less than the amount he or she originally claimed.

Pretrial activity in criminal cases. A good defense lawyer will also conduct a thorough investigation before trial in a criminal case, interviewing witness, visiting the scene of the crime, and examining any physical evidence. An important part of this investigation is determining whether the government can use certain items of evidence. For example, the government cannot use evidence that the defendant committed a previous crime to prove that the defendant committed a crime in another case. But there are some circumstances in which evidence of a previous crime may be used. Or, the defendant may argue that the government cannot use the defendant's confession because it was obtained in violation of the defendant's rights. Resolution of these evidentiary issues before the trial can result either in the government's dropping the charges or in the defendant deciding to plead guilty.

Jury selection. If the parties have chosen a jury trial, it begins with the selection of jurors. Citizens are selected for jury service through a process that is set out in laws passed by Congress and in rules adopted by the federal courts. First, citizens are called to court to be available to serve on juries. These citizens are selected at random from lists of all registered or actual voters in the district or from voter lists supplemented by some other sources of names, such as licensed drivers. The judge and the lawyers in each case then choose the persons who will actually serve on the jury.

To choose the jurors, the judge and sometimes the lawyers ask prospective jurors questions to determine if they will be able to decide the case fairly. This process is called voir dire. The lawyers may ask the judge to excuse any jurors they think may not be able to be impartial, such as those who know either party in the case or who have had an experience that might make them favor one side over the other. The lawyers may reject a certain number of jurors without giving any justification. Lawyers may not, however, reject jurors on the basis of race or gender.

Opening statements. Once the jury has been selected, the lawyers for both sides give their opening statements. The purpose of the opening statements is to allow each side to present its version of the evidence to be offered.

Direct and cross-examination. Introduction of evidence begins after the opening statements. First, the government's attorney, or the plaintiff's lawyer, questions his or her witness. When lawyers question the witnesses whom they have called to testify, it is called direct examination. After the direct examination of a government or plaintiff's witness, the defendant's lawyer may question the witness; this is called cross-examination. If, after the cross-examination, the plaintiff's lawyer wants to ask additional questions, he or she may do so on a redirect examination, after which the defendant's lawyer has an opportunity for a re-cross-examination. After all of the plaintiff's witnesses have been examined, the defense calls its witnesses, and the same procedures are repeated.

The lawyers often introduce documents, such as bank records, or objects, such as firearms, as additional evidence. These items are called exhibits.

Inadmissible evidence. The courts have established rules that must be observed in court proceedings to determine facts. For example, the Supreme Court has ruled that a defendant's out-of-court confession to a crime may not be used in a trial as evidence of the defendant's guilt if the confession resulted from coercion. The courts adopted this rule because forced confessions obviously aren't trustworthy.

The federal courts have also adopted a rule to prevent repeated injuries to others following a plaintiff's injury. To encourage the defendant to repair the faulty condition that may have caused the jury, the rule forbids the introduction of any evidence of such repair, which could be seen as an admission of guilt. Thus, a lawyer for a plaintiff who slipped on a wet sidewalk cannot introduce evidence that the defendant put up a "slippery when wet" sign after the plaintiff's accident. Without this rule, the act of putting up the sign could be interpreted as an admission that the sign should have been there at the time of the plaintiff's accident and that the defendant had a duty to warn the plaintiff of the hazardous condition. Such an admission would damage the defendant's case.

Another rule concerning the introduction of evidence prohibits the use of secondhand testimony, called hearsay. Under this rule, witness may not testify to something that they heard about from someone else. If John Smith, for example, testified, "Bill Jones told me he saw Frank Williams rob the Green Valley Bank," the testimony would be inadmissible as evidence. The courts have decided that hearsay is usually not very reliable and, therefore, cannot be used as evidence in a trial.

Sometimes a lawyer will break one of these rules, either inadvertently or on purpose, and will try to present evidence to the jury that it shouldn't be permitted to hear. If an opposing lawyer believes that testimony asked for or already given is improper, the lawyer may object to it and may ask the judge to instruct the witness not to answer the question or to tell the jury to disregard an answer that has already been given. The judge can either sustain the objection and do as the objecting lawyer requests, or overrule it and permit the testimony. When an objection is made, the judge alone decides whether the testimony is admissible.

Occasionally, the judge and the lawyers for both sides confer at the bench—sometimes called at sidebar—out of the jury's earshot but with the court reporter present to record what they say. At other times, they might confer in the judge's chambers. Often, they are discussing whether a certain piece of evidence is admissible. The court doesn't want the jurors to hear such a discussion because they might hear something that can't be admitted into evidence and that might prejudice them in favor of one side or the other.

Chapter 3
Federal Courts and What They Do

Closing arguments and instructions. After the evidence has been presented, the lawyers make their closing arguments to the jury, concluding the presentation of their cases. Like the opening statements, the closing arguments don't present evidence but summarize the most important features of each side's case. Following the closing arguments, the judge gives instructions to the jury, explaining the relevant law, how the law applies to the case being tried, and what questions the jury must decide. The jury then retires to the jury room to discuss the evidence and to reach a verdict. In criminal cases, the jury's verdict must be unanimous. In civil cases, the verdict must also be unanimous, unless the parties have agreed before the trial that they will accept a verdict that is not unanimous.

By serving on a jury, citizens have a unique opportunity to participate directly in the operation of our government. Jurors serve as a direct voice of the community in the judicial branch. They also make a vital contribution to the smooth functioning of our judicial system. To encourage citizens to participate, the courts try to make jury service as comfortable and rewarding as possible.

Posttrial matters and sentencing. In federal criminal cases, if the jury (or judge, if there is no jury) decides that the defendant is guilty, the judge sets a date for imposing the sentence. In federal courts, the jury doesn't decide the punishment; the judge does. But the judge's determination is controlled by sentencing statues passed by Congress and assisted by a set of guidelines, called sentencing guidelines, which take into account the nature of the particular offense and the offender's criminal history. A presentence report, prepared by one of the court's probation officers, assists the judge in determining the proper sentence under the applicable rules and guidelines.

In civil cases, if the jury (or judge) decides in favor of the plaintiff, the jury (or judge) usually orders the defendant to pay the plaintiff money (damages) or to take some specific action that will restore the plaintiff's rights. If the defendant wins the case, however, there is nothing more the trial court needs to do.

What Happens after the Trial or Guilty Plea?

A defendant who is found guilty in a federal criminal trial and the losing party in a federal civil case both have a right to appeal their case to the U. S. court of appeals. The grounds for appeal usually allege that the district judge made an error either in procedure (such as by admitting improper evidence) or in interpreting the law.

The government may not appeal if a defendant in a criminal case is found not guilty, because the double jeopardy clause in the Fifth Amendment to the Constitution provides that no person shall "be twice put in jeopardy of life or limb" for the same offense. This reflects our society's belief that, even if a second or third trial might finally find a defendant guilty, it is not proper to allow the government to harass an acquitted defendant through repeated retrials. The government may appeal in civil cases, as any other party may. Also, the losing party may not appeal if there was no trial—if the defendant decided to plead guilty or if the parties settled their civil case out of court. However, a defendant who pleads guilty may have the right to appeal his or her sentence. The government may also sometimes appeal a sentence.

An appeal in a federal criminal case usually proceeds in the following manner: Suppose a law is passed by Congress that prohibits demonstrations within 500 feet of any embassy. Following the enactment of the law, a group of six people stand on a street corner near the embassy of Malandia and ask passersby to sign a petition protesting Malandia's foreign policy. The six people are arrested and charged with committing a federal misdemeanor. At trial, they testify that they were careful to stay more than 500 feet away from the embassy. However, the U.S. attorney calls a police officer as a witness, and he testifies that the corner they were standing on is within 500 feet of the embassy.

Before the trial jury begins its deliberations, the lawyer for the defendants asks the district judge to instruct the jury that collecting signatures on a petition is not a "demonstration" and, therefore, if that was all they did, they weren't violating the law. The defendants' lawyer also argues that the law violated the First Amendment right to free speech, and therefore the case against them should be dismissed. The judge disagrees on both points. She instructs the jury that collecting signatures on a petition is a demonstration and refuses to dismiss the case, saying that Congress may prohibit demonstrations that pose a threat to foreign embassies without violating the First Amendment. To reach her

Chapter 3
Federal Courts and What They Do

decision, the judge consults precedents—similar cases that have already been decided by other courts. She pays special attention to prior decisions of the court of appeals for her circuit.

Because the judge has determined that collecting signatures is a demonstration and that Congress has the constitution power to prohibit a demonstration near an embassy, she instructs the jury to decide, on the basis of the evidence, whether the defendants collected signatures within 500 feet of the embassy.

Suppose that the jury finds that the defendants did collect signatures within 500 feet of the embassy, and the defendants are convicted of violating the law. The defendants may then appeal this decision to the U. S. court of appeals. A court of appeals would rarely throw out the jury's factual finding that the protesters were within 500 feet of the embassy. However, the court of appeals may decide that the district judge wrongly interpreted the law; it may decide that Congress didn't intend for the law to prohibit gathering signatures on a petition. After deciding this, the court of appeals will probably determine that it doesn't have to decide whether it was unconstitutional for Congress to prohibit demonstrations near embassies. That decision will have to wait for a case in which there is an actual demonstration.

If the court of appeals decides that the trial judge incorrectly interpreted the law, as in the example, then it will reverse the district court's decision. In other words, the court of appeals will say that the district judge made a mistake in interpreting the law, and thus the defendants are not guilty after all. However, most of the time—but certainly not always—courts of appeals uphold, rather than reverse, district court decisions.

Sometimes when a higher court reverses the decision of the district court, it will send the case back to the district court for another trial, or in legal terms, remand it. For example, in the famous *Miranda case*, the Supreme Court ruled that Ernesto Miranda's confession could not be used as evidence because he had not been advised of his right to remain silent or of his right to have a lawyer present during questioning. However, the government did have other evidence against him. The case was remanded for a new trial at which the improperly obtained confession was not used as evidence, and Miranda was convicted.

Appellate court procedure. The courts of appeals usually assign a panel of three judges to each case. The panel decides the case for the entire court. Sometimes, when the parties request it, or when there is a question of unusual importance, the entire appeals court, sitting en banc, will reconsider a panel's decision or hear the case anew.

In making its decision, the panel reviews key parts of the record on appeal, which consists of all the documents filed in the case at trial along with the transcript of the proceedings at the trial. The panel then learns about the lawyers' legal arguments from two sources. One is the lawyers' briefs. Briefs are written documents (often anything but brief) that explain each side's case and tell why the court should decide in its favor. The second source of information about the lawyers' legal arguments is the oral argument. If the court permits oral argument, each side's lawyers have a limited amount of time to explain its case to the judges in a formal courtroom session, and the judges frequently question them about the relevant law.

After the submission of briefs and oral argument, the judges discuss the case privately, consider any relevant precedents, and reach a decision. At least two of the three judges on the panel must agree with the decision. One of those who agree is chosen to write an opinion, which announces the decision and explains it. Any judge who disagrees with the majority's opinion may file a dissenting opinion, giving his or her reasons for disagreeing. Many appellate opinions are published in books of opinions called reporters. The opinions are read carefully by other judges and lawyers looking for precedents to guide them in their own cases. The accumulated judicial opinions make up a body of law known as case law, which is usually an accurate predictor of how future cases will be decided. Increasingly, the courts of appeals use short, unsigned opinions, which often are not published, for decisions that, in the judges' view, are important only to the parties and contribute nothing to the case law.

If you visit a court of appeals in session, you'll notice how it differs from the federal trial courts. There are no jurors, witnesses, or court reporters. The lawyers for both sides are present, but the parties usually are not.

The Supreme Court of the United States. The Supreme Court is the highest court in the nation. It is a different kind of appeals court—its major function is not correcting errors made by trial judges, but clarifying the law when other

Chapter 3
Federal Courts and What They Do

courts disagree about the interpretation of the Constitution or federal laws.

Unlike the U.S. courts of appeals, however, the Supreme Court does not have to hear every case that it is asked to review. The Supreme Court decides whether or not it will hear a case. Each year, losing parties ask the Supreme Court to review about 8,000 of the approximately 50 million cases handled by the state and federal courts. These cases come to the Court as petitions for writ of certiorari. The Court selects only about 80 of the most significant cases to review.

The decisions the Supreme Court hands down on cases appealed from lower courts set precedents for the interpretation of the Constitution and federal laws that all other courts, both state and federal, must follow. This power of judicial review makes the Supreme Court's role in our government vital. Judicial review is the power of any court, when deciding a case, to declare that a law passed by a legislature or an action of an executive official is invalid because it is inconsistent with the Constitution. Although district courts, courts of appeals, and state courts can exercise the power of judicial review, their decisions are always subject to review by the Supreme Court on appeal. When the Supreme Court declares a law unconstitutional, however, its decision can only be overruled by a later decision of the Supreme Court or by an amendment to the Constitution. Seven of the twenty-seven amendments to the Constitution have invalidated decisions of the Supreme Court. However, most Supreme Court cases don't concern the constitutionality of laws but the interpretation of laws passed by Congress.

Although Congress has steadily increased the number of district and appeals court judges over the years, the Supreme Court has remained the same size since 1869, with a Chief Justice and eight associate justices. Like all federal judges, the justices are appointed by the President with the advice and consent of the Senate. However, unlike the courts of appeals, the Supreme Court never sits in panels. All nine justices hear every case, and cases are decided by a majority ruling.

The Supreme Court begins its annual session or term on the first Monday of October. The term lasts until the Court has announced its decisions in all of the cases in which it has heard argument—usually until June. During the term, the

Court, sitting for two weeks at a time, hears oral argument on Monday through Wednesday and then holds private conferences to discuss the cases, reach decisions, and begin preparing the opinions. Most decisions, with their opinions, are released in the late spring and early summer.

The decisions of the Supreme Court affect the lives of millions of people, from magazine editors trying to decide whether publishing a disparaging article about a famous person may make them liable for damages, to taxpayers whose tax bill may be affected by rulings about state and federal tax laws. The widespread impact of some cases results in lively debates in the media. Rarely does everyone agree with an outcome.

Facts and Concepts You Should Remember About the Federal Courts

What is most noteworthy varies with an individual's point of view, but everyone should find the following points worth remembering:

• Federal and state courts exist side by side. State courts are courts of general jurisdiction and decide many more cases than federal courts. The federal courts' jurisdiction is much more limited than the state courts' jurisdiction.

• Courts resolve disputes through the adversary process, at both the trial and appellate levels, and rely on precedents for guidance in making decisions.

• Every individual has an absolute right to bring a case in federal court (assuming the court has jurisdiction), along with an absolute right of appeal for review of the district court's decision. Only in rare instances does a case go as far as the Supreme Court of the United States.

• In criminal cases, the courts provide legal assistance free of charge to defendants who cannot afford to pay for it themselves.

Exercises

Please choose the best answer to the following questions:

1. The states may, under the U. S. Constitution, do all of the following except _____.

   A. make their own laws regulating commerce within their borders.

Chapter 3
Federal Courts and What They Do

    B. maintain educational systems.

    C. set up their own police departments.

    D. provide for standing armies for self-defense.

2. A U. S. court of appeals is authorized by the Constitution to review _____

    A. a decision made by U. S. district court within its circuit.

    B. a decision made by a state agency, such as the board of education.

    C. a decision made by a state trial court.

    D. a decision made by any federal trial court.

3. When a lumberyard sues another under a contract for damages, it is seeking _____

    A. repair for what has been damaged.

    B. specific performance under the contract.

    C. monetary compensation.

    D. a fine forbreach of the contract.

4. A state court, having general jurisdiction, may hear a case that involves _____

    A. a reckless driver that causes an accident on the interstate highway.

    B. a landowner who complains about military aircraft flying over his home.

    C. a foreign spy that compromises the security system of a local company.

    D. a publisher who reproduces school books without permission.

5. The right to trial by jury (instead of by judge alone) is said to be absolute, because _____

    A. it is axiomatically a basic human right.

    B. it is guaranteed by the Constitution.

    C. it is fundamentally unfair to have a trial without a jury.

    D. it is judicially mandated and a party may not waive it.

6. If new evidence is found to prove the guilt of a murder defendant who has been exonerated at trial, he cannot be tried again for the reason of _____

    A. double jeopardy.   B. ex post facto law.

    C. adversarial process.   D. mistrial.

7. A judge who sits for life with salaries never reduced is called _____

    A. an honorable judge.   B. administrative law judge.

Part One Anglo-American Legal Culture

      C. article I judge.   D. article III judge.

8. When a witness testifies in court by saying that "I know it was John, because my classmate Rodney, who was at the scene of the crime, told me that he saw John angrily stabbed Smith several times." This is _____
    A. voir dire.   B. hearsay.
    C. direct evidence.   D. circumstantial evidence.

9. The Supreme Court of the United States reviews cases by the writ of certiorari, whereby it reviews _____
    A. about 80% of the petitions a year.   B. about 8,000 petitions a year.
    C. about 80 petitions a year.   D. about 80 petitions a month.

10. The important aspects of the federal courts include all of the following except _____
    A. both sides of the litigations, through their lawyers, will show up in court to argue their cases.
    B. if a criminal defendant does not have a lawyer to argue for him, the court can assign one for free.
    C. the Supreme Court of the United States reviews only a limited number of important cases.
    D. the federal and state courts run parallel to each other, and a plaintiff is free to choose either one.

Chapter 4

The Opinions of the Appellate Courts and Precedents

导 读 <<

判例通常是由上诉法院对法律的阐述而构成。上诉不是对案件进行二审或再审。通俗地讲,初审法院通过审理事实,依照法律(成文法或案例),裁定双方谁对谁错;上诉法庭仅审理下级法院判得对不对,通常仅就书面证据审理初审法院是否正确适用法律。因此,所谓"案例法"和法学院学生所要学习的内容大多是上诉法院的判决意见,其中包括分析意见和判决结果。

分析意见(dictum)通常不具有约束力,只具有说服力,而判决结果(holding)才是具有约束力的"判例法"。世上没有完全一模一样的案件事实,因此判决也会因事实的不完全一致而相应地具有适用的差别。

本章列举了一些对判决结果的适用度造成影响的因素。

The doctrine of stare decisis is founded on the primacy of the opinions of the appellate courts. These form the main and primary focus of study and analysis of jurists, lawyers, and judges. The formation of legal education is based on these opinions. We study them just like we study the advocacy of star lawyers for the best form of strategy and techniques. Ditto for the most preeminent among; jurists to ascertain the most comprehensive, extensive, and creative exposition and criticism of legal doctrines.

Factors Likely to Figure in Distinguishing Decisions

Many reasons work to scale down the mythical authority of judicial law. Judicial law developed on the basis of the rule of precedent is inherently distinguished and may be weighed down in authority in subsequent cases. Factors involved in distinguishing a previous decision include the following:

The **hierarchical**① status of the court deciding the case.

The reputation of the judges writing the opinion.

Is there a dissent or even a concurring opinion?

When was the case decided?

How does the precedent fit with the surrounding laws?

How has the decision been dealt with in later cases?

What authority does the precedent enjoy generally?

Conflicting precedents in different jurisdictions work to detract from the authority of individual decisions.

How does a decision fare in subsequent scholarly scrutiny (study and criticism)?

How does it fare in the hand of mass media? And what are the reactions of the general public?

Has it been affected or otherwise compromised by changes in social, political, or economic condition?

What are the reactions of the legislative branch and/or the executive branch?

Is it generally followed in fact?

---

① 按等级划分的，分层的

Chapter 4
The Opinions of the Appellate Courts and Precedents

Has it fallen into **desuetude**[①]?

Has the composition of the court changed?

Is it a memorandum decision, that is, a decision that sets forth no reason while affirming a decision of a lower court that stated the facts and its reasons in an opinion?

Opposing Treatments of Precedents

The doctrine of stare decisis requires that cases with the same fact-situation be treated the same way. But in actual fact, there are simply no two cases exactly alike. No two cases are on all four.

Essentially, methods are made possible that involve certain skillful manipulation of the nature, scope and significance of the holding of the earlier case(s) and the relevance and materiality of the facts in the case(s). Thus, the interchangeability between the holding of a case and its obiter dictum is very high and frequent.

To extend the principle of a prior decision to the present case is to profit from its wisdom and experience. Read the holding of the earlier decision more broadly; treat differences in the facts of the two cases as immaterial; regard as holding what might have been considered as dictum upon a narrow reading of the earlier case. In essence, this amounts to the formulation of broader legal principle to subsume under it both the facts of the earlier case and the case on hand.

If it seems undesirable to apply the rule of the earlier decision to the case at hand, just narrow the holding of an earlier case in order to distinguish it from the one before the court by treating differences in facts as material. What might have been considered as holding upon a broad reading of the earlier case will be regarded as dictum—as not necessarily for the disposition of the dispute before the court.

The role of distinguishing cases is essential to the development of new laws or new rules. Judges distinguish cases either by limiting or broadening the extent and wording of a rule which inevitably seems to have originally been

---

① 废弃不用,废止失效

expressed in too general or too narrow terms in the face of new fact-situations. Even here the more conservative majority tends to use this technique to temper the daring, sometimes the extravagances of their more progressive colleagues.

To Distinguish or to Overrule

Even a binding authority is not absolute. When a decision would be patently wrong by following a precedent, the court may refuse to follow it.

The court may overrule a precedent when the precedent is so old and altered conditions or changes of circumstance have made it in appropriate for the case at hand. The court is also inclined to overrule a precedent when the composition of the court may have changed so that what was formerly the view of a vehement minority is now that of the majority. This would be particularly needed on a constitutional issue where legislation is not an available remedial device. Please refer to the factor operative in opposing treatment of previous decisions mentioned above.

Distinguished decisions inevitably amount to overruled decisions. Tradition demands that where possible the doctrine of precedent be honored by careful distinguishing rather than outright overruling of objectionable decisions. But in point of fact the decision that has been distinguished and expressly limited to its particular facts by a later opinion is often so whittled down as to be virtually overruled.

When following precedent is a better option, such as in matter of commercial case or property law the court may just go ahead in spite of the injustice in the particular case. When so doing the court takes the view that any change to rectify the injustice should be left to the legislature to make.

Multi-legged Holding

This is another puzzle that adds to the complication of the doctrine of staredecisis. This concerns the weight to be given to a multi-legged holding—a decision that is based upon several grounds rather than a single-ground. For example, three distinct errors cited as reasons for reversal holdings by an appellate court. Could it be that either one without the other would have been sufficient for the reversal? Or neither one was necessary to the decision? Is there

Chapter 4
The Opinions of the Appellate Courts and Precedents

therefore no holding? And the entire opinion is a dictum? It is commonly accepted by prudent lawyer that precedents stay more firmly when they stand on only one leg and alternate grounds make a holding less reliable.

Exercises

Please choose the best answer to the following questions:

1. The doctrine of stare decisis is founded on the <u>primacy</u> of the opinions of the appellate courts.
   A. supramacy   B. prime   C. principle   D. printed matter

2. The force of a judicial decision could be <u>weighed down</u> by dissenting or even concurring opinions.
   A. vitiated   B. wiped out   C. enhanced   D. invalidated

3. To extend the principle of a prior decision to the present case is <u>to profit from</u> its wisdom and experience.
   A. to make money out of   B. to take advantage of
   C. to distinguish from   D. to gain advantage of

4. If it seems undesirable to apply the rule of the earlier decision to the case at hand, a judge can simply <u>narrow the holding of</u> an earlier case in order to distinguish it.
   A. pin it to the facts of   B. pay no attention to
   C. sharpen   D. twist

5. When a decision would be <u>patently</u> wrong by following a precedent, the court may refuse to follow it.
   A. partly   B. openly
   C. intellectually   D. conspicuously

6. When following precedent is a better option, the court may just <u>go ahead</u> in spite of the injustice in the particular case.
   A. proceed   B. go head on   C. go away   D. step aside

7. The court may <u>overrule</u> a precedent.
   A. dwell upon   B. reject   C. invalidate   D. follow

8. The plaintiff _____ the burden of proof.
   A. vests   B. bears   C. invokes   D. takes

Part One Anglo-American Legal Culture

9. The court _____ the defendant to cease the infringement, apologize publicly and pay the plaintiff $20,000 in damages.
   A. decreed   B. sentenced   C. found   D. ordered
10. After many months of extensive negotiations, teams of lawyers and bankers were finally about to _____ the deal, which involved the merger of two global players.
    A. close   B. carry out   C. bring   D. sign

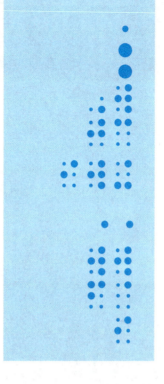

Introduction to American Laws

Part Two

Constitutional Law

> **导 读 <<**
>
> 美国宪法规划了法律的整体框架,是法律的灵魂。美国宪法的核心内容是对立法、司法、行政三权分立、相互制衡的制度设计。
>
> **一、司法权(judicial power)**
>
> 美国政府是一个权力有限的政府,只有经过宪法授权的行为才是合法行为。同时,宪法也在第3条中设定了联邦法院体系和联邦法院所管辖案件的范围。
>
> 联邦法院有两种:一种称作"第3条法院"(Article III Courts),也就是国会根据联邦宪法第3条第一款的规定设立的法院;一种叫做"第1条法院"(Article I Courts),也就是国会为了行使方方面面的立法权而设立的法院,这类法院不但有司法功能,有时候也具有行政功能。
>
> 联邦最高法院的管辖权,可以分为初审管辖权(original jurisdiction)和上诉管辖权(appellate jurisdiction)。初审管辖包括涉及大使、其他驻外高级外交使节与领事的案件,以及美国政府是一方当事人的案件。对于涉及宪法、国会制定的法律的案件,涉及国际条约的案件,除了国会规定的例外情况,最高法院都有管辖权。
>
> **二、立法权(legislative power)**
>
> 美国宪法以列举的方式授予了国会特定的权力,这些权力规定在第1条第8款,同时也通过"必要且适宜"条款(Necessary and Proper Clause)间接授予了国会辅助性的权力。

所谓必要且适宜的权力,就是为确保联邦政府任一分支机构权力的实施,国会有权制定所必须且适宜的法律。

宪法所列举的联邦国会的权力包括税收权、财政开支权、商务管理权、宣战权、调查权、财产处分权、破产规范权、邮政权与公民身份相关的权力、海事海商权(admiralty power)、货币制造与度量衡确定权、专利/著作权等。

三、对个人权利的保护与对政府行为或私人行为的限制

美国宪法的前10项修订条款,又称作权利法案,既是对个人权利的保护,又是对联邦政府权力的限制。

对私人行为的限制,主要体现在宪法的商务条款和外州公民权利条款,主要内容是联邦最高法院允许国会通过相关规定限制个人对他人的权利。

剥夺公民权法案(bills of attainder)是被宪法所禁止的。根据宪法第5条和第14条修正案,具有溯及力的立法和其他政府行为,可能会违背宪法的正当程序(due process)条款。条款规定,不经正当法律程序,政府不得剥夺个人的生命、财产和自由,强调程序的公正,至少要使当事人有机会向一个公正、中立的裁判者表达异议。

宪法的正当程序条款和平等保护条款的目的是保障法律的公平;实质性正当程序(substantive due process)是为了保证法律合理且不随意;平等保护条款则确保情况相似的个人受到相似对待。

法院审查有关法律是否违反上述条款时采取了一定的审查标准(standard of review),标准有三:严格审查标准(strict scrutiny)、中度审查标准(intermediate scrutiny)和最低审查标准(minimal scrutiny)。

平等保护条款对象限于各州行为,但是联邦政府明显不合理的歧视显然也是违反平等保护条款的。但是,如果立法行为或者政府行为仅仅具有歧视效果,并不足以启动严格审查或者中度审查程序。

四、基本权利

公民的基本权利包括隐私权、选举权、迁徙权等等。

公民的隐私权多种多样,包括婚姻、堕胎、生子等,都属于基本权利,对于影响这些基本权利的法律规定,要按照严格标准予以审查,只有在为保护极其重要的权益所必须时,这些法律才会得到支持。

年龄在18岁以上的美国公民都有选举权,包括全国性的和州内的选举。选举权也属于基本权利,通过严格审查后才能对这些权利予以限制。

迁徙权分为州际迁徙权和国际迁徙权。州际迁徙是基本权利,如果某个州要求达到一定居住年限的话,这一要求就必须通过严格审查标准才有效。至于国际迁徙,迄今联邦最高法院尚未将其宣布为基本权利,但是从正当程序规则中我们似乎可以推知,联邦政府不得随意干涉个人的国际间迁徙权。

Chapter 1

The Judicial Power

Marbury principle: Under *Marbury v. Madison*, it is the Supreme Court, not Congress, which has the authority and duty to declare a congressional statute unconstitutional if the Court thinks it violates the Constitution.

Congress has the general power to decide what types of cases the Supreme Court may hear, so long as it doesn't expand the Supreme Court's jurisdiction beyond the federal judicial power.

Congress also may decide what lower federal courts there should be, and what cases they may hear. Again, the outer bound of this power is that Congress can't allow the federal courts to hear a case that is not within the federal judicial power.

The federal judiciary may decide "cases" or "controversies" that fall within the federal judicial power.

I. Article III

The federal government is a government of limited powers, which means that for federal action to be legitimate, it must be authorized. The Constitution is the instrument that authorizes the federal government to act. Thus, whenever a question involves action by an entity of the federal government, the action will be valid only if it is authorized by the Constitution. The Constitution authorizes a federal court system in Article III, which provides that federal courts shall have Judicial Power over all "cases and controversies":

(1) Arising under the Constitution, laws, or treaties of the United States;

(2) Of admiralty and maritime jurisdiction;

(3) In which the United States is a party;

(4) Between two or more states;

(5) Between a state and citizens of another state;

(6) Between citizens of different states;

(7) Between citizens of the same state claiming lands under grants of different states; and

(8) Between a state or citizens thereof and foreign states, citizens, or subject.

II. Federal Courts

Only the action of Article III courts are the subject of our outline, but you should know that there are two types of federal courts.

1. Article III Courts

Article III courts are those established by Congress pursuant to the provisions of Article III, Section 1. Although Congress has **plenary power**① to delineate the jurisdictional limits, both original and appellate, of these courts, it is bound by the standards of judicial power set forth in Article III as to subject matter, parties, and the requirement of "case or controversy." Thus, Congress cannot require these courts to **render**② advisory opinions or perform administrative or non-judicial functions.

2. Article I Courts

Congress has created certain others, however, by way of implementing its various legislative powers; e.g. United States Tax Court, courts of the District of Columbia. Judges of such Article I courts do not have life tenure or protection from salary decrease as do Article III court judges. Article I courts are sometimes vested with administrative as well as judicial functions, and the congressional power to create such "hybrid" courts has been sustained by the Supreme Court.

---

① 全权;绝对权
② 作出(判决);执行,实施

Ⅲ. Jurisdiction of the Supreme Court

1. Original (Trial) Jurisdiction

Under Article Ⅲ, Section 2, the Supreme Court has original jurisdiction "in all cases affecting ambassadors, other public ministers and consuls, and those in which a state shall be a party." This provision is self-executing: Congress may neither restrict nor enlarge the Supreme Court's original jurisdiction, but Congress may give **concurrent jurisdiction**① to lower federal courts and has done so regarding all cases except those between states.

2. Appellate Jurisdiction

Article Ⅲ, Section 2 further provides that "in all other cases before mentioned [i. e., arising under the Constitution, Act of Congress, or treaty], the Supreme Court shall have appellate jurisdiction, both as to Law and Fact, with such Exceptions, and under such Regulations as the Congress shall make."

Ⅳ. Constitutional and Self-Imposed Limitations on Exercise of Federal Jurisdiction—policy of "Strict Necessity"

1. No Advisory Opinions

The Supreme Court's interpretation of the "case and controversy" requirement in Article Ⅲ bars rendition of "advisory" opinion. Thus, federal courts will not render decisions in moot cases, collusive suits, or cases involving challenges to governmental legislation or policy whose enforcement is neither actual threatened.

2. Ripeness—Immediate Threat of Harm

A plaintiff generally is not entitled to review of a state law before it is enforced (i. e., may not obtain a **declaratory judgment**②). Thus, a federal court will not hear a case unless the plaintiff has been harmed or there is an immediate threat of harm.

---

① 共同管辖权
② 宣告式判决,确认权利和义务的判决

3. Mootness

A federal court will not hear a case that has become moot; a real, live controversy must exist at all stages of review, not merely when the complaint is filed.

4. Standing

A plaintiff will be able to show a sufficient **stake**① in the controversy only if he can show an injury in fact—caused by the government—that will be remedied by a decision in his favor(i. e., causation and redressability).

(1) Injury

To be standing, a person must be able to assert that she is injured by a government action or that the government has made a clear threat to cause injury to her if she fails to comply with a government law, regulation, or order. Some specific injury must be alleged, and it must be more than the merely theoretical injury that all persons suffer by seeing their government engage in unconstitutional actions.

(2) Causation

There must be a causal connection between the injury and the conduct complained of—i. e., the injury must be traceable to the challenged conduct of the defendant and not be attributable to some independent third party not before the court.

(3) Redressability

In determining whether a litigant has a sufficient injury to establish standings, courts ask whether a ruling favorable to the litigant would eliminate the harm to him. If a court order declaring a government action to be illegal or unconstitutional (and ending that government action) would not eliminate the harm to the litigant, then that individual does not have the types of specific injury that would grant him standing to challenge the government action.

5. Adequate and Independent State Grounds

The Supreme Court will hear a case from a state court only if the state court judgment turned on federal grounds. The Court will refuse jurisdiction if it

---

① 风险,利害关系

finds adequate and independent nonfederal grounds to support the state decision.

(1) "Adequate"

The nonfederal grounds must be "adequate" in that they are fully dispositive of the case, so that even if the federal grounds are wrongly decided, it would not affect the outcome of the case.

(2) "Independent"

The nonfederal grounds must be "independent": If the state court's interpretation of its state provision was based on federal case law interpreting an identical federal provision, the state law grounds for the decision are not independent.

6. Abstention

(1) Unsettled State Law

When a federal constitutional claim is premised on an unsettled question of state law, the federal court should stay its hand ("abstain" temporarily), so as to give state courts a chance to settle the underlying state law question and thus potentially avoid the needless resolution of a federal constitutional issue.

(2) Pending State Proceedings

Generally, federal courts will not enjoin pending state criminal proceedings.

7. The Eleventh Amendment Limits on Federal Courts

The Eleventh Amendment is a jurisdictional bar that modifies the judicial power by prohibiting a federal court from hearing a private party's or foreign government's claims against a state government.

(1) What Is Barred?

The Eleventh Amendment's jurisdictional bar extends to the following:

a. Actions against state governments for damages;

b. Actions against state governments for injunctive or declaratory relief where the state is named as a party;

c. Actions against state government officers where the effect of the suit will be that retroactive damages will be paid from the state treasury or where the action is the functional equivalent of a quiet title action that would divest the state of owner ship of land; and

d. Actions against state government officers for violating state law.

(2) What Is Not Barred?

a. Actions Against Local Governments

The Eleventh Amendment protects only state governments. Local government (e. g., cities or counties) is not protected.

b. Actions by the United States Government or Other State Governments

Actions by the United States Government to other state governments are not barred.

Note: Native American tribes are treated as other private parties, and so they are barred from bringing an action against a state government in federal court.

(3) Exceptions to the Eleventh Amendment

a. Certain Actions Against State Officers

The Supreme Court allows the following actions to be brought against state officials despite the Eleventh Amendment:

(a) Actions against state officers for injunctions

(b) Actions against state officers for monetary damages from officer

(c) Actions against state officers for prospective payment from state

b. State Consents

A state may consent to suit in federal court. However, no consent will be found unless the state clearly waives its Eleventh Amendment immunity.

c. Congressional Removal of Immunity Under the Fourteenth Amendment

Congress can remove the states' Eleventh Amendment immunity under its power to prevent discrimination under the Fourteenth Amendment.

Chapter 2
Legislative Power

The power of congress is to make laws. Additionally, as an incident to that power, congress can conduct hearings and investigations, consider those matters that form the basis on which Congress may enact legislation, and perform other duties that are "necessary and proper" to the enacting legislation pursuant to Article I, Section I.

Ⅰ. Enumerated and Implied Powers

The Constitution grants Congress a number of specific powers, many of which are enumerated in Article I, Section 8. It also grants Congress auxiliary power under the Necessary and Proper Clause.

1. Necessary and Proper "Power"

The Necessary and Proper Clause grants Congress the power to make all laws necessary and proper (i.e., appropriate) for carrying into execution any power granted to any branch of the federal government.

2. Taxing Power

Congress has the power to lay and collect taxes, imposts, and excises, but they must be uniform throughout the United States. **Capitation**[①] or other direct taxes must be laid in proportion to the census, and direct taxes must be apportioned among the states.

---

① 人头税,按人头计算

3. Spending Power

Congress may spend to "provide for the common defense and general welfare." This spending may be for any public purpose—not merely the accomplishment of other enumerated powers. However, nonspending regulations are not authorized. Remember that the Bill of Rights still applies to this power.

4. Commerce Power

Article I, Section 8, Clause 3 empowers Congress to "regulate commerce with foreign nations and among the several states, and with the Indian tribes."

(1) Definition of Commerce

(a) Includes Basically All Activity Affecting Two or More States

Chief Justice Marshall in *Gibbons v. Ogden*, 22 U.S. 1(1824), defined commerce as "every species of commercial intercourse which concerns more states than one" and included within the concept virtually every form of activity involving or affecting two or more states.

(b) Include Transportation or Traffic

The Court has consistently regarded transportation or traffic as commerce whether or not a commercial activity is involved.

(2) "Substantial Economic Effect"

The Supreme Court has sustained congressional power to regulate any activity, local or interstate, that either it itself or in combination with other activities has a "substantial economic effect upon," or "effect on movement in," interstate commerce.

5. War and Related Powers

Article I, Section 8 gives Congress the power to declare war, raise and support armies, provide for and maintain a navy, make rules for the government and regulation of the armed forces, and organize, arm, discipline, and call up the militia. Of course, several other congressional powers may have direct or indirect application to military purpose: tax and spending power, commerce power, Senate's treaty consent power, maritime power, investigatory power, etc.

Chapter 2
Legislative Power

6. Investigatory Power

The power to investigate to secure information as a basis for potential legislation or other official action (such as impeachment or trying impeachments) is a well-established implied power. It is a very broad power, in that an investigation need not be directed toward enactment of particular legislation, but the following limitations on its use do exist.

7. Property Power

Congress has the power to "dispose of and make all needful rules and regulations respecting the territory or other property belonging to the United States." Many other congressional powers (war, commerce, postal, fiscal, etc.) obviously would be unworkable if the **ancillary power**① to acquire and dispose of property of all kinds—real, personal, and intangible—were not also implied from the main grants.

8. No Federal Police Power

Congress has no general **police power**② (i.e., power to legislate for the health, welfare, morals, etc., of the citizens.)

9. Bankruptcy Power

Article I, Section 8, Clause 4 empowers Congress "to establish uniform laws on the subject of bankruptcies throughout the United States." This power has been interpreted by the Supreme Court as nonexclusive; i.e., state legislation in the field is superseded only to the extent that it conflicts with federal legislation therein.

10. Postal Power

Article I, Section 8, Clause 7 empowers Congress "to establish post offices and post roads."

(1) Exclusive

The postal power has been interpreted as granting Congress a postal monopoly. Neither private business nor the states may compete with the Federal Postal Service absent Congress's consent.

---

① 附属权
② 治安权;社会综合治理权

(2) Scope of Power

Congress may validly classify and place reasonable restrictions on use of the mails, but may not deprive any citizen or group of citizens of the general mail "privilege" or regulate the mail in such a way as to abridge freedom of speech or press (except under valid standards, such as "obscenity") or violate the ban of the Fourth Amendment against unreasonable search and seizure.

11. Power over Citizenship

Article I, Section 8, Clause 4 empowers Congress "to establish a uniform rule of naturalization."

Exclusion of Aliens

Congress's power to exclude aliens is broad

(a) Nonresident Aliens

Aliens have no right to enter the United States and can be refused entry because of their political beliefs.

(b) Resident Aliens

Resident aliens are entitled to notice and hearing before they can be deported.

12. Admiralty Power

Although congressional power to legislate in maritime matters is not expressed in the Constitution, the Supreme Court has implied it from exclusive jurisdiction given the federal courts in this field by Article III, Section 2, supported by the Necessary and Proper Clause of Article I, Section 8.

13. Power to Coin Money and Fix Weights and Measures

Congress has the power to coin money and fix the standard of weights and measures under Article I, Section 8, Clause 5.

14. Patent/Copyright Power

Congress has the power to control the issuance of patents and copyrights under Article I, Section 8, Clause 8.

II. Delegation of Legislative Power

1. Broad Delegation Allowed

Congress has broad discretion to delegate its legislative power to executive

Chapter 2
Legislative Power

officers and/or administrative agencies, and even delegation of rulemaking power to the courts has been upheld.

2. Limitations on Delegation

(1) Power Cannot Be Uniquely Confined to Congress

To be delegable, the power must not be uniquely confined to Congress. For example, the power to declare war cannot be delegated, nor the power to impeach.

(2) Clear Standard

It is said that delegation will be upheld only if it includes intelligible standards for the delegate to follow. However, as a practical matter almost anything will pass as an "intelligible standard" (e. g., "upholding public interest, convenience, or necessary").

(3) Separation of Power Limitations

While Congress has broad power to delegate, the separation of powers doctrine restricts Congress from keeping certain over certain delegates. For example, Congress cannot give itself the power to remove an officer of the executive branch by any means other than impeachment (e. g., if Congress delegates rulemaking power to an executive branch agency (e. g., the FCC), it may not retain the power to fire the agency head). Similarly, Congress cannot give a government employee who is subject to removal by Congress (other than by impeachment) purely executive powers.

(4) Important Liberty Interests

If the delegate interferes with the exercise of a fundamental liberty to right, the burden falls upon the delegate to show that she has the power to prevent the exercise of the right and her decision was in furtherance of that particular policy.

Chapter 3

Executive Power

In its first three articles, the U.S. Constitution outlines the branches of the U.S. Government, the powers that they contain and the limitations to which they must adhere. Article II outlines the duties of the Executive Branch.

The President of the United States is elected to a four-year term by electors from every state and the District of Columbia. The electors make up the Electoral College, which is comprised of 538 electors, equal to the number of Representatives and Senators that currently make up Congress. The citizens of each state vote for slates of electors who then vote for the president on the prescribed day, selected by Congress.

In order to become president, a person must be a natural born citizen of the United States. Naturalized citizens are ineligible, as are persons under the age of 35. In the case that the president should be unable to perform his duties, be it by death or illness, the vice-president becomes the president. Amendment XXII placed a two-term limit on the presidential office.

I. Foreign Policy

1. Commander-in-Chief—President has board powers to use troops in foreign countries (case dismissed as *political question* or president wins because president has board power as commander in chief in domestic affairs)

2. Foreign affairs—paramount power, but shared with Congress (non-justiciable & inappropriate for judicial consideration); Congress has plenary power over foreign commerce

3. Treaties—agreements between the US & a foreign country that are

Chapter 3
Executive Power

negotiated by the President & are effective when ratified by the Senate

—State laws that conflict with treaties are invalid—Treaties prevail over conflicting state laws.

—If a treaty conflicts with a federal statute, the one adopted last in time controls.

—If a treaty conflicts with the United States Constitution, it is valid.

4. Executive agreements—an agreement between the US & a foreign country that is effective when signed by the President & the head of the foreign nation; NO Senate approval is required

—Executive agreements can be used for any purpose.

—Executive agreements prevail over conflicting state laws, but never over conflicting federal laws or the Constitution.

	Senate Approval Required	Conflict with State Law	Conflict with Federal Law	Conflict with Constitution
Treaties	YES	Treaty	Last in time	Constitution
Executive Agreements	NO	Executive Agreement	Federal Law	Constitution

II. Domestic Affairs

1. Appointment & removal power

(1) Appointment Power:

(i) Officers—Senate must approve(e.g. ambassadors, fed judges, officers of the US)

(ii) Inferior Officers—Congress may vest appointment in the President appointment

(a) Congress has some discretion in appointing inferior officers, and may vest the appointment of independent counsel in the lower federal courts

(b) Congress may not give itself or its officers the appointment power (that power is executive)(i.e. Congress cannot create a new executive agency where Congress appoints some of the members)

(2) Removal Power—unless removal is limited by statute, President may fire any executive branch official

(i) For Congress to limit removal power, it must be an office where independence from the President is desirable (i.e. it can limit removal of independent counsel, but not cabinet members)

（ii）Congress cannot prohibit removal, but can *limit* removal to good cause—this applies even to officers who should be independent from the President

2. Impeachment & removal: (i) the President, (ii) Vice President, (iii) fed judges, (iv) officers of the US can be impeached & removed from office for treason, bribery or for high crimes & misdemeanors

（1）Impeachment doesn't remove a person from office—it just means that there will be a trial in the Senate

（2）Impeachment by the House requires a majority vote, while conviction in Senate requires 2/3 vote

3. Executive Immunity—absolute immunity to civil suits for money damages while in office—BUT, President does not have immunity for actions that occurred *prior* to taking office

4. Executive privilege—applies to presidential papers & conversations, but such privilege must yield to other government interests (not absolute) i.e. need for evidence in a criminal trial (Watergate)

5. Power to pardon—BUT not for impeachment

（1）President may pardon only for fed crimes, NOT state crimes

（2）President may pardon only for criminal liability, NOT civil liability

United States v. Nixon
July 24, 1974

Facts of the Case

A grand jury returned indictments against seven of President Richard Nixon's closest aides in the Watergate affair. The special prosecutor was appointed by Nixon and the defendants sought audio tapes of conversations recorded by Nixon in the Oval Office. Nixon asserted that he was immune from the subpoena claiming "executive privilege," which is the right to withhold information from other government branches to preserve confidential communications within the executive branch or to secure the national interest. Decided together with *Nixon v. United States*.

Question

Is the President's right to safeguard certain information, using his "executive privilege" confidentiality power, entirely immune from judicial review?

Legal Provision: US Const. Art. II

Conclusion

No. The Court held that neither the doctrine of separation of powers, nor the generalized need for confidentiality of high-level communications, without more, can sustain an absolute, unqualified, presidential privilege. The Court granted that there was a limited executive privilege in areas of military or diplomatic affairs, but gave preference to "the fundamental demands of due process of law in the fair administration of justice." Therefore, the president must obey the subpoena and produce the tapes and documents. Nixon resigned shortly after the release of the tapes.

Chapter 4

Individual Guarantees Against Governmental or Private Action

Ⅰ. Constitutional Restrictions on Power and State Action Requirement

1. Bill of Rights

Twenty-seven amendments have been added to the Constitution since 1789. The first ten amendments, known as the Bill of Rights, were adopted as a unit in 1791. The Bill of Rights is the most important source of limitations on the federal government's power. By its terms, the Bill is not applicable to the states, although most of its safeguards have been held to be applicable to the states through the Fourteenth Amendment Due Process Clause.

2. The Fourteenth Amendment

The Fourteenth Amendment prohibits states (not the federal government or private persons) from depriving any person of life, liberty, or property without due process and equal protection of the law. As discussed above, this amendment is the most important source of limitations on the states' power over individuals, since through the Due Process Clause; most of the protections of the Bill of Rights are application to the states.

3. Commerce Clause

The Supreme Court has allowed Congress to use Commerce Clause to limit the power of individuals over other individuals—by adopting legislation barring private racial discrimination in activities "connected with" interstate commerce. Recall that under the affectation doctrine, almost any activity can be said to be

Chapter 4
Individual Guarantees Against Governmental or Private Action

connected with interstate commerce.

4. Rights of National Citizenship

The Supreme Court has also allowed Congress to limit the power of private individuals to infringe upon others' rights of national citizenship (e. g., the right of interstate travel, the right of assemble to petition Congress for redress), without pointing to any specific constitutional source for the power.

Ⅱ. State Action Requirement

1. Exclusive Pubic Functions

The Supreme Court has found that certain activities are so traditionally the exclusive **prerogative**① of the state that they constitute state action even when undertaken by a private individual or organization. To date, only running a town and running an election for public office have been found to be such exclusive pubic functions.

2. Significant State Involvement—Facilitating Private Action

"State action" also exists whenever a state affirmatively facilitates, encourages, or authorizes acts of discrimination by its citizens. Note, however, that there must be some sort of affirmative act by the state approving the private action; it is not enough that the state permits the conduct to occur.

---

① 特权

Chapter 5
Due Process

Due process is a difficult thing to define, and the Supreme Court has not been much help over the years. Due Process is mentioned in two places in the Constitution: in the 5th Amendment and in the 14th Amendment. The reference in the 5th Amendment applies only to the federal government and its courts and agencies. The reference in the 14th Amendment extends protection of due process to all state governments, agencies, and courts.

Due process, in the context of the United States, refers to how and why laws are enforced. It applies to all persons, citizen or alien, as well as to corporations.

Ⅰ. Basic Principle

The Due Process Clause of the Fifth Amendment (applicable to the federal government) and the Fourteenth Amendment (applicable to the states) provide that the government shall not take a person's life, liberty, or property without due process of law. Due process **contemplates**[①] fair process/procedure, which requires at least an opportunity to present objections to the proposed action to a fair, neutral decision-maker (not necessarily a judge).

1. When Is Individualized Adjudication Required?

There is a right to procedural due process only when the government acts to deprive an individual of life, liberty, or property (see below). There is no right to individualized adjudication when the government acts generally, even if

---

① 注重考虑,周密盘算

the action will result in burdening individuals' life, or property interests.

2. Intentional Deprivation v. Negligent Deprivation

Fair process is required for intentional acts of the government or its employees. If an injury is caused to a person through the mere negligence of a government employee, there is no violation of the Due Process Clause.

II. Is Life, liberty, or Property Being Taken?

Older Supreme Court cases indicated that due process protects "right," but not "privileges." This approach is no longer followed; rather the Court will determine whether a legitimate liberty or property interest is being taken.

1. Liberty

The term "liberty" is not specifically defined. It includes more than just freedom from bodily restraints (for example, it includes the right to contract and to engage in gainful employment). A deprivation of liberty occurs if a person:

(1) Loses significant freedom of action; or

(2) Is denied a freedom provided by the Constitution or a statute.

2. Property

"Property" includes more than personal belongings and realty, chattels, or money, but an abstract need or desire for (or a unilateral expectation of) the benefit is not enough. There must be a legitimate claim or "entitlement" to the benefit under state or federal law.

III. Relationship Between Substantive Due Process and Equal Protection

Generally where a law limits the liberty of all persons to engage in some activity, it is a due process question.

The Due Process Clause and the Equal Protection Clause guarantee the fairness of laws—substantive due process guarantees that laws will be reasonable and not arbitrary, and equal protection guarantees that similarly situated person will be treated alike. Both guarantees require the Court to review the substance of the law rather than the procedures employed.

IV. What Standard of Review Will the Court Apply?

The Court employs one of three tests in reviewing laws under these clauses, depending on the circumstances.

1. Strict Scrutiny (Maximum Scrutiny)

The Court uses the strict scrutiny standard when a suspect classification or fundamental right (these terms will be discussed infra) is involved. Under the strict scrutiny standard, a law will be upheld only if it is necessary to achieve a compelling or overriding government purpose. The Court will always consider whether less burdensome means for accomplishing the legislative goal are available. Most government action examined under this test fails.

2. Intermediate Scrutiny

The Court uses intermediate scrutiny when a classification based on gender or legitimacy is involved. Under the intermediate scrutiny standard, a law will be upheld if it is substantially related to an important government purpose.

3. Rational Basis (Minimal Scrutiny)

The rational basis standard is used whenever the other two standards are not applicable (i. e., most legislation). Under the rational basis standard, a law will be upheld if it is rationally related to a legitimate interest. It is difficult to fail this test; so most governmental action examined under this standard is upheld unless it is arbitrary or irrational.

Chapter 6

Equal Protection

The Equal Protection Clause of the 14th amendment of the U. S. Constitution prohibits states from denying any person within its jurisdiction the equal protection of the laws. In other words, the laws of a state must treat an individual in the same manner as others in similar conditions and circumstances. A violation would occur, for example, if a state prohibited an individual from entering into an employment contract because he or she was a member of a particular race. The equal protection clause is not intended to provide "equality" among individuals or classes but only "equal application" of the laws. The result, therefore, of a law is not relevant so long as there is no discrimination in its application. By denying states the ability to discriminate, the equal protection clause of the Constitution is crucial to the protection of civil rights.

Generally, the question of whether the equal protection clause has been violated arises when a state grants a particular class of individuals the right to engage in an activity yet denies other individuals the same right. There is no clear rule for deciding when a classification is unconstitutional. The Supreme Court has dictated the application of different tests depending on the type of classification and its effect on fundamental rights. Traditionally, the Court finds a state classification constitutional if it has "a rational basis" to a "legitimate state purpose." The Supreme Court, however, has applied more stringent analysis in certain cases. It will "strictly scrutinize" a distinction when it embodies a "suspect classification." In order for a classification to be subject to strict scrutiny, it must be shown that the state law or its administration is meant to discriminate. Usually, if a purpose to discriminate is found the classification will be strictly scrutinized if it is based on race, national origin, or, in some situations, non-U.S. citizenship (the suspect classes). In order for a classification to be found permissible under this test it must be proven, by the state, that there is a compelling interest to the law and that the classification is necessary to further that interest. The Court will also apply a strict scrutiny test if the classification interferes with fundamental rights such as first amendment rights, the right to privacy, or the right to travel. The Supreme Court also requires states to show more than a rational basis (though it does not apply the strictly scrutiny test) for classifications based on gender or a child's status as illegitimate.

The 14th amendment is not by its terms applicable to the federal government. Actions by the federal government, however, that classify individuals in a discriminatory manner will, under similar circumstances, violate the due process of the Fifth Amendment.

I. Constitutional Source

The Equal Protection Clause of the Fourteenth Amendment has no counterpart in the Constitution applicable to the federal government; it is limited to state action. Nevertheless, it is clear that grossly unreasonable discrimination by the federal government violates the Due Process Clause of the Fifth Amendment. Thus, there are really two equal protection guarantees. The Court applies the same standards under either constitutional provision.

II. Proving Discriminatory Classification

The mere fact that legislation or governmental action has a discriminatory effect is not sufficient to trigger strict scrutiny or intermediate scrutiny. There must be intent to discriminate on the part of the government. Intent can be shown in three ways: (i) facial discrimination; (ii) discriminatory application; (iii) discriminatory motive.

1. Facial Discrimination

A law may include a classification on its face. This type of law, by its own terms, makes an explicit distinction between classes of persons (perhaps by race or gender; e.g., all white males 21 or older may serve as jurors). In such cases the courts merely have to apply the appropriate standard of review for that classification.

2. Discriminatory Application

In some instances, a law that appears to be neutral on its face will be applied in a different manner to different classes of persons. If the persons challenging the governmental action can prove that the government officials applying the law had a discriminatory purpose (and used discriminatory standards based on traits such as race or gender), the law will be invalidated.

3. Discriminatory Motive

Sometimes a government action will appear to be neutral on its face and in its application, but will have disproportionate impact on a particular class of persons (such as a racial minority or women). Such a law will be found to involve a classification (and be subjected to the level of scrutiny appropriate to that classification) only if a court finds that the lawmaking body enacted or maintained the law for a discriminatory purpose. In such cases, the court should admit into evidence statistical proof that the law has a disproportionate impact on one class of persons. However, mere statistical evidence will rarely be sufficient in itself to prove that the government had a discriminatory purpose in passing a law. Statistical evidence may be combined with other evidence of legislative or administrative intent to show that a law or regulation is the product of a discriminatory purpose.

Ⅲ. Suspect Classifications

1. Race and National Origin

If governmental action classifies persons based on exercise of a fundamental right or involves a suspect classification (race, national origin, or alienage), strict scrutiny is applied. The result is invalidation of almost every case where the classification would burden a person because of her status as a member of a racial or national origin minority. The only explicit race discrimination upheld despite strict scrutiny was the wartime incarceration of United States citizens of Japanese ancestry on the West Coast.

(1) School Integration

Recall that only intentional discrimination will be found to create discriminatory classifications calling for strict scrutiny; thus, only intentional segregation in schools will be invalidated under equal protection.

(2) "Benign" Government Discrimination—Affirmative Action

Government action—whether by federal, state, or local governmental bodies—that favors racial or ethnic minorities is subject to strict scrutiny, as is government action discriminating against racial or ethnic minorities.

(3) Discriminatory Legislative Apportionment

Race can be considered in drawing up new voting districts, but it cannot be the predominant factor. If a plaintiff can show that a redistricting plan was draw up predominantly on the basis of racial considerations, the plan will violate the Equal Protection Clause unless the government can show that the plan is narrowly tailored to serve a compelling state interest.

(4) Private Affirmative Action

Private employees, of course, are not restricted by the Equal Protection Clause, since the Clause applies only to the government, and private employers lack state action. Nevertheless, Congress has adopted statutes regulating private discrimination by employers pursuant to its power under the enabling provisions of the Thirteenth and Fourteenth Amendments and the Commerce Clause. Thus, if ask whether private employer discrimination is valid, the answer generally cannot be based on equal protection.

2. Alienage[①] **Classifications**

(1) Federal Classifications

The standard for review of federal government classification based on alienage are not clear, but they never seem to be subject to strict scrutiny.

(2) State and local classifications

State/local laws are subject to strict scrutiny if based on alienage. A "compelling state interest" must be shown to justify disparate treatment. For example, a state law requiring United States citizenship for welfare benefits, civil service jobs, or a license to practice law will be struck down because there is no compelling interest justifying the requirement.

---

① 外国人身份

Chapter 6
Equal Protection

Ⅳ. Quasi-suspect Classifications

Classifications based on gender or legitimacy are almost always suspect. When analyzing government action based on such classifications, the Court will apply the intermediate standard and strike the action unless it is substantially related to an important government interest.

1. Gender

The Court has expressly held that government bears the burden of proof in gender discrimination cases and that an "exceedingly persuasive justification" is required in order to show that gender discrimination is substantially related to an important government interest.

(1) Intentional Discrimination Against Women

Gender classifications that intentionally discriminate against women will generally be invalid under the intermediate standard, because the government is unable to show the "exceedingly persuasive justification" that is required.

(2) Affirmative Action Benefiting Women

Classifications benefiting women that are designed to remedy past discrimination against women will generally be upheld.

(3) Intentional Discrimination Against Men

Intentional discrimination against men generally is invalid. However, a number of laws have been held valid as being substantially related to an important government interest.

2. Legitimacy Classification

Distinctions drawn between legitimate and illegitimate children are also reviewed under the intermediate scrutiny standard. Such classifications "must be substantially related to an important governmental objective."

(1) No Punitive Purpose

When the Court examines a classification based on illegitimacy, it gives greater attention to the purpose behind the distinction. It will not uphold discriminatory legislation intended to punish the offspring of illicit relationships.

(2) Immigration Preference to Legitimate Children—Permissible

Due to the plenary power over immigration, the Court upheld a federal law granting immigration preferences to legitimate children.

Chapter 7

Fundamental Rights

Fundamental rights are a group of rights that have been recognized by the Supreme Court as requiring a high degree of protection from government encroachment. These rights are specifically identified in the Constitution (especially in the Bill of Rights), or have been found under Due Process. Laws limiting these rights generally must pass strict scrutiny to be upheld as constitutional. Examples of fundamental rights not specifically listed in the Constitution include the right to marry and the right to privacy, which includes a right to contraception and the right to interstate travel.

I. Right of Privacy

Various private rights, including marriage, sexual relations, abortion, and childrearing, are fundamental rights. Thus, regulations affecting these rights are reviews under the strict scrutiny standard and will be uphold only if they are necessary to a compelling interest.

1. Marriage

The right of a male and female to enter into (and, probably, to dissolve) a marriage relationship is a fundamental right. Although not all cases examining marriage regulations clearly use the compelling interest standard, a law prohibiting a class of adults from marrying is likely to be invalidated unless the government can demonstrate that the law is narrowly tailored to promote a compelling or overriding or, at least, important interest.

Chapter 7
Fundamental Rights

2. Use of Contraceptives①

A state cannot prohibit distribution of nonmedical contraceptives to adults except through licensed pharmacists, nor prohibit sales of such contraceptives to persons under 16 who do not have the approval of a licensed physician.

3. Abortion

The Supreme Court has held that the right of privacy includes the right of women to have an abortion under certain circumstances without undue interference from the state. However, because the Court has held that the states have a **compelling interest**② in protecting the health of both the woman and the fetus that may become a child, it is difficult to apply the normal "strict scrutiny" analysis to abortion regulations since these two compelling interests may conflict with each other and with the regarding abortions and the Justices have not come to agreement on any applicable standard.

Ⅱ. Right to Vote

The right of all United States citizens over 18 years of age is mentioned in the Fourteenth, Fifteenth, Nineteenth, Twenty-Fourth, and Twenty-Sixty Amendments. It extends to all national and state government elections, including primaries. The right is fundamental; thus, restrictions on voting, other than on the basis of age, residency, or citizenship, are invalid unless they can pass strict scrutiny.

Ⅲ. Right to Travel

1. Interstate Travel

(1) Nature of the Right

Individuals have a fundamental right to travel from state to state, which encompasses the right: (i) to leave and enter another state, and (ii) to be treated equally if they become permanent residents of that state.

(2) Standard of Review

When a state uses a durational residency requirement (a waiting period) for

---

① 避孕用具
② 强制性利益,重大利益

dispensing benefits, that requirement normally should be subject to the "strict scrutiny" test. This means that the government must show that the waiting period requirement is tailored to promote a compelling or overriding interest. However, in some right to travel cases, the Court has not been clear as to whether it is using this strict scrutiny, compelling interest standard of review. The important point to note is that state residency requirements should not be upheld merely because they have some theoretical rational relationship to an arguably legitimate end of government.

2. International Travel

The Supreme Court has not yet declared that the right to international travel is fundamental, although the right appears to be protected from arbitrary federal interference by the Due Process Clause of the Fifth Amendment. The Court has held that this right is not violated when the federal government refuses to pay Social Security benefits to persons who leave the country. The test is "mere rationality, not strict scrutiny." Congress may give executive branch the power to revoke the passport of a person whose conduct in another country presents a danger to United States foreign policy. The Treasury Department, with congressional authorization, could restrict travel to and from Cuba without violating the Fifth Amendment.

Chapter 8

The First Amendment

Although the federal government is required by the provisions of the Constitution to respect the individual citizen's basic rights, such as right of trial by jury, the most significant guarantees for individual civil rights were provided by ratification of the Bill of Rights (Amendments 1—10). The First Amendment guarantees freedom of religion, speech, and the press, the rights of peaceful assembly and petition. Other amendments guarantee private property, fair treatment of those accused of crimes, such as unreasonable search and seizure, freedom from self-incrimination, a speedy and impartial jury trial, and representation by counsel.

Ⅰ. Free Speech Methodology

1. Content-based v. Content-neutral Restrictions:

(1) **Content-based** restrictions on speech generally must meet ***strict scrutiny***—2 types

(ⅰ) Subject matter restrictions—application of the law depends on the topic of the speech

(ⅱ) Viewpoint restrictions—application depends on the ideology of the message

(2) ***Content-neutral*** laws burdening speech generally need only meet intermediate scrutiny—must:

(ⅰ) further a significant government interest,

(ⅱ) narrowly tailored, AND

(ⅲ) leave open alternative channels of communication

2. **Prior Restraints**—Judicial orders to stop speech before it occurs (worst form of restraint on free speech)

(1) Court orders suppressing speech must meet strict scrutiny

(i) Procedurally proper court orders must be complied with until they are vacated or overturned—gag orders on press to prevent prejudicial pretrial publicity are NOT allowed

(ii) Collateral bar rule—a person who violates a court order is later barred from challenging it

3. **Vagueness & Overbreadth:**

(1) Vagueness—a law is unconstitutionally vague if not give reasonable notice of that is prohibited

(2) Overbreadth—a law is unconstitutionally overbroad if it regulates substantially more speech than is necessary

(3) **Fighting Words** (likely to provoke a violent response) laws are unconstitutionally vague & overbroad. HYPO: Appealing victim and nasty speaker—Answer is always that law prohibiting fighting words is unconstitutional.

4. **Symbolic Speech**—the government can regulate conduct that communicates IF (i) it has an important interest unrelated to suppression of the message, & (ii) the impact on communication is no greater than necessary to achieve the government's purpose

Constitutionally protected	Constitutionally NOT protected
—Flag burning —Burning of cross (unless there is intent to threaten) —Contribution limits for election campaigns	—Draft card burning —Nude dancing —Expenditure limitations

5. Anonymous speech is protected—protect right not to speak

II. What Speech Is Unprotected or Less Protected by the First Amendment

1. Incitement of Illegal Activity—government may punish speech if: (i) there's a substantial likelihood of imminent illegality, AND (ii) the speech is directed at causing the imminent illegality

Chapter 8
The First Amendment

2. **Obscenity & Sexually-oriented Speech:**

(1) Obscenity Test

(i) **appeal to the prurient interest** (a "shameful or morbid interest in sex")—local community standard;

(ii) **patently offensive under the law prohibiting obscenity**—local community standard; AND

(iii) **lack serious redeeming artistic, literary, political or scientific value**—national standard

(2) Zoning Permissible—government may use zoning ordinances to regulate the location of adult bookstores & movie theaters (Erogenous① Zoning is permissible)

(3) Child pornography—can be completely banned, even if not obscene②. (To be child pornography, it must be children, not adults that look like children or computer generated images)

(4) Punish private possession of obscene materials NOT allowed—BUT, may punish private possession of child pornography

(5) Government may seize the assets of businesses convicted of violating obscenity laws

(6) Profane & indecent speech—generally protected by the First Amendment, EXCEPT:

(i) broadcast media—broadcast is uniquely intrusive into the home, CAN censor profanity, (EXCEPT for cable television and the Internet which people choose to bring into their homes)

(ii) in schools(schools can punish profane and indecent language, including sexual innuendo)

3. **Commercial Speech:**

(1) False & deceptive ads—NOT protected by the First Amendment

(2) True commercial speech that inherently risks deception can be prohibited:

(i) Government may prohibit professionals from advertising or practicing under a trade name

(ii) Government may prohibit attorney, in-person solicitation of clients for

---

① 唤起情欲的,性感的
② 淫秽的,下流的

profit—BUT, if lawyers offer services for free or by letters, they can solicit

(iii) Government may NOT prohibit accountants from in-person solicitation of clients for profit

(3) Other commercial speech can be regulated if intermediate scrutiny is met (cannot solicit accident victims for 30 days was upheld)

(4) Commercial speech regulation must be *narrowly* tailored, but NOT need to be least restrictive alternative

4. **Defamation**—not protected, but the ability of a state to limit recovery is limited

actual malice[①]—knew the statement was false or acted with reckless disregard for the truth

Plaintiff	Liability Standard	Damages	Burden of Proof
Public official (or running for office)	actual malice	compensatory presumed/punitive	P must prove falsity by clear and convincing evidence
Public figure	actual malice	compensatory presumed/punitive	P must prove falsity by clear and convincing evidence
Private figure (matter of public concern)	negligence	compensatory for actual injury;	P must prove falsity and negligence on the part of the speaker
	actual malice	presumed/punitive damages require actual malice	
Private figure (matter of private concern)	unclear (negligence)	compensatory for actual injury	Unclear (burden on D to prove truth)
		presumed/punitive damages do not require actual malice	

5. **Privacy**

(1) Government may NOT create liability for the truthful reporting of information that was lawfully obtained from the government

(2) Liability is NOT allowed if the media broadcasts a tape of an illegally intercepted call, IF: (i) the media did not participate in the illegality, & (ii) it involves a matter of public importance

(3) Government may limit its dissemination of information to protect

---

① 真实恶意,实际恶意

private, but NOT in criminal trials—only the press has the First Amendment right in pre-trial criminal proceeding

6. Other government restrictions based on the content of speech—must meet strict scrutiny

III. What Places Are Available for Speech

1. **Public Forums**—government properties that the government id required to make available for speech (e.g. streets, sidewalks & parks)

(1) Regulations must be subject matter & viewpoint neutral

(2) Regulations must be a time, place, or manner regulation that serves an important government purpose & leaves open adequate alternative places for communication(e.g. No trucks with sound amplification equipment allowed in residential areas at night—UPHELD)

(3) *Narrowly tailored-government regulation of public forums need not use the least restrictive alternative* (e.g. city ordinance said concert in the park required city engineers for sound system—this is OK, because need not be least restrictive alternative)

(4) City officials can NOT have discretion to set permit fees for public demonstrations

2. **Limited/designated Public Forums**—government propertied that the government could close to speech, but chooses to open to speech; so long as government chooses to open property for speech, it must follow all of the above rules (e.g. school facilities are non-public forums in the evenings and on the weekends—Congress can open the place as a limited public form)

3. Non-public Forums—government properties that the government constitutionally can & does close to speech

(1) Government can regulate so long as the regulation on time, place & manner is (i) *reasonable* (rational basis), & (ii) viewpoint neutral

(2) Non-public forums include:

(i) military bases

(ii) Areas outside prisons & jails

(iii) Advertising space on city buses

(iv) Sidewalks on post office property

(v) Airports—may prohibit money solicitation; can NOT (vi) prohibit distribution of literature(fails rational basis review)

4. Private Property—the First Amendment right of access to private property (i.e. Shopping centers) for speech purposes.

	Subject matter neutral	Viewpoint neutral	Method of regulation allowed	Interest required
Public forums & Limited/designated public forums	YES	YES	time, place, or manner (i) open adequate alternative place (ii) narrowly tailored (NOT least restrictive)	important
Non-public forums	NO	YES	reasonable	legitimate
Private property	the First Amendment Right to use private property for speech purposes			

Ⅳ. Freedom of Association

1. Laws that *prohibit or punish group membership* must meet *strict scrutiny*—to punish a membership in a group, it must be proven that the person (i) actively affiliated with the group, (ii) knowing of its illegal activities, & (iii) with the specific intent of furthering those illegal activities.

2. Laws that require *disclosure of group membership*, where such disclosure would chill association, must meet strict scrutiny.

3. Laws that *prohibit a group from discriminating are constitutional*, UNLESS they are

 a. Intimate association (e.g., if you're not invited to a small dinner party, you can't sue), OR

 b. Expressive activity—discrimination is an integral part of the association (e.g., the KKK who have an anti-black messenger or Boy Scouts who had anti-gay message).

Ⅴ. Freedom of Religion

1. *Free Exercise Clause*

(1) Prohibits government interfere with religious *beliefs*

Member of the clergy *can* hold government office

Chapter 8
The First Amendment

(2) Allow regulation of general applicability (*conduct*)

Exception- Unemployment compensation (government may not deny benefits to individuals who quit their job for religious reasons)

2. ***Establishment Clause***

(1) Prohibits laws respecting the establishment of religion

(2) Test (SEX) (if any of these three are violated, it violates the Establishment Clause):

(i) Must be a Secular purpose for the law (e.g., 10 commandments can't be posted on public schools).

(ii) Effect must neither advance nor inhibit religion—government can't symbolically endorse religion, or a particular religion.

—plastic reindeer rule—if there are religious symbols accompanied by symbols from other religions, AND secular symbols (e.g., plastic reindeer), that's OK.

(iii) Must not be excessive entanglement with religion—government can't pay salaries of parochial school teachers because that would require too much supervision.

(3) Government can't discriminate *against* religious speech or among religions, unless strict scrutiny is met.

(4) Government sponsored religious activity in public schools is unconstitutional (e.g., school prayer, even moments of silence are unconstitutional, clergy delivered prayers at school graduations not allowed, student delivered prayers at football games not allowed), BUT religious students & community groups must have the same access to school facilities as non-religious groups.

(5) Government may give assistance to **parochial**[①] schools—so long as the money isn't used for religious instruction.

---

① 教区的

SCHENCK V. UNITED STATES

March 3, 1919

JUSTIE OLIVER WENDELL HOLMES, JR.: This is an indictment in three counts. The first charges a conspiracy to violate the Espionage Act of June 15, 1917... by causing and attempting to cause insubordination, etc., in the military and naval forces of the United States, when the United States was at war with the German Empire; to wit, that the defendant Charles T. Schenck willfully conspired to have printed and circulated to men who had been called and accepted for military service under the Act of May 18, 1917, a document set forth and alleged to be calculated to cause such insubordination and obstruction. The count alleges overt acts in pursuance of the conspiracy, ending in the distribution of the document set forth. The second count alleges a conspiracy to commit an offense against the United States; to wit, to use the mails for the transmission of matter declared to be non-mailed by... the Act of June 15, 1917, to wit, the above-mentioned document... The third count charges an unlawful use of the mails for the transmission of the same matter and otherwise as above. Schenck was found guilty on all the counts. He set up the First Amendment to the Constitution, forbidding Congress to make any law abridging the freedom of speech or of the press, and, bringing the case here on the ground, has argued some other points also of which we must dispose.

It is argued that the evidence, if admissible, was not sufficient to prove that the defendant Schenck was concerned in sending the documents. According to the testimony Schenck said he was general secretary of the Socialist party and had charge of the Socialist headquarters from which the documents were sent. He identified a book found there as the minutes of the executive committee of the party. The book showed a resolution of August 13, 1917, that 15,000 leaflets should be printed on the other side of one of them in use, to be mailed to men who had passed exemption boards, and for distribution. Schenck personally attended to the printing. On August 20 the general secretary's report said, "Obtained new leaflets from the printer and started work addressing envelopes," etc.; and there was a resolve that Comrade Schenck be allowed $15

Chapter 8
The First Amendment

for sending leaflets through the mail. He said that he had about fifteen or sixteen thousand printed. There were flies of the circular in question in the inner office which he said were printed on other side of the one-sided circular and were there for distribution. Other copies were proved to have been sent through the mails to drafted men... No reasonable man could doubt that the defendant Schenck was largely instrumental in sending the circulars about...

It is objected that the documentary evidence was not admissible because obtained upon a search warrant, valid so far as appears. The contrary is established. The search warrant did not issue against the defendant but against the Socialist headquarters at 1326 Arch Street and it would seem that the documents technically were not even in the defendants' possession... The notion that evidence even directly proceeding from the defendant in a criminal proceeding is excluded in all cases by the Fifth Amendment is plainly unsound.

The document in question upon its first printed side recited the first section of the Thirteenth Amendment, said that the idea embodied in it was violated by the conscription act and that a conscript is little better than a convict. In impassioned language it intimated that conscription was despotism in its worst form and a monstrous wrong against humanity in the interest of Wall Street's chosen few. It said, "Do not submit to intimidation," but in form at least confined itself to peaceful measures such as a petition for the repeal of the act. The other and later printed side of the sheet was headed "Assert Your Rights." It stated reasons for alleging that any one violated the Constitution when he refused to recognize "your right to assert your opposition to the draft," and went on, "If you do not assert and support your rights, you are helping to deny or disparage rights which it is the solemn duty of all citizens and residents of the United States to retain." It described the arguments on the other side as coming from cunning politicians and a mercenary capitalist press, and even silent consent to the conscription law as helping to support an infamous conspiracy. It denied the power to send our citizens away to foreign shores to shoot up the people of other lands, and added that words could not express the condemnation such cold-blooded ruthlessness deserves, &c., &c., winding up, "You must do your share to maintain, support and uphold the rights of the people of this country." Of course the document would not have been sent unless it had been intended to have some effect, and we do not see what effect it could be expected to have upon persons subject to the draft except to influence them to obstruct the carrying of it out. The defendants do not deny that the jury might find against them on this point.

But it is said, suppose that that was the tendency of this circular, it is protected by the First Amendment to the Constitution... We admit that in many places and in ordinary times the defendants in saying all that was said in the circular would have been within his constitutional rights. But the character of every act depends upon the circumstances in which it is done. The most stringent protection of free speech would not protect a man in falsely shouting fire in a theatre and causing a panic. It does not even protect a man from an injunction order to stop against uttering words that may have all the effect of force. The question in every case is whether the words used are used in such circumstances and are of such a nature as to create a clear and present danger that they will bring about the substantive evils that Congress has a right to prevent. It is a question of proximity and degree. When a nation is at war many things that might be said in time of peace are such a hindrance to its effort that their utterance will not be endured so long as men fight, and that no Court could regard them as protected by any constitutional right. It seems to be admitted that if an actual obstruction of the recruiting service were proved, liability for words that produced that effect might be enforced. The statute of 1917... punishes conspiracies to obstruct as well as actual obstruction. If the act, (speaking, or circulating a paper,) its tendency and the intent with which it is done are the same, we perceive no ground for saying that success alone warrants making the act a crime... But as the right to free speech was not referred to specially, we have thought fit to add a few words.

It is not argued that a conspiracy to obstruct the draft was not within the words of the Act of 1917. The words "obstruct the recruiting or enlistment service," and it might be suggested that they refer only to making it hard to get volunteers. Recruiting heretofore usually having been accomplished by getting volunteers the word is apt to call up that method only in our minds. But recruiting is gaining fresh supplies for the forces, as well by draft as otherwise. It is put as an alternative to enlistment or voluntary enrollment in this act. The fact that the Act of 1917 was enlarged by the amending Act of May 16, 1918... of course, does not affect the present indictment and would not, even if the former act had been repealed. Judgments affirmed.

Exercises

Ⅰ. Choose the best answer to the following questions:

1. Commerce clause is _____
   A. the constitutional provision giving the U.S. Congress power to legislate over matters that affect "interstate commerce."
   B. the power of the U.S. Congress to legislate over foreign affairs.
   C. the power of the president to regulate banks because of national economic and security considerations.
   D. the power of the President to regulate banks because of public safety issues.

2. A state has a total population of one million people, of whom only 4% are black. The question of whether to celebrate Martin Luther King Day was put on the ballot and failed to pass by the narrowest of margins. To ensure its passage in the next election, a local pastor sought to relocate elderly citizens to the state with "Friends of the King Holiday," a citizens' group operating in the state. The state has a 90-day residency requirement before a person can vote, and a one-year residency requirement before a person can receive state-funded medical assistance. An elderly woman relocated to the state two months before the election. She liked the state so much that she decided to remain permanently, and she applied for medical assistance the same day that she attempted to register to vote. The woman's application for state-funded medical assistance was denied, and the town clerk refused to allow her to register to vote.

   If the woman sues for medical benefits and the right to vote, what is the most likely outcome of the action?
   A. The court will order that the woman receive medical benefits.
   B. The court will order that the woman receive medical benefits and be permitted to register to vote, because she is a member of a suspect class.

Part Two Introduction to American Laws · Constitutional Law

    C. The court will deny the woman's claim for medical benefits and the right to vote, because she has resided in the state for only two months.

    D. The court will order that the woman be permitted to register to vote, because voting is a fundamental right that is not subject to state restrictions.

3. Congress recently enacted the Reproductive Health Act, and appropriated finds for the implementation of health education and clinical programs associated with sex education and pregnancy-related medical treatments. The sex-education programs were to provide clients with information about the prevention of sexually transmitted diseases, as well as information about all aspects of pregnancy prevention and termination. The president, who felt that homosexuality was immoral, ordered all executive branch personnel to refrain from discussing AIDS-related aspects of health care on the job. A physician's assistant working for the National Centers for Disease Control challenged the constitutionality of the president's order.

How is the court likely to find on the question of the constitutionality of the president's order?

    A. The order is constitutional, because the president has authority over executive branch employees.

    B. The order is constitutional, because the president has substantial discretion in executing the laws.

    C. The order is unconstitutional, because it violates the president's duty to faithfully execute the laws.

    D. The order is unconstitutional, because the president cannot refuse to spend funds as appropriated.

4. A city became a haven for protests of all kinds. Some of the protests and parades in the city had spawned counter-demonstrations, and on a couple of occasions, violent incidents erupted. The city council became worried when a budgetary analysis showed that the city spent $2,000,000 for extra police protection on weekends on which parades and rallies were held. Therefore, the city council passed an ordinance that provided that groups who applied for a permit to hold a parade or rally in the town could be charged up to a maximum of $2,500 for a permit, to be determined by the city manager,

Chapter 8
The First Amendment

based on how much police protection was anticipated to be needed. A group of radical environmentalists applied for a permit to hold a parade in the town. Knowing that one of the largest employers in a town was a lumber company, the city manager expected a counter-demonstration, and so he imposed a $1,000 fee for the permit. The environmentalists sued to enjoin the enforcement of the ordinance.

How should the court rule?

A. In favor of the city, because the fee was not based on the content of the message, was narrowly tailored to serve a significant governmental interest, and left open ample alternatives for communication.

B. In favor of the city, because the ordinance was a valid use of the city's police power to regulate for the city's safety and welfare.

C. In favor of the environmentalists, because the statute was facially void, not content-neutral, and gave the city manager overly broad discretion as to the price of the permit.

D. In favor of the environmentalists, because although the ordinance was content-neutral, it gave the city manager overly broad discretion as to the price of the permit.

5. A hearing officer has worked for a federal agency for 17 years. A federal statute provides that hearing officers and all other court employees, with the exception of Article III judges, must retire at age 70. The hearing officer, who is 69, is a highly productive employee, in good health, and could work for several years.

If the hearing officer seeks a declaratory judgment prohibiting her termination at age 70, which of the following is the strongest constitutional argument that the mandatory retirement statute is invalid?

A. The statute violates the powers granted to Congress under Article I.

B. The statute violates the Fourteenth Amendment Due Process Clause by depriving the hearing officer of a property right.

C. The statute violates the Fifth Amendment Due Process Clause by discriminating against the elderly.

D. The statute violates the Privileges and Immunities Clauses of Article IV and the Fourteenth Amendment.

6. A maintenance worker was hired by a city's parks department and is now in his third consecutive one-year contract. According to a city ordinance, he cannot acquire tenure until after five consecutive annual contracts. In his third year, the maintenance worker was notified that he was not being re-hired for the following year. Applicable state law and city department rules did not require either a statement of reasons or a hearing, and, in fact, neither was offered to him.

    Which of the following, if established, most strongly supports the parks department in refusing to give the maintenance worker a statement of reasons or an opportunity for a hearing?

    A. The maintenance worker's performance had been substandard.
    B. A speech he made that was critical of parks department policies violated a department regulation concerning employee behavior.
    C. The maintenance worker worked at the parks department for less than five years.
    D. The maintenance worker could be replaced with a more competent maintenance worker.

7. An army fort had been used as a military outpost for more than 100 years. Following the end of the Cold War, the federal government closed the fort and sold half of the property to the state, which used the land to build a university. The population at the school is now double the population that had existed at the base, straining the available water supply. The water source, while located on the land purchased by the state, supplies water to both halves of the property.

    As a humanitarian gesture in response to global events, the federal government agreed to take in 200 refugees from a war-torn country, and decided to place them in the barracks that remained on the portion of the land which the federal government still owned. The state then brought suit in federal court to prevent the refugee relocation, claiming that there would not be enough water for the existing population.

    What is the most likely outcome of the suit?

    A. The state will prevail, because a state may assert its regulatory authority over the federal government.

Chapter 8
The First Amendment

B. The state will prevail, because the source of the water is on state property.

C. The state will not prevail, because of the Supremacy Clause.

D. The state will not prevail, because a state may not assert its regulatory authority over a natural resource to be used by the federal government for the benefit of aliens.

8. For more than 100 years, the premier manufacturers of boats in the nation carried on their businesses in one particular state. There was little competition until recently, when out-of-state manufacturers began to take a significant portion of the boat-building business. At the same time, a global economic downturn affected the retail market for boats. Sales of boats manufactured in the state plummeted, layoffs followed on a massive scale, several builders closed their businesses permanently, and the surviving boat manufacturers turned to their state legislators for help.

   The legislature responded by enacting an excise tax on all boats purchased in the state but manufactured elsewhere. The amount of the tax on each boat was a percentage of its purchase price, with luxury vessels paying an additional surcharge. A manufacturer of recreational and luxury crafts in a bordering state had acquired a large market share of the retail boat business in the state prior to the tax being passed.

   In a challenge to the excise tax by the boat manufacturer in federal court, which of the following is the strongest constitutional argument against enforcement of the tax?

   A. The tax violates the Privileges and Immunities Clause.

   B. The tax imposes a burden on interstate commerce.

   C. The tax violates the Due Process Clause of the Fourteenth Amendment.

   D. The tax violates the Equal Protection Clause of the Fourteenth Amendment.

9. On the last day of its legislative session for 2009, a state legislature enacted the following statute, to go into effect on January 1, 2010: "Recycling creates many jobs in our great state, but many state citizens could benefit from increased demand for recycled products. Therefore, all offices in the state must use only 100% recycled paper in their copiers and printers." The governor signed the bill into law. On November 1, 2009, the state Chamber

of Commerce filed a complaint in state court challenging the constitutionality of the new law. The state filed a motion to dismiss.

Which argument would best support the state's motion?

A. The statute is constitutional, because the state's police power includes the authority to enact legislation for the health, welfare, and safety of its citizens.

B. The Chamber of Commerce does not have third-party standing.

C. The matter is not ripe for adjudication.

D. The complaint asks for an advisory opinion, which state courts are not permitted to render.

10. State law requires that any alcohol sold in the state must be sold through state-operated liquor stores. Recently, many of the stores in the state have had problems with employees belonging to a particular racial minority group. State legislators, aware that members of this minority group rarely graduate from college, passed a law that no person may apply for a job in a state-operated liquor store without a college degree. Members of the minority group who applied for jobs with the liquor stores and who were rejected on the basis that they lacked college degrees challenged the law as being discriminatory on the basis of race.

Which of the following correctly describes the level of scrutiny the court should use?

A. Strict scrutiny, because the classification is based on race.

B. Strict scrutiny, because even though the law is facially neutral, the state had a discriminatory purpose.

C. Strict scrutiny, because the law has a discriminatory effect against members of the racial minority.

D. Rational basis scrutiny, because the law is facially neutral and a mere discriminatory effect is insufficient to trigger strict scrutiny.

III. Essay Questions:

QUESTION 1

The Constitution of the State of America contains a due process clause whose language is identical to the Due Process Clause of the U. S. Constitution's Fourteenth Amendment. Tom was a teacher in the Town of Aaron, in

Chapter 8
The First Amendment

America. Because Tom's status was that of "probationary teacher," the custom in Aaron was that Tom could be fired at the end of any school year without cause. Tom was fired without cause. He sued Aaron in America state court. His suit was premised on the argument that his firing violated the America due process clause, in that he was not given a hearing before being fired. The Ames state court agreed, and the higherst appeals court in Ames affirmed. Now the Town of Aaron has appealed the case to the U. S. Supreme Court. May the U. S. Supreme Court hear the case? Give your reasons.

QUESTION 2

Five years ago, City adopted a municipal ordinance prohibiting the placing of "commercial" signs on rooftops within city limits. The stated purpose of the ordinance was "... improving the quality of life within City by emphasizing and protecting aesthetic values." The ordinance also provided that all signs in place on the date of its adoption in violation of its terms, must be removed within five years.

Three years ago, Rugged Cross Church (Church), with its church building situated within City's limits, placed a 20-foot blue neon-lighted sign in the shape of a cross on its church roof, with the message "Join and Support Our Church" in white neon lights inside the blue neon borders of the cross.

After the Church sign was in place, various citizens of City urged that the sign ordinance be amended to include all rooftop signs in City. Other citizens complained to City officials that Church's sign, in particular, was "an eyesore."

Effective two months ago, City amended its sign ordinance by deleting the word "commercial." City then notified Church that its rooftop sign would have to be removed within five years.

Church has brought suit against City in a state trial court of proper jurisdiction, claiming that the amended City sign ordinance is invalid under the United States Constitution, both (1) by its terms and general application, and (2) as City seeks to apply it to Church.

How should the court rule on each of Church's claims? Discuss.

Contracts

> **导 读** <<
>
> 普通法系强调合同是一种"允诺"(promise)。合同可以分为几种类别:(1) 已履行合同(executed contract)与待履行合同(executory contract);(2) 盖印合同(specialty contract)和简单合同(simple contract 或 parol contract);(3) 有效(valid)合同、无效(void)合同、可撤销(voidable)合同和不可执行(unenforceable)的合同。
>
> 合同的成立必须经过磋商过程,并且要有对价支持。磋商过程,一般表现为要约与承诺,并最终就主要条款达成一致。合同法要求要约必须清晰确定、向一个或数个具体相对人发出、足以表述要约人(offeror)受到约束(bound)的意思、到达受要约人(offeree)生效。要约不同于要约邀请(invitation offer),后者只是邀请别人向自己发出要约,而没有受到约束的意思。要约经过承诺(acceptance)后可以形成两种合同:双务合同、单务合同。要约在下列情形下终止:撤回(revocation)、受要约人拒绝(rejection by the offeree)、反要约(counter-offer)、期限届满(lapse of time)、任何一方死亡或无行为能力(incapacity),以及要约的条件未能满足。
>
> 所谓承诺,就是受要约人(offeree)依照要约要求的方式,向要约人做出接受其要约内容的意思表示。承诺要成立,必须遵循要约人明示或默示的方式,必须由受要约人或其代理人在要约规定的有效期内或者在合理的期限内做出,必须是无条件的,不能是反要约(counter-offer)。承诺可以通过履行或允诺做

出,但《合同法第二次重述》允许特殊情况下以沉默形式做出。做出的承诺要符合"镜像原则"(the mirror image rule)。承诺生效的时间,一般是投邮主义(Mail-box Rule),即以书信、电报作出承诺时,一经投至邮筒或者交至电报局即发生法律效力。

对价的主要特征是:必须真实且具有一定价值,不一定是充分的(adequate)(即不一定在价值上与要约对等或相等),但必须是合法的,必须由被允诺人提供,必须有被履行的可能性,不能是过去的(past consideration is no consideration),不能是既存义务或公共职责(public duty)。对价之要求有两个例外:(1)和解与清偿(accord and satisfaction),例如受要约人本应该支付特定款项,但是他如果答应提前支付或者在不同的地点支付部分款项以清偿所有欠款,那么要约人不再索要剩余款项的诺言就要受到约束;(2)衡平禁反言原则(doctrine of equitable estoppel)或允诺禁反言原则(doctrine of promissory estoppel)。即如果合同的一方当事人不受自己作为对价的允诺的约束,那么对方也不受约束,合同无效。

合同的条款就是界定合同当事人权利、义务关系的内容,包括明示条款(express term)、默示条款(implied term)和免责条款(exemption clause)。根据口头证据规则(the Parol Evidence Rule),"当事人签订正式书面合同"以作为正式协议时,"合同条款不得因此前的书面或口头协议而变更或推翻,但不排除与书面合同并无抵触的口头证据"。默示条款又可以分为三类:事实上的默示条款(term implied in fact)、法律上的默示条款(term implied in law)以及惯例性的默示条款(customary implied term)。许多大公司和公共机构会在合同中加入免责条款,使自己免负侵权责任。免责条款的适用要遵守一定的规则,其中包括不利于提供者原则(the contra proferentem rule)、矛盾解释规则(the repugnancy rule)以及四只角原则(the four corners rule)。

未成年人(minor)、精神病人(person of unsound mind)和公司法人(corporation)在缔约能力方面不尽相同。错误(mistake)、虚假陈述(misrepresentation)、胁迫(duress)、不当影响(undue influence)和非法(illegality)等也属于影响效力的因素。

两个当事人会为了第三方的利益签订合同,这个第三方叫做受益人,有意受益人(intended beneficiary)有权起诉要求执行前述两位当事人之间的合同,但意外受益人(incidental beneficiary)无此权利。

如果没有合法理由,一方当事人到期不履行合同、履行不符合约定,或者使自己无法履行合同,则为违约。如果到期之前当事人明确表示不履行合同或者使自己无法履行合同,则称为预期违约(anticipatory breach)。对于违约,普通法提供的救济有赔偿金(damages),商定金额之诉(action for an agreed sum)以及按照合理价格支付(quantum meruit);衡平法提供的救济由法庭自由裁量权,一般包括实际履行(specific performance)和禁止令(injunction)。合同的争议可以通过法院、替代性纠纷解决机制(alternative dispute resolution)或商业仲裁解决。

Chapter 1

Basics of Contracts

Contracts are promises that the law will enforce. The law provides remedies if a promise is breached or recognizes the performance of a promise as a duty. Contracts arise when a duty does or may come into existence, because of a promise made by one of the parties. To be legally binding as a contract, a promise must be exchanged for adequate consideration. Adequate consideration is a benefit or detriment which a party receives which reasonably and fairly induces them to make the promise/contract. For example, promises that are purely gifts are not considered enforceable because the personal satisfaction the grantor of the promise may receive from the act of giving is normally not considered adequate consideration. Certain promises that are not considered contracts may, in limited circumstances, be enforced if one party has relied to his detriment on the assurances of the other party.

Contracts are mainly governed by state statutory and common law and private law. Private law principally includes the terms of the agreement between the parties who are exchanging promises. This private law may override many of the rules otherwise established by state law. Statutory law may require some contracts be put in writing and executed with particular formalities. Otherwise, the parties may enter into a binding agreement without signing a formal written document. Most of the principles of the common law of contracts are outlined in the Restatement of the Law Second, Contracts, published by the American Law Institute. The Uniform Commercial Code, whose original articles have been adopted in nearly every state, represents a body of statutory law that governs important categories of contracts. The main articles that deal with the

Chapter 1
Basics of Contracts

law of contracts are Article 1 (General Provisions) and Article 2 (Sales). Sections of Article 9 (Secured Transactions) govern contracts assigning the rights to payment in security interest agreements. Contracts related to particular activities or business sectors may be highly regulated by state and/or federal law.

In 1988, the United States joined the United Nations Convention on Contracts for the International Sale of Goods which now governs contracts within its scope.

I. Definitions of Contracts

An agreement creats obligations enforceable by law. The basic elements of a contract are mutual assent, consideration, capacity, and legality. In some states, the element of consideration can be satisfied by a valid substitute. Possible remedies for breach of contract include general damages, consequential damages, reliance damages, and specific performance.

The Restatement Second of Contracts §1 in the United States defines a contract as "a promise or a set of promises for the breach of which the law gives a remedy, or the performance of which the law in some way recognizes as a duty."

Black's Law Dictionary defines a contract "an agreement between two or more parties creating obligations that are enforceable or otherwise recognizable at law, (a binding contract); the writing that sets forth such an agreement (a contract is valid if valid under the law of the residence of the party wishing to enforce the contract)."

The nature of contract, under civil law, is a "meeting of minds" or "mutual assent." Article 1101 of French Civil Code states: "Contract is a mutual assent with which one person or more is obligated to give a thing, to do or not to do a thing to one person or more persons."

II. Classification of Contracts

Contracts may be classified in the following categories:

1. Executed and Executory Contracts

Executed contracts are those in which the party or parties concerned have done all that they are, under the contract, required to do.

Executory contracts are those in which one or both sides have not yet performed the contractual obligations, for example, goods have not actually been delivered.

2. Specialty and Simple Contracts

A specialty contract is made by deed. It is legally binding because of the special solemnity attached to its form. It does not derive its legally binding quality from the operation of the law of contract but from its solemnity; so it does not need to be a true contract at all. To take effect as a deed, an instrument must make it clear on its face that it is intended to be a deed and must be validly executed.

Simple or "parole" contracts are not made by deed (e. g., orally, by conduct, or in writing). They derive their legal status entirely from the law of contract. It is with this kind of contracts that we are primarily concerned.

3. Void, Voidable and Unenforceable Contracts

A void contract is one which does not exist and which has never existed. A contract is void when it is destitute of all legal effect.

A contract is voidable when the law allows one of the contracting parties to withdraw from the contract if he so wishes.

The distinction between void and voidable contracts is crucial where the interest of a third party is involved. A voidable contract remains effective unless and until the innocent party chooses to avoid it; therefore, in case of a contract for the sale of goods, if the buyer resells the goods before the contract is avoided, the sub-buyer becomes the owner and retains the property provided that he took it in good faith. When a contract is void, ownership of the property which has been sole will not pass to the buyer, who will not be able to sell it to anyone else. The original seller will be able to recover the property from whoever has it.

A contract is unenforceable when, although it is valid if the parties perform it; it can not be enforced in the courts of law if either party fails to do so, thus, we call these contracts as unenforceable.

III. Formalities: Form of a Contract

Contracts may have the following four forms, which we will discuss in details in later section hereunder:

(1) Under seal;
(2) In writing;
(3) Evidenced in writing;
(4) Oral contracts.

IV. The Essentials of a Valid Contract

Under the common law, a valid contract is an agreement that contains all of the essential elements of a contract. As students of business law well know, a contract contains a number of elements:

(1) There must be an offer and acceptance: the agreement. If there is no agreement reached by the parties, of course there is no contract and no so-called valid contract.

(2) There must be consideration (unless the agreement is under seal).

(3) Certain types of agreement are only valid if made in a particular form, e.g., in writing.

(4) The contract parties must have the intention to create legal relations.

(5) The parties must have the appropriate capacity to contract.

(6) There must be genuine consent by the parties to the terms of the contract, and the terms shall be clear and certain.

(7) The contract must not have been concluded as a result of undue influence, duress or misrepresentation.

(8) The contract must not contradict public policy or be otherwise illegal.

(9) The contract must be capable of being performed.

(10) The contract must not be frustrated by an intervening event.

The civil law countries have similar stipulations to that except for the legally sufficient consideration. If a contact misses any one of these essential elements, it is a void, voidable or unenforceable contract.

Chapter 2
Contract Formation

First, students should get to know that a contract is an agreement and mutual assent reached through a negotiating process, which can be divided into two essential steps, offer and acceptance. Thus, students are required to pay much attention to the definition and requirements of and other relevant contents regarding offer and acceptance. Second, students may have a rough understanding about what a consideration is, its characters and its importance in common law.

Ⅰ. Mutual Assent

In general, before a contract can be formed the parties must mutually assent to the main terms of the agreement. For example, there usually must have mutual assent to the parties, the price, the time for performance, and the subject matter of the agreement. Whether there is mutual assent and the agreed-upon terms are measured from an objective standpoint. In other words, courts will look to what a reasonable person in the situation of the other party would conclude that his objective manifestation[①] of intent meant. The most common way that a contract is formed is through an offer and acceptance.

1. Offer

There are no magic words required to extend an offer, but all offers contain three elements:

(1) an expression of intent to enter a present contract;

---

① 表示,表现形式

Chapter 2
Contract Formation

(2) a sufficient articulation of the essential terms of the proposed bargain; and,

(3) communication of that intent and those terms to another person (the offeree) who is thereby endowed with the capacity to form a contract by a timely and conforming acceptance.

Therefore, it is different from:

An Invitation Offer, which is not to make an offer but, invites the other party to do so, it is not capable of being turned into a contract by acceptance, e. g. by displaying goods in a shop-window, or an indication of price at which petrol is to be sold at a filling station, or circulation of a price-list by a wine merchant.

Advertisement, which is addressed to public, not to specific one or more persons as required by an offer. Most of the nations recognize that an advertisement can never create the power of acceptance in a member of the public who reads the ad, but merely constitute an invitation. Meanwhile, however, it is recognized that if an advertisement is specific enough in describing the goods, their quantity and price, it may be considered an offer. Advertisement of rewards are generally considered as an offer, e. g. for the return of lost or stolen property, or for information leading to arrest or conviction of the perpetrator of a crime, are all treated as offers, because they are clearly made with the intension to be bound as no further bargaining is expected to result from them.

Auction: the putting up of goods for sale by auction is not an offer. The person who bids makes an offer which the auctioneer is free to accept or reject and the auctioneer's request for bids is merely an invitation to treat. The auctioneer's final decision of the successful bid is the only acceptance.

(4) Types of Contract

There are generally two different types of contracts contemplated by the offer:

a. Bilateral contract: an offer that promises to do something in exchange for another promise is an offer for a bilateral contract. The offer contemplates acceptance by a promise, with performance to follow. The contract is formed by the exchange of promises. For example, if John promised to pay Sally $50 in exchange for her promise to go to the grocery for him, this would be an offer for a bilateral contract.

b. Unilateral contract: an offer that promises something in exchange for performance of some act is an offer to enter into a unilateral contract. For example, if John promises to pay Sally $50 if Sally goes to the grocery for him, this is an offer for a unilateral contract. The offer contemplates acceptance by performance, and the contract is formed when performance is complete. A reward is generally an offer for a unilateral contract.

(5) Duration of an Offer

An offer terminates at the end of the time stated in the offer, and an attempted acceptance after that time is merely a counter offer. If no time is stated in the offer, it will lapse after a reasonable time. The duration of a reasonable time is a question of fact, dependent upon the nature of the contract, business usages, and other circumstances of which the offeree either knows or should knows.

(6) **Lapse**① of Offer

The offer remains open or valid until it is terminated in one of the following ways:

a. By revocation: revocation of offer means withdrawal of the offer and it will only be effective if it is communicated to the offeree before he accepts the offer.

As a general rule, an offer is not binding on the offeree. If the offeree does not accept it, he has no obligation to give a notice to the offeror. Whether or not an offer is binding on the offeror is rather complex. In common law, an offer generally is not binding on the offeror, due to the lack of consideration not being signed and sealed, and the offereror can withdraw the offer at any time before the offeree's acceptance.

Obviously, the above stipulation doesn't meet the development of modern economic life. UCC (Uniform of Commercial Code) has improved this and holds that an offer can't be revoked if (i) the offeror is merchant; (ii) it has a period of validity and (iii) the offer must be in writing and the offeror must

---

① （权利等的）失效,消失

sign on it. Article 14 of the CISG (United Nations Convention on Contract for the International Sale of Goods) states: (i) Until a contract is concluded an offer may be revoked if the revocation reaches offeree before he has dispatched an acceptance; (ii) However, an offer can't be revoked: if it indicates, whether by stating a fixed time for acceptance or otherwise, that it is irrevocable; or if it is reasonable for the offeree to rely on the offer as being irrevocable and the offeree has acted in reliance on the offer.

b. By rejection by the offeree, that is, by non-acceptance within the time prescribed for acceptance by the offeror.

Seller mails a letter to Buyer in which he offers to sell him Blackacre for $10,000, the offer to remain open for two weeks. Three days after receiving this offer, Buyer writes a letter to Seller informing him that he rejects it. Later Buyer writes a second letter to Seller stating that he has changed his mind and that he now accepts the offer. This letter reached Seller well within the period set for acceptance. Is Seller bound? It is generally assumed that a definite rejection once communicated extinguishes the offeree's power of acceptance, so that no contract would result on the facts stated. In one of the few discussions of the possible rationale of this rule it is said, "The real reason why a rejection... should terminate the power to accept seems to be the effect that it will probably have upon the thought and actions of the offeror." Corbin, Offer and Acceptance and Some of the Resulting Legal Relations, 1917, 26 Yale L.J. 169, 197.

c. **By counter-offer**[①], an acceptance is not a valid one and constitutes a new offer and a counter-offer if it contains additions or reductions or amendment to the offer, which may be accepted by the original offeror.

d. By lapse of time: an offer will expire after the expiration of a fixed time limit if it has been specified. If an offer doesn't express any provision limiting its duration, it will lapse after a reasonable time. What is a reasonable time will depend on the nature of the offer and the circumstances of the case.

e. By death of either party: an offer lapse on the death either of the offeror or the offeree before acceptance. Death after acceptance does not affect the

---

① 反要约,还价

obligations arising from a contract unless they are of a personal nature.

Restatement Second §48 provides that "an offeree's power of acceptance is terminated when the offeree or offeror dies or is deprived of legal capacity to enter into the proposed contract." According to this Section, the offeror's death or incapacity extinguishes the offeree's power to create a contract by acceptance even though the offeree did not know of the death or incapacity at the time he accepted.

Where the proposed contract is of such a nature that it would itself be dissolved by the death or incapacity of one of the parties after it was entered into, it is, of course, unnecessary to inquire whether the death or incapacity of the offeror revoked the offer. For example, a contract of personal employment is normally regarded as dissolved by the death of either the employer or employee. It would therefore be pointless to insist that an offer of employment survived the death of the offeror, since the contract itself would be incapable of surviving that **contingency**①. The problem of the continued existence of the offeree's power of acceptance does, however, become material in cases where the proposed contract, if once validly concluded, would survive the death or incapacity of a party.

f. By failure of a condition subject to which the offer was made. If the offer was made subject to a condition and that condition is not fulfilled, the offer is incapable of acceptance.

Akers v. J. B. Sedberry, Inc.
39 Tenn. App. 633, 286 S. W. 2d 617(1955).

Facts: Sedberry (D), through majority shareholder Mrs. Sedberry, entered into a contract with Akers (P) whereby Akers would serve as Chief Engineer for five years. Sedberry entered into a similar five year employment contract with Whitsitt (P). Akers and Whitsitt were to perform their duties at the Jay Bee Manufacturing Company in Tyler, Texas.

Mrs. Sedberry later purchased stock in Jay Bee owned by Jay Bee's general

---

① 意外事故,偶发事件

manager, who was then replaced by Sorenson. Ps had difficulty working with Sorenson and Jay Bee owed large amounts of money to a bank whose officials were concerned the company would fail under Sorenson. The bank addressed its concerns to Ps, who then met with Sedberry without Sorenson's knowledge to discuss possibilities for the refinancing of Jay Bee. As a show of good faith, Ps offered their resignations on ninety days notice; Sedberry refused. Ps returned to Jay Bee with instructions; however, the next day Mrs. Sedberry informed Ps that their resignations were accepted effective immediately.

Ps sued D for breach of their employment contracts and contended that Mrs. Sedberry had refused their resignations and that no offer remained open. The trial court awarded damages to Ps and D appealed.

Issue: If two parties are in each other's presence and one party extends an offer without indicating any time period for acceptance, for how long will the offer remain open?

Holding and Rule: If two parties are in each other's presence and one makes an offer without indicating any time for acceptance, an inference will be drawn that that offer will not extend beyond the time of the conversation unless special words or circumstances indicate a contrary intention on the part of the offeror.

An employee's tender of resignation is not binding until it has been accepted by the employer. Such an offer must be accepted according to its terms and within the time fixed. An offer may be terminated by: (1) rejection, or (2) failure to accept within the time fixed, or (3) failure to accept within a reasonable time if no time is fixed.

A determination of what constitutes a "reasonable time" is a question of fact depending on the nature of the contract proposed, usages of business, and other factual circumstances. An offer made by one to another face to face is deemed to continue only to the close of their conversation and cannot be accepted thereafter (Restatement (2d) of Contracts 40).

The court held that in this case Ps' face to face offer was terminated when Mrs. Sedberry rejected it. The attempt by D to terminate the contract the following day was a breach and Ps were entitled to the recovery granted by the trial court.

2. Acceptance

As with the offer, neither common nor statutory law imposes any mandatory words or acts as constituting an acceptance of an offer and formation of a bargain. However, there is a mandatory formula. An acceptance consists of an expression of present, **unequivocal**①, unconditional assent by the offeree to each and every term of the offer. This expression must be communicated to the offeror at a time prior to revocation or termination of the offer. The UCC has made a radical change in the rules respecting the content of an effective assent if the subject matter of the attempted exchange is the sale of goods.

(1) Definition of Acceptance

The Restatement defines an acceptance as the offeree's manifestation of assent to the terms of the offer, made in a manner invited or required by the offer. In general, only those persons in whom the offeror intended to create a power of acceptance may accept an offer. In addition, a person usually can only accept an offer if he knew of the offer at the time of the acceptance. For example, most courts have held that persons cannot claim rewards for a particular act if they performed the act without knowledge of the reward offer.

(2) Requirements of Acceptance

a. Acceptance must be made in the manner expressly or impliedly prescribed by the offeror;

b. Acceptance must be made by the offeree or by someone acting with his authority;

c. Acceptance must be made within the period of validity of the offer, or within the reasonable time;

d. Acceptance must be unqualified and should be distinguished from a counter-offer, a conditional assent, a standing offer.

(3) Mode of Acceptance

In general, the offeror may specify the required means of acceptance, because the offeror is the "master of the offer." The Restatement provides that if the method of acceptance is not specified, acceptance may be given in any manner and by any medium that is reasonable under the circumstances.

---

① 明确的,毫不含糊的

Chapter 2
Contract Formation

a. If the offer is an offer to form a unilateral contract (i. e., where the offer seeks an acceptance of an act, rather than a return promise), the offeree can usually only accept by full performance. If the offeree has begun the performance, however, the offer generally becomes temporarily irrevocable as to that offeree. (However, once performance has started, the offeree is not obligated to complete the performance.) The offeree generally must give the offeror notice that he has performance.

b. If the offer is for a bilateral contract (i. e. where the offer seeks acceptance by a return promise), the offeree may accept by words or actions that indicate the offeree intends to enter a contract. In general, the offeree must communicate his acceptance to the offeror within the time set forth in the offer, or if no time is stated, within a reasonable time.

c. If the offer is unclear as to the modes of acceptance, an offeree can accept either by promising to perform or by actually performing. The UCC, which applies to transactions involving the sale of goods, also provides that an offer or request to ship goods can be accepted by either promising to ship the goods or actually shipping the goods.

d. Acceptance by Silence. The Restatement allows a party to accept by silence in the following situations: where the offeror gives reason to understand that silence may constitute acceptance; an offeree that silently accepts services will be held to have accepted a contract for them if the offeree had an opportunity to reject them and knew or should have know that the provider expected compensation for his services; or where the parties have in the past allowed the offeree to accept by silence.

(4) Battle of the Form

Most countries follow the mirror image rule. It requires that an acceptance be unconditional and that it not attempt to change any of the terms proposed in the offer; otherwise, the acceptance contained different or additional terms is considered a counter-offer and thus a rejection of the original offer.

These requirements present special problems when both parties, buyer and seller, negotiate back and forth via "standard" business forms. The seller might rely on an order confirmation form or sales forms. Typically, these forms leave room on the front so the parties may insert important contract terms such as price, quality, or ship date. The reverse side often contains detailed provisions or standard clauses, often called terms and conditions, or general conditions of sale. They are often drafted by attorneys to protect their client's right, placing greater liability on the other party. In international trade practices, both parties may not even be aware of the legal significance of these seldom read provisions on the reverse side, because they usually read carefully the crucial terms. Usually the preprinted terms on these forms differ, sometimes in significant ways and thus cause potential conflict. When this occurs, it is called a battle of forms.

(5) Time of Acceptance

Under the common law, a contract is formed when the acceptance is dispatched by the offeree. Each contract comes into being at the moment of acceptance. It is therefore often important to determine the time and place the acceptance becomes effective.

Under the common law, a contract is formed when the acceptance is dispatched by the offeree. The general rule of contacts made by post is that, offers and revocations are effective only upon receipt, but acceptances are effective upon posting. When acceptance is by post and telegram, it is generally deemed to occur as soon as the letter or telegram is posted. This is known as "Mail-box rule."

There are two exceptions to this rule:

a. The postal rule can be excluded by the terms of the offer. If the negotiating parties do not intend to have a binding agreement until the party accepts an offer or exercises an option, then there will be no contract unless acceptance is actually communicated.

b. The postal rule does not apply to acceptances made by some instantaneous mode of communication. An offer by telex is not accepted until notice of the acceptance is received by the offeror. The same rule will apply to facsimile transmittal or by telephone.

Another exception relates to the acceptance by performance. If the court treats an offer as one which invites acceptance either by promise or by performance, then the beginning of performance binds the offeror without regard to whether the offeror is aware of this event.

II. Consideration

Something bargained for and received by a promisor from a promisee. Common types of consideration include real or personal property, a return promise, some act, or a forbearance. Consideration or a valid substitute is required to have a contract. Consideration is one of the three basic elements of contract formation in common law, the other two being offer and acceptance. It is not present in other legal systems.

1. Definition of Consideration

There are various definitions to consideration, like:

Consideration is some benefit received by a party who gives a promise or performs an act, or some detriment suffered by a party who receives a promise.

"A valuable consideration, in the sense of the law, may consist either in some right, interest, profit of benefit accruing to one party or some forbearance, detriment, loss or responsibility given, suffered or undertaken by the other."

Consideration means something which is of some value in the eye of the law, moving from the plaintiff; it may be some detriment to the plaintiff or some benefit to the defendant, but at all events it must be moving from the plaintiff.

Accordingly, consideration is either some detriment to the promisee or some benefits to the promisor. A valid consideration must be executory or executed; it cannot be past.

Executory—a promise to do something in the future (e.g. A promises to deliver goods to B and B promises to pay for the goods);

Executed—an act constituting the consideration is wholly performed (e.g. the payment of money for goods; the return of a lost dog, for which a reward has been offered).

Consideration is something bargained for and given in exchange for a promise. That "something" may be an act, a **forbearance**[①], or a return

---

① 缓期,宽容,忍耐

promise. It may either be a benefit to the promisor or a **detriment**[①] to the promisee. To constitute consideration, there must be a detriment to the promisee.

Consideration is some benefit received by a party who gives a promise or performs an act, or some detriment suffered by a party who receives a promise. A valid consideration must be executory or executed; it cannot be past.

2. Characteristics of Consideration

(1) It must be real and of some value. It must not be vague, indefinite or abstract.

(2) It need not be adequate. This principle is sometimes explained as "consideration need not be equal to the promise" or "consideration may not be adequate but must be sufficient."

(3) It must be legal. An illegal consideration makes the whole contract invalid.

(4) It must move from the promisee, i.e. only the person who has paid the price for a promise can sue on it.

(5) It must be possible to perform. A promise to do the impossible would not be accepted as consideration.

(6) It must not be past. If the act put forward as consideration was performed before any promise of reward was made it is not valid consideration. The general rule is that "past consideration is no consideration."

(7) Performance of an existing contractual duty, or a public duty imposed on the promisee by law, these will not amount to consideration unless the promisee goes beyond what he is required to do.

3. Exceptions to the Consideration Requirement

A contract without consideration can be invalid or unenforceable unless it is under seal. This doctrine is not suitable to the practice of today; therefore, there are two exceptions to this doctrine. They are:

(1) Accord and Satisfaction

The general rule of common law is that a creditor is not bound by an

---

① 损失，损害

undertaking to accept part payment in full settlement of debt. An accrued debt can be discharged only by accord and satisfaction. The actual part payment is no satisfaction, that is to say, "payment of a lesser sum on the day in satisfaction of a greater sum cannot be any satisfaction for the whole."

This rule is finally approved by the House of Lords in *Foakes v. Beer*. For example, if A owes B $1,000, his undertaking to pay, say, $900, is no consideration for B's promise not to sue for the remaining balance. B may accept the $900 then sue for the balance, despite his promise. In addition, B may insist to claim interest notwithstanding that the principal sum has been settled.

But if the promisee has undertaken to do something different from what he was bound to do, this will amount to consideration. So it has been held that where, at the promisor's request, the promisee pays a smaller amount, e.g. at an earlier date, or in a different place, there is consideration for a promise not to sue for the balance, for he has gone beyond the scope of what he is bound to do. This exception dates back to 1602 in Pinnel's case.

Therefore, at common law if A owes B $1,000 and wishes to discharge that obligation by paying B $900 he must: (i) obtain the agreement (accord) of B; and (ii) provide B with some consideration (satisfaction) for giving up his right to $1,000 unless the release is under seal.

(2) Doctrine of Equitable (Promissory) Estoppel

A promise made by the promisor intended to create legal relations and intended to be acted upon by the promisee, may be enforced by the promisee (despite that he gave no consideration for it), if in fact he relied upon it to his detriment. The promisor is prevented (estopped) from denying his promise.

The doctrine is subject to the following qualifications:

a. that the other party has altered his position;

b. that the promisor can withdraw his promise on giving reasonable notice, which need not be formal notice, provided the promisee is able to resume his position;

c. the promise only becomes final and irrevocable if the promisor cannot resume his former position.

The essentials of the traditional version of estoppel were stated by Lord Birkenhead in *Maclaine v Gatty* [1921]:

Where A has by his words or conduct justified B in believing that a certain state of facts exists, and B has acted upon such belief to his prejudice, A is not permitted to affirm against B that a different state of facts existed at the same time.

A classic example of estoppel is if one party represents to another that A has authority to contract on his behalf, when in fact he has not so authorized A. If in reliance on this representation the other party enters a contract with A as agent, the first party (the principal) is estopped from denying that A has authority to act as his agent, and the contract made through A will be binding on him.

4. The Problem of Mutuality

In hundreds of American cases, it has been asserted as a general rule of contract law that both parties must be bound or neither is bound. This motion has usually been called "the principle of mutuality."

This principle obviously needs more qualification than it usually receives in judicial opinions.

First, the principle has no application to a unilateral contract. In a bilateral contract, the parties exchange a promise for a promise. (For example, Seller agrees to sell Buyer a used car for $2,000, delivery in three days, and Buyer agrees to pay $2,000 on delivery.) In a unilateral contract, the parties exchange a promise for an act. (For example, A promises to pay B $50 for mowing A's lawn and makes clear that only B's act of mowing the lawn, not B's promise to do so, will suffice.) In such bargains, the party who exchanges an act for promise may never be bound, because he is not bound to do anything before he chooses to do the act and he may not be bound to do anything after he does the act. Thus suppose, in the last example, that B mows the lawn. B was not bound to mow the lawn before he mowed it, and is not bound to A in any way he moved it. Nevertheless, A is bound to B.

Second, the principle of mutuality is not to bargains in which both parties have made real promises but one party is not legally bound by this promise. For example, suppose A fraudulently induces B to agree to buy Blackacre. Although B is not legally bound, he can enforce the contract notwithstanding the doctrine of mutuality. The same result follows in many other kinds of cases, such as those in which one but not both parties has a defense under the Statute of Frauds or a defense of incapacity.

SCOTT v. MORAGUES LUMBER CO.
Supreme Court of Alabama, 1918
202 Ala. 312, 80 So. 394.

Suit by the Moragues Lumber Company, a corporation, against J. M. Scott, or damages for breach of an agreement of charter party. Judgment for plaintiff, and defendant appeals. Affirmed.

Count 2 of the complaint as amended is as follow:

"The plaintiff claims of the defendant $13,000 as damages from breach of an agreement entered into between the plaintiff and the defendant on the 27th day of June, 1917, consisting of an offer by the defendant that, subject to his buying a certain American vessel, 15 years old, which he was then figuring on and which was of about 1,050 tons and then due in Chile, he would charter said vessel to the plaintiff for the transportation of a cargo of lumber from any port in the Gulf of Mexico to Montevideo or Buenos Aires, for the freight of $65 per thousand feet of lumber, freight to be prepaid, free of discount and of insurance, and the vessel to be furnished to be plaintiff within a reasonable time after its purchase by the defendant, which said offer was accepted by the plaintiff, and the plaintiff avers that although the defendant purchased said vessel, and although the plaintiff was at all times ready, willing, and able to comply with all the provisions of said contract on its part, the defendant without notifying the plaintiff of said purchase, and before said vessel was delivered to him, chartered said vessel to a third person, and thereby rendered himself unable to comply with the said contract."

SAYER, J. It is said, in the first place, that the alleged contract between the parties was conditioned upon the will of appellant, defendant and was therefore void for want of consideration or mutuality of obligation. A valid contract may be conditional upon the happening of an event, even though the event may depend upon the will of the party, who afterwards seeks to avoid its obligation. This principle is illustrated in *McIntyre Lumber Co. v. Jackson Lumber Co.*, 165 Ala. 268, 51 So. 767, 138 Am. St. Rep Appellant was not bound to purchase the vessel; but, when he did, the offer—or the contract, if the offer had been accepted—thereafter remained as if this condition had never been stipulated, its mutuality or other necessary incidents of obligation depending upon its other provisions and the action of the parties thereunder. *Davis v. Williams*, 121 Ala. 542, 25 So. 704; 3 Page on Contracts, §1358. See, also, Jones v. Lanier, 198 Ala. 363, 73 So. 535.

The effect of appellee's acceptance, if communicated while the offer was yet open, was to convert it into a binding contract. 6 R. C. L. p. 605, §27. In substance, it is alleged in the complaint that appellant's offer was accepted; that appellant purchased the vessel; that appellee was able, ready, and willing to perform the contract on its part; but that appellant disabled himself, or failed and refused to perform on his part. From the order in which the facts are alleged it is to be inferred that appellee accepted appellant's offer before the latter purchased the vessel, and there is no ground of demurrer questioning the sufficiency of the complaint to that effect. Thereupon the offer was converted into a binding contract to be performed, if not otherwise stipulated, within a reasonable time; the promise on either hand constituting the consideration of the promise on the other. Appellant's purchase of the vessel was a condition precedent to the existence of a binding contract, it is true; but that was alleged, as it was necessary that it should be. 13 C. J. pp. 724, 847. citing *McCormick v. Badham*, 191 Ala. 330, 67 So. 609; *Long v. Adix*, 184 Ala. 236, 63 So. 982; *Flouss v. Eureka Co.*, 80 Ala. 30. And so with respect to appellee's acceptance of the offer. It was necessary that appellee communicate its acceptance to appellant. 1 Page, §43. But this communication was a part of the acceptance and was covered by the general allegation of acceptance.

Affirmed.

Ⅲ. Terms of a Contract

The terms of a contract define the rights and duties of the parties arising under the contract. Terms may be expressly agreed by the contracting parties or implied by the courts or by statutory legislation.

1. Express Terms

Express terms are those specifically mentioned and agreed by the contracting parties at the time when the contract is made, whether it is done in writing or verbally.

(1) Conditions and Warranty

Contractual terms, oral or written, differ in importance and may be further classified into conditions and warranties. A condition is an important term which goes to the root of the contract, so that its non-observance will frustrate the main purpose of the contract. Breach of a condition will give the innocent party a right to rescind or repudiate the contract. However, the innocent party may on his own **volition**[①], elect to go on with the contract.

A warranty is a less important contract term, breach of which will only give the innocent party the right to sue for damages but not to treat the contract as discharged.

Many express terms are difficult to classify so neatly in advance at the time when the contract is made and they can only be classified by reference to the nature of the breach. A minor breach of the term might only be a breach of warranty, whereas a serious breach or a breach which has serious consequence might be a breach of condition. Both conditions and warranties are terms in condition or a warranty having regard to the intentions of the parties. The significance lies in the remedy in the event of breach.

(2) The Parol Evidence Rule

The parol evidence rule is a substantive common law rule in contract cases that prevents a party to a written contract from presenting extrinsic evidence that discloses an ambiguity and clarifies it or adds to the written terms of the contract that appears to be whole. The term of art *parol* means "oral" and comes from Anglo-French, Anglo-Norman, or Legal French.

The supporting rationale for this rule is that since the contracting parties have reduced their agreement to a single and final writing, extrinsic evidence of past agreements or terms should not be considered when interpreting that writing, as the parties had decided to ultimately leave them out of the contract. In other words, one may not use evidence made prior to the written contract to contradict the writing. A common misconception is that it is a rule of evidence

---

① 意愿,选择

(like the Federal Rules of Evidence), but that is not the case.

If a contract is in writing and final to at least one term (integrated), parol or extrinsic evidence will generally be excluded. To take an example, Carl agrees in writing to sell Betty a car for $1,000, but later, Betty argues that Carl earlier told her that she would only need to pay Carl $800. The parol evidence rule would generally prevent Betty from testifying to this alleged conversation because the testimony ($800) would directly contradict the written contract's terms ($1,000).

(3) Certainty of Terms

A contract will be void for uncertainty unless the parties make their contract in terms which are certain.

Moreover, there cannot be a contract to make another contract. The parties cannot, in other words, reach an agreement to keep in the future. The parties must agree on the terms which are definite or capable of being made definite without further agreement.

However, if the parties have agreed on a procedure whereby the terms could determine either by conferring on a court of law or an arbitrator the power to fill in a term in their agreements, then the contract is binding.

If the whole contract consists of meaningless terms, the contract is void. However, if the meaningless terms are secondary, the contract may be held valid and the meaningless terms will be disregarded in law.

2. Implied Terms

Implied terms may be divided into three groups:

(1) Terms Implied in Fact

Terms implied in fact refer to terms which are not expressly set out in the contract, but which the parties must be intended to include.

One test for the implication of a term in fact is the "officious bystander" test, by which the courts decides whether, if it had been suggested at the time the contract was made that the clause should be included, the parties would have readily agreed. For a term to be implied into a contract it must be obvious and essential. It is not sufficient that the term should be reasonable.

A second test for the implication of a term in fact is that of "business efficacy," the judge regarding himself as doing merely what the parties themselves would have done in order to cover the situation if they had addressed themselves to it, and to make these contract workable, that is to say, to give them "business efficacy."

(2) Terms Implied in Law

Terms implied in law refer to terms imported by operation of law, although the party may not have intended to include them.

There are, for example, a series of rights and duties implied into contracts of agency, employment and tenancy. Under a contract of employment, an employer owes an implied duty to take reasonable care for the safety of his employees, not to endanger the employees' health and not to require to the employees to do any unlawful act; and an employee owes a duty to show good faith, to obey lawful and reasonable instructions, and not to act against the employer's interest.

(3) Customary Implied Terms

A contract may be subject to customary terms not specifically mentioned by the parties. However, customary terms will not be implied if the express terms of the contract reveal that the parties had a contrary intention.

3. Exemption Clauses

Many large companies and public authorities impose conditions in their contracts exempting or excluding themselves from liability for torts, particularly negligence, arising from contracts. The rules applicable in such situations may be summarized as follows:

(1) An exemption clause can be incorporated in the contract by signature, by notice or by course of dealing:

a. Where the terms are signed, the parties are bound as a general rule even if the plaintiff has not read it;

b. The inserter of exemption clauses must do all that is reasonability necessary to the notice of the person subject to the clause or to draw his attention to it;

c. The conditions must be brought to the notice of the offeree either before or at the same time when the contract is made;

d. An exemption clause printed on a receipt is not an integral part of the contract.

(2) The party who wishes to rely on an exemption clause must show that the breach and loss are covered by the clause. If there is any doubt as to the scope of an exemption clause, it will be construed under the following rules:

a. The contra proferentem rule. If there is any ambiguity or room for doubt as to the meaning of an exemption clause, it will be construed against the person who puts it into the contract;

b. The **repugnancy rule**①. If an exemption clause is in direct contradiction to another term of the contract, the exemption clause can be struck out;

c. The four corners rule. Exemption clauses only protect a party when he is acting within the four corners of the contract. Thus he is liable for damage which occurs when he deviates from contract and he would not be protected by any exemption clause.

(3) The Control of Exemption Clauses Ordinance came into force in December 1990. It limits the extent to which civil liability for breach, or for negligence or other breach of duty, can be avoided by means of contract terms or by warning notices. The main purpose of the legislation is to prevent absolute attempts to exclude liability for death or personal injury and to place limitation on unfair exemption clauses used in the course of a business.

The essential elements of this Ordinance are as follows:

a. No contact term or notice is able to exclude or restrict a person from liability for death or personal injury resulting from negligence;

b. For negligence causing damage other than death or personal injury, the exemption clause will only be effective if the term or notice is reasonable having regard to all circumstances;

c. Where a business contracts on its own written standard terms, it cannot exclude or vary its liability for breach of contract unless it can show that the exemption is reasonable;

d. For contracts imposing an indemnity, no person dealing as a consumer can be made to indemnify another in respect of liability incurred by the other's negligence or breach of contract unless the contract term imposing such an indemnity is reasonable.

---

① 矛盾解释规则

Chapter 3

Capacity of a Contract

In contract law, capacity refers to a person's ability to satisfy the elements required for someone to enter binding contracts. For example, capacity rules often require a person to have reached a minimum age and to have soundness of mind.

Ⅰ. Minors

A minor becomes an adult at the first instance of his eighteenth birthday. Minor's contracts are roughly divided into two classes: valid or voidable.

1. Valid Contracts for Necessaries

Where necessaries are sold and delivered to an infant or minor, or to a person who, by reason of mental incapacity or drunkenness, is incompetent to contract, he must pay a reasonable price therefore.

Necessaries are defined as "goods suitable to the condition in life of such infant and to his actual requirements at the time of sale and delivery." But the term includes services as well as goods, and, if a minor is married, necessaries for his family are also included.

The onus of proof is upon the seller, i.e. it is for him to prove that any goods supplied were necessaries. If he proves that the goods are necessaries, the minor will be liable to pay a reasonable price but not the contract price for them.

2. Voidable Contracts

There are some contracts under which a minor will have interest of a continuous nature in a subject-matter, such as land, stock or shares. Such contracts are binding on a minor but they may be **repudiated**[①] by the minor before he becomes of age (or within a reasonable time thereafter). By doing so, he will escape any future liabilities under the contract, but not those which have already accrued. He cannot recover money paid unless there has been a "total failure of consideration."

3. Other Contracts

There are contracts for non-necessary goods or contracts for loans which are not binding on the minors unless they ratify them after reaching the age of 18. No fresh consideration is needed on ratification.

4. Age of Majority (Related Provisions) Ordinance

Apart from declaring that the legal capacity of a natural person at 18, it has the following important provisions applicable to the rules of contract:

(1) Guarantees of minors' contracts: any guarantee in relation to an obligation of a minor under a contract shall not for the reason of infancy alone be unenforceable against the guarantor.

(2) When a person makes a contract with a minor and the contract is unenforceable against that minor, that person can apply to the court on just and equitable grounds for an order to return to that person any property acquired by the minor under the contract, or any property representing it.

This creates a new remedy against the infant. It is similar to the equitable remedy of restitution which may arise in the limited circumstances where an infant, by fraudulently misrepresenting his age, obtains non-necessary goods or money. In such a case, equity will compel that infant to restore the actual goods or money so obtained. If the subject-matter is in fact necessary goods, an equitable right of subrogation will then arise and the infant will be made liable to pay a reasonable price for the necessary goods.

However, this section would not apply where the minor had dissipated the property acquired under the contract or its proceeds, e.g. where he had bought a bottle of wine and consumed it, or where he had sole property acquired under the contract for cash and had used the money to pay for a holiday.

---

① 拒不履行(法律义务)

II. Persons of Unsound Mind

Contracts made by persons of unsound mind are valid unless at the time when the contract was made:

(1) Such person did not know what he was doing; and

(2) The other party was or should have been aware of this.

Therefore, if the party does not know of the patient's disability, the contract is valid.

A person under the influence of drink is considered being in exactly the same position as a person of unsound mind.

However, where necessaries are sold to a person of mental incapacity or in a state of drunkenness, he must pay a reasonable price.

III. Corporations

Corporations can make any contracts within the power granted to them as from the time of their incorporation or thereafter.

Chapter 4

Vitiating Factors

These are the factors affecting the validity of an otherwise effective contract. They include mistakes, misrepresentation, duress, undue influence and illegality.

I. Mistakes

Mistakes under common law mean a misunderstanding about a fact between the parties to a contract. The general rule is that mistake does not affect the validity of a contract. For example, where a buyer is mistaken as to the nature of value of what he buys, this is his misfortune and the court will not rewrite the contract to reflect what the court believes the contract ought to be. In some cases, however, some mistakes operate on the agreement and really undermine it so that there is no true consent. This is called an operative mistake, the effect of which is to render the contract either void at common law or liable to be set aside in equity.

There are some kinds of mistakes when the parties enter into a contract and each may lead to different results.

1. Operative Mistakes

There are three types of operative mistakes, which are mistakes of fact:

(1) Common or identical mistake: where both parties make the same mistake, e.g. A agrees to buy a ring from B which they both think it is gold, but is not.

(2) Mutual or non-identical mistake: where the parties misunderstand each other, e.g. A thinks that he has agreed to buy a gold ring, but B thinks that he

Chapter 4
Vitiating Factors

is agreeing to sell a platinum ring.

(3) Unilateral mistake: where one party alone makes a mistake, of which the other is (or ought to be) aware, e.g. A thinks he is agreeing to buy a gold watch; B knows what A thinks, and knows that the watch is not gold.

In case (1) there is agreement between the parties, but it is based on a false promise. In case (2) and (3) the effect of the mistake is that the agreement never exists.

Common or Identical Mistakes

Where the common or identical mistake involves the existence of the subject-matter, the contract is void, for the parties are about to enter into a contract on something that does not exist.

For example, a salvage firm won the contract to raise an oil tanker from a reef off Papua New Guinea. The salvage firm was unable to find the tanker, despite following explicit instructions given by the Common-wealth Disposal Commission which had advertised for tenders. Later evidence revealed that no tanker had ever gone down in the area. The salvage firm sued to recover the money it would have eared under the contract and for other losses. The Commission claimed there had been a common mistake because both parties believed the tanker was in the area. The High Court held that the advertisement calling for tenders implied that the tanker did, in fact, exist and that the salvage firm had submitted a tender based on that representation. There was no common mistake and the Commission was bound to meet its obligations.

A common or identical mistake regarding any assumption that is fundamental to the contract will render it void. It can be a fundamental misapprehension as to a state of affaires, or facts forming the basis of the contract. For example, the contract will be void if a dead man's life is insured or unmarried persons make a separation agreement. The mistake must relate to the fundamental nature of the subject-matter. Simple mistakes as to the value or quality of the subject-matter, even though common to both parties, generally will not render the contract void.

Mutual or Non-identical Mistakes

When A and B are both mistaken as to a fundamental fact concerning contract but each party has made a different mistake, the court must decide if:

(1) There is a contract in the sense intended by A (e.g. a contract for the sale of a ring), or

(2) There is a contract in the sense intended by B, or

(3) There is a no true agreement at all and the contract is void for mistake.

This occurs when the parties to an apparent contract misunderstanding each other regarding an essential fact. A typical instance is where each party is mistaken about the other's intension. If mutual mistake is proved, then there is no agreement and the apparent contract is **void ab initio**[①].

Unilateral Mistakes

This arises where one of the parties is mistaken as to some fundamental fact concerning the contract, and the other party knew, or ought to have known of this mistake.

The rule is that the contract is void if the mistake affects the nature of the offer (and so relates to the "fundamental character of the agreement"); but not if it affects something less, such as the quality of goods.

(1) Once an offer has been accepted it cannot be withdrawn merely because the offeror made a mistake, provided the offeree was not aware of that mistake. If the offoree knows that the offeror is mistaken, the contract may be void for unilateral mistake.

(2) Unilateral mistakes arise most frequently where one party is mistaken as to the identity of the other. In such a case the contract will be void if he can prove that:

(a) He had no intention to contract with that other party, but with someone else;

(b) The other party was aware of this;

(c) At the time of negotiating the agreement, he regarded the identity of the other party to the contract of crucial importance; and

(d) He took reasonable steps to verify the identity of that party.

---

① 自始无效

Chapter 4
Vitiating Factors

RUSHLIGHT AUTOMATIC SPRINKLER CO. v. PORTLAND
189 Or. 194, 219 P.2d 732 (1950)

"We believe that in the state an offer and an acceptance are deemed to effect a meeting of minds, even though the offeror made a material mistake in compiling his offer, provided the acceptor was not aware of the mistake, and if it was basic, or if the circumstances were such that he, as a reasonable man, should have inferred that a basic mistake was made, a meeting of the minds does not occur... [A]s stated in §94 of Williston on Contracts, Rev. Ed.: ...The offeree will not be permitted to snap up an offer that is too good to be true; no contract based on such an offer can then be enforced by the acceptor."

"When the City officials opened the plaintiff's bid they surmised that it was too good to be true. When they went through the form of accepting it, they knew that the paper in their hands did not represent the plaintiff's intent. They had no occasion to doubt the truth, which was apparent, that the paper, although it bore the plaintiff's signature, was not in fact the plaintiff's offer. When they adopted their resolution, no meeting of minds occurred."

UNITED STATES v. METRO NOVELTY MFC. CO.
125 F. Supp. 713 (S. D. N. Y. 1954)

Cross the motions are presented for summary judgment. Plaintiff seeks to recover $12,000 damages from defendant for its failure to carry out a $6,000 bid for uniform ornaments. Defendant claims a mistake in the computation of the bid. Plaintiff admits that the error was so gross that it was placed on notice. It further admits that the only consequence of defendant's failure to perform was the acceptance of the second lowest bid and that there was no damage to the government from the delay in execution which resulted from defendant's participation in the biding. Plaintiff's purchasing agent sought to avoid the force of *Kemp v. United States*, D. C. Md. 1941, 38 F. Supp. 568 [holding that a seller was not bound to perform his contract where the defendant must have known that his bid was mistaken], by telephoning the defendant and asking for a "verification" of the bid and by having it "confirmed" by telephone and letter from defendant's president. Plaintiff, however, did not put defendant on notice of the mistake which it surmised. Reaffirmation of the bid under these circumstances does not bar the defense of rescission. Defendant's motion for summary judgment is granted.

It is sometimes said that relief for unilateral mistake will not be granted unless the parties "can be placed in status quo in the equity sense, i.e. rescission must not result in prejudice to the other party expect for the loss of his bargain." [*James T. Taylor & Son, Inc.* Arlington Independent School District, 60 Tex. 617,335 S. W. 2d 371(1960).] Taken literally, this would preclude relief when there has been any reliance by the non-mistaken party. Such a rule would be unnecessary to serve the purposes intended, and expressions like that in James T. Taylor should be read to mean that relief will not be granted unless the other party has either not relied or cannot be restored to his precontractual position by the award of reliance damages.

2. Documents Mistakes Signed

Generally a person who signs a contract is bound by it, even if he has not read it. But there is an exception that he could plead **non est factum**①: it is not my deed, e.g. a deed releasing all claims was read to an illiterate woman and she executed it on being told that it concerned arrears of rent. Held: the deed was null and void.

The defense of *non est factum* operates to avoid the contract and is open to a person who has signed a document by mistake. The mistake must be "radical" or "fundamental," specifying the kind of document it was, not merely its exact contents. The party relying on this defense must prove that he made the mistake notwithstanding that reasonable care had been taken.

A plea of *non est factum* is likely to succeed by a particularly vulnerable person in special circumstances, or it will be successful if:

(1) The person signs a contractual document in the mistaken belief that it is a totally different document;

(2) He was not negligent when he signed;

(3) His signature was procured by a fraudulent act.

---

① 否认订立合同的抗辩:"这不是我的契约"

Chapter 4
Vitiating Factors

II. Misrepresentation

A misrepresentation is an untrue statement of fact, made by one contracting party to the other, which statement was intended to, and did, induce the other party to enter into the contract.

1. The Meaning of Representation and Inducement

A representation is a statement made by a party to another to induce him to enter a contract. It must be a positive statement of some existing facts or past events, and so the following are excluded:

(1) Statement of law;

(2) Promises as to future behavior or conduct;

(3) Statements of intention—unless it can be proved as a matter of fact that there was no such intention;

(4) Statement of opinion—unless it can be proved as a matter of fact that the speaker does not have any such opinion;

(5) Mere "puffing," as for example, any statement used in advertising;

(6) Silence does not normally amount to representation, except in the following cases:

a. Where it distorts a positive representation—a half-truth may have the same effect as a lie;

b. Where a statement, true when it is made, subsequently becomes false before the conclusion of the contract;

c. As regards contracts where statute requires disclosure;

d. As regards contracts of the utmost good faith, such as contracts of insurance and family settlements where full and frank disclosure must be made;

e. In cases of concealed fraud.

2. Inducement (Misrepresentation)

The representation must be material, i. e. it must lead to the plaintiff's entering into the contract and also that it was relied on. There will be no inducement if:

(1) The plaintiff did not know that there had been a misrepresentation;

(2) The plaintiff would have made the contract relied on his judgment

despite the representation;

(3) The plaintiff knew the statement was false.

3. Types of Actionable Misrepresentation

(1) Fraudulent Misrepresentation

Fraud is a serious charge which must be clearly and distinctly proved. A party who has been deceived by a fraudulent misrepresentation has the following remedies open to him. He may:

a. Bring an action in tort for damages for deceit or under the Misrepresentation Ordinance for damages for fraudulent misrepresentation;

b. Bring an action for rescission with or without a claim for damages;

c. Repudiate the contract and refuse further performance;

d. Affirm the contract;

e. Prosecute, or notify the police of an apparent crime (obtaining property or pecuniary advantage by deception under the Theft Ordinance).

The party which was deceived may treat the contract as voidable. He may choose to affirm the contract or not. In effect, it is up to him to seek any of the above remedies or to treat the contract as binding by affirming it. If he is being sued, he may plead fraud as a defence and counterclaim for damages.

(2) Innocent or Negligent Misrepresentation

In the past, all misrepresentation which were not fraudulent was described as "innocent." Now, innocent misrepresentation is further divided into innocent statements made negligently or wholly innocent statements.

In modern law, a misrepresentation is negligent if it is made carelessly and in breach of a duty owed by the representor to the representee to take reasonable care that the representation is accurate. Where the representor can prove that he made the statement with reasonable grounds to believe that it is true, the statement so made, if turn out to be untrue, is innocent misrepresentation.

The remedies for innocent or negligent misrepresentation are:

a Damages;

b Rescission either by the innocent party canceling the contract himself or by the court;

c Refusal of further performance, and if being sued, by using the other side's misrepresentation as a defense;

Chapter 4
Vitiating Factors

d Affirmation of the contract.

4. The Limitation of Right to Rescission

The right to set a contract aside for misrepresentation will be lost where:

(1) The injured party has affirmed the contract, fully aware of his rights.

(2) *Restitutio in integrum* (restoration in full) has become impossible.

(3) An innocent third party has acquired for value an interest in the subject-matter. It should be noted that it is vital to avoid a contract induced by fraud as soon as possible since misrepresentation at most makes a contract voidable (and not void); if the rogue sells the goods to a third party before avoidance, he passes a good title and the original owner will have to assume the loss. If the rogue "sells" after avoidance he cannot pass title, thus it is the third party to whom he has "sold" who must bear the loss.

(4) The plaintiff delays unreasonably in seeking rescission, the court may refuse to grant to him the equitable remedy of rescission which is discretionary in nature.

5. Contract of *Uberrimae Fidei* (of the Utmost Good Faith)

Although disclosure is not a general requirement, in some exceptional cases the law imposes a special duty to act with the utmost good faith, i.e. to disclose all material information.

So, failure to disclose renders the contract voidable at the option of the party, for example:

(1) Contract of insurance.

(2) Contract of family arrangement, for the settlement of family property, etc.

(3) Company prospectus.

III. Duress

Duress is wrongful coercion that induces a person to enter or modify a contract. There are three categories.

1. Duress to a Person

It refers to the actual or threatened violence to, or the actual or threatened unlawful imprisonment of, a person or a near relative of that person, which pressures them into entering into a contract.

2. Duress to Goods

Where persons have been pressured into entering a contract because of wrongful threats to seize or damage or destroy their goods of property, the contract is voidable on the grounds of duress to goods.

Duress (i.e. compulsion) at common law makes a contract voidable, not void. At one time, the common law concept is limited to physically violence (or threats of immediate physical violence) to the person. As his consent was not freely given, such contracts are voidable at his option. This view was rejected and suggested that it is not only duress to person, which will invalidate a contract, but it is now a plea of "compulsion or coercion" which would also be available in other circumstances. This view was accepted in later cases, so that the question is no longer what was threatened, but whether the effect of the threat was to bring about a "coercion of the will, which vitiates consent."

3. Economic Duress

Economic duress is a vitiating factor under the common law, which derives from commercial or financial pressure. This is therefore an abuse of a dominant bargaining position to the extent that the will of the weaker party is not freely exercised. To be capable of giving rise to such duress, the threat must be illegitimate either because:

(1) What is threatened is a legal wrong;

(2) The threat itself is wrongful; or

(3) It is contrary to public policy.

Whether the threat actually gives rise to duress must then be considered by reference to its coercive effect in each case. In determining whether there has been such a coercion, the court will consider the following:

(1) Whether the person alleged to have been coerced did or did not protest;

(2) Whether at the time he was allegedly coerced into making the contract, he did or did not have an alternative course open to him, such as an adequate legal remedy;

(3) Whether he had received independent advice;

(4) Whether after entering into the contract, he took steps to avoid it.

Chapter 4
Vitiating Factors

IV. Undue Influence

In contract law, a defense can be used by a party to argue against the formation of a binding contract between two parties. The use of undue influence by one party over another puts the free will of one of the parties entering the contract into question, and therefore leads to the contract being unenforceable and voidable by the victim party. To prove undue influence, a party must show that one party to the contract is a person with weaknesses which make him likely to be affected by such persuasion, and that the party exercising the persuasion is someone in a special relationship with the victim that makes the victim especially susceptible to such persuasion.

The purpose of undue influence is to protect the old, the timid, and the physically or mentally weak from those who gain their confidence and attempt to take advantage of them.

1. Two Types of Undue Influence

(1) **Actual**

The party who claims relief on the ground of actual influence must show that such influence existed and had been exercised, and that the transaction resulted from that influence. There is no further requirement in cases of this kind that the transaction must be shown to be to the manifest disadvantage of the party seeking to set it aside.

(2) **Presumed**

In some situations, where there is fiduciary relationship between the parties, undue influence is presumed by the court that there was not genuine consent; such influence will prevail unless rebutted by the party benefiting from the transactions by proving the plaintiff understood the contract and entered it voluntarily.

Currently, the presumption arises in relationship as following categories:

a. Parent and child;

b. Trustee and beneficiary;

c. Solicitor and client;

d. Doctor and patient;

e. Guardian and ward;

f. Religious adviser and devotee

Thus, in these situations, there is no need to show that undue influence existed and had been exercised.

2. Effect on the Contract

A contract induced by undue influence is voidable, and confers a right to rescission.

If no legally recognized special relationship exists, there is no presumption of undue influence. The plaintiff must satisfy the onus of proof by showing, on the balance of probabilities, that he or she was dominated by the defendant and did not understand the contract. Proof that the defendant did not encourage the plaintiff to obtain independent legal or financial advice would help the plaintiff's case.

The mere existence of a close or dependent relationship between the parties that results in economic advantage to one of them is not sufficient for undue influence. It must also appear that the weaker person entered the contract because he was subject to unfair methods of persuasion. In determining this, a court will look at all of the surrounding facts and circumstances, e.g.:

(1) Was the person isolate and rushed into the contract or did he have access to outsiders for advice and time to consider his alternatives?

(2) Was the contract discussed and consummated at an unusual time or in an unusual place?

(3) Was the contract a reasonably fair one that a person might have entered voluntarily? or

(4) Was it so lopsided and unfair that one could infer that he probably would not have entered it unless he had been unduly influenced by the other party?

The answer to these and similar questions help determine whether the line between permissible and impermissible persuasion has been crossed.

3. Inequality of Bargaining Power

This may also be regarded as undue influence. In this regard, law gives relief to one who, without independent advice, enters into a contract on unfair terms or transfers property for a consideration which is mostly inadequate, where his bargaining power in grievously impaired by his own ignorance or infirmity, coupled with undue influence or pressures brought on him by or for the benefit of the other.

In Unconscionable Contract Ordinance, a contract may be voidable on the ground of unconscionable conduct. The plaintiffs who enter a contract must prove that:

(1) Their "disability" made them the weaker party in contract negotiations;

(2) The stronger party took unfair advantage of this disability; and

(3) This prevented them from making an independent decision about the contract.

The courts have interpreted disability to mean a marked disadvantage and have recognized a wide range of situations, including illiteracy, limited education, illness, poverty, age-related problems and lack of access to legal advice.

V. Illegal Contracts

Illegal contract does not merely imply criminal activity; it also means that neither party can get the assistance of the courts to enforce a contract which is, in the courts' view, injurious in some way to society. Such illegal contracts can be mainly divided into two classes:

1. Illegal Contracts Strictly So Called

(1) Illegal contracts are those which:

a. commit a crime, a tort or a fraud on a third party;

b. are sexually immoral;

c. are prejudicial to the public safety, such as contracts with alien enemies in wartime;

d. are prejudicial to the administration of justice, such as agreements to obstruct criminal prosecutions;

e. tend to promote corruption in public life;

f. are designed to defraud the revenue;

g. are prohibited by statute. For instance the Banking Ordinance provides that only a bank can carry on banking business;

h. tend to defraud or deceive a third party.

(2) Such contract may be either:

a. Illegal as formed, i.e. agreements which cannot be lawfully performed, such as an agreement to rob a bank; or

b. Illegal as performed, i.e. where a contract is innocent in origin and intention, but one party performs his side of the agreement in an illegal manner.

(3) The effect of contracts illegal as formed

The contract is void, and neither party has any claim under it: *ex turpi causa non oritur actio* (no disgraceful matter can ground an action).

(4) The effect of contracts illegal as performed

The guilty party cannot sue in respect of the contract. But the position of the innocent party is a strong one. He can:

a. Sue on a *quantum meruit* (as much as he has earned) for work done or *quantum valebant* (as much as they were worth) for goods supplied;

b. Sue on a separate promise, if any promise has ever been made, that the work would be performed legally;

c. Recover money paid or property transferred;

d. Recover damages for breach of contract.

2. Illegal Contracts Traditionally So Called

Examples of such contracts are:

(1) Agreements to oust the jurisdiction of the courts.

(2) Agreements in restraint of trade.

The question whether a restraint is valid must be determined by reference to the circumstances in existence when the contract was made. Restraints may take many forms, but the following are the main categories:

a. Contracts of employment may have terms to provide that the employee may not compete with his present employer either by setting up in business on his own or by working for a rival business after leaving his present employment. It is a general view that such restraint will be uphold if it is reasonable in its limits of time and space and that the public interest as a whole should not suffer from the particular restraint.

b. Upon a sale of business, the purchaser will normally impose terms on the vendor whereby the vendor promises that he will not carry on rival business in competition with the purchaser in future after the sale of business;

c. Retailers sometimes make "*solus*①" agreement whereby a trader agrees to restrict his orders of goods to only one supplier or to sell only that supplier's brand of goods.

The test of validity of a covenant was whether it was wider than reasonably necessary to protect the plaintiff's goodwill. Both the interests of the parties and the public interest must be considered, but the public interest, being the foundation of the doctrine, is more important. The nature of the restraint, its geographical area, the duration for which it is to operate, and all other relevant factors must be no more than are necessary to protect the interest in question.

The party who seeks to enforce the term has the responsibility of showing that it is reasonable. Any attempt to impose restraints by indirect means will be subject to the same test.

(3) The effect of illegal contracts traditionally so called

Such contracts are not wholly void. They are void only when they are contrary to public policy. Money paid and property transferred is recoverable. And the doctrine of severance applies, i.e. lawful promises, if they can be severed from the unlawful part, will have to be carried out.

VI. Problems Involving Persons Other Than the Parties to the Original Contract

In some cases, two parties may form a contract for the benefit of a third party. For example, suppose B promises to deliver merchandise to A. In exchange, A promises B to pay $100 to C. In this situation, C is an intended third-party beneficiary of the A-B agreement.

1. Intended Beneficiaries

Only those beneficiaries deemed "intended beneficiaries" are entitled to sue to enforce an agreement between two other parties. In the above example, if C was an intended beneficiary she would likely be able to sue upon the A-B contract. Before a court will find that a party is an "intended beneficiary," it must find that:

---

① 单独的

(1) Giving that party the right to sue would effectuate the intentions of the parties; and

(2) The performance of the promise will satisfy an obligation of the promise to pay money to the beneficiary, or

(3) The circumstances indicate that the promise intends to give the beneficiary the benefit of the promised performance.

2. Incidental Beneficiaries

If the beneficiary is merely an "incidental beneficiary" of a contract, he will not be allowed to sue. For example, suppose A contracts with B, a car dealer, to purchase a Ford Mustang. While the Ford Motor Company obviously would benefit from this transaction, it would only be an incidental beneficiary and could not sue A if he failed to perform.

When deciding whether a beneficiary is an intended or incidental beneficiary, courts will usually look at whether the promise intended that the third party have the benefit of the contract. In other words, courts will try to determine to whom the performance was run. If it was to run directly to the promise, the third party is normally an unprotected incidental beneficiary. If the performance is to run directly to the third party, however, they are likely an intended beneficiary.

3. Impairment or Extinguishment of Third-Party Rights by Contract Modification or Mutual Rescission

After rights have been created in a third-party beneficiary, the original parties' ability to modify or discharge the contract ends when the beneficiary—before having notice of the modification or discharge—takes the following actions: (i) materially changes his position in justifiable reliance upon the promise; or (ii) brings suit on the promise; or (iii) manifests assent to it at the request of either party.

4. Enforcement by the Promisee

If the promisor breaches the contract, most courts allow the promisee to file suit against the promisor for the benefit of an intended third-party beneficiary. Thus, a third-party beneficiary contract can be enforced by the promisee or by the intended third-party beneficiary.

Chapter 5
Discharge

Once it is determined that a party is under an immediate duty to perform, the duty to perform must be discharged. A contract may be discharged in one of the following ways.

I. By Performance

The most obvious way to discharge a contractual duty is, of course, by full and complete performance.

II. By Tender of Performance

Good faith tender of performance made in accordance with contractual terms will also discharge contractual duties. Note that the tendering party must possess the present ability to perform; a mere promise of performance will not suffice.

III. By Frustration (Impossibility or Impracticability of Performance)

The legal basis of the doctrine of frustration rest in the disappearance of a foundation that the parties assumed to be at the basis of their contract, the disappearance of the foundation renders performance impossible.

(1) A contract is said to be frustrated when:

a. There is an intervening (or "supervening") event;

b. It is entirely beyond the contemplation of the parties when the contract was made;

c. It causes fundamental change in circumstances that it affects the root of the agreement;

d. It is not self-induced.

There are different opinions as to the reason for the doctrine. The best view is that the new event has caused a "change in obligation" and that it would be unfair to impose the new obligation on the party affected.

(2) Examples of frustrating events are:

a. Where the whole basis of the contract is the continued existence of a specific thing which is destroyed;

b. Where the whole basis of the contract is the occurrence of an event which does not occur but the contract would not be frustrated if some other purposes of the contract were or could still be performed;

c. The death or illness of a party to a contract for personal services;

d. Government prohibition (provided that the period of prohibition is sufficiently long);

e. The passing of a statute making performance of the contract illegal.

(3) Effects of frustration

The effect of frustration is to discharge the contract from the moment of the frustrating event, not to make it void from the start. At common law, the loss is counted when the contract starts to fail, except that money paid was recoverable if there was a total failure of consideration.

IV. By Operation of Law

The law provides for automatic discharge in the following circumstances:

(1) Where a contract is formed for a specific period, it is discharged at the expiry of that time.

(2) Where a simple contract is subsequently incorporated into a deed, the former is discharged by merger.

(3) A written contract or deed is discharged by a material alteration in its terms.

(4) Bankruptcy or death or mental incapacity of a party discharges a contract for personal services.

Ⅴ. By Occurrence of Condition Subsequent

The occurrence of a condition subsequent will serve to discharge contractual duties.

Ⅵ. By Illegality

If the subject matter of the contract has become illegal due to subsequently enacted law or other governmental act, performance will be discharged. This is often referred to as "supervening illegality."

Ⅶ. By Rescission

Rescission will serve to discharge contractual duties. This rescission may be either mutual or unilateral.

(1) Mutual rescission: The contract may be discharged by an express agreement between the parties to rescind. The agreement to rescind is itself a binding contract supported by consideration, namely, the giving up by each party of his right to counter-performance from the other. The reasons for entering into such an agreement are immaterial absent duress or fraud.

(2) Unilateral rescission: Unilateral rescission results when one of the parties to the contract desires to rescind it but the other party desires that the contract be performed according to its terms. For unilateral rescission to be granted, the party desiring rescission must have adequate legal grounds. Most common among these are mistake, misrepresentation, duress, and failure of consideration. Where the nonassenting party refuses to voluntarily grant rescission, the other party may file an action in equity to obtain it.

Ⅷ. By Novation

A novation occurs when a new contract substitutes a new party to receive benefits and assume duties that had originally belonged to one of the original parties under the terms of the old contract. A novation will serve to discharge the old contract. The elements for a valid novation are as follows:

(1) A previous valid contract;

(2) An agreement among all parties, including the new party (or parties)

to the new contract;

(3) The immediate extinguishment of contractual duties as between the original contracting parties; and

(4) A valid and enforceable new contract.

IX. By Cancellation

The destruction or surrender of a written contract will not usually by itself discharge the contact. If, however, the parties manifest their intent to have these acts serve as a discharge, it will usually have this effect if consideration or one of its alternatives is present.

X. By Release

A release and/or contract not to sue will serve to discharge contractual duties. The release or contract not to sue usually must be in writing and supported by new consideration or promissory estoppel elements.

XI. By Substituted Contract

A contract may be discharged by a substituted contract. This occurs where the parties to a contract enter into a second contract that immediately revokes the first contract.

XII. By Accord and Satisfaction

(1) Accord: an accord is an agreement in which one party to an existing contract agrees to accept, in lieu of the performance that she is supposed to receive from the other party to the existing contract, some other different performance.

(2) Satisfaction: satisfaction is the performance of the accord agreement. Its effect is to discharge not only the original contract but the accord contract as well.

XIII. By Account Stated

An account stated is a contract between parties whereby they agree to an amount as a final balance due from one to the other. This final balance encompasses a number of transactions between the parties and serves to merge all of these transactions by discharging all claims owed. In other words, all rights as to the individual, original transactions are discharged and the new agreement is enforceable. It is necessary, in order for the agreement to qualify as an account stated that the parties have had more than one prior transaction between them.

XIV. By Lapse

Where the duty of each party is a condition concurrent to the other's duty, it is possible that on the day set for performance, neither party is in breach and their contractual obligations lapse.

XV. Effect of Running of Statute of Limitations

Where the statute of limitations on an action has run, it is generally held that an action for breach of contract may be barred. Note, however, that only judicial remedies are barred; the running of the statute does not discharge the duties.

Chapter 6

Breach of Contract

I. Breach of Contract

A breach of contract is committed when a party without lawful excuse fails or refuses to perform what is due from him under the contract, or performs defectively or incapacitates himself from performing. That is, breach of contract may occur by a party's:

(1) Express repudiation;

(2) Disabling himself from performing;

(3) Failure to perform by the due time.

In the first two cases, the breach may occur before the time due for performance. It is then known as "anticipatory breach[①]."

II. Excuses for Non-performance

Where the contract has been frustrated there is no liability for breach of contract because both parties have been provided with a "lawful excuse" for their non-performance.

1. Impossibility of Performance

Impossibility would excuse nonperformance in cases involving:

(1) The death of one of the parties;

(2) The destruction of the specific subject matter of the contract;

(3) When performance of the contract has been rendered illegal or made

---

① 预期违约

impossible due to the fault of the other party.

2. Supervening Illegality

A contract becomes impossible to perform and the parties excused when performance becomes illegal. For instance, suppose that a company is under contract to ship computers to Iraq. After Iraq's invasion of Kuwait, the U.S. government declared that conducting business with Iraq or shipping goods there was illegal. Since the contract has been rendered illegal, performance is discharged.

3. Frustration of Purpose

In a leading English case, *Knell v. Henry* (1903), a party leased a room overlooking the coronation route of the king. When the king took ill and the coronation canceled, the court ruled that the party was excused from paying rent on the room, because the coronation was essential to the purposes of the contract. Although it had been possible to perform the party would have realized no value in doing so.

4. Commercial Impracticability

Courts hesitate to excuse parties from contracts. Accordingly, the non-breaching party will be excused only if performance would result in extreme hardship, difficulty, or unreasonable expense as a result of an unforeseen event.

The courts have experienced some difficulty in determining what a "hard ship" is and how much additional cost is "unreasonable." If the cost of performing the contract becomes so excessive that performance is rendered unrealistic and senseless, and threatens the viability of the business itself, performance may be excused.

Ⅲ. Force Majeure Clauses

A Force Majeure Clause[①] in a contract is an exculpatory clause; it excuses a party from failing to perform on the occurrence of an event specified in the clause itself—a force majeure.

Courts do not like to release parties to a contract on the basis of an excuse.

---

① 不可抗力条款

Under the rule of commercial impracticability, a party will not be excused if the risk was foreseeable, because the party is assumed to have provided for that excuse in the contract itself. As a result, lawyers frequently advise their clients to incorporate a force majeure clause into a contract.

In drafting force majeure clauses, attention should not be paid only to standard contingencies such as those listed, but also to the special nature of the contract and the type of business involved. A model of comprehensiveness is better recommended because this form leaves the least out in the contract.

Chapter 7

Remedies for Breach of Contract

Both common law and equity provide remedies for breach of contract. The common law remedies include damages, action for an agreed sum, and a claim for *quantum meruit* [①]. The equitable remedies comprise of specific performance and injunction which are awarded at the court's discretion.

Ⅰ. Damages and General Principle of Remedies

In breach of the contract cases, the usual remedy granted by common law courts to both buyers and sellers is the legal remedy of money damages. Article 74 of the CISG provides: "Damages for breach of contract by one party consist of a sum equal to the loss, including loss of profit, suffered by the other party as a consequence of the breach. Such damages may not exceed the loss which the party in breach foresaw or ought to have foreseen at the time of the conclusion of the contract, in the light of the facts and matters of which he then knew or ought to have known, as a possible consequence of the breach of contract."

The claim for damages involves a consideration of two questions:

1. Damages

For what type of damages or loss should the plaintiff be entitled to receive compensation? (Remoteness of Damage)

Remoteness of damage in contract is governed by the rule in *Hadley v. Baxendale* 1854, that damages are recoverable for loss which either:

(1) Arises naturally, i.e. according to the usual course of things from the

---

① 应得数额,合理金额

breach of contract; or

(2) Was within the parties' contemplation at the time of the contract as the probable result of breach.

These principles were reformulated in later cases and it was held that normal business profits would be recoverable but not exceptional profits as the loss was "reasonably foreseeable as liable to result from the breach." The word "foreseeability" to test remoteness in contract refers to a higher degree of probability than in tort.

2. The Doctrines of Compensation (Measure of Damages)

In respect of each type of damage or loss recoverable in law, how much should the plaintiff be entitled to receive? (*Quantum* of Damages)

The general rule is that the plaintiff is entitled to recover his actual loss so that he is placed in the same position as if the contract had been performed.

In practice, for breach of contract, the innocent party could claim compensation on one of a number of different grounds.

(1) The expectation interest, which is based on the injured party's hopes at the time of making the contract, but on the actual value that the contract would have had to the injured party had it been performed.

(2) The reliance interest, which means that the claimant has acted to his detriment in entering the contract when the defendant's promised to perform his contractual obligations. The aim is to put the claimant in as good a position as he was in before the defendant's promise was made, i.e. as the contract hadn't been concluded.

(3) The restitution interest. A claimant who claims the protection of his restitution interest does not wish to be compensated for the loss which he has suffered; rather, he wishes to deprive the defendant of a gain which he has made at the claimant's expense.

3. Mitigation (Limitation) of Damages

The plaintiff has the obligation to do what he reasonably can to minimize or mitigate the damage caused; damage attributable to his failure to do so is not recoverable.

Chapter 7
Remedies for Breach of Contract

4. Liquidated Damages and Penalties

Damages for breach of contract are intended to compensate the plaintiff, not to punish the defendant. Where the amount of compensation claimed is left to be assessed by the court; they are called "unliquidated damages."

Where the parties have agreed in advance on a sum to be payable in the event of a breach, the sum would only be recoverable if it is found by the court to be a genuine pri-estimate of damages ("liquidated damages") but not if it was imposed with the intention to penalize or threaten. Rules were laid down in some cases to distinguish the two:

a. The sum is a penalty if it is extravagant;

b. It is a penalty if it is the payment of a larger sum for failure to pay a smaller sum;

c. Subject to the above, it is likely to be liquidated damages if there is only one event of which the sum is payable;

d. It is a penalty if the same sum is payable upon trifling as upon serious events.

Clearly, a penalty clause is invalid and unenforceable. Where liquidated damages clause is characterized as a penalty, the claimant is entitled to sue for damages and have them quantified by a court, and the measure of damage will be the actual loss proved.

A simple form of liquidated damages clause is: "In the event that delivery of the goods is delayed, the supplier shall pay the customer the sum of $100.00 each day until the day of delivery to a maximum of $1,000.00."

II. Anticipatory Breach in Common Law and Its Remedies

Where breach of contract may occur in two cases, i.e. by a party's express repudiation, or disabling himself from performing before the time due for performance. It is known as "anticipatory breach." Under these circumstances, the innocent party can ask for a remedy immediately, rather than waiting till the time due for performance.

Repudiation by one party allows the innocent party:

(1) To sue at once, or

(2) To treat the contract as still continuing and to wait until the time for

performance arrives.

In the later case, the contract continues in existence; the party in default may take advantage of any circumstances or events which may subsequently release him from liability under the contract.

III. Specific Performance

Specific performance is an order of the court and constitutes an express instruction to a party to a contract to perform the actual obligation which he undertook under its terms.

In a proper case, the court will insist on the parties carrying out their agreement. A party may be forced to perform his side of the contract where damages would be an inadequate remedy. This applies especially to contracts connected with land.

Because the remedy is an equitable one it is discretionary and unlike common law remedies which can be obtained as of right. Thus the court will apply the equitable maxims of "he who seeks equity must do equity" and "he who comes to equity must come with clean hands."

Specific performance will not normally be granted where:

(1) Damages would be an adequate remedy;

(2) Constant supervision is required to make sure that the defendant complies with the decree;

(3) Is not available to either party, e. g. specific performance will not apply to a minor;

(4) In a contract for personal services, or

(5) In a contract to lend money, however, the remedy is available in appropriate circumstances to enforce a payment of money.

The Duty to Perform in Good Faith Under the UCC Restatement Second

UCC §1-203 provides that "every contract or duty within this Act imposes an obligation of good faith in its performance or enforcement." This concept permeates the entire UCC. Thus, according to Summers, "good faith" in General Contract Law and the States Provisions of the Uniform Commercial Code, 54 Va. L. Rev. 195, 21, 219 n. 91(1968), thirteen provisions in Article 2 explicitly use the term "good faith," and nineteen more have

Chapter 7
Remedies for Breach of Contract

comments which use the term. For example, UCC §2-311(1) provides that "An agreement for sale which is otherwise sufficiently definite... to be a contract is not made invalid by the fact that it leaves particulars of performance to be specified by one of the parties. Any such specification must be made in good faith and within limits set by commercial reasonableness." Similarly, UCC §2-305 provides that "a price to be fixed by the seller or by the buyer means a price for him to fix in good faith."

Exactly what constitutes good faith within the meaning of given UCC provision is not always so clear. In Article 1 ("General Provisions"), UCC §1-201(19) defines "good faith" to mean "honesty in fact in the conduct or transaction concerned." However, In Article 2 (Sales), §2-103(1)(b) provides that "unless the context otherwise requires... 'good faith' in the case of a merchant means honesty in fact and the observance of reasonable commercial standards of fair dealing in the trade" (Emphasis added). In some cases, the meaning may be made more specific by the Official Comment. Thus Comment 3 to §2-305, supra, states that "in the normal case a 'posted price' or a future seller's or buyer's given price,' 'price in effect,' 'market price,' or the like satisfies the good faith requirement."

In accord with UCC §1-203, Restatement Second has added a new provision, §205: "Every contract imposes upon each party a duty of good faith and fair dealing in its performance and its enforcement." The comments to §205 state:

a. Meanings of "good faith." The phrase "good faith" is used in a variety of contexts, and its meaning varies somewhat with the context. Good faith performance or enforcement of a contract emphasizes faithfulness to an agreed common purpose and consistency with the justified expectations of the other party; it excludes a variety of types of conduct characterized as involving "bad faith" because they violate community standards of decency, fairness or reasonableness. The appreciate remedy for a breach of the duty of good faith also varies with the circumstances.

b. Good faith performance. Subterfuges and evasions violate the obligation of good faith in performance even though the actor believes his conduct to be justified. But the obligation goes further: bad faith may be overt or may consist of inaction, and fair dealing may require more than honesty. A complete catalogue of types of bad faith is impossible, but the following types are among those which have been recognized in judicial decision: evasion of the spirit of the bargain, lack of diligence and slacking off, willful rendering of imperfect performance, abuse of a power to specify terms, and interference with or failure to cooperate in the other party's performance.

IV. Injunction

An injunction is an order restraining a person from doing some act. This remedy will be granted to enforce a negative stipulation in a contract where damages would not be an adequate remedy; like specific performance, it is an equitable and discretionary remedy. It can be applied to cases where there is no actual negative stipulation but where one may be inferred.

In suitable cases an injunction may be used as an indirect means of enforcing a contract for personal services, but here a clear negative stipulation is required.

Types of injunctions may be:

(1) Interlocutory—granted before the hearing of the action; the plaintiff would be responsible for any damage caused to the defendant if in the subsequent action the plaintiff does not succeed.

(2) Perpetual—granted after a trial and when the point at issue has been finally determined.

(3) Prohibitory—stops a certain positive act from being performed.

(4) Mandatory—a certain positive act shall be performed.

A Mareva injunction is an order of the court restraining the defendant, pending trial, from dissipating or disposing of his assets in or outside the jurisdiction of the court before the judgment of the action.

The injunction may be granted if it appears likely that the plaintiff will succeed in the action and there are reasons to believe that the defendant may deal with his assets in such a way which will be untraceable or not recoverable, will not be untraceable when judgment is given against him.

Chapter 7
Remedies for Breach of Contract

V. Dispute Settlement

1. Settlement of Disputes Through Municipal Courts

(1) Choice of Forum Clause

During the initial drafting of the contract the parties should decide which court shall have jurisdiction, and then specify that court in a Forum Selection Clause. That clause should both specify the court which has jurisdiction and state that that court has exclusive jurisdiction to preclude other courts from entering the case.

(2) Choice of Law Clauses

Generally, in common law and civil law jurisdictions, parties may choose the law which they wish to govern their contract relationship, as long as the law chosen is that of a place which has a substantial relationship to the parties and to the international business transaction, and is not contrary to a strong public policy of the place where suit is brought.

2. Alternative Dispute Resolution

It is known to all that litigation as a means of settling disputes presents a number of problems at the international level. Consequently, many parties are turning to other ways of resolving problems, named, negotiation, mediation, Mini-trial, etc, which are known collectively as alternative dispute resolution (ADR).

3. Commercial Arbitration

In international business practices most disputes are resolved by arbitration if the parties fail to reach an agreement. Arbitration in contrast with litigation has a number of special advantages.

Arbitration Agreement and Arbitration Clauses

The agreement to arbitration is the foundation stone of international commercial arbitration, which serves to evidence the consent of the parties to submit to arbitration.

There are two basic types of arbitration agreement:

1) The first and more common is to submit future disputes to arbitration.
2) To submit existing disputes to arbitration.

Part Two Introduction to American Laws · Contracts

Exercises

I. Choose the best answer to the following questions:

1. Unilateral contract is _____
   A. A contract for the sale of only a single item or service.
   B. An unenforceable contract.
   C. A contract where there is no "meeting of the minds."
   D. A contract where only one party makes a promise or undertakes performance.

2. Caveat emptor is _____
   A. Election made by parties to a letter of credit to apply the Uniform Customs and Practice for Documentary Credits.
   B. Principle to protect consumers from unscrupulous sellers.
   C. A Latin term for "let the buyer beware."
   D. Implied warranty of fitness for use.

3. Option contract is _____
   A. A contract that is not binding because performance is optional.
   B. A binding agreement in which the owner agrees to sell the property to a prospective purchaser, at a specified price, within a stated period of time.
   C. An offer that can be revived after being rejected by the offeree.
   D. In securities law, a purchasing mechanism that is used only on the New York Stock Exchange.

4. According to the Uniform Commercial Code, which of the following would most likely NOT be considered "goods"?
   A. A TV valued at $300.
   B. A refrigerator valued at $900.
   C. Unborn cattle.
   D. 300 acres of growing corn.

5. The consent of the parties to a contract should be _____
   A. free.
   B. mutual.
   C. communicated by each to the other.
   D. all of the answers provided.

Chapter 7
Remedies for Breach of Contract

6. A contract in which one party makes a promise in order to induce another party to do something is a _____ contract.
   A. bilateral
   B. unilateral
   C. executed
   D. none of the answers provided.

7. If a party to a contract is under the influence of alcohol or drugs during the signing of the agreement, a case could be made to make the contract voidable due to _____
   A. undue influence or duress.
   B. mutual mistake.
   C. fraud.
   D. misrepresentation.

8. An elderly man who lived by himself started repainting his house. Because the elderly man was having a difficult time with the project, his son hired a contractor to do the job. Their contract provided that the contractor would receive payment after completion of the work. When the contractor was halfway done with the job, the elderly man died.
   Which of the following is correct?
   A. The contract is discharged and the contractor will receive no payments, because he did not complete the work.
   B. The contract is discharged, but the contractor will receive payment for work completed.
   C. The contract is not discharged, but the contractor must receive half of the payment before continuing work.
   D. The contract is not discharged, and the contractor must complete the repainting project.

9. An uncle wanted his nephew to quit smoking, because smoking is unhealthy. The uncle attempted to convince the nephew to quit, but the nephew would not agree. The uncle then offered to pay the nephew $5,000 if the nephew quit smoking for one year. It was the uncle's hope that if he could get the nephew to stop smoking for one year, he would not pick up the unhealthy habit again. The nephew agreed, and signed a contract to that effect with the

161

uncle. The nephew quit smoking for one year, but afterward, restarted smoking. He asked for the $5,000, but the uncle refused to pay. The nephew has now filed suit against the uncle.

What is the likely outcome of the case?

A. The uncle is liable, because there was a bargained-for exchange.

B. The uncle is liable, because the nephew relied to his detriment on the uncle's promise.

C. The uncle is not liable, because the consideration was inadequate.

D. The uncle is not liable, because the uncle did not receive a benefit and the nephew did not suffer a detriment.

10. A woman had lived in Apartment 123 in the same apartment complex for six years. On many prior occasions, the woman had hired the same handyman to perform odd jobs in her apartment. The woman, who was leaving town on vacation, telephoned the handyman and said, "If you will replace the tile in my bathroom while I'm on vacation, I will pay you $700. You can get the keys from the superintendent."

The handyman responded, "It's a deal." During their telephone conversation, the woman failed to tell the handyman that she no longer lived in Apartment 123, but had moved down the hall into Apartment 132. The handyman came to the apartment complex, got the key for Apartment 123 from the superintendent, and re-tiled the bathroom. When the woman returned from her vacation, she noticed that her bathroom tile had not been replaced. She contacted the handyman, who then informed her that he had replaced the tile in Apartment 123. The handyman demanded that the woman pay him $700, but the woman refused.

If the handyman sues the woman for payment of the $700 and the woman claims mistake, for whom should the court award judgment?

A. The handyman, because the woman should have realized that he would replace the tile in Apartment 123.

B. The handyman, because even though no contract existed, he is entitled to quasi-contractual relief under the circumstances.

C. The woman, because the handyman did not replace the tile in the woman's bathroom.

Chapter 7
Remedies for Breach of Contract

D. The woman, because no contract existed due to the mutual mistake of the parties.

II. **Essay Questions:**

QUESTION 1

Please explain what competent means regarding the requirement that an agreement be between competent parties in order for a contract to be effective?

QUESTION 2

My 15-year old son, who looks older, just signed a contract joining a health club which has "dues" of $50.00 a month. Is this contract valid?

QUESTION 3

At the wedding of Tom and Mary, Tom's father, Frank, told them that he wanted them to live with him and to care for him for the rest of his life. He said, "If you agree to do this, I will deliver to you, within a year, a deed to my home." Tom and Mary told Frank they accepted his offer and promised to look after Frank with loving care in Frank's home. They immediately moved in with him. Soon after moving into Frank's home, Tom and Mary used their own money to add a new wing to the house, pay the outstanding property taxes, and pay off an existing mortgage of $25,000. One year after Tom and Mary moved into the home, Tom reminded Frank of his promise to convey the property to them. Frank became angry, refused to execute the deed, and ordered Tom and Mary to leave the premises.

Tom and Mary consult you concerning the rights and remedies that may be available to them.

How would you advise them? Discuss.

Torts

> **导 读** <<
>
> 侵权行为法涉及的不法行为主要包括对人身、财产、名誉等合法权益进行侵害的行为。
>
> 根据侵权法中的归责原则,侵权行为可分为故意、过失、无过失(严格责任)三种。常见的故意侵权行为包括:(1) 殴打(battery),成立要件包括身体接触、有害或冒犯性、故意;(2) 恐吓(assault),指行为人故意做出的令他人产生会发生暴行的担忧;(3) 非法监禁(false imprisonment),指故意非法将他人拘禁于一定区域之内的行为,包括将他人限定于行为人设定的区域、行为人的行为直接或者间接产生他人被迫置身于行为人设定的区域,以及被限定活动范围的人意识到这一限制或者因限制而受害;(4) 侵害动产(trespass to chattel),指故意侵害他人所有或占有的动产,因而产生损害,例如造成财产价值的减损、妨害他人占有权或者所有权、侵夺他人所有物或占有物等;(5) 侵入土地(trespass to land),指故意非法进入他人所有或占有的土地;(6) 故意施加精神痛苦(intentional infliction of emotional distress),指故意以极端且粗暴的行为造成他人严重的精神痛苦;(7) 侵占(conversion),指被告对原告的动产权益进行完全处分的行为。
>
> 在故意侵权中,被告具有充分的确定性(substantial certainty)知道自己的行为会侵害他人权益,但是在过失侵权案中,被告往往是在对风险的存在缺乏充分注意的情况下行事,从而对原告产生损害,案件的焦点往往在于风险是否具有可预

见性,被告的行为是否达到了普通正常人(reasonable person)对可预见风险的注意程度。要想认定过失的存在,必须具备几个要件:注意义务的存在,注意义务的违反,损害结果的发生,因果关系。其中注意的标准,是采用普通正常人标准。对于过失侵权行为的抗辩理由,主要有三种:一是共同过失(contributory negligence,即原告也有过失);二是比较过失(comparative negligence);三是自冒风险(assumption of risks)。

无过失责任又称严格责任,指侵权行为的成立不以行为人的故意或过失为要件,没有过错也应当负责。这种类型的责任主要包括动物饲养人或占有人的责任,异常危险活动的责任以及产品责任三种。野生或者驯养动物的管理者一般要对其动物的侵犯承担责任,不管其自身有没有过错。如果一项活动本身具有固有的危险性,即使他人小心采取措施也无法绝对避免,这种活动就是一场危险的活动。产品责任是指卖方由于产品的瑕疵而给购买、使用的人或者他人带来伤害时所负的责任,责任当事人之间可以有合同关系,也可以没有合同关系。

侵权法的其他重要问题还包括因果关系与损害赔偿。因果关系的认定,是英美侵权法中非常复杂的问题,涉及事实上的因果关系和近因关系两种。关于事实上的因果关系的判断,传统上采取"如果没有此种加害,则不会发生此种损害"标准,即"but for"标准。一旦确定了事实原因,原告就必须也确立近因。近因是法律上承认的原因。并非所有由被告"实际"造成的伤害都被看做由近因造成的,因此,近因理论是对法律责任的限制。近因的一般规则是,对属于被告行为造成的正常后果或增加的危险,被告须为其一切有害结果负法律责任。

行为人承担责任的情况中,如果是共同侵权行为,被害人可能同时对几个人都有损害赔偿的请求权,共同侵权人因而需要负连带责任(joint and several liability)。雇主对雇员的职务行为侵权时也应承担代理责任,也即连带赔偿责任。损害赔偿一般包括三类:(1)补偿性损害赔偿(compensatory damages),即针对实际损害所为的赔偿金,一般的赔偿金多为此种性质。(2)象征性损害赔偿(nominal damages),指没有发生或者没有证明有实际损害,但是仍然象征性地请求赔偿金以显示被害人的权利已被侵害的情形,例如请求一元赔偿。(3)惩罚性损害赔偿(punitive damages),指针对主观恶意较高的情况,以高出实际损害的巨额赔偿金来惩罚加害人,达到吓阻不法行为的目的。

Chapter 1
Intentional Torts

An intentional tort is a category of torts that describes a civil wrong resulting from an intentional act on the part of the tortfeasor. The term negligence, on the other hand, pertains to a tort that simply results from the failure of the <u>tortfeasor</u>① to take sufficient care in fulfilling a duty owed, while strict liability torts refers to situations where a party is liable for injuries no matter what precautions were taken.

Ⅰ. Battery and Assault

Battery is the intentional tort that protects a person's interest in freedom from unwanted bodily contact. To maintain a battery action, a plaintiff must establish three elements: (i) a contact; (ii) that is harmful or offensive; and (iii) that the defendant caused the contact intentionally.

Tort law also protects plaintiffs from the apprehension of such contact, even if contact never occurs. This protection is accomplished through the tort of assault. Like battery, assault developed from the writ of trespass and has a long history in the common law system. Here is a very early example of an assault case. The defendant arrived at the plaintiff's tavern, looking for wine. Upset that the tavern was closed, the defendant beat on the door with a <u>hatchet</u>②. The plaintiff's wife put her head out the window and told the defendant to stop hitting the door. The defendant then swung his hatchet again, although he did not strike the wife. Despite the lack of contact, the court ruled that he had

---

① 侵权人,侵权行为者
② 短柄斧,斧头

committed a trespass by making an "assault upon the woman."

Although colloquially used interchangeably, in many jurisdictions, assault and battery are distinct crimes. In such jurisdictions, assault (also called attempted battery) is a threat or physical act that creates a reasonable apprehension of imminent harmful or offensive contact, whereas battery is a physical act that results in that harmful or offensive contact. Assault is a lesser included offense of battery, meaning that assault merges into battery and that a defendant may be punished for one but not both crimes.

II. False Imprisonment

A person commits false imprisonment when he commits an act of restraint on another person which confines that person in a bounded area. An act of restraint can be a physical barrier (such as a locked door), the use of physical force to restrain, a failure to release, or an invalid use of legal authority. Threats of immediate physical force are also sufficient to be acts of restraint. An area is only bounded if freedom of movement is limited in all directions. If there is a reasonable means of escape from the area, the area is not bounded.

False imprisonment is the third intentional tort that grew from the old writ of trespass to protect an individual's physical integrity. False imprisonment differs from battery and assault in that it does not protect against contact or apprehension of contact. Rather, it protects an individual's right to move freely from place to place as she sees fit. The Restatement of Torts Second defines false imprisonment as follows:

An actor is subject to liability to another for false imprisonment if

(1) He acts intending to confine the other or a third person within boundaries fixed by the actor, and

(2) His act directly or indirectly results in such a confinement of the other, and

(3) The other is conscious of the confinement or is harmed by it.

As a practical matter most false imprisonment cases turn on the issue of whether the plaintiff was truly "confined" to a bounded area.

The Restatement indicates that a plaintiff seeking recovery for false imprisonment must prove that the defendant confined him within boundaries fixed by the defendant. Sometimes it is easy to recognize the bounded area (as in the *Teichmiller* case, where the defendants blocked the plaintiff's exit from the room). Other times, however, the "bounded area" requirement is a bit more difficult to conceptualize. For example, in the famous case of *Whittaker v. Sandford*, 85 A. 339 (Me. 1921), a member of a religious sect in Jaffa(today Tel Aviv) decided to leave the sect and return to the United States. The leader of the sect offered the member passage to Maine (where the sect maintained another colony) on his yacht. The member accepted the offer. However, when the yacht arrived in port, the leader refused to furnish her with a boat to go ashore. The plaintiff eventually freed herself, and she later sued the sect leader for false imprisonment. In affirming a jury verdict in favor of the plaintiff, the Supreme Judicial Court of Maine compared the plaintiff's **plight**① to that of a person locked in a room:

If one should, without right, turn the key in a door, and thereby prevent a person in the room from leaving, it would be the simplest form of unlawful imprisonment. The restraint is physical. The four walls and the locked door are physical impediments to escape. Now it is different when one who is in control of a vessel at anchor, within practical rowing distance for the shore, who has agreed that a guest on board shall be free to leave, there being no means to leave except by rowboats, wrongfully refuses the guest the use of the boat? The boat is the key. By refusing the boat he turns the key. The guest is as effectively locked up as if there were walls along the sides of the vessel. The restraint is physical. The impassable sea is the physical barrier.

With respect to the intent element of false imprisonment, it is only necessary for the plaintiff to prove that the defendant had a purpose to confine her, or that the defendant was substantially certain that his conduct would cause **confinement**②. The defendant's motive for confining the plaintiff is irrelevant, at least so far so the prima facie case goes. The distinction between intent and words such as "motive," or "malice" can be difficult to sort out. In trying to understand the terms, consider the following passage from a South Carolina

---

① 境况,困境,誓约
② 监禁,关押,约束,限制

appellate court decision:

Volition is the actor's willingness to do an act. Deliberation is the thinking out or weighing of the act before it is done. Purpose is the result act. Malice is the actor's feeling of ill will or hatred towards the victim of the act.

Intent is proved by showing that the actor acted willingly (volition) and that he knew or [was substantially certain] the result would follow from his act. Neither deliberation nor malice is necessary elements of intent.

Ⅲ. Trespass to Land and Chattels

Trespass is defined by the act of knowingly entering another person's property without permission. Such action is held to infringe upon a property owner's legal right to enjoy the benefits of ownership. Actions violating the real property of another are handled as Trespasses to Land. Violations to personal property are handled as Trepass to Chattels.

Under Tort Law, a property owner may bring a Civil Law suit against a trespasser in order to recover damages or receive compensatory relief for injury suffered as a direct result of a trespass. In a tort action, the plaintiff must prove that the offender had, but knowingly violated, a legal duty to respect another person's right to property, which resulted in direct injury or loss to the plaintiff.

The Restatement of Torts defines trespass to land as follows:

One is subject to liability to another for trespass, irrespective of whether he thereby causes harm to any legally protected interest of the other, if he intentionally

(1) Enters land in the passion of the other, or causes a thing or a third person to do so, or

(2) Remains on the land, or

(3) Fails to remove from the land a thing which he is under a duty to remove.

Note that the Restatement suggests the imposition of liability without regard to whether the defendant harmed the plaintiff. This reflects the fact that trespass to land developed as a mechanism to enforce property boundaries, not as an action to compensate individuals for actual harm. This development reflects the great importance that people in early England placed on possessory rights in land. Professor Richard Epstein, for example, traces the roots of the tort to the Crown's need to maintain social order. "One symptom of the high levels of disorder was the frequency with which owners were dispossessed of their land by strangers." Epstein, Torts §1.10 at 22. As one means to respond to attacks on property, according to Professor Epstein, "the common law developed the action trespass *quaere clausam fregit*, or trespass qcf: why did D break into P's 'close,' or close historical connection between trespass and civil order, and it reminds us that in early intentional trespasses, deliberate seizure and destruction of land were the chief targets of the versatile trespass action." *Id*. At 22—23.

Despite the ability to maintain an action without regard to damages, plaintiffs did need to demonstrate that the plaintiff's invasion of land was tangible, for example, an invasion by the plaintiff's own body or by the building of a fence post.

Trespass to **chattels**① grew from the common law writ of *trespass de bonis asportates*—literally, the asportation or carrying away of chattels. Courts later expanded the action to include situations where the defendant did not literally take the chattel, but instead simply damaged it. Today, the law reflects a position that allows a plaintiff to maintain an action in a broad range of situations where a defendant dispossesses another of his chattel, or where a defendant "uses" or "intermeddles" with another's possessory interests in personal property.

One can imagine a number of straightforward situations that would give rise to a trespass to chattels claim. For example, a vandal who purposely scratched your car would be liable for cost of repainting the vehicle. Or a classmate who purposely spilled coffee into the keyboard of your laptop would be responsible for subsequent repairs. In recent years, however, the advent of technology has forced courts to consider some interesting issues concerning the concept of what constitutes "property" itself.

---

① 动产

Chapter 1
Intentional Torts

IV. Conversion

Conversion[①] is an intention act by a defendant causing the serious and substantial interference with or the destruction of the chattel of the defendant. However, one should understand two important wrinkles to this rule. First, a defendant need not physically damage a plaintiff's property to convert it. In other words, asserting domination over a plaintiff's property can suffice. Second, courts historically have allowed a plaintiff to recover the full value of converted property, even if the defendant has not damaged the property. Thus, it is sometimes said that the primary distinctions between conversion and trespass to chattels are the degree of the invasion and the "forced sale" remedy.

Why is this a "conversion" case instead of a "trespass to chattels" case? The Restatement of Torts distinguishes the two actions by defining conversion as an act that "so seriously interferes with the right of another to control the property that the actor may justly be required to pay the other the full value of the chattel."

The Restatement then sets forth factors that courts can use in determining the seriousness of the interference:

(1) The extent and duration of the actor's exercise of domination or control;

(2) The actor's intent to assert a right in fact inconsistent with the other's right of control;

(3) The actor's good faith;

(4) The extent and duration of the resulting interference with the other's right of control;

(5) The harm done to the chattel;

(6) The inconvenience and expense caused to the other.

V. Intentional Infliction of Emotional Distress

The law has been hesitant to allow recovery for emotional distress apart from any invasion of a personal or property interest. In fact, it was not until

---

① 财产的转换,转变,换位

about 100 years ago that courts began to allow recovery in such situations. The classic case is *Wilkinson v. Downton*, 2 Q. B. D. 57 (1897), in which the defendant played a "practical joke" on the plaintiff by telling her that her husband has broken both of his legs in an accident and that she should go pick him up immediately. The "joke" severely distressed the plaintiff, and she suffered permanent physical consequences as a result. The court allowed the plaintiff to recover damages despite the fact that the case did not fit any of the traditional trespassory action.

In the early part of the twentieth century, American courts slowly began to follow the lead of *Wilkinson*. In 1948, the American Law Institute recognized an action for intentional infliction of emotional distress in the First Restatement of Torts. Today, the Restatement defines the action as follows: "One who by extreme and outrageous conduct intentionally or recklessly causes severe emotional distress to another is subject to liability for such emotional distress, and if bodily harm to the other results from it, from such bodily harm." Restatement (second) of Torts §46(1) (1965). Despite widespread recognition of this "new" cause of action for intentional infliction of emotional distress, the hurdles for a plaintiff remain high. The defendant's conduct must be "extreme and outrageous," and the plaintiff's distress must be "severe."

Chapter 2

Defenses to Intentional Torts

Even those plaintiffs who establish a prima facie case are not automatically entitled to compensation. Defendants may try to justify their conduct through the use of various defenses. This means that even if a plaintiff proves all of the elements of her claim, a defendant can avoid liability by proving a different set of facts to support the defense.

Ⅰ. Consent

When a person voluntarily and willfully agrees to undertake an action that another person suggests, the consenting person must possess sufficient mental capacity. Consent is a defense to an intentional tort claim. The defense derives from the common law principle *volenti non fit injuria*[①]—to one who is willing, no wrong is done. Content poses few complications when a plaintiff verbally expresses assent to an otherwise tortuous invasion. For example, if you point to your nose and tell your classmate to "go ahead and hit me," your will not be able to maintain a battery action if he accepts your invitation.

But consent extends beyond verbal expressions. For example, a plaintiff may communicate consent by actions as well as words. The famous case of *O'Brien v. Cunard Steamship Co.*, 28 N. E. 266 (Mass. 1891), demonstrates this principle. In *O'Brien*, the plaintiff silently extended her arm toward a doctor to receive a smallpox vaccination that was required for her entry into the United States. The plaintiff later claimed that she did not want the shot, and she

---

① (Latin: "to a willing person, injury is not done") 自愿承担风险(受损害人明知且明确同意了活动中可能存在的风险,他就不得在事后就该活动导致的损害要求赔偿)

sued the doctor for battery. The trial court directed a verdict in favor of the doctor, and the Supreme Judicial Court of Massachusetts affirmed:

In determining whether the act was lawful or unlawful, the surgeon's conduct must be considered in connection with the surrounding circumstances. If the plaintiff's behavior was such as to indicate consent on her part, he was justified in his act, whatever her unexpressed feelings. There was nothing in the conduct of the plaintiff to indicate to the surgeon that she did not wish to obtain a card which would save her from detention at quarantine, and to be vaccinated, if necessary for that purpose. Viewing his conduct in the light of the surrounding circumstances, it was lawful; and there was not evidence tending to show that it was not.

To what extent do participants in athletic events consent to contact? According to the Restatement of Torts: Taking part in a game manifests a willingness to submit to such bodily contacts or restrictions of liberty as are permitted by its rules or usages. Participating in such a game does not manifest consent to contacts which are prohibited by rules and usages of the game if such rules and usages are designed to protect the participants and not merely to secure the better playing of the game as a test of skill. This is true although the player knows that those with or against whom he is playing are habitual violators of such rules.

II. Self Defense

According to the Restatement of Torts:

An actor is privileged to use reasonable force, not intended or likely to cause death or serious bodily harm, to defend himself against unprivileged harmful or offensive contact or other bodily harm which he reasonably believes that another is about to inflict intentionally upon him.

III. Defense of Property

The question of when an individual can engage in otherwise tortious activity to protect property is similar to the question of when an individual can do so in self defense. In general, a person may use reasonable force to protect property when she reasonably believes that force is necessary to prevent the intrusion.

The issue of what constitutes reasonable force sometimes poses problems. As with self defense, the use of force must be proportional to the threatened interest. Proportionality generally does not exist, however, when a person uses deadly force to protect property alone. For example, in the famous English case of *Bird v. Holbrook*, 4 Bing. 628, 130 Eng. Rep. 911 (C. P. 1828), the defendant set a spring gun in his garden to prevent the theft of his tulips. Subsequently, the plaintiff climbed a wall to enter the garden in search of his neighbor's peahen, triggered the gun, and was seriously injured. The court found the defendant liable for the plaintiff's injuries.

Ⅳ. Necessity

Defense to liability for unlawful activity where the conduct cannot be avoided and one is justified in the particular conduct because it will prevent the occurrence of a harm that is more serious. In tort law, there are two different categories of the necessity defense that can be employed: public necessity and private necessity.

1. Private Necessity

The law permits interference with another's property in certain emergency situation. Courts and commentators divide this "necessity" privilege into two categories—public necessity and private necessity (which is discussed in a separate section below) provide defendants with an absolute privilege to interfere with the property of others to avoid a "public disaster." Private necessity, on the other hand, provides defendants with a qualified privilege to interfere with property to protect their own interests, or those of a small group of others. Private necessity is a qualified privilege because it still requires the defendant to compensate the property owner for any damage caused. The Restatement of Torts explains:

One is privileged to commit an act which would otherwise be a trespass to the chattel of another or a conversion of it, if it is or is reasonably believed to be reasonable and necessary to protect the person of property of the actor, the other or a third person from serious harm, unless the actor knows that the person for whose benefit he acts is unwilling that he shall do so.

Where the act is for the benefit of the actor or a third person, he is subject to liability for any harm caused by the exercise of the privilege.

2. Public Necessity

The Restatement (second) of Torts §262 provide:

One is privileged to commit an act which would otherwise be a trespass to a chattel or a conversion if the act is or is reasonably believed to be necessary for the purpose of avoiding a public disaster.

As noted in the introduction to this section, the most important distinction between public necessity and private necessity is that public necessity is an absolute privilege—in other words, a defendant who successfully raises the privilege need not compensate the plaintiff for his loss. For example, in a famous nineteenth century house in order to prevent a fire from spreading. The plaintiff sought recovery for the value of property inside the house that he did not have time to recover. A jury ruled for the plaintiff, but the Supreme Court of California reversed.

Chapter 3
Negligence

Ⅰ. Introduction

Generally speaking, today, intentional torts involve claims that the defendant knew with "substantial certainty" that his actions would invade the interests of another. By contrast, negligence cases involve claims that the defendant engaged in behavior without due care for the risks involved. With negligence, the focus is on whether the risk was foreseeable, and whether defendant's conduct fell below the level expected of a reasonable person in light of the foreseeable risks. In order for a plaintiff to be successful in bringing a negligence cause of action, the plaintiff must prove all the following elements of a negligence claim.

1. A Duty of Due Care

In general, a duty exists if it is foreseeable that the defendant's conduct creates unreasonable risks of harm.

2. Breach of the Duty

Plaintiff must prove that the defendant failed to use reasonable care to avoid causing harm.

3. Causation

The causation element has two parts. Plaintiff must first prove "cause in fact" that the defendant's breach of duty (the negligent conduct) in some way brought about the plaintiff's injury. Plaintiff must then prove "proximate cause" that the causal connection between the negligent conduct of the defendant and the plaintiff's injury was close enough that the defendant should be held liable.

4. Damages

The plaintiff must prove that actual injury resulted from the defendant's conduct. Nominal damages are not awarded for negligent conduct that does not cause injury.

The concept of "negligence" is difficult to define. There is a certain vagueness, yet common sense understanding to the meaning of the term. Society recognizes the common sense nature of the determination by placing the power to determine negligence primarily in the jury. Negligence seems to be **blameworthy**① behavior that requires less in the way of intent, but is deemed blameworthy because a jury finds that the defendant's behavior falls below the reasonable person standard of care.

II. Applying the Reasonable Person Standard

We continue our study of negligence with a description of the standard of care, starting with what some have described as the "general duty" that applies whenever a person is acting in a way that can potentially cause harm to others. For the purpose of our discussion, we will presume that the act itself is not so dangerous that it is automatically negligent, that it assumes the risk, or that it is so inherently dangerous as to be covered in strict liability. The general duty is to act as a reasonable person. The jury is asked to make an objective rather than subjective determination. The person who acts is not required to do his or her own best, but is required to act as a hypothetical reasonable person who would act in similar circumstances.

There are three parts to the jury's finding of "negligence." The first is whether a duty exists at all. The second question presumes the existence of a duty, and focuses on how the judge describes the duty to the jury. Finally, once the jury is told what the duty is, the jury must apply the law to the facts to determine whether the defendant has breached that duty.

Should the "reasonable person standard" be based on the characteristics of the people involved?

---

① 负有责任的,该受指责的

Chapter 3
Negligence

1. Minors

All states define an "age of majority," usually 18. Persons younger than this age are considered minors, and must be under the care of a parent or guardian unless they are emancipated. Minors are treated differently from adults for many legal purposes including privacy of official records, punishment in criminal matters, or the ownership or transfer of property. In many cases, even with minors, there is no question that a duty exists. For example, if a fifteen-year-old driver with a learner's permit, driving with his mother, causes an automobile accident that results in injury to another, there is no question that some duty exists, although there may be a question as to the nature of that duty and whether it was breached. In these cases the important question is how the court should instruct the jury concerning the standard of care required of a driver of lesser age and experience. It is only in the light of this jury instruction that the jury will need to determine whether the fifteen-year-old breached the duty that existed in the circumstances described by the witness.

2. The Elderly

Senior citizens are held to the ordinary adult standard of care, unless they are the plaintiff, and then the standard is affected more by physical disability, than just simply by age. In determining the contributory negligence of an elderly person, a court may measure his conduct against the standard of conduct of the ordinary person suffering from the same or similar **infirmities of old age**[①]. According to the Restatement (Second) of Torts, the weakness of age is treated merely as part of the "circumstances" under which a reasonable person must act. There is not a different standard from that of the reasonable person, but an application of it to the special circumstances of each case.

In *Estate of Burgess v. Peterson*, 537 N. W. 2d 115 (Wis. 1995), the court examined the reasoning behind the principle that in assessing the negligence of an adult, age may be considered only in the limited circumstances where old age was the cause of a physical infirmity. The logic of this position is that, while it is impossible to quantify or measure the degree to which age slows thought

---

① 老年疾病

processes, physical infirmities (e. g. , arthritis, osteoporosis, etc.) have physical manifestations than can be objectively observed and measured. This allows for positive proof that a person is suffering from a certain condition. It assures that elderly persons who are negligent will not be shielded from liability for their acts by claiming that they "aren't as sharp as they used to be." Absent evidence that an individual suffered from an age-related disability affecting his cognitive abilities, the individual's age should not be considered when assessing his negligence.

3. Drunkenness, Blackouts, Seizures, and Sudden Mental Illness

The line between physical deficiency and mental deficiency is not always easy to draw. While the drunk may be entitled to a safe street, he or she should not get behind a wheel of a car. Of course, just having a drink does not make a driver negligent: to be relevant, there needs to be a showing that drinking affected the driver's behavior.

Blackouts[①] and seizures often present jury questions concerning the level of notice to the sufferer of their condition before they got behind the wheel of their car.

IV. The Role of Custom

One tool that courts allow juries to use in determining the reasonableness of the plaintiff actor's behavior is to refer the jury to the custom of actors similarly situated. There are a number of reasons for this. Custom may militate the otherwise *expost facto* nature of the jury decision and answer the actor's complaint, "How was I to know what is reasonable?" In addition, custom is evidence of the cost benefit analysis that actors similarly situated engage in, or have done unconsciously, as they decide how fast to drive on a particular road, or what amount of a drug to prescribe to given patient in a given situation.

On the other hand, there is nothing to guarantee that custom will set the standard at the right height. The truthfulness of belief does not depend on how long it has been held, or how many people hold such a belief. (Consider that,

---

① 封锁,管制

at one time, most people believed that the world was flat.) As a result, the courts have struggled with how much weight the juror should give to "custom" in processing of the question of neglect.

V. Calculus of Risk

One rule that you might take away from the materials on custom is that custom will dictate care unless the costs to the actor are less than the risk of injury—the probability of injury multiplied by the extent of the expected injury—the actor's conduct creates. Yet as the Helling case points out, there is certain arrogance for a court to say that it does the calculus of risk better than the actors who have set the custom. Still, it does seem appealing that the law of negligence set the level of care with an eye to efficiency. After all, if all actors took the responsibility for protecting others from injury which they could most cost effectively prevent, then our tort law would create a more efficient use of its resources, and everyone would benefit.

VI. Proof of Negligence

*Res Ipsa Loquitur*① is a doctrine in negligence law that allows a plaintiff to survive the defendant's motion to dismiss at the close of the plaintiff's case. It means the court feels that the jury, having heard these facts, could reasonably conclude that there is negligence on the part of the defendant. The facts are said to speak for themselves.

BYRNE v. BOADLE
159 Eng. Rep. 299 (Ex. 1863)

Plaintiff's proof was that he was passing along the highway in front of defendant's premises when he was struck and badly hurt by a barrel of flour that was apparently being lowered from a window above which was on the premises of the defendant, a dealer in flour. Several witnesses testified that they saw the barrel fall and hit plaintiff. The defendant claimed that "there was no evidence

---

① 事实自证原则

of negligence for the jury." The trial court, agreeing, nonsuited plaintiff after the jury had awarded the damages at £ 50 and the trial court gave plaintiff leave to move the Court of Exchequer to enter a verdict for him in that amount. Having obtained a rule nisi to enter a verdict for plaintiff "on the ground of this direction [of the trial court] in ruling that there was not evidence of negligence on the part of the defendant," the defendant's attorney showed cause, arguing that it was consistent with the evidence that the purchaser of the flour or some complete stranger was supervising the lowering of the barrel of flour and that its fall was not attributable in any way to defendant or his servants. It was presumed that the defendant's servants were engaged in removing the defendant's flour. Defendant's attorney observed that "Surmise[①] ought not to be substituted for strict proof when it is thought to fix a defendant with serious liability. The plaintiff should establish his case by affirmative evidence. The plaintiff was bound to give affirmative proof of negligence. But there was not a scintilla of evidence, unless the occurrence is of itself evidence of negligence." The court then commented, "There are certain cases of which it may be said *res ipsa loquitur* and this seems one of them. In some cases the Court had held that the mere fact of the accident having occurred is evidence of negligence, as, for instance, in the case of railway collision."

Then followed a discussion between the defendant's counsel and the judges of the Court of Exchequer over the relevance of certain precedents involving railroads.

Pollock, C. B. We are all of opinion that the rule must be absolute to enter the verdict for the plaintiff. The learned counsel was quite right in saying that there are many accidents form which no presumption of negligence can rise, but I think it would be wrong to lay down as a rule that in no case can presumption of negligence arise from the fact of an accident. Suppose in this case the barrel had rolled out of the warehouse and fallen on the plaintiff, how could he possibly ascertain from what cause it occurred? It is the duty of persons who keep barrels in a warehouse to take care that they do not roll out, and I think that such a case would, beyond all doubt, afford prima facie evidence of

---

① 推测,猜想

Chapter 3
Negligence

negligence. A barrel could not roll out of a warehouse without some negligence, and to say that a plaintiff who is injured by it must call witness from the warehouse to prove negligence seems to me preposterous. So in the building or repairing a house, or putting pots on the chimneys, if a person passing along the road is injured by something falling upon him, I think the accident alone would be prima facie evidence of negligence. Or if an article calculated to cause damage is put in a wrong place and does mischief, I think that those whose duty was to put it in the right place are prima facie responsible, and if there is any state of facts to rebut the presumption of negligence, they must prove them. The present case upon the evidence comes to this, a man is passing in front of the premises of a dealer in four, and there falls down upon him a barrel of flour. I think it apparent that the barrel was in the custody of the defendant who occupied the premises, and who is responsible for the acts of his servants who had the control of it; and in my opinion the fact of its falling is prima facie evidence of negligence, and the plaintiff who was injured by it is not bound to show that it could not fall without negligence, but if there are any facts inconsistent with negligence it is for the defendant to prove them.

Guest Statues and *Res Ipsa Loquitur*

A quick note about guest statutes. For a number of years, if a person was injured in an automobile accident where he was riding as a guest of the driver, the person injured could only recover if he or she could prove that the driver was grossly negligent. The courts reasoned that the guest gave up reasonable care when the guest was not paying his or her own way. It also reasoned that the possibility of collusion between driver and passenger to get at the insurance coverage of the driver was just too tempting.

Fortunately for torts students, this issue—the difference between negligence and gross negligence—in guest statutes has been resolved through a combination of insurance practices and state Supreme Court due process jurisprudence. A number of state supreme courts ruled that legislation that barred recovery by a passenger violated due process and equal protection rights provided by the state constitutions. These cases are remarkable for their willingness to challenge the presumed rationality of their state legislatures by examining the reasoning above and finding that the state was acting irrationally when it enacted the legislation. In addition, the insurance companies were more than willing to fold coverage in for the passenger in an auto accident, in exchange for a higher premium charged the driver/owner of the car. Since most drivers wanted to provide coverage if their negligence would cause injury to a passenger in their car, the market seems to have taken care of the problem which suits posed to the courts.

Chapter 4
Cause in Fact

This chapter will begin by examining how courts approach the issue using the "but-for" test of causation, which asks whether the accident would have occurred "but for" the defendant's negligent conduct. The question requires us to imagine what would have occurred if we remove only the element of the defendant's negligent conduct while holding all other facts of the situation constant.

I. "But-for" Causation

The "but-for" test is applied by considering only the negligent aspect of the defendant's conduct. In the Lyons case followed, for example, it is clear that the conduct of driving the truck caused the accident, in the sense that had the defendant not driven at all, the accident would not have occurred. This is not the issue, however. Instead, the court focuses on whether the accident would have occurred but for the defendant's negligent conduct.

LYONS v. MIDNIGHT SUN TRANSPORTATION SERVICES
928 P. 2d 1202

Per Curiam.
Esther Hunter-Lyons was killed when her Volkswagen van was struck broadside by a truck driven by David Jette and owned by Midnight Sun Transportation Services, Inc. When the accident occurred, Jette was driving south in the right-hand lane of Arctic Boulevard in Anchorage. Hunter-Lyons pulled out of a parking lot in front of him. Jette braked and steered to the left,

but Hunter-Lyons continued to pull out further into the traffic lane. Jette's truck collided with Hunter-Lyons's vehicle. David Lyons, the deceased's husband, filed suit, asserting that Jette had been speeding and driving negligently.

At trial, conflicting testimony was introduced regarding Jett's speed before the collision. Lyons's expert witness testified that Jette may have been driving as fast as 53 miles per hour. Midnight Sun's expert testified that Jette probably had been driving significantly slower and that the collision could have occurred even if Jette had been driving at the speed limit, 35 miles per hour. Lyons's expert later testified that if Jette had stayed in his own lane, and had not steered to the left, there would have been no collision. Midnight Sun's expert contended that steering to the left when a vehicle pulls out onto the roadway from the right is a normal response and is generally the safest course of action to follow...

The jury found that Jette, in fact, had been negligent, but his negligence was not a legal cause of the accident. The jury finding of negligence indicates that the jury concluded David Jette was driving negligently or responded inappropriately when Ms. Hunter-Lyons entered the traffic lane and, thus, did not exercise the care and prudence a reasonable person would have exercised under the circumstances. Although the jury found Jette to have been negligent, it also found that this negligence was not the legal cause of the accident. Duty, breach of duty, causation and harm are the separate and distinct elements of a negligence claim, all of which must be proven before a defendant can be held liable for the plaintiff's injuries.

We cannot say that the jury's finding of lack of causation was unreasonable. There was evidence presented at trial from which the jury could reasonably have drawn the conclusion that even though Jette was driving negligently, his negligence was not the proximate cause of the accident. Midnight Sun introduced expert testimony to the effect that the primary cause of the accident was Ms. Hunter-Lyons's action in pulling out of the parking lot in front of an oncoming truck. Terry Day, an accident reconstruction specialist testified that, depending on how fast Ms. Hunter-Lyons was moving, the accident could have happened even if Jette had been driving within the speed limit. Midnight Sun also introduced of an automobile in his traffic lane. Although all of this testimony was disputed by Lyons, a reasonable jury could have concluded that Ms. Hunter-Lyons caused the accident by abruptly pulling out in front of an oncoming truck, and that David Jette's negligence was not a contributing factor. With the element of causation lacking, even the most egregious negligence cannot result in liability.

AFFIRMED

II. Proving But-for Cause: The Slip and Fall Case

Proving "but-for" causation can be a challenge even in fairly ordinary fact situation. Consider, for example, that staple of tort litigation known as the "slip and fall." Even if the plaintiff can prove that the defendant negligently created a dangerous situation—a pool of spilled liquid or a banana peel left on the floor, a slippery or poorly lighted staircase—the plaintiff must still prove that the dangerous condition caused the fall. In many cases that has proved surprisingly difficult to do.

Chapter 5

Proximate Cause

The term "proximate cause" is as mysterious as any in law, and many have criticized the very use of the term to describe this next stage of the analysis, proposing such alternative descriptions as "legal cause" (itself hardly illuminating) or "scope of liability." The point is to emphasize that this inquiry asks different questions than the preceding cause in fact analysis. Granting that the negligent conduct of the defendant was in some way the cause of the harm, we now ask whether or not the defendant should in fact be held liable for it.

After establishing that the defendant's negligent conduct was the cause in fact of the plaintiff's injury, the next step in the negligence analysis is determining whether the negligence was the "proximate cause" as well.

I. Introductory Problem: Jury Instructing on Proximate Cause

As noted, proximate cause in theory is a distinct step in the analysis, which is reached if and only if actual cause is established. In practice, unfortunately, the two issues are not always kept clearly separated. Consider, for example, the following jury instructions, which will serve to introduce the type of issues presented in proximate cause analysis, as well as to present the two dominant approaches used in resolving them:

1. Jury Instruction: Direct Cause

The "proximate cause" is that which produces an injury directly, or in the natural and normal sequence of events without the intervention of any independent, intervening cause. It is the direct and immediate cause, the predominant cause which, acting directly or in the natural sequence of events, produces the accident and resulting injury, and without which the injury would not have occurred.

2. Jury Instruction: Foreseeability of Injury

The "proximate cause" of a jury is a cause which in its natural and continuous sequence produces an event, and without which the event would not have occurred. In order to warrant a finding that the defendant's negligence is the proximate cause of an injury, it must appear from a preponderance of the evidence that facts and circumstances existed that were such a person of ordinary prudence would have reasonably foreseen that the injury would be the natural and probable consequence of the negligence.

Examine these jury instructions. Both contain a "but-for" cause element ("and without which the event would not have occurred"). But they also contain an additional requirement, and it is those additional elements that will be the focus of study in this chapter. In the "Direct Cause" instruction, the emphasis, as the name suggests, is on the directness of the causation and the lack of any "independent, intervening causes." The second instruction also speaks to the sequence of events, but adds the requirement that the defendant be able to foresee that the injury would be the result of the negligence.

II. Foreseeability and Intervening Cause

The final issue to be considered in this chapter concerns the proper treatment of what are called "intervening causes." The cause presenting this problem usually presents the same general fact pattern. First, the defendant will act negligently. This negligent conduct may not immediately cause the plaintiff any harm at all. Instead, the negligence creates a dangerous situation or, more broadly, places the plaintiff in a position of vulnerability. Some other actor or force then comes into play to trigger the potential danger created by the defendant and to thereby cause injury to the plaintiff. This other actor or force is the intervening cause. The difficulty is to decide whether or not this intervening force is so extraordinary or so independent of the original negligent conduct that the defendant should be excused from liability. (If the intervening cause is deemed to be so significant that it excuses the defendant, it is referred to as a "superseding cause.")

Chapter 6

Multiple Tortfeasors

Ⅰ. Joint and Several Liability

1. Under the rule of joint and several liabilities, each negligent defendant is fully responsible for a plaintiff's damages, assuming that the defendants caused an indivisible harm. However, liability is several only where defendant cause distinct or separable components of a plaintiff's harm.

2. Should comparative fault states continue to apply joint and several liabilities? No **consensus**① has emerged. In fact, jurisdictions are so splintered that the Restatement refused to endorse a position. Instead, the Restatement sets out five separate "tracks" to describe the competing approaches. The first track reflects approximately eleven jurisdictions that have retained joint and several liabilities even after adopting comparative fault. The second track describes the opposite approach (adopted by approximately 14 states) of applying only several liability to multiple defendants who have caused indivisible harm. The remaining tracks reflect jurisdictions that have come down somewhere in the middle. One of the remaining tracks suggests the imposition of joint and several liabilities, subject to a reallocation of unenforceable shares to all parties in proportion to their share of comparative responsibility. Another track suggests the imposition of joint and several liabilities for a plaintiff's economic damages, but only several liabilities for noneconomic damages, such as pain and suffering. A fifth track suggests the imposition of joint and several liabilities only against defendants who are assigned "a percentage of comparative

---

① 一致,合意,一致同意

responsibility equal to or in excess of the legal threshold." Among states that follow this approach, the "threshold" runs from 10% to 60%. Below the threshold, defendants are only severally liable for a plaintiff's harm.

3. Where a defendant commits an intentional tort, the Restatement suggests joint and several liabilities for indivisible harm regardless of which "track" a jurisdiction follows in cases involving negligent tortfeasors.

II. Indemnity and Contribution

1. The contribution and indemnity are the primary methods by which jointly-responsible tortfeasors seek reimbursement from one another. Indemnity is a rule that compels one tortfeasor to completely reimburse another who has paid a judgment to a plaintiff. Often, the rule applies where one party has contractually agreed to reimburse another. However, indemnity also applies in several other circumstances. For example, a defendant whose liability was premised on vicarious liability can seek indemnity from the "active" tortfeasor who actually harmed the plaintiff. In addition, indemnity can apply where tortfeasors have committed wrongs of a different "magnitude" against the plaintiff. (Noting that a comment to the Restatement of Torts Second §866B allows for indemnity by a negligent actor against intentional, reckless, or even grossly negligent actors). Finally, product retailers or wholesalers sometimes can seek indemnity against manufacturers in a products liability action. (Permitting retailer to seek indemnity against manufacturer where retailer's liability was based on duplication of manufacturer's warning label).

2. As an "all or nothing" rule, indemnity is consistent with traditional tort principles such as contributory negligence and joint and several liability. This is not true of contribution, which envisions joint tortfeasors sharing responsibility for a plaintiff's harm. As recently as the 1970s, only a handful of American jurisdictions permitted contribution absent legislative action. The District of Columbia, which still retains the rule of contributory negligence, was one of those jurisdictions, and the Ahmadi decision from that jurisdiction reflects the basic contribution rule whereby jointly-liable tortfeasors can seek "pro rata" contribution from one another. Today, however, a majority of states have enacted statutes that permit contribution on a comparative basis; such statutes are consistent with states' adoption of comparative fault.

Chapter 7
Damages for Personal Injuries

Damages are a separate element of the causes of action in negligence and strict liability cases. With the trepassory intentional torts, general damages will be awarded once the jury finds that the intentional tort has been committed. In other words, damages are not a separate required element.

The amount of damages is a question of fact for the jury, (or judge, when the judge is the fact finder.) Jurors are told that they are to compensate the injured to the extent possible, so as to place the person injured by the defendant into a position he or she would have been in had the defendant not injured him or her. To the common law, though money may never be a sufficient compensation, it is better than nothing at all, and theoretically substitutes for violence and provides for the peaceful resolution of disputes.

Ⅰ. Economic Loss

A prominent element of economic loss is an award of lost wages. In general, the calculation of lost wages relies on the following variables: the person's present wages and benefits, expected wage growth due to expected increase in job responsibility and benefits, expected wage growth due to expected increase in job responsibility and promotion, years of work expectancy, a subtraction for other employment in mitigation, a discounting to present value, and a determination of the tax effect on the award, if any.

A person's wage can be difficult to determine. For example, if a ball player is injured just when he is about to sign a pro contract, past wages are not relevant to his reasonably expected wage. And how is the law to deal with children, who are permanently disabled or killed before they ever worked? One way is to use average wages of others similarly situated. Here, damages experts can consult national labor statistics for information about average wages, average wage growth, and averages work expectancies. There may be personal characteristics of the injured person that may reasonably affect these averages.

Whether to discount to present value is also a matter of debate. Some jurisdictions determine that wage growth and inflation will balance out any need to discount total wages to its present value. Others recognize that paying a lump sum up front for all the wages a person would have lost over a number of years doesn't account for the fact that investing the unused portion of that money during that work expectancy of the injured person will produce an income stream well in excess of the lost wages. And so damages experts try to calculate a figure which will pay the expected wage of the individual, invest the excess, and thereby produce a stream of income equal to the exact amount of money a person would have been paid over their work expectancy. One way of looking at what the damages expert is doing is to ask yourself how much life insurance you would need to buy to pay your family what you would have made for them over the years you would be working. You would buy too much insurance if you just multiplied the number of years you would work time your expected wages, because of the investment factor.

Again, figuring past medical expenses is also fairly easy, but determining future medical expenses requires predicting the future. Will continuing care be more or less expensive? What if a miracle cure is found? What incentives are there for the patient to try to get better, compensate for their injury and move on with life? How do you factor in all these uncertainties and come up with any reasonably accurate figure for future medical expenses?

One way to handle the uncertainty of future damages is for the parties to enter into structured settlements. These agreements are contracts that provide payment for certain needs, if and when they arise. One danger of structured settlements is that they may cause the plaintiff to malinger in order to get the future payment. Also, if there is a fair way to determine the total sum of the future damages, there is no economic reason to favor the defendant keeping the unpaid sum for reinvestment, over the plaintiff getting the sum and investing it for the plaintiff. Each will take risks in investing the money that or may not pan out. Yet despite these difficulties, structured, or "periodic," payments is the method of payment provided by worker's compensation statues, because the conduct and health of the plaintiff can be effectively monitored by the worker's compensation system of providing health benefits.

II. Non-Economic Loss: Pain and Suffering

One type of damage that is recoverable in a personal injury case is for "pain and suffering." Pain is the physical pain that plaintiff suffers from his injuries (i.e., the loss of a leg). Suffering is the psychological pain that plaintiff feels because of his condition.

The difficulty is that, unlike lost wages or medical expenses, few "pain and suffering" cases can truly be measured in dollar terms. Consider the prior problems in which one plaintiff suffered paralysis, another suffered facial disfiguration and a third suffered brain injury. All of these injuries may involve a great deal of pain. They may also impose psychological suffering on the plaintiff subjected to them.

III. Loss of Consortium

Loss of consortium claims is wrapped in the sexism of early English common law. And even as late as 1952, in England, while a husband was allowed compensation for loss of society and sexual services of his wife, a wife was not allowed compensation for the loss of her husband. *Best v. Samuel Fox and Co. Ltd.* [1052] A. C. 716. The wife was treated like the man's property or as a servant. The American cases, however, since the 1950s, universally vest the action for loss of consortium[①] in the wife as well as the husband.

The debate over the loss of consortium has now shifted to suits by children whose parents have been injured or killed. The leading case against providing for the loss of a parent by a minor child is *Borer v. American Airlines*, Inc., 563 P. 2d 858, 860—61(Cal. 1977), where Justice Torbiner rejected the damage claims of the injured party's nine children. Michigan is mixed, allowing

---

① 配偶的地位和权利

recovery to parents for loss of their children *Berger v. Weber*, 303 N. W. 2d 424(Mich. 1981) but not to children for loss of their parents. *Sizemore v. Smock*, 422 N. W. 2d 666 (Mich. 1988). More recently, a different perspective emerged in *Villareal v. Arizoma*, 774 P. 2d 213(Ariz. 1989). The Arizona rule allows parents to recover for the loss of companionship of their adult children, even though the parents were not dependent upon those adult children for financial support. To the Arizona courts, the nature of the loss—companionship, love and support—required recovery without regard to the archaic pecuniary theory of parental rights.

Ⅳ. Future Damages

Many personal injury cases involve a claim for future earnings and future medical expenses. One issue is whether awards for these types of damages should be reduced to present value.

Let's start by looking at future earnings. Suppose that, absent a **debilitating**[①] accident, plaintiff might have expected to work for 20 more years at a wage of $40,000 per year. In order words, he might have expected to receive $800,000. If plaintiff is given the entire $800,000 at the conclusion of the law suit, and can invest it in a safe security, for example, at 5% per annum, he will earn, on interest alone, before taxes, $40,000 a year. Won't the plaintiff be overcompensated? Plaintiff will receive the expected $40,000 per year at the end of each of the twenty years, for twenty years, but will have the entire $800,000 left at the end of the 20 years. Some argue that such an award represents overcompensation because the award should only compensate plaintiff for his actual loss ($40,000 per year for 20 years) and not provide him with a windfall (the remaining $800,000). As a result, some argue that the award should be reduced to present value—giving plaintiff the amount needed to generate $40,000 a year for 20 years, but exhausting the principal at the end of that time. Some might disagree with the "windfall" analysis. After all, inflation is a fact of life. So is expected wage growth, as responsibility rises, and a person becomes more efficient and experienced, and so can take on more

---

① 使虚弱,使衰弱

V. Punitive Damages

work.

In resent years there has been a proliferation of claims for punitive damages in tort cases, and to some, the awards of punitive damages have grown too high. Accompany this increase in punitive damages claims is renewed criticism of the concept of punitive damages in a tort system that is designed primarily to compensate injured parities for harm. The result has been for states to examine characterizations of a defendant's conduct in the light of the historic objectives of punitive damages, try to more precisely define the nature of the conduct potentially subject to a punitive damages award, and heighten the standard of proof required of someone seeking an award of punitive damages. Moreover, some argue that if the punishment in a given case is too great, it may be arbitrary, may violate due process, and may violate both state and the federal constitutions.

Chapter 8

Limited Duties: Special Limitations on the Scope of Duty

As we have seen, there can be no negligence unless the plaintiff establishes that the defendant has breached some legally-recognized duty of care. In most cases that we have studied thus far, the alleged negligence has been based upon some type of affirmative misconduct (i.e., **misfeasance**①) between the parties. In this Chapter we examine a variety of situations where the defendant has done nothing at all (i.e., non-feasance) under circumstances where The law imposes an affirmative duty to act in a certain manner, as well as in situations when the law simply does not recognize that any legal harm has occurred.

Ⅰ. "Misfeasance" v. "Non-Feasance"

The traditional common law "no duty" to rescue rule seems particularly harsh because it offends commonly accepted notions of morality. Most people in a civilized society are morally outraged by any person's refusal, as in *Yania*, to render aid or assistance to someone who is in life-threatening peril, especially when to do so does not subject the rescuer to any personal danger. Nevertheless, as one commentator has observed: "The law has persistently refused to recognize the moral obligation of common decency and common humanity, to come to the aid of another human being who is in danger."

At the opposite end of the moral **spectrum**②, however, the imposition of

---

① 不法行为,不当行为
② 范围

Chapter 8
Limited Duties: Special Limitations on the Scope of Duty

an affirmative legal duty to render aid may be just as offensive to society's notions of individual autonomy and the freedom to act (or not to act) in a certain way. Historically, courts have sometimes attempted to balance these competing interests by characterizing the actor's conduct as one involving either "misfeasance" or "nonfeasance."

II. Public versus Private Duties

It is one thing for the court to impose an affirmative duty to act upon a private individual; it is quite a different matter to impose such a duty upon a public entity. The potential economic implications of requiring public entities to take affirmative action in various potential negligence situations have led many courts to refrain from imposing affirmative duties to act, at least absent some special circumstance. As we have seen already, if the public entity (even though under duty to take action) nevertheless voluntarily acts so as to induce the plaintiff, a duty may be imposed. Likewise, if some "special relationship" can be shown to exist between the plaintiff and the public entity, an affirmative duty to act may be recognized.

III. Negligence Infliction of (Solely) Emotional Injuries

One of the most controversial areas of negligence law is duty as it relates to emotional distress injuries sustained by "bystanders" and caused (either directly or indirectly) to a third-party victim. The tort cause of action is generally referred to as "negligence infliction of emotional distress" (i.e., NIED). In this tort, however, the plaintiff has suffered no actual physical harm that can be directly attributed to the defendant's alleged negligence. Instead, the plaintiff seeks to recover for purely emotional distress injuries (which may or not be accompanied by some physical symptoms or manifestations) that are allegedly caused by the actor's original negligence toward some other person with whom the plaintiff claims some type of close or other special relationship.

At the outside, it must be noted that "negligence infliction of emotional distress" cases can be analyzed from either a "no duty" or "no proximate cause" perspective. Although considerable debate among courts continues to surround this basic question, the legal distinction between these two very different analytical approaches was nicely explained in *Ballard v. Uribe*, 715 P. 2d 624 (Cal. 1986):

A court's task—in determining "duty"—is not to decide whether a particular plaintiff's injury was reasonably foreseeable in light of a particular defendant's conduct, but rather to evaluate more generally whether the category of negligence conduct at issue is sufficiently likely to result in the kind of harm experienced that liability may appropriately be imposed on the negligence party.

The jury, by contrast, considers "foreseeability" in two more focused, fact-special settings. First, the jury may consider the likelihood or foreseeability of injury in determining whether, in fact, the particular defendant's conduct was negligent in the first place. Second, foreseeability may be relevant to the jury's determination of whether the defendant's negligence was a proximate or legal cause of the plaintiff's injury.

IV. Negligent Infliction of (Solely) Emotional Injuries

1. The "Impact Rule"

As discussed in Dziokonski (*Dziokonski v. Babineau* 380 N. E. 2d 1295 (Mass. 1978)), the "impact rule" (referred to as the "Spade" rule in Massachusetts, after its namesake, *Spade v. Lynn & Boston R. R.*, 168 Mass. 285(1897), denies recovery for all emotional distress injuries received by anyone who was not also physically impacted by the actor's original negligence. The reasons most often given for this rule are set forth in the main opinion in Dziokonski. The legal effect of the "impact rule" is to deny recovery by even the closed relatives of the victim of a negligence inflicted injury in any case where they merely witnessed or (as in Dziokonski) where they learned nearly contemporaneously of the victim's injury, but were not themselves physically harmed by the actor's negligence. As indicated by Dziokonski, most (although not all) courts have abandoned the "impact rule."

2. The "Zone of Impact Rule"

Dziokonski, also discusses the "zone of impact" rule that permits recovery for purely emotional distress injuries to persons who, although not themselves physically impacted by the actor's negligent conduct toward a third-person, are so closely situated to the accident scene (i.e., within the "zone of impact") that they could have been physically impacted. The rationale is that such person is just as foreseeable victims of the actor's negligence as those who are, in fact, actually impacted. Thus, under this rule there is no legal justification for denying recovery to such closely-situated (i. e., foreseeable) bystanders.

The "zone of impact" rule expands the scope of potential liability, but it still does not permit recovery for emotional distress injuries sustained by those persons (even though close relatives as in Dziokonski) who are not physically situated within close proximity to the actual scene of the victim's injury. Courts often become occupied with trying to delineate the precise limits of the permissible "zone" of impact.

3. The "Dillon Rule[①]"

Dissatisfied with the inconsistent results produced under the "impact" rule and the "zone of impact" rule, the California Supreme Court in *Dillon v. Legg*, 441 P. 2d 912(Cal. 1968), articulated a new "rule" relative to the recovery of emotional distress injuries by bystanders in negligent infliction cases. Instead of relying solely upon the occurrence of a physical impact (i. e., the "impact" rule) or the physical location of the bystander relative to the location of the injured victim (i. e., the "zone of impact" rule), the court in Dillon adopted a test for the imposition of duty that was determined simply by the foreseeability of the bystander's emotional distress injury under the circumstances. To aid courts in identifying the types of situations most likely to produce foreseeable emotional distress injuries, Dillon identified three distinct "factors" to be taken into consideration in determining whether a duty was owed in a given case. Specifically, these factors included:

(1) Whether plaintiff [the bystander] was located near the scene of the accident (as contrasted with one who was a distance away from it);

(2) Whether the shock resulted from a direct emotional impact upon plaintiff from the sensory and contemporaneous observance of the accident (as contrasted with learning of the accident from others after its occurrence); and

(3) Whether plaintiff and the victim were closely related (as contrasted with the absence of any relationship or the presence of only a distant

---

① 狄龙规则(是一项限制地方政府权力的原则)

relationship).

Although the Dillon factors were merely intended as guidelines to be used in determining the ultimate issue: foreseeability of emotional distress under the specific circumstances involved, the so-called Dillon test, by which it is now often referred to, has taken on a "life" of its own. Some courts have ignored the Dillon factors altogether, or applied them only occasionally, as needed to justify a particular desired result. Other courts have treated them as a rigid set of requirements for the imposition of a duty in bystander negligent infliction of emotional distress cases. In any event, the flexibility that was intended by Dillon has produced no less certainty and predictability than its predecessor rules as the following cases illustrates.

Chapter 9

Premises Liability: Duties of Owners and Occupiers of Land

As we have seen, the political, social, and economic influences of early English feudal society played an important role in shaping tort law. At that time, England was a rural, essentially **agrarian**① society, in which not only land, but wealth and power were directly associated with the ownership of real property. Not surprisingly, the newly-developed English common law rules reflected this feudal heritage by creating various "status" categories which often favored the landowner in claims brought by injures entrants. These categories involved simplistic classifications based solely upon the legal "status" of the injured entrant—trespasser, licensee, and invitee.

When the American colonies become states, formed their own governments and created their own judicial systems, they adopted legal precedents from the existing body of English common law. Since the early American society was also largely rural and agrarian. American courts gave a warm reception to the English common law "status" categories. Just like their English counterparts, American courts strictly enforced and rigidly applied the categories. The results were often harsh and uncompromising, frequently favoring the landowner.

As both English and American societies evolved, becoming more urban and industrialized, the legal rules that had once favored the feudal landowners began to change. Courts recognized new subcategories of entrants such as "discovered trespassers" and "child trespassers." Desirous of achieving more just and fair

---

① 土地的，农业的

results, courts began to blur the once clear distinctions between the original status categories. By the middle of the twentieth century, virtually every American jurisdiction had developed an impressive array of legal rules, exceptions, limitations and even "fictions," each patterned around the traditional tri-partite common law "status" categories. The resulting body of law has persisted largely intact today in most American jurisdictions, despite continued and often severe criticisms from both courts and legal commentators. For example, in 1959 decision that rejected the traditional common law distinctions between "licensees" and "invites" in admiralty law, the United States Supreme Court characterized this myriad of common law rules as a "semantic morass①."

Most of these traditional doctrines continue to be recognized and applied, in at least some form, in virtually every American jurisdiction. To understand why, it is necessary to examine the historical doctrines, as well as the modern pressures for change. The resulting body of case law, often referred to as "premises liability" law, represents one of the most litigious and diverse areas in all of torts today. Concerned primarily with myriad of tort liabilities that arise out of conditions existing on real property, as well as the various activities which are conducted thereon, the law of premises liability encompasses for more than the ubiquitous "slip and fall" case. Indeed, there may be no single area of modern tort litigation that involves so diverse and complex an array of legal issues as that of "premises liability."

Ⅰ. Common Law "Status" Categories of Entrants

Common law negligence is the most frequently asserted cause of action in premises liability cases. However, sometimes plaintiffs also rely on other tort theories, such as those involving various intentional torts, nuisance, or even strict liability. Moreover, there are an ever-increasing number of statues and ordinances that regulate individual aspects of the law governing the tort liability of owners and occupiers of legal property.

The duty of care owned by a landowner of occupant of real property to

---

① 困境,陷阱

persons injured on the premises is dependent, in whole or in part, upon the legal "status" of the entrant as either a trespasser, a licensee, or an invitee. Absent a statute or some other special circumstance to the contrary, the landowner ordinarily owes no duty with respect to a mere trespasser, and only a limited duty with respect to licensees. In fact, the only category of entrants to whom the landowner owes a traditional duty of reasonable care is the invitee. Of course, as will become evident, there are numerous exceptions to these general rules for determining the landowner's duty of care in common law negligence actions.

II. Special Categories of Entrants

1. Trespassing Children

Young children who are injured after trespassing onto the land of another have always created special problems under the traditional common law scheme for determining the landowner's duty of care. Because of their tender age and lack of experience in recognizing potential which might be encountered, young children, even though technically classified as trespassers, have generally been treated less harshly than other types of trespassers. Known variously as the "turntable doctrine," "the playground theory," the "dangerous instrumentality doctrine" or most commonly as the doctrine of "attractive nuisance," these rules represent an attempt to avoid the harsh effects of the traditional "no duty" rule applies to ordinary trespassers in whose special situations where the injured entrant is a young child.

Under the "attractive nuisance" doctrine, the child's legal status as a trespasser is not conclusive with respect to the landowner's duty of care. Instead, it represents merely one of many factors that must be considered by the trier of fact. Thus, a duty of reasonable care may still be imposed upon a landowner who has reason to anticipate the presence of trespassing young children on the premises and the danger created by some dangerous condition existing on the property is of such a nature that the injured child, because of his/her young age, inexperience, or other circumstances is not otherwise likely to have appreciated it. Historically, the name of this doctrine derives from the fact that the injury-causing condition or activity must have actually "lured" or "enticed①" the child to commit the trespass. However, this requirement is no longer necessary in the majority of jurisdictions which continue to apply the doctrine today.

2. Firefighters, Police Officers and Other Public Officials

Firefighters, police of entrants that deserves special attention is that of firefighter, police officers, and other public officials who enter onto the premises while performing their official duties. Under the traditional status classifications, these entrants would naturally fall into the "invitee" category, to which the landowner owes a duty of reasonable care under the circumstances since the presence of such entrants on the premises is due solely to their performance of some official duty or an employment-related function from which the landowner typically derives a distinct benefit. Thus, it is not surprising that various types of public officials and employees, including postal workers, trash collectors and numerous government inspectors, who enter on premises have been classified as "invitees" for purposes of defining the landowner's duty of care.

Despite the classification of various types of government and public officials as invitees, there is one particular subgroup within this general category of entrants (consisting solely of firefighters and police officers) that traditionally has been denied invitee status by many jurisdictions, and treated, instead, as mere "licensees." Typically referred to as the "firefighter's rule," this special treatment has been justified by the argument that it would be unfair to impose a duty of reasonable care upon landowners to protect such entrants from injuries due to the unusual circumstances which often necessitate their entry. Other courts continue to support the "firefighter's rule" on the basis that firefighters and police officers have been specially trained to confront dangerous situations as a necessary part of their occupations, and should be denied the favored "invitee" status by virtue of their assumption of the risk with respect to such dangers. Some courts have justified their continued adherence to this rule on the basis that firefighters and police officers are specially compensated for

---

① 诱惑，怂恿

Chapter 9
Premises Liability: Duties of Owners and Occupiers of Land

their high-risk occupations. Whatever the justification, the application of the "firefighter's rule" typically bars recovery by an injured firefighter or police for those injuries which have been caused by the same conduct or activity that is responsible for the entrant's original presence at the scene, just as any true "license" would be barred. It is only when the injury to a public safety officer results from some cause that is truly separate and distinct from those circumstances which necessitated the original entry that the landowner or occupant will normally be held liable. Of course, when a firefighter or police officer has been classified as a "license" under the "firefighter's rule," the landowner still remains subject to the same limitations which are applicable to any other "license." Thus, the landowner may still have a duty to warn firefighters and police officers who enter the premises as to the presence of certain hazards which are known to exist, as well as refrain from inflicting any willful or wanton injury.

While a few jurisdictions have abolished the "firefighter's rule" in favor of a standard based upon reasonable care under the circumstances, the majority of jurisdictions continue to recognize the landowner's limited liability relative to this special category of public safety officers.

3. Social Guests

Another category of entrants in premises cases which requires special consideration is that of social guests. A social guest is one who has been expressly invited onto the premises for some social, non-business purpose. Despite the fact that such persons have been invited to enter the premises, the majority of American jurisdictions treat them as mere licensees, to whom the landowner's only duty is to provide a warning of known, hidden dangers. This is true, where the social guest also provides some service or other incidental benefit to the landowner while on the premises.

The rationale most frequently offered in support of this reduced duty of care owned to invited social guests on the premises is that such persons should be entitled to no greater protection from hazards on the host's premises than would any other member of the host's own family. Since the host is not required to inspect the premises to discover and remove hazards which might injure members of his own family, such an inspection (ordinarily required to prepare the premises for an invitee) should also not be required for the visit of a mere social guest. Not surprisingly, however, this harsh treatment of social guests has been the subject of much criticism and debate among courts and legal commentators.

III. Recreational Premises

The application of the common law tri-parties scheme or classifying entrants to land has been particularly troublesome in situations involving persons who are injured after having been gratuitously permitted to enter land for recreational purposes. Under the traditional scheme such person could possibly be classified as "invitee," to whom a duty might be owned by the landowner either to warn or remove known dangers from the premises. However, such duties have been perceived as particularly burdensome on recreational landowners. As a result, the legislatures in almost every state have enacted statutes (referred to as "recreational use" statutes) that expressly articulate a lesser duty of care in certain recreational settings. Basically, these statutes treat recreational entrants as "licensees" rather than "invitees," and impose only a duty to refrain from intentionally inflicting an injury to the recreational entrant.

IV. Criminal Assailants

Traditionally, the common law declined to impose any liability for negligence against the owners or possessors of property for injuries inflicted upon entrants by the criminal actions of unknown third parties. The reason most often given by courts for such a no-duty rule relates to the absence of foreseeability by the landowner or occupant with respect to criminal attacks by third party assailants. For example, in *Doe v. Manheimer*, 563 A. 2d 699 (Conn, 1989), the plaintiff pedestrian was abducted from a public sidewalk and subsequently sexually assaulted by an unknown assailant as she walked adjacent to the defendant landowner's vacant lot that was overgrown with brush and tall grass. The court held that even if the defendant had been negligent in allowing the lot to become overgrown with weeds, such negligence was not the proximate cause of the plaintiff's assault injuries. Instead, applying the traditional rationale based upon the absence of foreseeability, the court concluded that the intentional misconduct of the assailant constituted an independent cause that superseded any such negligence by the defendant.

Despite the traditional rationale for this no-duty rule, certain specific types of criminal activity by third parties are not always unforeseeable.

V. Lessors of Real Property

Unlike the traditional rules regarding liability for ordinary landowners with respect to premises-related injuries, lessors of real property enjoyed much greater common law immunity. Even though the tenant/lessee might be classified as an "invitee" on the leased premises, most courts refused to impose any common law duty of care whatsoever upon the lessor with respect to injured tenants, or even their injured guests (licensees). By analogy to the common law sales doctrine of caveat emptor ("let the buyer beware"), this traditional rule of nonliability of lessors has sometimes been referred to as caveat lessee ("let the lessee beware"). Over the years, the harshness of this rule of nonliability has given rise to the creation of numerous "exceptions" whereby a duty of reasonable care has been imposed against lessors of real property in a wide variety of special situations.

Chapter 10

Defenses

Ⅰ. Defenses Based on the Plaintiff's Conduct

Courts have long recognized the importance of considering the plaintiff's own conduct in determining whether the plaintiff is entitled to recover compensation. At one time the basis for such decisions may have been the moral notion that the plaintiff's own misconduct somehow cancelled out the defendant's negligence or otherwise rendered the plaintiff undeserving. In some recent times law and economics scholars have justified such policies on the basis of efficiency and incentives. The plaintiff may be the party who can most easily and cheaply take precautions to avoid an accident, and denying or reducing recovery when the plaintiff fails to do so will provide an important incentive to take appropriate precautions.

1. Contributory Negligence

Contributory negligence is the plaintiff's failure to use due care for his or her own safety, which is an actual and proximate cause of the plaintiff's injuries. His defense originally was a complete bar to all recovery by the plaintiff.

2. Comparative Negligence

The "all or nothing" aspect of contributory negligence provoked increasing criticism through the first half of the twentieth century. Many argued that the defense produced unfair results since it often let a negligent defendant escape without liability. The justification for the doctrine—that the plaintiff's negligence disqualified him from recovery—could be used against the defendant. If the plaintiff's fault made it unjustified to throw the entire loss on the defendant, the defendant's fault made it unjustified to leave the entire loss with the plaintiff. Others were concerned that efforts to escape the doctrine, such as last clear chance, unnecessarily confused and complicated the law. There was also a concern that the doctrine encouraged unprincipled behavior by the jury, which might decide in the plaintiff's favor on contributory negligence, in spite of the evidence, but then surreptitiously reduce the damage. Better, it as felt, to handle this explicitly by adopting a rule that would mitigate the all or nothing aspect of contributory negligence, while retaining its effect of penalizing the plaintiff whose lack of care contributed to her own injury. This was the adoption of what's generally referred to as comparative negligence. As the materials below illustrate, comparative negligence (for some variation thereof) has been adopted by statute in many jurisdictions, and by judicial decision in a few others. However the doctrine is adopted, there are certain basic choices that must be made.

3. Assumption of the Risk

The common law took the position that there was no legal injury to one who consented to bear a risk. In tort law, this maxim became the doctrine of assumption of the risk. One aspect of this doctrine involves the explicit release of liability by contact. The more difficult problem is whether one can imply such an "agreement" to bear the risk from the plaintiff's conduct.

(1) Express Assumption of the Risk

A party may agree by contract to bear a risk. But courts are wary lest such agreement undermine the safety and compensation policies of tort law. When such a release is challenged, courts must decide whether or not to enforce the release of liability.

(2) Implied Assumption of the Risk

Implied assumption of the risk involves situations where the plaintiff has voluntarily encountered a known risk. Should this be construed as an implied agreement to release from liability the party that created the risk? The courts must decide what the consequences of such an implied agreement should be. One of the problems with this doctrine is deciding whether it is really something distinct from ordinary contributory negligence.

II. Other Defenses: Limitations and Immunities

This section deals with other types of defense that do not involve the issue of the plaintiff's conduct. Statutes of limitation and repose are designed to prevent the litigation of claims after the passage of a sufficient period of time. Immunities, on the other hand, are bars to litigation based on the status of the defendant.

1. Statutes of Limitation and Repose

Statutes of limitation and statutes of repose both operate to bar claims after a specified period of time has elapsed since the claims "accrued." These statutes express the decision of the legislature that after a certain period of time, such claims have become too old or, as they are often described, "state." The reasons for barring stale claims are many, but the most important usually put forward are, first, the loss of evidence over time and, second, the need eventually to put disputes to rest. The first reason recognizes that the passage of time creates unfairness as evidence disappears, memories fade, and witnesses die or disappear. The defendant who did not preserve, or cannot now find, exculpatory evidence may therefore be prejudiced if a claim can be pursued many years after the events that gave rise to it. It is worth nothing, however, that in theory a statute of limitations bars the claim simply by the passage of time. The defendant asserting the statute does not need to prove that prejudice would in fact occur in order to make use of the defense. The second reason is founded on the problems that can occur when settled expectations are overturned after many years. There is a value placed on prompt assertion of rights and in the security of knowing that a dispute cannot be pursued after the passage of a certain number of years. Here again, however, the defendant is not obligated to prove that any settled expectations will in fact be upset. The passage of the prescribed time period without filling suit is sufficient to allow the defense.

Statutes of limitation must begin to run at some identifiable point in time. Usually this is said to be at the moment the cause of action "accrues." Accrual occurs at the moment the cause of action is complete, in that all the events necessary to satisfy the elements of the cause of action have occurred so that the case is now ripe for the plaintiff to file suit. Because negligence cases, for example, require actual damages in order to be actionable, the statute of limitations in most personal injury cases begins to run at the moment the plaintiff is injured. While this moment is readily identifiable in accident cases, it may be much harder to pinpoint in toxic exposure cases, in which exposure may occur over a period of many years, and symptoms of illness only gradually manifested themselves. To start the statute running at the first exposure would likely mean that the cause of action was barred before the plaintiff ever knew that a problem can occur in medical malpractice cases in which the existence of a problem, such as a misdiagnosis, is not discovered until several years after the doctor's act.

Statutes of repose also imposes a time limit, but it is calculated in a wholly different fashion. Statutes of repose are designed to place an outer limit on the responsibility of a party for a particular act, without regard for the timing of the injury to the plaintiff. An example is the construction statute of repose, which bars suits against the architects and builders of an improvement to real property a specified number of years after the substantial completion of construction. For example, if the statute of repose barred suits after ten years, the plaintiff who injured because of a defect in design or construction of the building eleven years after substantial completion would be barred from suing, no matter how quickly the suit was filed after the injury occurred. In other words, the suit would be effectively barred even before the injury occurred. Similar statutes are on the books in some jurisdictions to protect manufacturers of durable products against product liability suits. Such product liability statutes of repose would typically begin to run on the date the defendant sold the defective product that caused the injury.

The operation of both types of limit can be harsh and arbitrary, and tend to cut against the preference of courts to decide cases on the merits. As might be predicted, some courts have developed doctrines to allow a certain amount of flexibility in the application of the statutes, although usually at some expense to clarity and ease of administration. Some of these doctrines are illustrated below.

As a final note of caution, it should be kept in mind that the failure to meet the statute of limitations is one of the most common complaints in legal malpractice suits. This may be in part because the determination of the proper statute of limitations can be difficult, as surprising as that may sound. The first step is to look the statutes up and determine which statute applies to a particular case. That is not quite the statement of the obvious that it may appear. First, it may not be clear from the text of the statute itself what categories of cases it applies to, and in some cases more than one statute can appear to govern. Research into the application of the statutes is often necessary to determine how the courts actually apply the statutes. Furthermore, different statutes may apply to the same claim depending on the legal theory used. For example, a personal injury caused by a defective product might be brought as a claim in tort for strict product liability or as claim for breach of implied warranty. Very different statutes of limitations are likely to apply depending upon the theory chosen, and it can happen that claim is time barred under one theory but not the other. Sometimes a plaintiff can obtain a longer statute by suiting the defendant in a different jurisdiction. Finally, many **ameliorating**[①] doctrines exist that may toll the running of the statute for a period of time. Because many legislatures in recent years have altered or reformed these statutes and how they operate, there is no substitute for thorough understanding of a particular jurisdiction's current statutes and their application.

2. Immunities

"Immunities" are generally protections against being sued based on the status of the defendant. For our purposes the most common immunities are the family immunities (based on the status of the defendant as a member of the plaintiff's family), charitable immunities (based on the defendant's statue as a charitable organization) and the governmental immunities. Recent court decisions and legislative changes have tended to narrow or even eliminate the protection of the family and charitable immunities. Governmental immunities are still very much alive but are frequently subject to limited waives by statute.

(1) Family Immunities

The origin of family immunities lies in the common law doctrine that husband and wife were a single legal person. For that reason one spouse could not sue the other for a tort, because it would be as if a person were suing herself

---

① 改良的,改善的

Chapter 10

Defenses

or himself. This was thought to be a logical impossibility. Logical or not, the strictness of this rule began to erode in the nineteenth century as legislatures began to pass legislation, called Married Woman's Property Acts, that granted women the right to own property separately from their husbands and to sue to protect it if need be. Courts joined in this trend by allowing spouses to sue each other to recover for intentional torts. From that point on the spousal immunity continued to weaken to the point that, today, it is generally abrogated. The Restatement of Torts Second §895F, for example, now takes the position that no immunity exists between spouses solely because of the marriage relationship.

A separate doctrine, traceable to the Mississippi case of *Hewlett v. George*, 9 So. 895 (Miss. 189), recognized parental immunity from tort actions filed by their children. No legal fiction about oneness of parent and child supported this immunity, which came to be justified by a variety of somewhat inconsistent argument. One concern was that allowing such actions would potentially disrupt family harmony and interfere with the right of the parents to discipline their children. A separate concern, which likely became more acute as automobiles and automobile insurance became more common, was that such actions would encourage collusive lawsuits. For example, if Parent got into an accident while driving the family car with Child as a passenger. Child could sue Parent alleging negligent driving. If Parent had automobile insurance, there would be every incentive on Parent's part to tearfully confess to negligence and thereby collect on the automobile liability policy in Child's behalf. (You will note that family harmony seems to survive in this example). If Parent were immune from suit, however, the insurer would be safe from such suits.

As with spousal immunity, parental immunity has gradually eroded. Courts began to allow suits when the child was injured while working in the parents' commercial endeavors. Some courts then began to allow suits for intentional torts. Others allowed suits in exactly the situations that most worried the insurers: for automobile accidents or, more generally, whenever insurance was available to pay the claim. The concern with collusion tended to get brushed aside as insufficient to justify the total ban on liability. Today, many jurisdictions have totally abolished the immunity. With abolition (or steps toward abolition) new problems began to arise under the general heading of "negligent supervision." As example of this type of issue, consider the parent who allows a five-year-old child to play in the front yard without supervision. If the child wanders into the street and it struck by an automobile, should the child have an action against the parent for negligent supervision? Is this careless parenting, or proper encouragement of the child's independence? The implications of this sort of liability on proper parental discretion are troubling to some courts that have otherwise abolished the immunity. In New York, for example, the Court of Appeals refused to allow an action for negligent supervision. *Holodook v. Spencer*, 324 N. E. 2d 338 (N. Y. 1974). California and some other jurisdictions, by contrast, have abolished the immunity and replaced it with a "reasonable parent" standard of care that is supposed to allow sufficient leeway for the proper exercise of parental discretion and discipline. *Gibson v. Gibson*, 479 P. 2d 648 (Cal. 1971). In the view of these courts, the proper limitation is not absolute or even limited immunity but a sensibly drawn substantive rule of liability.

Even if the "correct" standard of liability is adopted, once the parental immunity is abolished, some interesting new possibilities are opened up.

(2) Charitable Immunity

The immunity of charitable organizations from suit by those injured by their beneficent activities is also something of an historical curiosity whose time has largely passed. Courts put forward various explanations and justifications for the immunity, none of which were totally satisfactory and all of which the critics of the rule have attacked and debunked. In recent times courts and legislatures have tended to abrogate the immunity more or less completely, although it survives in some jurisdictions in limited forms thanks to legislative action. The rule applied in one's own jurisdiction must therefore be researched before any counsel is provided on this topic.

Courts seem to have originally embraced the immunity out of a sense that it would product and encourage those who tried to provide charitable benefits to others. Perhaps there was a time when most charities were small, underfunded affairs in need of such protection, and perhaps courts were right to be concerned that the threat or liability would mean that, for example, there would be no health care at all for the poor. Today the charitable or non-profit hospital is apt to be multi-million dollar concern that, at the very least, is able to purchase adequate liability insurance. As the perception of the nature of the charitable enterprise changed, the attitude of the courts towards the charitable immunity changed as well. As a result, the Restatement of Torts Second §895E today takes the position that "one engaged in a charitable, educational, religious or benevolent enterprises or activity is not for that reason immune from tort liability." Most jurisdictions today agree.

(3) Governmental Immunity

The liability of governmental entities for torts committed by their agents and employees is a huge topic. Whole treatises have addressed the problems involved in suing governing entities. Because governmental liability is subject to many specific local variations, no detailed examination of the topic is possible here. This section will attempt only to provide an overview of a few of the issues raised by this type of tort liability.

At the outset, it should be understood that governmental tort liability can potentially create separation of powers problems, as the courts attempt to assess liability for the actions of the executive and legislative branches. For example, a litigant **disgruntled**① by the way that police protection is distributed in a municipally might sue, claiming that the decision creates unreasonable risks of harm to persons living in a particular neighborhood that receives less coverage than others. But these decisions are the executive's to make, not the court's. Allowing second guessing of such decision via the courts would be a judicial usurpation of the executive function. On the other hand, many injuries inflicted by governmental agents raise no issue of governmental authority. If a city employee negligently drives a city vehicle on city business and injuries a pedestrian, it is hard to see how imposing liability on the municipality is any different from imposing **vicarious liability**② on a delivery company for the negligent driving of an employee. A third type of litigation involves government action that violates fundamental constitutional rights. The difficulty in defining governmental tort liability is constructing a system that allows recovery to

---

① 不满的,不高兴的
② 替代责任

injured victims in appropriate situations, without allowing improper interference with the lawful authority of the legislature and executive.

It is also important to understand that not all governmental entities are treated the same way. The federal government and the states are considered "sovereign" and therefore enjoy sovereign immunity. The doctrine of sovereign immunity began with the rule that the king, as the "sovereign," could not be sued. The immunity was then transferred from the person of the king to the abstract entity of the government itself. In the process, the rule was justified on the theory that the sovereign authority, which is the source of laws and rights and creates the courts and gives them their powers, cannot be made to answer in those same courts. The effect of this doctrine in its pure form was to bar totally all suits against the sovereign. This result solves the problem of improper interference by the courts in government affairs, but at the cost of leaving victims of injuries inflicted by government agents without a remedy against the government. One possibility for relief would be suit against the government agent personally, since the doctrine of sovereign immunity did not protect the individual government official from suit. As a practical matter, however, this remedy was often unsatisfactory, since the individual official might not have sufficient assets to pay a judgment, or in some cases was protected by some form of official immunity. In the federal system, the doctrine of immunity meant that the only way to get redress from the federal government was to persuade Congress to pass a private bill authorizing compensation. The pressure of dealing with vast numbers of these private bills finally persuaded Congress in 1946 to pass the Federal Tort Claims Act (FTCA). The FTCA waived federal sovereign immunity in certain specified types of claims. It is considered below.

The sovereign immunity of the states underwent a similar development. In some states the legislature passed a limited waiver of immunity, allowing suit on certain types of claims such as automobile accident. In some states the courts took the lead in abolishing sovereign immunity, *Cf. Muskopf v. Corning Hospital Dist.*, 359 P. 2d 457 (Cal. 1961). When this occurred, the legislature was usually spurred to action to pass a statute defining the scope of governmental liability. These statutes vary greatly, but all are designed to try to answer, to some degree, the question of the proper scope of government liability. Both state and federal tort claims statutes require careful reading and research by the attorney in order to determine not only the scope of the waiver and what suits are permitted, but also to learn the required procedure for making a claim against the government.

(4) Municipal Immunity

In contrast, municipal government was not considered to be sovereign, and therefore could not take advantage of sovereign immunity. Municipalities were creatures of state law, similar to corporations, and as such were **amenable**① to suit. Municipalities, however, were authorized to discharge government functions, and to that extent the problem of the proper scope of municipal liability presented many of the same issues as did sovereign immunity. For that reason, courts developed the rule that municipalities were immune from suit for injuries caused by "governmental" activities, but could be sued if the activities were "**proprietary**②," which meant the sort of activities that a private corporation might engage in. Unfortunately, the distinction between the two types of activities was uncertain, and as a result the decisions about when to allow or deny the right to sue were often arbitrary.

In many jurisdictions today the immunity for governmental decisions has either been abolished or more clearly defined by statute.

---

① 有义务的,经得起检验的
② 专有的,专利的,所有的

Chapter 11

Vicarious Liability

The concept of vicarious liability refers to the legal principle whereby tort liability is imposed against one party for a tort actually committed upon the victim by another. In the eyes of the law, the liability of the party committing the **tortuous**① act is "**imputed**②" to a different party who, although innocent of any actual wrongdoing, is nevertheless held responsible for the harm to the plaintiff. The most commonly asserted legal justification for imputing tort liability is the existence of some type of "special relationship" between the tortfeasor and the party held legally responsible. Usually, this special relationship arises out of an employer-employee relation, but as we will see, there are many other bases for imputing vicarious liability.

Unlike the bases of liability that we have studied thus far, the imposition of liability vicariously is not dependant upon any notion of fault or wrongdoing by that party. Instead, liability is imputed for reasons of policy or practicality. In this sense, vicarious liability is often said to relate more loosely to strict liability than either negligence or intentional tort liability. In this Chapter we will also examine the specific policy argument typically offered in support of vicarious liability.

Ⅰ. Respondeat Superior

Traditionally, courts imposed vicarious liability when some type of employer-employee relationship existed between the party held legally

---

① 扭曲的,不正当的
② 把(错误等)归咎于

responsible and the party (also legally responsible) who actually inflicted the injury. Vicarious liability derives from the doctrine of *respondeat superior*, which, in Latin meant literally to "let the superior respond" (by paying for the damages), and was originally applied by English common law courts against "masters" for various injuries tortiously inflicted by their "servants" in pursuit of their masters' business purposes. Today, the term is still used to refer to the vicarious liability of employers for torts committed by their employees in the scope of their employment. However, the scope of the traditional "employer-employee" relationship is applied much more broadly to include situations where no formal employer-employee relationship exists at all.

II. Employer-Employee Relationship

1. Who Is an "Employee?"

In the majority of situations involving the doctrine of *respondeat superior* in work-related environments, the success or failure of plaintiff's claim depends upon the resolution of two basic questions. First, was the person who caused the plaintiff's injury properly classified as an "employee"? Only if an employer-employee relationship exists between the defendant and the tortfeasor does the analysis proceed to the second question: whether the employee was acting within the "scope of employment" at the time of the injury-causing event? If the tortfeasor is not found to be an "employee," he or she will likely be classified as an "independent contractor" and held accountable in a purely individual capacity, subject to the various limitations discussed in Section C, infra. Although many *respondeat superior* cases seem to focus almost entirely on the second of these questions (i. e., whether the tortfeasor was acting within the "scope of employment" at the time of the injury-causing accident), if the requisite employer-employee relationship is not first established there can be no vicarious liability against the employer.

2. Employer's Vicarious Liability for Intentional Torts

A surprising number of claims arising from employment situations involve willfully or intentionally inflicted injuries. However, unlike "negligence" analysis which treats most intentionally inflicted injuries as unforeseeable and, thus, not proximately caused by the tortfeasor's alleged negligent act(s), in many types of employment-related situations certain intentional torts may be entirely foreseeable as apart of the employment. For example, when a tavern owner hires a "bouncer" to remove drunken or disorderly patrons from the premises, it is certainly foreseeable; indeed even likely, that a patron will sustain injury from the intentional acts of an over-exuberant bouncer, ever though the bouncer is acting entirely within the scope of employment. Other employment relationships present similar opportunities for the commission of intentional torts that are within the scope of employment and very foreseeable.

3. Joint Enterprises, Joint Ventures, and Partnerships

Apart from employer-employee relationships, the law also recognizes a variety of other situations in which vicarious liability maybe imputed. As with most other situations in which the doctrine of respondeat superior is asserted, some type of "special relationship" is still required before such liability may be imputed from one person to another person or legal entity. One particular setting in which vicarious liability is frequently asserted involves situations when the defendant has agreed, either expressly or by implication, in advance of the activity, to participate with other persons in some type of common enterprise or activity. The materials which follow discuss various legal distinctions that exist among the most common types of such agreements.

FARMERS INSURANCE EXCHANGE v. PARKER
936 P. 2D 1088 (Utah Ct. App. 1997)

Billings, Judge:

On June 19, 1994, appellant and three friends were climbing near the Storm Mountain Slide Area in Big Cottonwood Canyon. Appellant was an experienced climber and chose the particular climb. During the climb, the group was forced to cross a rock slide area without knocking any rocks onto the road. Another climber, who followed appellant across the rocks, accidentally dislodged some rocks which rolled down to the road below.

At approximately the same time, Farmers' insurance was driving up the canyon. Despite his best efforts, the insured was unable to avoid all of the rocks on the road and was forced to drive over one of them, causing $2746.47 of

Chapter 11
Vicarious Liability

damage to his van.

After the accident an officer arrived on the scene and saw the rocks on the road as well as several individuals up the mountain, including one in the middle of the slide area. He immediately ordered the individuals to come down. Eventually, appellant made his way down the mountain to offer assistance and speak with the officer. Once down, he informed the officer that he was the leader of the climb.

Farmers brought suit against appellant for the damage to the car of its insured. The trial court found appellant one-hundred percent liable for the damage because (i) appellant was the leader of the expedition and had "assumed the duties and risks associated with the expedition," and (ii) appellant was liable for the negligence of the others in the expedition because he failed to join any of the other parties in the litigation so as to have their fault apportioned.

Appellant first claims the trial court erred in holding him liable because he was the leader of the non-commercial hiking party. While the trial court expressly found there was no pecuniary interest between appellant and the other climbs, the court still found appellant vicariously liable for the negligence of the other climbers because he had assumed the risks involved by "leading" the climbing party. Appellant argues that he could not be vicariously liable for the negligence of others in the hiking party because there was no pecuniary interest between himself and the other climbers, and thus, there was no joint enterprise that would create vicarious liability. We agree.

The elements of joint enterprise are: "(i) An agreement, express or implied, among the members of the group; (ii) a common purpose to be carried out by the group; (iii) a community of pecuniary interest in that purpose, among the members; and (iv) an equal right to a voice in the direction of the enterprise, which gives an equal right of control."

Utah Farm Bureau Mut. Ins. Co. v. Johnson
738 P.2d 652,655 (Utah Ct. App. 1987)

The Utah Supreme Court considered an analogous claim in *Hall v. Blackham*, 18 Utah 2d 164, 417 P.2d 664 (1966). In hall, four friends were returning home from a duck hunting trip when they were involved in an accident, causing the death of one individual. The plaintiffs sued, claiming, among other things, that the passengers were liable because they were involved in a joint venture. In affirming the trial court's refusal to submit an instruction to the jury based on joint enterprise liability, the supreme court stated: "The mere association of persons riding together in an automobile belonging to one of them for a common purpose of pleasure such as was done here not provide sufficient basis for finding a joint venture." Thus, the Supreme Court refused to find vicarious liability in a situation where four friends were engaged in a mutual, pleasurable, non-commercial activity.

Our sister jurisdictions have also been faced with similar claims. In *Masell v. Ginner*, 119 Idaho 702, 809 P. 2d 1181 (Idaho Ct. App. 1991), two friends received permission from a landowner to cut timber on his land. When the two arrived at the property they found that a gate was locked, so one friend went to get a key from the owner while the other friend began cutting trees. The woodcutter felled a tree that struck an electrical wire and began a fire causing damage to the landowner's property. The landowner sued the woodcutter's friend under a theory of joint enterprise liability. Id. The Idaho court refused to hold the friend liable under such a theory because the woodcutter and the friend "did not intend to harvest the timber for sale, nor was their purpose to provide a compensable service to the landowner." The court concluded "that where the community of interest in the common purpose is personal as to an individual, a family, or a household rather than business-related, joint enterprise liability will not be imposed."

These cases make clear that an individual is not vicariously liable for the negligence of others when all individuals involved are simply engaging in non-commercial, pleasurable adventures. In this case, four friends went on a climbing **excursion**① for pleasure. No money was exchanged, nor was any expected. Although appellant may have been the most experienced of the climbers, and hence the "leader," there is nothing in the record indicating appellant had the right to control any of the actions of the other climbers. Thus,

---

① 远足,游览,短途旅行

Chapter 11
Vicarious Liability

the trial court erred in concluding appellant was vicariously liable for the negligence of the other climbers in the group. As there was nothing in the record to indicate appellant was individually negligent, we reverse and vacate the judgment against appellant.

We conclude the trial court erred in determining appellant was vicariously liable for the negligence of the other climbers in his group. As there is no evidence of any individual negligence on the part of appellant, we reverse the judgment of the trial court.

Chapter 12

Products Liability

Products liability deals with the problem of injuries accidentally inflicted on people by "defective" products. As will be seen in the following materials, injured parties have employed a number of legal theories in seeking a remedy for product harms. The most important of these are negligence, warranty, and strict liability.

The development of products liability law was long hampered by the doctrine of privity of contract. The privity doctrine provided that a party who manufactured or sold a defective product owed a duty with respect to that product only to the immediate purchaser, the party with whom the seller was in privity of contract. If a third party were injured because of a defect in the product, the courts would hold that there could be no liability because no duty ran to the injured third party. We therefore begin our examination of products liability with the negligence cause of action, because here the law first began its assault on the "**citadel**①" of privity.

Ⅰ. Strict Liability in Tort

The plaintiff in *Greenman v. Yuba Power Products*, 377 P. 2d 897 (Cal. 1963), was severely injured while working with a Shopsmith lathe manufactured by the defendant. The injury occurred when the piece of wood on which the plaintiff was working came loose and flew out of the machine, striking him in the forehead. The plaintiff demonstrated at trial that the piece of

---

① 要塞,大本营,根据地

Chapter 12
Products Liability

wood came loose because "inadequate set screws were used to hold parts of the machine together so that normal vibration caused the tailstock of the lathe to move away from the piece of wood being turned permitting it to fly out of the lathe." The plaintiff's experts also testified "that were other more positive ways of fastening the parts of the machine together, the use of which would have prevented the accident." The court noted that this evidence could establish both negligence on the part of the manufacturer or breach of warranty. However, the defendant claimed that the warranty claim must fail because the plaintiff had not provided the notice called for by the sales act. Rather than placing the basis of liability in the breach of warranty, however, the court explicitly adopted strict liability in tort as the appropriate basis for liability of a manufacturer to a consumer injured by a defective product: "A manufacturer is strictly liable in tort when an article he places on the market, knowing that it is to be used without inspection for defects, proves to have a defect that causes injury to human being. Recognized first in the case of unwholesome food products, such liability has now been extended to a variety of other products that create as great or greater hazards if defective."

Although in these cases strict liability has usually been based on the theory of an express or implied warranty running from the manufacturer to the plaintiff, the abandonment of the requirement of a contract between them, the recognition that the liability is not assumed by agreement but imposed by law and the refusal to permit the manufacturer to define the scope of its own responsibility for defective products make clear that the liability is not one governed by the law of conduct warranties but by the law of strict liability in tort. Accordingly, rules defining and governing warranties that were developed to meet the needs of commercial transactions cannot properly be invoked to govern the manufacturer's liability to those injured by their defective products unless those rules also serve the purposes for which such liability is imposed."

The adoption of section 402A as part of the Second Restatement of Torts sealed this development, as strict products liability quickly swept the nation, with many courts explicitly adopting the standards set forth by 402A. It is therefore important to become familiar with section 402A's formulation of strict products liability, both in the text of the section itself and in the accompanying "comments." It is equally important to recognize 402A's limitation, and to understand the ways in which the courts have to expend on the outline of liability found there. The development in the courts has recently led to a new attempt to restate the law of products liability, the Third Restatement of Torts. The relevant sections of the Third Restatement will be used to introduce the relevant topics as we address them.

402A. SPECIAL LIABILITY OF SELLER OF PRODUCT FOR PHYSICAL HARM TO USER OR CONSUMER

(1) One who sells any product in a defective condition unreasonably dangerous to the user or consumer or to his property is subject to liability for physical harm thereby caused to the ultimate user or consumer, or to his property, if

(a) The seller is engaged in the business of selling such a product, and

(b) It is expected to and does reach the user or consumer without substantial change in the condition in which it is sold.

(2) The rule stated in Subsection (1) applies although

(a) The seller has exercised all possible care in the preparation and sale of his product, and

(b) The user or consumer has not bought the product from or entered into any contractual relation with the seller.

Caveat:

The Institute expresses no opinion as to whether the rules stated in this section may not apply

(1) To harm to person other than users or consumers;

(2) To the seller of a product expected to be processed or otherwise substantially changed before it reaches the user or consumer; or

(3) To the seller of a component part of a product to be assembled.

II. The Definition of "Defective"

The definition of "defective condition" found in Comment g to section 402A was written with manufacturing defects in mind. These are defects in which the products leave the control of the manufacturer in a condition that is different from what the manufacturer intended. In other words, the product was not made correctly and the mistake escaped the manufacturer's quality control. When the mistake makes the product unreasonably dangerous, it is considered "defective" under section 402A. Comment j also recognized that a product could be defective if the manufacturer failed to provide the consumer with necessary warnings or instructions for use. The *Greenman* case itself imposed liability for a defect in the design of the product. Courts soon recognized that all types of defect could result in strict liability under section 402A. Courts also recognized, however, that each different type of defect called for different standards for the imposition of liability. In dealing with manufacturing defects, for example, it was always possible to compare the product to the standard manufacturer itself had established. With both design and warning defects, however, the product had to be compared to an external standard of "proper" design or warning. The establishment of different standards for each type of defect will be examined in the sections that follow. The new Third Restatement has recognized the development of these three types of defect, defining them as follow:

RESTATEMENT OF THE LAW (THIRD) TORTS: PRODUCTS LIABILITY

§2. CATEGORIES OF PRODUCT DEFECT

A product is defective when, at the time of sale or distribution, it contains a manufacturing defect, is defective in design, or is defective because of inadequate instructions or warnings. A product:

(1) contains a manufacturing defect when the product departs from its intended design even though all possible care was exercised in the preparation and marketing of the product;

(2) is defective in design when the foreseeable risks of harm posed by the product could have been reduced or avoided by the adoption of a reasonable alternative design by the seller or other distributor or a predecessor in the commercial chain of distribution, and the omission of the alternative design renders the product not reasonably safe;

(3) is defective because of inadequate instructions or warnings when the foreseeable risks of harm posed by the product could have been reduced or avoided by the provision of reasonable instructions or warnings by the seller or

other distributor, or a predecessor in the commercial chain of distribution, and the omission of the instructions or warnings renders the product not reasonably safe.

III. The Definition of "One Who Sells"

§8. LIABILITY OF COMMERCIAL SELLER OR DISTRIBUTOR OF DEFECTIVE USED PRODUCTS

One engaged in the business of selling or otherwise distributing used products who sells or distributes a defective used product is subject to liability for harm to persons or property caused by the defect if the defect:

(1) arises from the seller's failure to exercise reasonable care, or

(2) is a manufacturing defect under §2(a) or a defect that may be inferred under §3 and the seller's marketing of the product would cause a reasonable person in the position of the buyer to expect the used product to present no greater risk of defect than if the product were new; or

(3) is a defect under §2 or §3 in a used product remanufactured by the seller or a predecessor in the commercial chain of distribution of the used product; or

(4) arises from a used product's noncompliance under §4 with a product safety statute or regulation applicable to the used product.

A used product is a product that, prior to the time of sale or other distribution referred to in this Section, is commercially sold or otherwise distributed to a buyer not in the commercial chain of distribution and used for some period of time.

Chapter 13
Defamation

Defamation protects an individual's interest in reputation. At common law, defamation was both a crime and a tort. In a number of early cases, individuals were punished for "sedition libel." The most famous criminal libel case occurred in 1735 when John Peter Zenger was prosecuted in New York for criticizing the government. The case was aggravated by the fact that the Chief Justice of the Province of New York disbarred two lawyers who tried to represent Zenger. Andrew Hamilton ultimately represented Zenger and gained acquittal for him.

On the civil side, defamation was divided into "slander" and "libel." Slander included defamatory statements made orally while libel included written statements. As a general rule, libel was actionable without proof of damage. Slander required damage except when the communication constituted "slander per se": it carried the imputation that plaintiff had committed a criminal offense, suffered from a loathsome or venereal disease, engaged in conduct incompatible with one's profession, or—in the case of woman—had engaged in acts of unchastity.

Ⅰ. Defamation Defined

1. A dead person cannot be defamed.

No right of action existed at common law for damages for the defamation of the dead, in favor of the surviving relative who themselves are not defamed.

One reason for the rule is that the action is personal. The injury must be the reputation of the plaintiff. No action lies by a third person for a libel directed at another. "A party cannot support a charge of libel by showing that the same publication libeled another. To make a case, the publication must be libelous as to the plaintiff, not another. The malice supporting the charge must flow from defendant to plaintiff and be personal to him alone and not another.

The intent of the General Assembly was not to modify the common law by creating an entirely new cause of action for the recovery by surviving relatives and friends of damages for the defamation of a dead person.

2. Corporations cannot sue for defamation. However, they can sue for commercial disparagement.

Ⅱ. The Constitutionalization of Defamation

From the founding of the United States until the early 1960s, the Court treated libel as speech that raised no First Amendment issues. As the Court stated in *Beauharnals v. Illinois*, 343 U.S. 250(1952), "libellous utterances are not within the area of constitutionally protected speech" because they have "such slight social value as a step to truth that any benefit that may be derived from them is clearly outweighed by the tort of defamation and to determine the scope of recovery. Some states readily imposed liability inaccurate statements.

Ⅲ. "Public Figures" and "Private Plaintiffs"

In *Curtis Publishing Co. v. Butts*, 388 U. S. 130 (1967), the Court extended *New York Times* protections to defamatory statement made regarding public figures. *The Saturday Evening Post* alleged that Butts, the Athletic Directors at the University of Georgia, had conspired to fix a football game. Butts had previously served as the University's head football coach and was a well-known and respected figure in coaching ranks. The jury returned a verdict of $60,000 in general damage and $3,000,000 in punitive damages. The companion case of *Associated Press v. Walker*, 388 U. S. 130(1967), involved an eyewitness account of a riot on the University of Mississippi campus. *The Associated Press* article claimed that Walker, a private citizen who had been in the United States Army, had taken command of a violent crowd and had personally led a charge against federal marshals sent to enforce a court degree and to assist in preserving order. The article described Walker as encouraging rioters to use violence and giving them technical advice on combating the effects of tear gas. A verdict of $500,000 compensatory damages and $300,000 punitive damages was returned. In a plurality opinion written by Mr. Justice Harlan, the Court treated both Butts and Walker as public figures:

The public interest in the circulation of the materials here involved, and the publisher's interest in circulating them, is not less than that involved in *New York Times*. Both Butts and Walker commanded a substantial amount of independent public interest at the time of the publications; both, in our opinion, would have been labeled "public figures" under ordinary tort rules. Butts may have attained that status by position alone and Walker by his purposeful activity amounting to a thrusting of his personality into the "vortex" of an important public controversy, but both commanded sufficient continuing public interest and had sufficient access to the means of counterargument to be able "to expose through discussion the falsehood and fallacies" of the defamatory statements. Libel actions of the present kind cannot be left entirely to state libel laws, unlimited by any overriding constitutional safeguard.

Mr. Chief Justice Warren concurred:

Although they are not subject to the restrains of the political process, "public figures," like "public officials," often play an influential role in ordering society. And surely as class these "public figures" have as ready access as "public officials" to mass media communication, both to influence policy and to counter criticism of their views and activities. Our citizenry has a legitimate and substantial interest in the conduct of such persons, and freedom of the press to engage in uninhibited debates about their involvement in public issues and events is as crucial as it is in the case of "pubic officials." The fact that they are not amenable to the restrains of the political process only underscores the legitimate and substantial nature of the interest, since it means that public opinion may be the only instrument by which society can attempt to influence their conduct.

Chapter 14

Competitive Torts

To this point, you have been focusing almost exclusively on tort claims brought by individuals. Although corporations have been involved in many of these cases, they have been the defendants, not the plaintiffs. But tort law does not exist only to protect individuals. Instead, in certain types of situations, it will also afford protection to corporations and other sorts of business concerns.

Of course, a business cannot suffer a personal injury like a broken arm. The injuries that a business suffers are instead purely financial in nature.

Do not assume that area of the law is completely divorced from the other torts. The field of competitive torts does share certain core principles with the torts you have studied so far. On the other hand, the field also has its own **idiosyncratic**① policy concerns and practical features, both of which affect how the rules in this area have evolved.

Ⅰ. Competition as a Tort

The Competition "Exception." Putting to one side for moment the particulars of Katz, (*Katz v. Kapper*, 44P. 2d 1060 (Cal. Ct. App. 1935)) consider the basic premise of the court's opinion competition is ordinarily not a tort. The proposition may seem unremarkable at first glance. But consider how it relates to other areas of tort law. Competition, after all, involves a party who knowingly and intentionally causes economic harm to another.

---

① 怪异的

Chapter 14
Competitive Torts

II. Unlawful Means: Lying, Cheating the Process of Competition

1. Lying: The Law of False Advertising

From almost the very beginning, courts have recognized that lying to customers constitutes a form of "unfair" competition. As the case law developed, courts began to distinguish between several categories of cases. The first, commonly called "passing off" or "palming off," involved a defendant who had represented to consumers that its product had actually been produced or approved by the plaintiff. In order to prevent a competitor from preying on the goodwill of a more established seller, courts routinely allowed plaintiff to recover in these cases.

The "passing off" branch of unfair competition law has evolved into the modern cases of trademarks, service marks, and trade names. Most nations encourage the use of these commercial symbols by providing a registry. A party who registers its mark with the government typically receives a number of added benefits, such as a presumption that the registrant "owns" the symbol. Nevertheless, the basic principles of trademark law still reflect the common-law origins. A study of the fascinating but complex law of trademarks is deferred to specialized course.

The "lying" branch of unfair competition was not limited to cases where a defendant misrepresented the source of its product. Courts also routinely declared that it was unfair to allow a defendant to lie about the quality of good being sold in the marketplace. However, the common-law tort of unfair competition proved much less effective in dealing with these types of misrepresentations.

2. Cheating: The Limits of Competitive Behavior

Economic theory can prove quite useful in analyzing the law of unfair competition. In conditions of perfect competition, sales below cost would not be a problem, as no competitor could afford to take losses for any appreciable period. Moreover, even if a seller could absorb short-term losses, it would need some time after competition is destroyed to recoup those losses. During that recoupment period, the seller would need to sell at well above its cost. However, other companies could theoretically enter the market at that point and undercut the seller. That sales below cost (often called "dumping") do occur, then, is a sign that a "market imperfection" exists, i. e., that there is not perfect competition.

In the "real world," large companies may have the wherewithal to operation at a loss for a significant period of time. The defendant in Barco, for example, could offset its losses in one market by its sales in other markets. In other cases, the start-up costs involved in marketing a particular goods or service make it difficult for others to jump into the market once the seller raises its prices after the competition is destroyed. Although some commentators question whether these conditions will actually exist very often, there is no doubt that sales below cost occur often enough to present a real-world problem.

In recognition of this threat, both the federal government and some states have enacted statutes prohibiting, or at least limiting, sales below cost. At the national level, section 3 of the Robinson-Patman Act (part of the antitrust laws) makes it a crime to sell goods at "unreasonably low prices for the purpose of destroying competition or eliminating a competitor."

Exercises

Ⅰ. **Choose the best answer to the following questions:**

1. Intentional Infliction of Emotional Distress (IIED)
    A. A cause of action that allows for recovery after a person is insulted.
    B. A cause of action for the intentional breach of a contract obligation.
    C. A cause of action arising when a defendant's behavior toward a plaintiff is so outrageous and extreme that it proximately causes serious emotional distress.
    D. A cause of action for putting another person in fear of being hit.
2. A man purchased a new bike. One day, he rode the new bike to a local movie theater for the eight o'clock show and parked his bike out front. As it was a small town, he felt comfortable leaving his bike on the rack without locking it. While the man was in the movie theater, the ticket agent decided to take the bike out for a spin. The ticket agent rode the bike once around the block before placing it back in the rack just as the man had left it. As the ticket

Chapter 14
Competitive Torts

agent was placing the bike back in the rack, the handlebars gently rubbed against the rail. After the movie, the man retrieved the bike, and had no idea that it had been moved until he noticed a small scratch on the handlebars.

If the man files suit against the ticket agent, will he prevail?

A. No, because the man was unaware of the ticket agent's use.

B. No, because there was insufficient damage to the man's bike.

C. Yes, for trespass to a chattel.

D. Yes, for conversion.

3. An artist and a firefighter were neighbors who had been feuding for some time. One afternoon, the artist found some trash in her yard next to the fence that separated her and the firefighter's properties. Convinced that the firefighter had deposited the trash on her property, the artist picked it up and threw it onto the firefighter's property. The firefighter saw the artist throw the trash onto his property and immediately ran up to the artist with a sledgehammer in his hand, got to within inches of the artist's face, and shouted, "If you ever do something like that again, I'll break your leg!" The firefighter then stormed off, leaving the artist shaken by the encounter. The artist subsequently brought an action against the firefighter for intentional infliction of emotional distress.

What is the likely outcome of the case?

A. Judgment for the firefighter, because he did not threaten any immediate physical harm.

B. Judgment for the firefighter, as long as the artist experienced no physical harm as a result of the firefighter's actions.

C. Judgment for the artist, if the firefighter intended that the artist experience an apprehension of a harmful physical contact.

D. Judgment for the artist, if she suffered severe emotional distress as a result of the firefighter's actions.

4. A man owned an independent grocery store in an upscale urban area. The grocer prided himself on his high-end deli meats and cheeses and his large selection of expensive wines. The grocer had recently noticed, however, that one of the freezers in the store leaked from time to time, causing the

tiles underneath the freezer to become wet. The grocer had called the freezer company to repair the freezer, but the freezer company had not yet sent a technician to repair it.

While the grocer was preparing for the lunchtime rush, a man came into the store and slipped on a portion of the floor that was wet due to the freezer leakage. The man landed awkwardly on his knee, shattering his kneecap.

If the man brings suit against the grocer, how should the court rule?

A. Judgment for the grocer, because by calling the freezer company to fix the freezer, the grocer took reasonable care to prevent the injury.

B. Judgment for the man, but only if the grocer knew that the leakage had expanded to the area around the freezer.

C. Judgment for the man, if the grocer could have discovered the risk posed by the freezer leakage by a reasonable inspection of his property.

D. Judgment for the man, because the grocer is liable for any condition on his premises that injures a customer.

5. Sunday was generally family day at the shopping mall. One Sunday, like many others, two parents took their two children, a six-month-old daughter and a seven-year-old son, to the mall. At their son's insistence, the parents decided to let him push the courtesy stroller provided by the mall that was carrying the daughter, while the father held the handle. The son proudly pushed the stroller, grinning from ear to ear as he walked along the main promenade.

The father's former high school basketball coach smiled as he passed the family. Ten minutes later, the coach passed the family again. At that moment, the father let go of the handle of the stroller in order to bend down and pick up the daughter's pacifier, and the son became temporarily distracted. In his moment of distraction, the son ran the stroller into the coach. The collision caused the coach to fall to the ground, and he sustained a broken elbow.

If the coach sues the son, what is the son's best defense?

A. The coach assumed the risk when he saw the son pushing the stroller.

B. The son was exercising the care appropriate for a reasonable child of like age, knowledge, and experience.

Chapter 14
Competitive Torts

C. A seven-year-old is presumed incapable of negligence.

D. The son did not intend to strike the coach.

6. A ski instructor purchased a new brand of sunscreen made especially for the sensitive skin on a person's face and neck. He took the unopened product to his first ski class of the day and offered it to one of his students, who had forgotten her own sunscreen. When the student opened the sunscreen, all of the skiers in her vicinity noticed a very strong chemical odor. The student didn't believe that the unpleasant smell came from the product, though, and applied the sunscreen to her face and neck. With minutes, a painful rash had broken out on the student's face. It was later determined that the manufacturer of the sunscreen had inadvertently included a harsh cleaning agent in the batch of sunscreen used by the student. The student filed a strict products liability claim against the manufacturer. The manufacturer claims that the student should not recover because she assumed the risk by applying a sunscreen with such a strong chemical odor.

Is the manufacturer likely to succeed in asserting this defense?

A. No, because the student did not comprehend the risk.

B. No, because a plaintiff's conduct cannot negate or reduce the plaintiff's strict products liability claim.

C. Yes, because the student could smell the chemical odor and exposed herself to it nonetheless.

D. Yes, because the student assumed the risk by applying the sunscreen.

7. A bar manager told one of his bartenders that there was a new type of home blender on the market that could handle the ingredients of any drink, as well as the ingredients to make salsa and other chopped foods. The manager intended to wait in line to buy the blender at a special sale, and the bartender asked the manager to pick an additional blender up for the bartender as well. The manager purchased three blenders, and kept one for himself. He sold one to the bartender for the sale purchase price, and gave the third to his sister as a gift. Two weeks later, the manager came across information on the Internet that the blender manufacturer was recalling the blenders because the motors could overheat and throw sparks, causing a fire. The manager called his sister right away and left a message, but she didn't get it in time. Her

blender sparked, causing a fire in her kitchen that burned her right hand and caused major property damage. The bartender was also burned by his blender, although he didn't suffer nearly as much property damage. The manager apologized to the bartender for not having told him about the recall. If the sister and the bartender file a strict products liability action against the manager for damages, what is the likely outcome?

A. The bartender and the sister will prevail against the manager, because the manager is strictly liable.

B. The bartender, but not the sister, will prevail against the manager, because the manager failed to warn the bartender about the recall.

C. Neither the bartender nor the sister will prevail against the manager, because the manager is not a commercial seller.

D. Neither the bartender nor the sister will prevail against the manager, because the manager did not tamper with the blender.

8. In preparing for her law school examinations, a student invited a few classmates to her apartment for a study group. The student, who loved spiders, kept a pet tarantula caged in her apartment. When the student purchased the tarantula, she had the poisonous venom removed so that it would be harmless.

During the study group session, the student brought out the cage with the tarantula to show her friends. When she was placing the cage down on the kitchen counter, the student carelessly left the cage door slightly ajar. Moments later, the tarantula crawled out of the cage and crept toward one of the classmates. The classmate, who was deathly afraid of spiders, saw the tarantula and tried to run away. As she did so, she tripped over a chair and fell down, fracturing her wrist.

If the classmate files suit against the student to recover damages for her injury, who will prevail?

A. The classmate, because the student was negligent in leaving the cage door open.

B. The classmate, because the student is strictly liable.

C. The student, because the spider did not directly cause the classmate's injury.

Chapter 14
Competitive Torts

D. The student, because a spider is not a wild animal.

9. A company was engaged in transporting liquids. As is normal, the company was hired to deliver a container of highly flammable chemicals to a local plant. The company required all of its employees to engage in extensive training. On the day of the delivery, the trucker hauling the chemicals noticed a stalled car ahead of him in the right lane. There was no way for the trucker to avoid the car. As he tried to maneuver around it, some of the chemicals spilled out of the container and ended up on the car. The car's driver, who had been smoking a cigarette with his windows rolled down while waiting for a tow truck, quickly caught fire, and later died. The driver's estate now brings a strict liability action.

Will the company be liable for the injuries caused to the car's driver?

A. No, because the trucker and the company exercised due care.

B. No, because the driver should have removed the car from the road.

C. Yes, because transporting flammable liquid is an abnormally dangerous activity.

D. Yes, because transporting flammable liquid is illegal.

10. Trespass to chattels may be defined as _____.

A. dispossess or intermeddles with another's chattel or possessory

B. enter land or cause a thing or a third person to enter land

C. dispossess the plaintiff of an interest in personal property completely

D. damage a plaintiff's property to convert it

Ⅱ. Essay Questions:

QUESTION 1

Star stored furniture in a warehouse owned by Ware and prepaid one month's storage fees. At the end of the month, Star demanded return of his furniture. Ware, claiming in good faith that unpaid storage fees were due, refused to surrender the furniture. Ware informed Star that he would check to determine if the fees had been paid, and would call Star if he determined payment had been made. Star heard nothing further from Ware.

The day following Star's demand, Exco, a licensed exterminator who had been hired to free the warehouse of rats, began his work. Ware and Exco had agreed that a poisonous gas would be used for this purpose (which gas Exco claimed was the most effective). All decisions about the work were left to Exco.

Two days after Exco had commenced, but not completed, the job, two things happened. First, some of the gas escaped from the warehouse into the adjoining building. Otis, the owner of that building, was injured by inhalation of the gas. There is no evidence as to how the gas escaped. All of the usual precautions had been taken to seal all exits and openings in the warehouse. Second, gas fumes exploded later that day when they came into contact with an open flame in the warehouse. The explosion destroyed Star's furniture. For Exco, this was the first instance in which this gas had exploded. The accepted opinion of experts was that the gas was not flammable or explosive.

What are the rights of Otis against Exco? Against Ware? Discuss.

What are the rights of Star against Exco? Against Ware? Discuss.

QUESTION 2

Phil, who was a dignified banker and president of several civic organizations, was walking down Main Street when he discovered that his shoestring had come untied. When he stooped down to retie it, Cam, a commercial photographer, snapped his picture.

Cam takes pictures of people on public sidewalks while they are unaware of what is happening. He then hands each such person a ticket bearing a serial number corresponding to the number on the exposed film of the picture taken. The holder is invited to write his name and address on the ticket and send it to Cam's studio with one dollar, for which he receives a print of his photo. If this is done, the correspondingly numbered film is developed and printed. Otherwise, the film is destroyed.

When Phil was handed his ticket, he threw it on the sidewalk. The next passerby was Joker, a wealthy socialite and friend of Phil's. Cam also took Joker's photo. Joker accidentally dropped and then attempted to retrieve the numbered ticket which he was handed by Cam. By mistake, Joker picked up Phil's discarded ticket. Thinking it was his own, Joker filled the ticket out and sent it to Cam's studio with a dollar. Cam mailed him the corresponding picture in a sealed envelope.

The picture of Phil which Joker received gave the impression that Phil was

Chapter 14
Competitive Torts

reaching down to pick up a discarded cigar butt on the sidewalk, although anything but the most casual observation would have revealed that this was only a photographic illusion. Joker was highly amused at the picture, and posted it on the bulletin board on the lobby of a country club "Club" to which both he and Phil belonged. The manager of the Club allowed the picture to stay there for several weeks. It became the subject of hilarious conversation among the members. Finally, one member of Club, who was an editor of *Town Topics*, a local paper, removed the picture and published it in the Hobby section of his paper in connection with an article entitled: "Can you trust your camera?"

What are Phil's rights against Cam? Joker? Club? *Town Topics*? Discuss.

QUESTION 3

An unprecedented storm in City X caused the electrical wiring that controlled a traffic signal at an intersection to short circuit. As a result, a green "go" light was continuously displayed both to north-south and east-west traffic. When this confusing situation first occurred, a City X policeman observed it. He did nothing, however, since he had received a call that stores about one mile away were being looted.

Two hours later, the lights were still green in both directions. Peter, driving his car northbound, observed a green traffic light and proceeded directly toward the intersection. At the same time, Simon, who was operating his car in violation of a criminal statute prohibiting driving while intoxicated, approached the intersection heading west. Simon saw the green signal facing him and proceeded to cross. He assumed that any cars coming from the south would halt as they approached what had to be a "red" signal. Peter, in turn, saw Simon as he proceeded into the intersection. Peter made an effort to stop and could have done so if the brake fluid in his car's master cylinder had not been low. A reasonable inspection would have disclosed to Peter that his brakes were defective for this reason. In the collision that followed, Simon's car was struck broadside and injuries were sustained by both Peter and Simon.

Discuss the possible liabilities of City X and each driver.

Property Law

> **导 读** <<
>
> 财产法根源于英国的封建土地法,由于动产在现代社会中已多被置于其他民事法律部门之下,所以美国财产法的主要内容是不动产(real or immovable property)。
>
> **一、财产的取得** 财产的取得方式多种多样:包括捕获野生动物、发现、时效占有(adverse possession)和寄托(bailment)。通过发现取得财产,必须事实上发现该物,而且具有占有的意图。时效占有要求排他、实际、公开、公然、敌对和持续占有不动产达到一定期间。寄托的要求有三:交付、转移占有、接受。
>
> **二、占有地产权** 土地产权是当前所占有的,或者可能要占有的权益,通过时间的持续期间予以测算。占有地产权是持有人的当前占有权;未来权益(future interests)是将来要或可能要占有的权利。不动产权还可以分为自由保有地产权(freehold)和非自由保有地产权(non-freehold)。自由保有地产权可以无限期持续,而非自由保有地产权于特定日期终止。非限定继承不动产(fee simple)就属于自由保有地产权,下分绝对非限定继承不动产、可终止的非限定继承不动产、附条件的非限定继承不动产三类。限嗣继承不动产(fee tail)也属于自由保有地产权,只是将继承人限于直系亲属。终身产权(life estate)是在一个或一个以上的人生存期间存在的产权,不得随意取消,但是不得长于一个或者一个以上的人的生命持续期间。
>
> 未来权益虽然不能让所有人取得当前占有,但是该权益是

现实的、受法律保护的,而不只是预期的或者不确定的。

共同占有地产权(concurrent estates),指两个或者两个以上的当事人在相同的不动产之中同时拥有权益。可以分为普通共有(tenancy in common)、共同保有(joint tenancy)、夫妻共同保有(tenancy by the entirety)等。

三、租赁保有 租赁保有(leasehold)是一种土地产权,承租人对出租的不动产拥有现实的占有权益,出租人拥有未来权益。出租人与承租人之间的关系衍生出特定的权利与义务,租赁保有地产权主要有三种:定期租赁(tenancies for years);不定期租赁(periodic tenancies);任意租赁(tenancies at will)。

出租人义务由租赁协议确定,法律也对出租人施加了一定义务,包括保证承租人对租赁不动产的占有,保证承租人对租赁不动产的安宁享受权,保证用于居住目的的租赁不动产适宜居住。关于出租人是否有默示义务将租赁不动产交付给承租人占有,美国法认为出租人有义务确保承租人对租赁不动产有法律上的占有权,但无义务确保承租人实际占有租赁不动产。

根据传统规则,若承租人转让余下租赁期的全部利益,则构成转让;若承租人转让余下租赁期的部分利益,则构成转租。不动产可因赠予、买卖等原因转让。

四、不动产附着物(fixtures) 所谓附着物,指附着于土地上的动产(chattel),且因为该附着方式而不再保持动产特性,而成了不动产的一部分。研究不动产附着物问题,必须区分共同所有与区分所有两种情况。共同所有指将动产附着于不动产之上的人,既拥有该不动产,又拥有该动产。区分所有指该人或者只拥有动产附着物,或者只拥有不动产。不管哪种情况,只要动产并入不动产后失去了独立存在的条件,就成了不动产的一部分,如砖头砌入房屋的情况。

五、不动产买卖 不动产买卖通常都要订立不动产买卖合同。不动产买卖合同在合同形式上受欺诈法的约束,通常需要具有书面形式方有强制执行力。不动产买卖合同的卖方和货物买卖合同卖方一样要承担默示担保义务,包括不动产所有权的可销售性担保,向买方披露不动产潜在缺陷的义务,及对质量的默示担保。违反不动产买卖合同的救济主要包括实际履行、损害赔偿和解除合同。

《反欺诈行为法》规定,出售不动产合同应采用书面形式,并经被执行人签字,合同方能被强制执行。对此主要有两个例外:一是部分履行,另一个是禁止反言。

六、妨害行为(nuisance) 妨害行为指一个人对自己的土地的不合理使用实质性减损了他人对自己土地的使用和享受,妨害分为对私人的妨害和对公众的妨害。

关于妨害的诉讼一般有四种解决方式:认定有关行为不构成妨害,驳回相关诉讼请求;认定有关行为构成妨害,发布禁令禁止该行为;认定有关行为构成妨害,但在被告进行损害赔偿的情况下允许该行为继续;在原告支付赔偿金的情况下禁止该行为。

Chapter 1

Acquisition of Property

Ⅰ. Capture of Wild Animals

"Mere pursuit" is not possession, because capture of wild animals requires actual capture.

Ⅱ. Acquisition by Find

A finder taking possession of personal property must: (i) actually come upon or discover the thing and (ii) have an intent to take possession of it.

(1) Prior possessor has superior right; finder has rights superior to all except true owner.

(2) Categories of Found Property (state of mind of the owner determines status)
   a. Lost;
   b. Mislaid;
   c. Abandoned.

Armory v. Delamirie
(1722) 1 Strange 505; 93 E.R. 664 (Court of King's Bench)

The plaintiff being a chimney sweeper's boy found a jewel and carried it to the defendant's shop (who was a goldsmith) to know what it was, and delivered it into the hands of the apprentice, who under pretence of weighing it, took out the stones, and calling to the master to let him know it came to three halfpence, the master offered the boy the money, who refused to take it, and insisted to have the thing again; whereupon the apprentice delivered him back the socket without the stones. And now in <u>trover</u>① against the master these points were ruled:

1. That the finder of a jewel, though he does not by such finding acquire an absolute property or ownership, yet he has such a property as will enable him to keep it against all but the rightful owner, and subsequently may maintain trover.

2. That the action well lay against the master, who gives a credit to his apprentice, and is answerable for his neglect.

3. As to the value of the jewel several of the trade were examined to prove what a jewel of the finest water that would fit the socket would be worth; and the Chief Justice directed the jury, that unless the defendant did produce the jewel, and shew it not to be of the finest water, they should presume the strongest case against him, and make the value of the best jewels the measure of their damages: which they accordingly did.

III. Adverse Possession

Adverse possession is a doctrine under which a person in possession of land owned by someone else may acquire valid title to it, so long as certain common law requirements are met, and the adverse possessor is in possession for a sufficient period of time, as defined by a statute of limitations.

The common law requirements have evolved over time, and the articulation of those requirements varies somewhat from jurisdiction to jurisdiction. Typically, adverse possession, in order to ripen into title, must be:

1. *Continuous*; this means *continual*.

2. *Hostile* to the interests of the true owner; this is the *adverse* part of adverse possession.

3. *Open and notorious*, so as to put the true owner on notice that a trespasser is in possession.

4. *Actual*, so that the true owner has a cause of action for trespass, on

---

① 追索侵占物诉讼

which the true owner must act within the statute of limitations.

5. *Exclusive*, in order that there be no confusion as to who acquires title once the time has run.

The statute of limitations: A typical statute will require possession for 7 years, if under color of title, or 20 years, if not.

A mnemonic① may help with remembering the decisional and statutory elements of adverse possession; think of it as inchoate ownership which becomes **choaTe** [(i. e. **c**ontinuous, **h**ostile, **o**pen, **a**ctual, for the requisite period of **T**ime, and **e**xclusive). Decisional pieces are indicated in lowercase, statutory ones in uppercase.]

Ⅳ. Bailment

A "bailment" is a non-ownership transfer of possession. Under English Common Law, the right to possess a thing is separate and distinct from owning the thing. In some jurisdictions, an owner of an object can steal his own property, a curious result of the distinction. In context, an owner who lends someone else an article, then secretly takes it back, can be stealing.

When a bailment is created, the article is said to have been "bailed." One who delivers the article is the bailor. One who receives a "bailed" article is the bailee.

1. Requirements of a Bailment

(1) Delivery

Delivery can be actual, constructive, or symbolic.

(2) Transfer of possession

(3) Acceptance

2. Creation

To create a bailment, the alleged bailee must assume actual physical control with the intent to possess.

---

① 记忆法,助记符

Chapter 2
Possessory Estates

The concept of estates in Anglo-American law arose out of the feudal system in England. The concept underlies American present system of real property law. Estates in land are interests which presently are or may become possessory and which are measured by a period of time. Possessory estates give the holder the right to immediate possession. Future interests are estates that will or may become possessory in the future. Estates in realty are further categorized as freehold or non-freehold. Freehold estates continue indefinitely or until the occurrence of some event. Non-freehold estates end on a particular date.

Ⅰ. The Fee Simple

1. Fee Simple Absolute

Fee simple absolute is an estate that has the potential of enduring forever. The largest estate permitted by law is the fee simple absolute. The holder of this estate has full possessory rights now and in the future for an infinite duration. There are no limitations on its inheritability, it cannot be divested and it will not end upon the happening of any event. However, the holder of the estate can sell it or any part of it during his lifetime and dispose of it by will at his death.

2. Fee Simple Determinable

Fee simple determinable, also called a determinable fee, is an estate that automatically ends on the happening of a stated event and goes back to the grantor. It is created by the use of durational, adverbial language, such as "for so long as", "while", "during" or "until". A fee simple determinable can be conveyed by the owner thereof, but his grantee takes the land subject to the termination of the estate by the happening of the event.

3. Fee Simple Subject to Condition Subsequent

Fee simple subject to condition subsequent is created when the grantor retains the power to terminate the estate of the grantee upon the happening of a specified event. Upon the happening of the event stated in the conveyance, the estate of the grantee continues until the grantor exercises her power of termination by bringing suit or making reentry.

II. Fee Tail

Fee tail, typically created by the words "to A and the heirs of his body," limited inheritance to lineal① descendants of the grantee. If no lineal descendants survived at the grantee's death, the property either reverted to the grantor or her successors or passed to a designated remainderman②. Today, most United State jurisdictions have abolished the fee tail and have enacted statute under which any attempt to create a fee tail results in the creation of a fee tail.

1. Characteristics

(1) During Tenant's Life

The tenant in fee tail can do nothing to defeat the rights of the tenant's lineal descendants. In practical effect, he has only a life estate.

(2) On Tenant's Death

The fee tail can be inherited only by the issue of the original grantee, and not by his collateral kin. If the blood descendants of the original owner run out, the property is returned to the original grantor or his heirs, or to any holder of the remainder named in the grant creating the fee tail.

2. Types of Fee Tail

(1) Fee Tail Male

Fee tail male is limited succession to male descendants of the grantee, i.e., "to A and the male heirs of his body."

---

① 直系的
② 不动产继承人

(2) Fee Tail Special

Fee tail special is inheritable only by the issue of a specific spouse, i.e., "to A and the heirs of his body by his wife, B."

Ⅲ. The Life Estate

A life estate endures for a period of one or more human lives that is not terminable at any fixed or computable period of time, but cannot last longer than the life or lives of one or more persons. It may arise by operation of law or may be created by an act or agreement of the parties.

1. Life Estate by Marital Right

Such estates arise under dower and curtesy, the common law interests of wife and husband, respectively, in real property of which the other spouse was seized during marriage. At common law, a surviving wife's dower right entitled her to a life estate in an undivided one-third of her husband's lands.

2. Conventional Life Estate

(1) For Life of Grantee

The usual life estate is measured by the life of the grantee and is called simply a life estate. It may be indefeasible, or it may be made defeasible in the same ways that fee estates can be defeasible.

(2) Life Estate *Pur Autre Vie*

A life estate *pur autre vie* is a life estate measured by the life of someone other than the life tenant. Such an estate can be created directly by the grantor, e.g., "to A for the life to B."

3. Rights and Duties of Life Tenant—Doctrine of Waste

A tenant for life is entitled to all the ordinary uses and profits of the land; but he cannot lawfully do any act that would injure the interests of the person who owns the remainder or the reversion. If he does, the future interest holder may sue for damages and/or enjoin such acts.

Chapter 3

Future Interests

A future interest is an estate that does not entitle the owner thereof to possession immediately but will or may give the owner possession in the future. A future interest is a present, legally protected right in property; it is not an expectancy.

I. Reversionary Interests—Future Interests in Transferor

1. Possibilities of Reverter and Rights of Entry

These future interests are discussed above in connection with the present estates to which they are attached.

2. Reversions

A person owning an estate in real property can create and transfer a lesser estate. The residue left in the grantor, which arises by operation of law, is a reversion.

Reversions are transferable, devisable by will, and descendible by inheritance. The holder of a reversion may sue a possessory owner for waste and may recover against third-party wrongdoers for damages to the property.

3. All Reversionary Interests Are "Vested"

Although a reversionary interest becomes possessory in the future, it is a vested interest, not a contingent interest, because both the owner and the event upon which it will become possessory are certain. This is true even if the reversionary interest is determinable or defeasible. Because it is a vested interest, a reversionary interest is not subject to the Rule Against Perpetuities.

Chapter 3
Future Interests

II. Remainders

A remainder is a future interest created in a transferee that is capable of taking in present possession and enjoyment upon the natural termination of the preceding estates created in the same disposition. Unlike a reversion, which arises by operation of law from the fact that the transferor has not made a complete disposition of his interest, a remainder must be expressly created in the instrument creating the intermediate possessory estate.

III. Executory Interests

Here is a good shorthand rule for classifying executory interests. Remember that there are two and only two future interests that can be created in a transfer: remainders and executory interests. If it is not a remainder because the preceding estate is not a life estate, then it must be an executory interest. Thus, an executory interest is any future interest in a transferee that does not have the characteristics of a remainder, i.e., it is not capable of taking on the natural termination of the preceding life estate. More specifically, an executory interest is an interest that divests the interest of another.

IV. Importance of Classifying Interests "in Order"

Future interests are classified clause by clause—which will often mean that the label appended to the first future interest created in a disposition will determine the label to be appended to a second future interest created in the same disposition. For instance, if the first future interest is a contingent remainder, subsequent future interests must also be contingent remainders. Similarly, if the first future interest is a vested remainder subject to divestment, the following future interests will be executory interests.

V. Transferability of Remainders and Executory Interests

1. Vested Remainders Are Transferable, Devisable, and Descendible

At common law and in all jurisdictions today, vested remainders are fully transferable during life, devisable by will, and descendible by inheritance. This is true of all types of vested remainders: indefeasibly vested, vested subject to open, and vested subject to total divestment.

2. Contingent Remainders and Executory Interests Are Ttransferable *Inter Vivos*

At common law, contingent remainders and executory interests were not assignable. While this is still the rule in a few states, most American courts hold that these interests are freely transferable.

3. Any Transferable Future Interest Is Reachable by Creditors

The rule followed in nearly all states is this: if a future interest can, under the laws of the state, be transferred voluntarily by its owner, it is also subject to involuntary transfer; that is, it can be reached by the owner's creditors by appropriate process.

Ⅵ. Survival

As a general rule, all future interests can pass at death by will or inheritance; *i.e.*, they are descendible and devisable. This is true unless the interest's taking is subject to an expressed or implied contingency of survival.

Chapter 4

Concurrent Estates

An estate in land in which two or more parties have a contemporaneous interest in the same realty is a concurrent estate.

I. Tenancy in Common

In a tenancy in common, each tenant has an undivided interest in the entire property. Each tenant has the right to possession of the whole property. There is no right of survivorship. Each tenant has a distinct proportionate interest in the property, which is alienable by *inter vivos* or testamentary transfer and passes by succession. There is a presumption that a conveyance to two or more persons is a tenancy in common.

II. Joint Tenancy

In this type of tenancy each tenant owns an undivided share of the estate. There is a right of survivorship. Thus, on the death of one joint tenant the survivor retains an undivided right to the entire estate, which is not subject to the rights of the deceased cotenant.

1. Creation

At common law, four unities are required to create a joint tenancy:

(1) Unity of time

(2) Unity of title

(3) Unity of interest

(4) Unity of possession

Under modern law, joint tenancies are disfavored. Hence, there must be a clear expression of intent to create this estate, or it will not be recognized. The usual language required is "to A and B as joint tenants with right of survivorship." Today, when two or more persons take property by a single conveyance, a tenancy in common, not a joint tenancy, is presumed. A joint tenancy results only when an intention to create a right of survivorship is clearly expressed.

2. Severance

A joint tenancy can be terminated by a suit for partition, which can be brought by any tenant. It may also be terminated by various acts by any joint tenant.

III. Tenancy by the Entirety

This is a marital estate which can only be created between a husband and wife. It is similar to a joint tenancy except that the right of survivorship cannot be destroyed, since severance by one tenant is not possible. An existing marriage is requisite for a tenancy by the entirety. In many states there is a presumption that a tenancy by the entirety is created in any conveyance to a husband and wife. Half of the states, however, have abolished this type of tenancy. In New York, the tenancy by the entirety exists as to realty but not personality.

1. Right of Survivorship

The estate carries a right of survivorship, which operates in the same manner as the right of survivorship incident to a joint tenancy.

2. Severance Limited

The major distinction between a joint tenancy and a tenancy by the entirety concerns severance. A tenancy by the entirety cannot be terminated by involuntary partition.

3. Individual Spouse Cannot Convey or Encumber Tenancy

In most states, an individual spouse may not convey or encumber tenancy by the entirety property. A deed or mortgage executed by only one spouse is ineffective.

4. Tenancy in Common

Tenancy in common is a form of concurrent ownership wherein each co-tenant is the owner of a separate and distinct share of the property, which has not been divided among the co-tenant. Each owner has a separate undivided interest in the whole.

IV. Incidents of Co-Ownership

1. Possession

Each co-tenant has the right to possess all portions of the property; no co-tenant has the right to exclusive possession of any part. A co-tenant out of possession cannot bring a possessory action unless there has been an "ouster" by the tenant in possession. A claim of right to exclusive possession can constitute an ouster.

2. Rents and Profits

In most jurisdictions, a co-tenant in possession has the right to retain profits gained by her use of the property. A co-tenant in possession need not share such profits with co-tenants out of possession, nor reimburse them for the rental value of her use of the land, unless there has been an ouster or an agreement to the contrary.

3. Effect of One Concurrent Owner's Encumbering the Property

A joint tenant or tenant in common may place a mortgage on her interest, but may not, of course, **encumber**[①] the other co-tenant's interest. Likewise, if a joint tenancy is involved and the mortgage itself does not sever the joint tenancy, the mortgagee can foreclose on the mortgagor/co-tenant's interest and the foreclosure sale itself will cause a severance. But in the case of a joint tenancy, the mortgagee runs the risk that the mortgaging co-tenant will die before foreclosure, extinguishing the mortgagee's interest. The same principles apply to judgment liens obtained against an individual co-tenant.

4. Ouster

Under the unity of possession, each co-tenant is entitled to possess and

---

① 妨碍,阻碍

enjoy the whole of the property subject to the equal right of her co-tenant. If one tenant wrongfully excludes another co-tenant from possession of the whole or any part of the premises, there is an ouster. The ousted co-tenant is entitled to receive his share of the fair rental value of the property for the time he was wrongfully deprived of possession.

5. Remedy of Partition

A joint tenant or tenant in common has a right to judicial partition, either in kind or by sale and division of the proceeds.

6. Duty of Fair Dealing Among Co-tenants

A confidential relationship exists among co-tenants. Accordingly, the acquisition by one co-tenant of any outstanding title or lien that might affect the estate held by all the co-tenants is deemed to be an acquisition on behalf of all the other co-tenants as well. Thus, when one co-tenant purchases or otherwise acquires a lien holder's claim against the co-tenancy property, she must give the other co-tenants a reasonable time to pay their share and acquire a proportionate interest. Courts carefully scrutinize the fairness of transactions between co-tenants. Lastly, it is difficult for one co-tenant to adversely possess against other co-tenants.

Chapter 5

Landlord and Tenant

Ⅰ. Instruction of Leasehold

A <u>leasehold</u>① is an estate in land. The tenant has a present possessory interest in the leased premises, and the landlord has a future interest. Certain rights and liabilities flow from this property relationship between landlord and tenant. The three major types of leasehold estates are tenancies for years, periodic tenancies, and tenancies at will. There is a fourth category called tenancies at sufferance.

1. Tenancies for Years

A tenancy for years is one that is to continue for a fixed period of time. It may be for more or less than a year; it may be determinable or on condition subsequent. The termination date of a tenancy for years is usually certain. As a result, the tenancy expires at the end of the stated period without either party giving notice to the other. Even if the date of termination is uncertain, most courts hold that if the parties have attempted to state some period of duration, the lease creates a tenancy for years.

2. Periodic Tenancies

A periodic tenancy is a tenancy that continues from year to year or for successive fractions of a year until terminated by proper notice by either party. The beginning date must be certain, but the termination date is always uncertain until notice is given.

---

① 租赁权,租赁物,租赁保有

All conditions and terms of the tenancy are carried over from one period to the next unless there is a lease provision to the contrary. Periodic tenancies do not violate the rules limiting the length of leaseholds because each party retains the power to terminate upon giving notice.

3. Tenancies at Will

A tenancy at will is an estate in land that is terminable at the will of either the landlord or the tenant. To be a tenancy at will, both the landlord and tenant must have the right to terminate the lease at will.

4. Tenancies at Sufferance

A tenancy at sufferance arises when a tenant wrongfully remains in possession after the expiration of a lawful tenancy. Such a tenant is a wrongdoer and is liable for rent. The tenancy at sufferance lasts only until the landlord takes steps to evict the tenant. No notice is required to end the tenancy, and authorities are divided as to whether this is even an estate in land.

5. The Hold-over Doctrine

When a tenant continues in possession after the termination of his right to possession, the landlord has two choices of action:

(1) Eviction

The landlord may treat the hold-over tenant as a trespasser and evict him under an unlawful detainer statute.

(2) Creation of periodic tenancy

The landlord may, in his sole discretion, bind the tenant to a new periodic tenancy.

II. Leases

A lease is a contract containing the promises of the parties. It governs the relationship between the landlord and tenant over the term of the lease. In general, covenants in a lease are independent of each other; i.e. one party's performance of his promise does not depend on the other party's performance of his promise. Thus, if one party breaches a covenant, the other party can recover damages, but must still perform his promises and cannot terminate the landlord-tenant relationship.

III. Tenant Duties and Landlord Remedies

1. Tenant's Duty to Repair

A tenant cannot damage—commit waste on—the leased premises. The rules governing waste in the leasehold context are very much like those governing waste in the context of the life estate.

2. Duty to Not Use Premises for Illegal Purpose

If the tenant uses the premises for an illegal purpose, and the landlord is not a party to the illegal use, the landlord may terminate the lease or obtain damages and injunctive relief.

3. Duty to Pay Rent

At common law, rent is due at the end of the leasehold term. However, leases usually contain a provision making the rent payable at some other time.

4. Landlord Remedies

At common law, a breach, such as failure to pay rent, resulted only in a cause of action for money damages; a breach by either party did not give rise to a right to terminate the lease. Most leases, however, grant the nonbreaching party the right to terminate. Furthermore, nearly all states have enacted an unlawful detainer statute, which permits the landlord to evict a defaulting tenant. These statutes provide for a quick hearing, but severely limit the issues that may be raised. Under most statutes, the only issue properly before the court is the landlord's right to rent and possession. The tenant cannot raise counterclaims.

IV. Landlord Duties and Tenant Remedies

Subject to modification by the lease, a statute, or the implied warranty of habitability, the general rule is that a landlord has no duty to repair or maintain the premises. Leases, however, commonly prescribe landlord liability to tenant in several areas. If a lease does not expressly prescribe landlord duties, some duties will be implied.

V. Assignments and Subleases

Absent an express restriction in the lease, a tenant may freely transfer his leasehold interest, in whole or in part. If he makes a complete transfer of the entire remaining term, he has made an assignment. If he retains any part of the remaining term, the transfer is a sublease.

VI. Condemnation of Leaseholds

1. Entire Leasehold Taken by Eminent Domain—Rent Liability Extinguished

If all of the leased land is condemned for the full balance of the lease term, the tenant's liability for rent is extinguished because both the leasehold and the reversion have merged in the condemnor and there is no longer a leasehold estate. Absent a lease provision to the contrary, the lessee is entitled to compensation for the taking of the leasehold estate.

2. Temporary or Partial Taking—Tenant Entitled to Compensation Only

If the taking is temporary, or if only a portion of the leased property is condemned, the tenant is not discharged from the rent obligation but is entitled to compensation for the taking.

Chapter 6

Fixtures

A "fixture" is a chattel that has been so affixed to land that it has ceased being personal property and has become part of the realty. For example, S and B contract to sell and buy a house. Before vacating, S removes a built-in refrigerator. B claims that the item was "part of the house." Is the refrigerator a "fixture"? If so, B is entitled to its return or appropriate compensation.

It is important in dealing with "fixture" problems to distinguish between *common ownership* cases and *divided ownership* cases. Courts treat them differently even though they often purport to apply the same tests. "Common ownership" cases are those in which the person who brings the chattel onto the land owns both the chattel and the realty (e.g., X installs a furnace in her own home). "Divided ownership" cases are either ones where the person who owns and installs the chattel does not own the land (e.g., T installs a furnace in her rented home, which belongs to L); or the person owns the land but does not own the chattel. In addition, there are cases involving more than two persons.

I. Chattels Incorporated into Structure Always Become Fixtures

In both common ownership and divided ownership cases, where the items become incorporated into the realty so that they lose their identity, they become part of the realty. Examples include bricks built into a building or concrete poured into a foundation. Similarly, where identification is possible, but removal would occasion considerable loss or destruction, the items are considered fixtures, *e.g.* heating pipes embedded in the wall or floor of a house.

II. Divided Ownership Cases

In divided ownership cases, unlike the ones just discussed, the chattel is owned and brought to the realty by someone who is not the landowner. The question is whether the ownership of the chattel has passed to the landowner. Courts often say that the intention test is to be applied in these cases, too. But the exceptions disprove the rule.

1. Landlord-tenant

Early English law favored the landlord. However, American law created a trade fixtures exception under which tradesmen-tenants could remove an item that otherwise would have been a "fixture." Later, this exception was expanded to include all tenants generally. Some courts have treated the trade fixtures exception as consistent with the annexor's-intention test; i.e. a tenant's **annexations**① are removable because "it was not the intention of the tenant to make them permanent annexations to the freehold and thereby donations to the owner of it."

2. Life Tenant and Remainderman

The same rules should apply here as in the landlord-tenant cases. Historically, however, results have been more favorable to the remaindermen. Apart from statute, the removal privilege has been unrealistically limited to the duration of the term.

3. Licensee and Landowner

Licenses to bring items onto land usually contain agreements respecting removal. In the absence of agreement, licensees are permitted to remove the items subject to a duty to repair damages caused thereby.

4. Trespasser and Landowner

Trespassers normally lose their annexations whether installed in good faith or not. This follows from the intention test: The good faith trespasser, believing the land to be her own, normally intends annexation of an item to be permanent.

---

① 附加物,合并物

Chapter 7

Rights in the Land of Another—Easements, Profits, Covenants, and Servitudes

Ⅰ. Easements

The holder of an easement has the right to use a tract of land for a special purpose, but has no right to possess and enjoy the tract of land. The owner of the servient tenement continues to have the right of full possession and enjoyment subject only to the limitation that he cannot interfere with the right of special use created in the easement holder. Typically, easements are created in order to give their holder the right access across a tract of land, e.g., the privilege of laying utility lines, or installing sewer pipes and the like. Easements are affirmative or negative, appurtenant or in gross.

1. Types of Easements

(1) Affirmative Easement

The owner of an affirmative easement has the right to go onto the land of another and do some act on the land. Most easements are affirmative.

(2) Negative Easement

The owner of a negative easement can prevent the owner of the servient land from doing some act on the servient land.

2. Creation

Easement may be created by express grant or reservation, by implication, or by prescription.

(1) Creation by Express Grant

Because an easement is an interest in land, the Statute of Frauds applies.

Therefore, any easement must be in writing and signed by the grantor unless its duration is brief enough to be outside a particular state's Statute of Frauds' coverage. An easement can be created by conveyance. A grant of an easement must comply with all the formal requisites of a deed. An easement is presumed to be of perpetual duration unless the grant specifically limits the interest.

(2) Creation by Reservation

An easement by reservation arises when the owner of a tract of land conveys title but reserves the right to continue to use the tract for a special purpose after the conveyance. In effect, the grantor passes title to the land but reserves unto himself an easement interest.

(3) Creation by Implication

Implied easements are limited to 2 kinds (i) an intended easement based on an apparent use existing at the time the servient tenement is separated from the dominant tenement, and (ii) an easement by necessity.

(4) Creation by Prescription

Acquiring an easement by prescription is **analogous**[①] to acquiring property by adverse possession. Many of the requirements are the same: to acquire a prescriptive easement, the use must be open and notorious; adverse and under claim of right; and continuous and uninterrupted for the statutory period. Note that the public at large can acquire an easement in private land if members of the public use the land in a way that meets the requirements for prescription.

Requirements of Prescription are:

(1) Open and notorious use;

(2) Under a claim of right;

(3) Continuous use;

(4) Uninterrupted use.

3. Termination of Easements

An easement, like any other property interest, may be created to last in perpetuity or for a limited period of time. To the extent the parties to its original creation provide for the natural termination of the interest, such limitations will control.

---

① 相似的,可比拟的

Chapter 7
Rights in the Land of Another—Easements, Profits, Covenants, and Servitudes

II. Profits

Like an easement, a profit is a nonpossessory interest in land. The holder of the profit is entitled to enter upon the servient tenement and take the soil or a substance of the soil. Also, like an easement, a profit may be appurtenant or in gross. In contrast to easement, however, there is a constructional preference for profits in gross rather than appurtenant.

1. Creation

Profits are created in the same way as easements.

2. Alienability

A profit appurtenant follows the ownership of the dominant tenement. A profit in gross may be assigned or transferred by the holder.

3. Exclusive and Nonexclusive Profits Distinguished

When an owner grants the solo right to take a resource from her land, the grantee takes an exclusive profit and is solely entitled to the resources, even to the exclusion of the owner of the servient estate. By contrast, when a profit is nonexclusive, the owner of the servient estate may grant similar rights to others or may take the resources herself. Ordinarily, profits are construed as nonexclusive.

4. Termination

Profits are terminated in the same way as easements. In addition, misuse of a profit, unduly increasing the burden, will be held to surcharge the servient estate.

III. Covenants Running with the Land at Law

A real covenant, normally found in deeds, is a written promise to do something on the land or a promise not to do something on the land. Real covenants run with the land at law, which means that subsequent owners of the land may enforce or be burdened by the covenant. To run with the land, however, the benefit and burden of the covenant must be analyzed separately to determine whether they meet the requirements for running.

1. Requirements for Burden to Run

If all requirements are met for the burden to run, the successor in interest to the burdened estate will be bound by the arrangement entered into by her predecessor as effectively as if she had herself expressly agreed to be bound.

(1) Intent;

(2) Notice;

(3) Horizontal privity;

(4) Vertical privity;

(5) Touch and concern.

2. Requirements for Benefit to Run

(1) Intent;

(2) Vertical privity;

(3) Touch and concern.

3. Remedies—Damages Only

A breach of a real covenant is remedied by an award of money damages, not an injunction. If equitable relief, such as an injunction, is sought, the promise must be enforced as an equitable servitude rather than a real covenant. Note that a real covenant gives rise to personal liability only. The damages are collectible out of the defendant's general assets.

4. Termination

As with all other nonpossessory interests in land, a real covenant may be terminated by:

(1) The holder of the benefit executing a release in writing;

(2) Merger;

(3) Condemnation of the burdened property.

Ⅳ. Equitable Servitudes

If a plaintiff wants an injunction or specific performance, he must show that the covenant qualifies as an **equitable servitude**①. An equitable servitude is a covenant that, regardless of whether it runs with the land at law, equity will

---

① 衡平法上的地役权

Chapter 7
Rights in the Land of Another—Easements, Profits, Covenants, and Servitudes

enforce against the assignees of the burdened land that have notice of the covenant. The usual remedy is an injunction against violation of the covenant.

1. Creation

Generally, equitable servitudes are created by covenants contained in a writing that satisfies the Statute of Frauds. As with real covenants, acceptance of a deed signed only by the grantor is sufficient to bind the grantee as promisor. There is one exception to the writing requirement: Negative equitable servitudes may be implied from a common scheme for development of a residential subdivision.

2. Enforcement

For successors of the original promise and promisor to enforce an equitable servitude, certain requirements must be met.

(1) Requirements for Burden to Run

a. Intent;

b. Notice;

c. Touch and concern.

(2) Requirements for Benefit to Run

The benefit of the equitable servitude will run with the land if the original parties so intended and the servitude touches and concerns the benefited property.

(3) Privity Not Required

The majority of courts enforce the servitude not as an in personal right against the owner of the servient tenement, but as an equitable property interest in the land itself. There is, therefore, no need for privity of estate.

3. Termination

Like other nonpossessory interests in land, an equitable servitude may be terminated by a written release from the benefit holder, merger of the benefited and burdened estates, or condemnation of the burdened property.

Chapter 8

Conveyancing

Ⅰ. Finding the Property

Real estate is often purchased and sold with the assistance of a real estate broker. Brokers may be employed to sell property, in which case their duty is to act honestly toward the principal and obtain the highest price possible. They may also be employed by a purchaser to locate property, in which case their duty is to secure the property at the lowest possible price. The broker's duty is a general one of an agent to principal. A broker's contract is not required to be in signed and in writing in many states, as Statutes of Frauds only applies to direct transfers of realty, and not actions to enforce brokerage contracts.

It is a general rule that the broker becomes entitled to a commission when they complete the services they are hired to perform. In the event that the brokers are employed to obtain purchasers, they are entitled to their commission when they introduce a person to the principal who is ready, willing and able to purchase on the terms requested. Accordingly, it is advisable for the person who hires brokers to enter into an agreement with them whereby it is agreed the broker will not be entitled to a commission until the transaction and closing are fully completed. There are various types of brokerage agreements which are as follows:

1. Non-exclusive Agreement

This is also known as an open listing. Under this type of agreement several brokers may be hired by the owner. A broker is only entitled to commission when a buyer is procured.

2. Exclusive Agency Agreement

Under this type of agreement the seller can only hire one broker. The owner, however, can sell or lease the property without a broker, in which case the owner is not liable to the broker his or her commissions.

3. Exclusive Right to Sell

Under this type of agreement, the broker has the exclusive right to sell, and receives a commission if the sale is **consummated**[①] by him or her or the owner.

4. Multiple Listings

This is an arrangement among a group of brokers whereby a participating broker can sell property that is exclusively listed with any of the other participating brokers. The "listing broker" obtains the listings and the "selling broker" sells the property. These two brokers split the commission and the listing service receives a small fee.

5. Net Listings

This is an agreement whereby the seller indicates a specific price for which the property is to be sold. The broker's commission is the difference between that price and the sales price received. These types of listings are prohibited in New York.

Ⅱ. Financing

Purchasers of real property obtain financing from various sources. Mortgages are commonly used to finance the acquisition of real property, since the lender receives a lien that may be enforced on the default of the purchaser. The buyer retains title to the property unless the mortgage lien is foreclosed. The lender, who may be the seller or a third party, can enforce the mortgage by foreclosing the lien. The borrower can redeem the property by reinstatement or payment of the loan prior to foreclosure. Certain states are considered "title theory states" and treat title to mortgaged premises as being in the mortgagee. Other states are considered "lien theory states" and consider that the legal title to

---

① 完成,达成

the mortgaged premises remains in the mortgagor and the mortgagee merely has a lien on the property. A mortgage loan can be structured in a variety of ways and can have fixed or adjustable rates.

Purchasers of **condominiums**[①] also obtain financing from various sources. Commonly, as with the purchase of a home, a mortgage which can be foreclosed upon is held as security for the loan.

The loans which are obtained by purchasers of cooperative apartments are generally secured by pledges of the purchaser's stock in the entity and an assignment of the proprietary leases.

Ⅲ. Land Sale Contract

Most transfers of land are preceded by contracts of sale. These normally contemplate escrows before closing.

1. Statute of Frauds Applicable

To be enforceable, a land contract must be in writing and signed by the party to be charged. The writing needs not be a formal contract; a memorandum suffices, e.g., escrow instructions can be the contract of sale. The Statute of Frauds requires that the writing contains all "essential terms" of the contract. These are:

a. A description of the property;

b. Identification of the parties to the contract;

c. The price and manner of payment.

Incidental matters can be determined by custom; they need not appear in the writing nor even have been agreed upon.

2. Doctrine of Equitable Conversion

Under the doctrine of equitable conversion, once a contract is signed and each party is entitled to specific performance, equity regards the purchaser as the owner of the real property. The seller's interest, which consists of the right to the proceeds of sale, is considered to be personal property. The bare legal title that remains in the seller is considered to be held in trust for the purchaser as

---

① 公寓,公寓住房

security for the debt owed the seller. But note that possession follows the legal title; so even though the buyer is regarded as owning the property, the seller is entitled to possession until the closing.

3. Marketable Title

There is an implied warranty in every land sale contract that at closing the seller will provide the buyer with a title that is "marketable."

4. Tender of Performance

In general, the buyer's obligation to pay the purchase price and the seller's obligation to convey the title are deemed to be concurrent conditions. This means that neither party is in breach of the contract until the other party tenders her performance, even if the date designated for the closing has passed.

5. Remedies for Breach of the Sales Contract

(1) Damages

The usual measure of damages is the difference between the contract price and the market value of the land on the date of the breach. Incidental damages, such as title examination and moving or storage costs, can also be recovered.

(2) Specific Performance

a. Buyer's Remedy

A court of equity will order a seller to convey the title if the buyer tenders the purchase price. The remedy at law is deemed inadequate because the buyer is getting land and land is unique.

b. Seller's Remedy

Somewhat illogically, the courts also generally will give a specific performance decree for the seller if the buyer is in breach. This is sometimes explained as necessary to have "mutuality of remedy."

6. Risk of Loss

The common law rule with regard to risk of loss is that if the property is destroyed between the time the contract is signed and the time of transfer of the deed, and such destruction is not the fault of either party, then as a result of the doctrine of equitable conversion, equitable title was passed to the buyer upon signing the contract. Consequently, the risk of loss has passed to the buyer. However, some states have adopted the Uniform Vendor and Purchasers Risk

Act, which puts the risk of loss on the seller until the buyer takes title or possession.

IV. Deeds—Form and Content

The actual transfer of title to real property generally occurs by a deed. It usually occurs at a closing where it is executed, acknowledged and delivered. There are various types of deeds. The principal types are quitclaim deed, warranty deed with full covenants, and bargain and sale deed. A quitclaim deed contains no covenants by the grantor. A warranty deed with full covenants contains covenants by the grantor of right to convey, against encumbrances, of further assurances, and of quiet enjoyment and warranty. A general warranty deed warrants title against defects arising before as well as during the time the grantor has title. A special warranty deed contains the same covenants, but only warrants against defects arising during the time the grantor has title. A bargain and sale deed contains the basic covenants against grantor's acts.

A deed must be in writing, it must identify the parties and the land involved and it must be acknowledged and delivered.

A deed must satisfy various formalities required by statute, here are the formalities:

1. Statutes of Frauds;
2. Description of land and parties;
3. Words of intent;
4. Consideration not required;
5. Seal is unnecessary;
6. Attestation and acknowledgement generally unnecessary;
7. Signature.

V. Delivery and Acceptance

1. Delivery

A deed is not effective to transfer an interest in realty unless it has been delivered. Physical transfer of a deed is not necessary for a valid delivery. Nor does physical transfer alone establish delivery. Rather, "delivery" refers to the grantor's intent; it is satisfied by words or conduct evidencing the grantor's intention that the deed has some present operative effect; i. e. , that title passes immediately and irrevocably, even though the right of possession may be postponed until some future time.

2. Acceptance

(1) Usually Presumed

There must be an acceptance by the grantee in order to complete a conveyance. In most states, acceptance is presumed if the conveyance is beneficial to the grantee. In other states, acceptance is presumed only where the grantee is shown to have knowledge of the grant and fails to indicate rejection of it. Acceptance is presumed in all states if the grantee is an infant or an incompetent.

(2) Usually "Relates Back"

Acceptance usually "relates back" to the date of "delivery" of the deed in escrow. However, many courts refuse to "relate back" an acceptance where it would defeat the rights of intervening third parties such as BFGs, attaching creditors acceptance if doing so defeats the devisees of the grantor.

3. Recordation

In order to protect a purchaser or lender from the subsequent rights of third parties over the real estate, it is essential to record the relevant documents by filing in a public recording office. Generally the recordation of contracts, deeds and mortgages occurs at the county level. Significant differences with regard to recording procedures and requirements exist from county to county.

(1) Contracts

There is no requirement that a real estate contract be recorded, and quite often it is not recorded. However, if an executory contract is recorded, the purchaser may enforce his right to performance against a person who after the recording, purchases or acquires by exchange, the same realty or any part thereof from the seller's devisees or distributes.

(2) Deeds

There are three major types of recording statutes that may protect subsequent bona fide purchasers of land by putting them on notice of competing interests in land. Most states have adopted one of the three types of statutes:

(i) Notice Statutes invalidate the purchase of a subsequent bona fide purchaser with actual or constructive notice of another grantee. Approximately half of the states have adopted notice statutes. (ii) Race Statutes: Under these types of statutes whoever records first regardless of notice is deemed to be the legitimate owner of the property. (iii) Race Notice Statutes: Under these statutes a subsequent bona fide purchaser is only protected if he or she records before the other person claiming on the interest and without notice of that interest.

Most recording statutes provide that the deed must be acknowledged before a notary public to be recorded. There are differences from jurisdiction to jurisdiction as to the formalities required for recordation. Approximately half of the states including New York are "race-notice" jurisdictions. Every prior conveyance not recorded is void as against any such person who subsequently purchases in good faith without notice and whose conveyance contract or assignment is fully recorded.

4. Closing

The closing is the ceremony at which the property transaction is consummated. Closing practices are dictated by custom, which varies from region to region. Generally, all necessary parties are present, their identity is verified, the documents are finalized, financial calculations and adjustments are reviewed and documents, money and information are exchanged. The closing usually takes place at the office of the seller's attorney but occasionally at the office of the lenders' counsel. There are various costs which are payable at closing, which vary according to jurisdiction. Costs typically paid by a purchaser include fees to record the deed and the mortgage, utility bills, escrow fees, attorney fee for the bank attorney, taxes, special assessments, financing charges, inspection fees, origination fees, rent payable if possession is taken before closing and adjustments.

Hannan v. Dusch
Supreme Court of Appeal of Virginia, 1930
154 Va. 356, 153 S. E. 824, 70 A. L. R. 141

PRENTIS, C. J., delivered the opinion of the court. The declaration filed by the plaintiff, Hannan, against the defendant, Dusch, alleges that Dusch had on August 31, 1927, leased to the plaintiff certain real estate in the city of Norfolk, Virginia, therein described, for fifteen years, the term to begin January 1, 1928, at a specified rental; that it thereupon became and was the duty of the defendant to see to it that the premises leased by the defendant to the plaintiff should be open for entry by him on January 1, 1928, the beginning of the term, and to put said petitioner in possession of the premises on that date; that the petitioner was willing and ready to enter upon and take possession of the leased property, and so informed the defendant; yet the defendant failed and refused to put the plaintiff in possession or to keep the property open for him at that time or on any subsequent date; and that the defendant suffered to remain on said property a certain tenant or tenants who occupied a portion or portions thereof, and refused to take legal or other action to oustsaid tenants or to compel their removal from the property so occupied. Plaintiff alleged damages which he had suffered by reason of this alleged breach of the contract and deed, and sought to recover such damages in the action. There is no express covenant as to the delivery of the premises or for the quiet possession of the premises by the lessee.

The defendant **demurred**① to the declaration on several grounds, one of which was that under the lease set out in said declaration the right of possession was vested in said plaintiff and there was no duty as upon the defendant, as alleged in said declaration, to see that the premises were open for entry by said plaintiff.

The single question of law therefore presented in this case is whether a landlord, who without any express covenant as to delivery of possession leases property to a tenant, is required under the law to oust trespassers and wrongdoers so as to have it open for entry by the tenant at the beginning of the term—that is, whether without an express covenant there is nevertheless an implied covenant to deliver possession.

For an intelligent apprehension of the precise question it may be well to observe that some questions somewhat similar are not involved.

---

① 表示异议,反对

It seems to be perfectly well settled that there is an implied covenant in such cases on the part of the landlord to assure to the tenant the legal right of possession—that is, that at the beginning of the term there shall be no legal obstacle to the tenant's right of possession. This is not the question presented. Nor need we discuss in this case the rights of the parties in case a tenant rightfully in possession under the title of his landlord is thereafter disturbed by some wrongdoer. In such case the tenant must protect himself from trespassers, and there is no obligation on the landlord to assure his quiet enjoyment of his term as against wrongdoers or intruders.

Of course, the landlord assures to the tenant quiet possession as against all who rightfully claim through or under the landlord.

The discussion then is limited to the precise legal duty of the landlord in the absence of an express covenant, in case a former tenant, who wrongfully holds over, illegally refuses to surrender possession to the new tenant. This is a question about which there is a hopeless conflict of the authorities. It is generally claimed that the weight of the authority favors the particular view contended for. There are, however, no scales upon which we can weigh the authorities. In numbers and respectability they may be quite equally balanced.

It is then a question about which no one should be **dogmatic**[①], but all should seek for that rule which is supported by the better reason.

It is conceded by all that the two rules, one is called the English rule, which implies a covenant requiring the lessor to put the lessee in possession, and the other called the American rule, which recognizes the lessee's legal right to possession, but implies no such duty upon the lessor as against wrongdoers, are irreconcilable.

The English rule is that in the absence of stipulations to the contrary, there is in every lease an implied covenant on the part of the landlord that the premises shall be open to entry by the tenant at the time fixed by the lease for the beginning of his term.

It must be borne in mind, however, that the courts which hold that there is such an implied covenant do not extend the period beyond the day when the

---

① 教条的,固执己见的

lessee's term begins. If after that day a stranger trespasses upon the property and wrongfully obtains or withholds possession of it from the lessee, his remedy is against the stranger and not against the lessor.

It is not necessary for either party to involve himself in an uncertainty, for by appropriate covenants each may protect himself against any doubt either as against a tenant then in possession who may wrongfully hold over by refusing to deliver the possession at the expiration of his own term, or against any other trespasser.

As has been stated, the lessee may also protect himself by having his lessor expressly covenant to put him in possession at a specified time, in which case, of course, the lessor is liable for breach of his covenant where a trespasser goes into possession, or wrongfully holds possession, and thereby wrongfully prevents the lessee from obtaining possession.

A case which supports the English rule is *Herpolsheimer v. Christopher*, 76 Neb. 352, 107 N.W. 382, 111 N.W. 359, 9 L.R.A.(N.S.) 1127, 14 Ann. Cas. 399 note. In that case the court gave these as its reasons for following the English rule: "We deem it unnecessary to enter into an extended discussion, since the reasons pro and con are fully given in the opinions of the several courts cited. We think, however, that the English rule is most in consonance with good conscience, sound principle, and fair dealing. Can it be supposed that the plaintiff in this case would have entered into the lease if he had known at the time that he could not obtain possession on the 1st of March, but that he would be compelled to begin a lawsuit, await the law's delays, and follow the case through its devious turnings to an end before he could hope to obtain possession of the land he had leased? Most assuredly not. It is unreasonable to suppose that a man would knowingly contract for a lawsuit, or take the chance of one. Whether or not a tenant in possession intends to hold over or assert a right to future term may nearly always be known to the landlord, and is certainly much more apt to be within his knowledge than within that of the prospective tenant. Moreover, since in an action to recover possession against a tenant holding over, the lessee would be compelled largely to rely upon the lessor's testimony in regard to the facts of the claim to hold over by the wrongdoer, it is more reasonable and proper to place the burden upon the person within whose knowledge the facts are most apt to lie. We are convinced, therefore, that the better reason lies with the courts following the English doctrine, and we therefore adopt it, and hold that, ordinarily, the lessor impliedly covenants with the lessee that the premises leased shall be open to entry by him at the time fixed in the lease as the beginning of the term."

So let us not lose sight of the fact that under the English rule a covenant which might have been but was not made is nevertheless implied by the court, though it is manifest that each of the parties might have provided for that and for every other possible contingency relating to possession by having express covenants which would unquestionably have protected both.

Referring then to the American rule: Under that rule, in such cases, the landlord is not bound to put the tenant into actual possession, but is bound only to put him in legal possession, so that no obstacle in the form of superior right of possession will be interposed to prevent the tenant from obtaining actual possession of the demised premises. This quoted language is Mr. Freeman's.

So that, under the American rule, where the new tenant fails to obtain possession of the premises only because a former tenant wrongfully holds over, his remedy is against such wrongdoer and not against the landlord—this because the landlord has not covenanted against the wrongful acts of another and should not be held responsible for such a tort unless he has expressly so contracted. This accords with the general rule as to other wrongdoers, whereas the English rule appears to create a specific exception against lessors. It does not occur to us now that there is any other instance in which one clearly without fault is held responsible for the independent tort of another in which he has neither participated nor concurred and whose misdoings he cannot control.

For the reasons which have been so well stated by those who have enforced the American rule, our judgment is that there is no error in the judgment complained of.

Affirmed.

Chapter 9

Cooperatives, Condominiums, Zoning and Nuisance

Ⅰ. Cooperatives

In the most common form of housing cooperative, title to the land and buildings is held by a corporation that leases the individual apartments to its shareholders. Thus, the residents in a cooperative are both tenants of the cooperative and owners of the cooperative. Stock interests in the cooperative are not transferable apart from the occupancy lease to which they are attached.

Ⅱ. Condominiums

In a condominium, each owner owns the interior of her individual unit plus an undivided interest in the exterior and common elements.

1. Restriction on Transfer of Interests

Because condominium unit ownership is treated as fee ownership, the ordinary rules against restraints on alienation apply.

2. Mortgages

Each unit owner finances the purchase of her unit by a separate mortgage on her unit. Consequently, unit owners need not be as concerned about defaults by others as they must be in a cooperative.

3. Maintenance Expenses

Each unit owner is personally liable on her own mortgage and each pays her own taxes. In addition, each unit owner is liable to contribute her proportionate share to the common expenses of maintaining the common elements, including insurance thereon.

III. Zoning

The state may enact statutes to reasonably control the use of land for the protection of the health, safety, morals, and welfare of its citizens. Zoning is the division of a jurisdiction into districts in which certain uses and developments are permitted or prohibited. The zoning power is based on the state's police power and is limited by Due Process Clause of the Fourteenth Amendment. Other limitations are imposed by the Equal Protection Clause of the Fourteenth Amendment and the "no taking without just compensation" clause of the Fifth Amendment. Cities and countries can exercise zoning power only if authorized to do so by state enabling acts. Ordinances that do not conform to such acts are "ultra vires" and void.

IV. Nuisance

There are two types of nuisance: "public" nuisance and "private" nuisance. A "private" nuisance is one that unreasonably interferes with the use and enjoyment of nearby property. A "public" nuisance "is a species of catch-all criminal offense, consisting of an interference with the rights of the community at large, which may include anything from the obstruction of a highway to public gaming-house or indecent exposure."

Private nuisance is like negligence in that courts weigh and balance a number of factors to decide whether a particular activity constitutes a nuisance.

Carpenter v. Double R. Cattle Co.
701 P. 2d 222 (Idaho 1985).

Dissenting Justice Bistline found a nuisance:

We have before us homeowners complaining of a nearby feedlot—not a small operation, but one which holds 9,000 cattle. The homeowners claim that the odor, manure, dust, insect infestation[①] and increased concentration of birds

---

① （害虫、盗贼等）群袭，出没，横行

Chapter 9
Cooperatives, Condominiums, Zoning and Nuisance

constituted a nuisance. If the odoriferous quagmire created by 9,000 head of cattle is not a nuisance, it is difficult to imagine what is. While it may be desirable to have a serious nuisance continue because the utility of the operation causing the nuisance is great, those directly impacted by the serious nuisance deserve some compensation for the invasion they suffer as a result of the continuation. This is exactly what the more progressive provision of §826 (b) of the Restatement (Second) of Torts address. What §826(b) adds is a method of compensating those who must suffer the invasion without putting out of business the source or cause of the invasion. The fairness of it is overwhelming.

The majority disagreed and held that defendant's cattle feedlot did not constitute a nuisance. The majority rejected subsection(b), Section 826, of the Restatement (Second) of Torts, which permits a finding of nuisance even though the gravity of harm is outweighed by the utility of the conduct if the harm is "serious" and the payment of damages is "feasible" without forcing the business to discontinue.

Exercises

I. Choose the best answers to the following questions:

1. Who has the ultimate ownership rights to land in the United States?
   A. The person who buys the land.   B. The federal government.
   C. The local government.   D. A homeowners' association

2. Under what conditions may the U.S. government take your land?
   A. For a private purpose and with just compensation.
   B. For a public purpose and with just compensation.
   C. Whenever it pays fair market value for the land.
   D. For a public purpose, with just compensation and the landowner's consent.

3. Frank leases an apartment from Conway. In this situation, Conway is known as _____.
   A. the lessor   B. the lessee   C. the tenant   D. the debtor

4. A homeowner obtained and moved onto a large plot of land, occupying a significant portion of the property. The homeowner lived on that portion of

the land for more than 22 years, believing that the whole plot was his own. Recently, however, the homeowner learned that the deed he had acquired was in fact defective. Now, a person with a valid deed is claiming the entire plot of land for himself. The statutory period for adverse possession in this jurisdiction is 20 years.

What rights, if any, does the homeowner have with respect to the plot of land?

A. The homeowner owns the whole plot of land, because he acquired title to the land by adverse possession.

B. The homeowner owns the portion of the property on which he lived, but not the whole plot, because he did not possess the whole plot.

C. The homeowner does not own any part of the land, because his possession was not hostile.

D. The homeowner does not own any part of the land, because he did not possess the whole plot of land.

5. Developer purchased a lot in the downtown business district of a city. For years, the lot had been used as a for-pay parking lot. Developer obtained the required city zoning approvals and building permits to construct an office building on the lot. The proposed office building would be twice as tall as an older high-rise apartment building on an adjacent lot. Believing that his tenants would be unhappy about the loss of light and of their former view of a large city park on the other side of Developer's lot, the owner of the apartment building brought an action to enjoin the construction of the office building.

Will the owner succeed in obtaining injunctive relief?

A. Yes, because a subsequent use of property must not unreasonably interfere with the light and air of existing adjacent uses.

B. Yes, if the parking lot and any prior uses of Developer's property permitted light and air to reach the apartment building for the statutory period required for adverse possession.

C. No, unless the owner has a cognizable property interest in light and air.

D. No, because Developer received the necessary city approvals and permits.

Chapter 9
Cooperatives, Condominiums, Zoning and Nuisance

6. At the start of the basketball season, a team's coach decided not to start a player who was a long-time fan favorite. As the team started to lose on a consistent basis, one season ticket holder became disgusted with the coach and began wearing a T-shirt suggesting that people stop attending the team's games. During the games, the fan would walk in front of TV cameras with his T-shirt slogan prominently displayed.

   As the season progressed, many other fans joined in heckling the coach and wearing similar T-shirts. Soon thereafter, the fan received a notice from the team's management revoking his season tickets. The fan was informed that he would not be allowed to attend any more games, but would receive full reimbursement for all remaining games.

   If the fan brings an appropriate action against the team challenging the revocation of his season tickets, will he prevail?

   A. Yes, because he was entitled to express his rights of free speech.

   B. Yes, because he had paid for the tickets for the whole season.

   C. No, because his license to attend games was revocable.

   D. No, because obscene speech is not constitutionally protected.

7. Alvin held a life estate in a commercial building, where he ran a music store. His sister Belva held a contingent remainder in the building. Alvin insisted that vinyl records would be popular again in the future, and so he spent all of his money stocking up on old rock and roll records. Over the years, Alvin allowed the premises to become dilapidated—the ceiling sagged, the basement had water damage, and one of the main structural walls showed significant cracking. Belva visited the music store and was horrified to see the condition of "her" building. She subsequently sued Alvin to prevent future damage to the building.

   Should the court rule in favor of Belva?

   A. Yes, because Alvin committed voluntary waste.

   B. Yes, because a remainderman has standing to sue to prevent future waste.

   C. No, because a remainderman does not have standing to sue for damages.

   D. No, because a life tenant is not responsible for permissive waste.

8. A landowner conveyed his property "to A, her heirs and assigns, so long as it is used by the people to gather for purposes of public assembly and debate,

then to B and his heirs."

Which of the following best describes A's interest in the property?

A. A fee simply absolute.

B. A fee simply determinable.

C. A fee simply subject to a condition subsequent.

D. A fee simply subject to an executory interest.

9. A man entered into a lease for a period of five years. Planning to open a hardware store, the man hired a contractor, who installed overhead lighting and built wooden shelves that were nailed into the walls. The contractor also constructed freestanding tables for displaying merchandise. In addition, the man hired a builder to construct a second-floor loft that was structurally attached to the main building. At the expiration of the lease, the man decided to vacate the premises and remove the improvements that he made. He began disassembling the loft and started removing the lighting, shelving, and freestanding tables. The landlord immediately filed suit seeking to enjoin the man from removing these items.

What items will the court most likely allow the man to remove?

A. Everything.

B. Everything except the loft.

C. Everything except the loft and the lighting.

D. The freestanding tables only.

10. A landlord and a tenant signed a lease agreement for a one-year term. One month into the lease term, the tenant changed jobs and abandoned the apartment, because his new job was an inconvenient commute from the apartment. The landlord did not find a replacement tenant. At the end of the lease term, the landlord sent the tenant a bill for the unpaid rent.

In determining how much tenant owes, to which of the following would most courts give the greatest weight?

A. How burdensome the tenant's new commute is.

B. Whether the lease contained a covenant of quiet enjoyment.

C. Whether the landlord has met his burden of showing that he attempted to find a replacement tenant.

D. Whether the tenant has met his burden of showing that the landlord failed to attempt to find a replacement tenant.

Chapter 9
Cooperatives, Condominiums, Zoning and Nuisance

II. **Essay Questions:**

QUESTION 1

Owen owned Blackacre, which consisted of a house on a lot. He conveyed Blackacre to his two children, Sam and Doris, by a deed that reads as follows: "Owen hereby grants Blackacre to Sam and Doris, to be held by them jointly." The deed was duly recorded.

Thereafter, Sam borrowed money from Bank and gave Bank a mortgage on Blackacre to secure repayment of the loan. In the mortgage document, Sam covenanted for himself, his successors and assigns, that Blackacre would not be used for any purpose other than as a single-family residence.

Sam died before the loan became due. His will left all his property to his friend Tom. As applicable law permits, Bank elected not to file a claim against Sam's estate or to call the loan, but rather to rely on whatever rights it had under the mortgage.

Shortly after Sam's death, the area in which Blackacre is located was rezoned to permit multiple-family dwellings. Tom decided to convert the house on Blackacre into a three-unit apartment building.

Bank, upon learning of Tom's plans, sought an injunction against Tom to prohibit the conversion.

Doris brought an action against Bank and Tom to quiet title to Blackacre in herself.

Discuss the result in each case.

QUESTION 2

L and T entered into a written lease of a completely furnished dwelling for a period of one year at a rental of $250 per month, commencing on September 1, 2002. The lease contained a clause allowing T "to give up possession and terminate his liability for rent if the premises, through no fault on T's part, are destroyed or damaged so as to be uninhabitable."

X, the previous tenant of L under a lease that expired August 31, 2002, wrongfully held over and remained on the premises until December 1, 2002, when T took possession. During this period, L refused to take any action to oust X, although repeatedly requested to do so by T.

Shortly after going into possession, T was injured when a bedroom chair collapsed under his weight. Several of the screws pulled loose and came out of the softwood frame. There is no evidence that L knew of the chair's defective construction or that L was negligent.

On March 1, 2003, T paid his rent up to date, surrendered possession, and moved out because the roof had deteriorated and had begun to leak badly. L informed T that he refused to accept the surrender, but he would attempt to relet the dwelling for T's account. On May 1, 2003, T relet the premises to Y for the remainder of the term at a rental of $200 per month.

There are no applicable statutes. Discuss any rights and duties of L and T.

Evidence Law

导 读 <<

证据法在美国通常被称为证据规则(rules of evidence),一般是指规范哪些证明可以在庭审过程中用作证据的一套规则和标准。目前美国影响最大的证据规则是1975年通过的《联邦证据规则》(the Federal Rules of Evidence,缩写为 Fed. R. Evid.)。美国证据法不区分民事证据法和刑事证据法,而是采取二者合一的立法模式。

一、证据的可采性

证据法可以简单地概括为:具有实质性和相关性的有效证据就是可以采纳的。如果当事人提出的一项证据与案件的一项实体法律争点有联系,即满足了实质性要件。为此,有几个问题值得思考:提出的证据要证明什么争点?该争点对案件的实体性诉讼理由或抗辩重要吗?回答这些问题,就取决于诉讼文件中的实体性法律争点。

相关性或证明力(probativeness)指的是主张与证明之间的联系。有效性(competency)存在的条件,是证据没有违反排除规则(exclusionary rule)。

证据有两种基本类型(types of evidence)和三种基本形式(forms of evidence)。两种基本类型是直接证据(direct evidence)和间接证据(indirect evidence),间接证据又被称为旁证(circumstantial evidence)。三种基本形式包括言词证据(testimonial evidence)、书面证据(documentary evidence)和实物证据。言辞证据是证人宣誓后提供的口头证据。书面证据是以书面形式做出的证据,如合同书或者认罪书。实物证据指的是由实实在在的东西构成的证据,而不是证人关于事物的观点主张。

二、相关性与司法认知(relevance and judicial notice)

从证明力角度,相关性就是处理证据对某个事实的证明或否定的倾向性问题。一般可以认为,如果具有关联性的证据是以一种无可辩驳的形式和方式提交的,那么这个证据就是可采用的。

司法认知,指没有经过正式的证据提交就对某事实予以承认和接受,这主要是针对不证自明的主张(self-evident propositions),以绕开成本高昂、费时甚多的正式证明程序。

三、传闻证据排除规则(hearsay rule)与例外原则(hearsay exceptions)

《联邦证据规则》将传闻证据定义为:"在庭审过程中,宣誓作证的人提供的他人做出的陈述,以作为证据来证明当事人主张的真实性"。对传闻证据的排除规则,是证据法中重要的排除规则。

排除传闻证据的重要理由,就是无法进行交叉询问。美国证据法认为,一名证人如果在法庭亲自宣誓说真话,且他在作证时经过对方律师的交叉询问,其证词才有可信性,可被接受为证据。如果一个人的供述不在法庭宣誓并接受交叉询问,他就不算正式证人,其供述就是缺乏可靠性的"传闻",审判时要被排除使用。传闻证据排除规则是以证人中心主义为制度基础的。在案件事实的证明中,证人作证都需要真实的保障,传闻证据规则就是对证人证言提供真实性保障的机制。

传闻证据例外原则通常与两个理念相关。首先,一些庭外陈述由于在某些特殊的情形下做出,而具有了先天的可靠性。其次,在某些情况下法院必须在也许不可靠性的证据与没有任何证据之间做出选择。有时必要性要求证据应当被采纳,否则,将得不到公正的结果。《联邦证据规则》第801条d款规定两类陈述为非传闻陈述:(1)证人的先前陈述;(2)对方当事人承认。

四、特免权制度(privileged rules)

特免权规则是指允许人们在诉讼程序中拒绝透露和制止他人透露某种情报的权利。常见的特免权制度包括:(1)不得被迫自证其罪;(2)律师—委托人特免权;(3)婚姻特免权;(4)医生—病人特免权。

五、证明责任(burden of proof)

证明责任是指当事人如不能证明自己的主张,就要对该主张承担败诉风险的责任。证明责任包含举证责任(burden of production)和说服责任(burden of persuasion)两方面。

Chapter 1

General Considerations

Ⅰ. Threshold Admissibility Issues

A shorthand summary of evidence law might be stated in one sentence: Material and relevant evidence is admissible if competent.

1. Materiality: The Proposition to Be Proved

Materiality exists when the proffered evidence relates to one of the substantive legal issues in the case. The key questions to ask regarding materiality are: What issue is the evidence offered to prove? Is that legal issue material to the substantive cause of action or defense in the case? The answer to these questions and the determination of materiality depend upon the substantive legal issues framed by the pleadings. Thus, evidence is immaterial if the proposition for which it is offered as proof is not a legal issue in the case.

2. Relevance: Probativeness—The Link Between Proof and Proposition

Probativeness embraces the test of materiality and something more. Probative evidence contributes to proving or disproving a material issue.

3. Federal Rules—Materiality and Probativeness Combined

In the Federal Rules of Evidence, as in most modern codes, the requirements of materiality and probativeness are combined into a single definition of relevance. Thus, Federal Rule 401 provides that "relevant evidence" means evidence tending to prove (probativeness) any fact of consequence to the action (materiality).

4. Competence

As mentioned above, material and relevant evidence is admissible and competent. Evidence is competent if it does not violate an exclusionary rule. Basically, then, if evidence is material and relevant, the only reason such evidence would not be admitted is it is prohibited by a special exclusionary rule and evidence.

II. Evidence Classifications

1. Direct or Circumstantial

(1) Direct evidence goes directly to material issue without intervention of an inferential process. Evidence is direct when the very facts in dispute are communicated by those who have actual knowledge by means of their senses.

(2) Circumstantial evidence relies on inference. Circumstantial evidence is indirect and relies on inference. It is evidence of a subsidiary or collateral fact from which, alone or in conjunction with a cluster or other facts, the existence of the material issue can be inferred.

2. Testimonial, Documentary, or Real

(1) Testimonial evidence is oral evidence given under oath. The witness responds to the questions of the attorneys.

(2) Documentary evidence is evidence in the form of a writing, such as a contract or a confession.

(3) Real evidence is the term applied to evidence consisting of things as distinguished from assertions of witnesses about things. Real evidence includes anything conveying a firsthand sense impression to the trier of fact, such as knives, jewelry, maps, or tape recordings.

III. Limited Admissibility

1. Admissible for One Purpose But Not Another

The use of admissible evidence is a frequently encountered problem. It often happens that evidence is admissible for one purpose but is not admissible for another purpose.

Chapter 1
General Considerations

2. Admissible Against One Party But Not Another

It is also possible that the evidence is admissible against one party but is not admissible against the other party.

3. Jury Must Be Properly Instructed

As a general rule, if evidence is admissible for one purpose, it is not excluded merely because of the danger that the jury may also consider it for another incompetent purpose. When the evidence is admissible as to one party or for one purpose but is not admissible as to another party or for another purpose which is admitted, the court must, upon request, restrict the evidence to its proper scope and instruct the jury accordingly.

Chapter 2
Relevance and Judicial Notice

Relevance, in the sense of **probativeness**①, has to do with the tendency of evidence to prove or disprove a material issue, to render it more probably true, or untrue, than it would have been without the particular evidence. Relevance is concerned with the substance or content of the evidence, not with the form or manner in which it is offered (e. g., hearsay rule, and best evidence rule). It can be stated, as a general proposition, that all relevant evidence is admissible if it is offered in an unobjectionable form and manner.

Ⅰ. Determining Relevance

Relevant evidence is evidence having any tendency to make the existence of any fact that is of consequence to the determination of an action more probably than it would be without the evidence.

Exceptions—Certain Similar Occurrences Are Relevant

Despite the above rule, previous similar happenings and transactions of the parties and others similarly situated may be relevant if they are probative of the material issue involved and if that probative value outweighs the risk that the evidence will confuse the jury or result in unfair prejudice. Of course, whenever a similar occurrence is offered to establish an inference about the subject occurrence, the quality of the inference depends on the similarity between the other happening and the one in issue.

---

① 检验,证明力

Chapter 2
Relevance and Judicial Notice

II. Discretionary Exclusion of Relevant Evidence (Pragmatic Relevance)

A trial judge has broad discretion to exclude relevant evidence if its probative value is substantially outweighed by the danger of unfair prejudice, confusion of the issues, or misleading the jury, or by consideration of undue delay, waste of time, or needless presentation of cumulative evidence. [Fed. R. Evid. 403] "Unfair surprise" is listed as an additional basis for exclusion under some state rules, but it was omitted under the Federal Rules on the theory that surprise can be prevented by discovery and pretrial conference or mitigated by granting a continuance.

Certain items of evidence may be directed to material issue in the case and may be very probative of that issue, but they are excluded because of predictable polities designed to ensure an orderly and efficient proceeding and to encourage certain public policy solutions to legal problems.

III. Exclusion of Relevant Evidence for Public Policy Reasons

Certain evidence of questionable relevance is excluded by the Federal Rules because public policy favors the behavior involved. For example, the law encourages the repair of defective premises that cause injury, and consequently, evidence of the subsequent repair may not be admitted to prove antecedent negligence, even though it may be probative of the issue. Evidence excluded for public policy reasons is set forth below.

1. Liability Insurance

2. Subsequent Remedial Measures

(1) Inadmissible to Prove Negligence or Culpable Conduct

Evidence of repairs or other precautionary measures made following an injury is inadmissible to prove negligence, culpable conduct, a defect in product or its design, or a need for a warning or instruction. [Fed. R. Evid. 407] The purpose of the rule is to encourage people to make such repairs.

(2) When Admissible

Although evidence of subsequent repairs is not admissible to prove negligence, etc., this evidence may still be admissible for other purposes. Some of these purposes are:

1) To Prove Ownership or Control
2) To Rebut Claim that Precaution Was Not Feasible
3) To Prove Destruction of Evidence

3. Settlement Offers—Negotiations Not Admissible

Evidence of compromises or offers to compromise is inadmissible to prove liability or invalidity of a claim that is disputed as to validity or amount. [Fed. R. Evid. 408] Rationale: Public policy favors the settlement of disputes without litigation, and settlement would be discouraged if either side were deterred from making offers by the bar that they would be admitted in evidence.

The Federal Rules also exclude "any conduct or statement" made in the course of negotiating a compromise, as well as the offer to compromise itself; therefore, admissions of fact made during compromise negotiations are inadmissible. This position encourages settlements by allowing complete candor between the parties in negotiations. [Fed. R. Evid. 408]

But note: Rule 408 des not exclude evidence that would otherwise be discoverable because it was presented during compromise negotiations. Thus, if defendant presents a document to plaintiff during compromise negotiations to facilitate a compromise and the document was discoverable by plaintiff, it will be admissible in evidence notwithstanding that it was presented during compromise negotiations.

4. Withdrawn Guilty Pleas and Offers to Plead Guilty Not Admissible

Under the Federal Rules neither withdrawn guilty pleas, pleas of nolo contendere, offers to plead guilty, nor evidence of statement made in negotiating such pleas are admissible in any proceeding. [Fed. R. Evid. 410] Most jurisdictions concur. The evidentiary value of a withdrawn plea of guilty as an admission is deemed offset by the prejudicial effect of the evidence. Moreover, it is felt that the judge who permitted the withdrawal of the guilty plea must have decided that there was a good reason to withdraw it and, under these circumstances, the significance of the initial plea is minimal. Most courts exclude offers to plead guilty on reasoning similar to that advanced for not admitting offers to compromise as proof of liability in civil cases.

5. Payment of Medical Expenses Not Admissible

Similarly, evidence that a party paid (or offered to pay) the injuries party's medical expenses is not admissible to prove liability for the injury. [Fed. R. Evid. 409] This rule is based upon the concern that such payment might be promoted solely by "humanitarian motives." However, unlike the situation with compromise negotiation, admissions of fact accompanying offers to pay medical expenses are admissible.

IV. Character Evidence—A Special Relevance Problem

The rules regarding use of character evidence are affected by three major concerns. These are: (i) the purpose for which evidence of character is offered; (ii) the method to be used to prove character; and (iii) the kind of case, civil or criminal.

1. Purposes for Offer of Character Evidence

(1) To prove character when character itself is ultimate issue in case.
(2) To serve as circumstantial evidence of how a person probably acted.
(3) To impeach credibility of witness.

2. Means of Proving Character

Depending upon the jurisdiction, the purpose of the offer, and the nature of the case, the following types of evidence may be used to prove character:

(1) Evidence of specific acts as demonstrating character.
(2) Opinion testimony.
(3) Testimony as to person's general reputation in community.

3. Generally Not Admissible in Civil Cases

Evidence of character to prove the conduct of a person in the litigated event is generally not admissible in civil case. The reasons given are that the slight probative value of character is outweighed by the danger of prejudice, the possible distraction of jury from the main question in issue, and the possible waste of time required by examination of collateral issues.

4. Accused in a Criminal Case—Prosecution Cannot Initiate, but Accused Can

The general rule is that the prosecution cannot initiate evidence of the bad character of the defendant merely to show that she is more likely to have committed the crime of which she is accused. However, the accused may introduce evidence of her good character to show her innocence of the alleged crime.

5. Specific Acts of Misconduct Generally Inadmissible

The basic rule that when a person is charged with one crime, extrinsic evidence of her other crimes or misconduct is inadmissible if such evidence is offered solely to establish a criminal disposition. Thus, this statement of Federal Rule 404(b) is merely another way of saying that the prosecution may not show the accused's bad character to imply criminal disposition. The danger against it is that the jury may convict the defendant because of past crimes rather than because of her guilt of the offense charged.

V. Judicial Notice of Fact

Judicial notice is the recognition of a fact as true without formal presentation of evidence. In most instances the costly, time-consuming, and cumbersome process of formal proof is required to ensure fact-finding accuracy. However, self-evident propositions need not be subjected to this process, but instead may be judicially noticed. Judicial notice, like the presumption, is a judicial shortcut, a substitute for proof. The underlying policy considerations include expediting the trial and avoiding judicial disrepute where the lack of evidence might result in a conclusion contrary to well-known facts. For example, requiring proof that Washington, D. C., is the capital of the United State would require unnecessary time in a situation where a contrary conclusion would be ridiculous.

Chapter 3

Real Evidence

Ⅰ. In general

1. Addressed Directly to Trier of Fact

Real or demonstrative evidence is addressed directly to the trier of fact. The object in issue is presented for inspection by the trier of fact. Ordinarily the evidence is addressed to the sense of sight (e. g. , exhibition of injured arm to jury to demonstrate extent of injury), but it may be directed to other senses as well (e. g. , sound recording of factory noise played during a nuisance trial).

2. Special Problems

This form of proof, which allows the triers of fact to reach conclusions based upon their own perceptions rather than relying upon those of witnesses, frequently involves special problems. Often there is concern regarding proper authentication of the object: additionally, the possibility exists that physical production of the thing may be too burdensome or may inspire prejudicial emotions outweighing its probative value to the litigation.

Ⅱ. Types of Real Evidence

1. Direct

Real evidence may be direct evidence, i. e. , it may be offered to prove the facts about the objects as an end in itself.

2. Circumstantial

Real evidence may also be circumstantial, i. e. , facts about the object are proved as a basis for an inference that other facts are true.

3. Original

Real evidence may be original, i.e., it may have had some connection with the transaction that is in question at the trial.

4. Prepared

Real evidence may also be prepared; e.g., sketches or models may be made to be shown to the trier of fact. This category of real evidence is called "demonstrative evidence."

III. General Conditions of Admissibility

Real evidence, like all other forms of evidence, must be relevant to the proposition in issue. The admissibility of real proof also depends on additional legal requirements, such as those that follow.

1. Authentication

The object must first be identified as being what the proponent claims it to be. Real evidence is commonly authenticated by recognition testimony or by establishing a claim of custody.

2. Condition of Object and Useful Probativeness

If the condition of the object is significant, it must be shown to be in substantially the same condition at the trial. Moreover, the object must be logically helpful or reliable in tending to prove the proposition in issue.

3. Legal Relevance

Assuming the object has been properly identified and is probative, the discretion of the trial judge is called upon to decide whether some auxiliary policy or principle outweighs the need to admit the real evidence.

IV. Particular Types of Real Proof

1. Reproduction and Explanatory Real Evidence

When properly authenticated, relevant photographs, movies, diagrams, maps, sketches, or other reproductions are admissible if their value is not outweighed by the danger of unfair prejudice. On the other hand, items used entirely for explanatory purpose (such as skeletons, anatomy[①] charts, etc.) are permitted at a trial, but are usually not admitted into evidence and are not given to the jury during its deliberations. These items are not represented to be reproductions of the real thing, but are merely used as aids to testimony.

2. Maps, Charts, Model, Etc.

Maps, charts, models, etc., are usually admissible for the purpose of illustrating testimony. Since these are all reproductions, they must be authenticated by testimonial evidence showing that they are faithful reproductions of the object or thing depicted. As with other real evidence, introduction of these items is within the discretion of the court, and they may be excluded where they would be wasteful of time or where they would unduly impress the Trier of fact with the importance of the material.

3. Exhibition of Child in Paternity Suits

Almost all courts permit exhibition of the child for the purpose of showing whether it is of the race of the putative father. The courts are divided with respect to the propriety of exhibiting the child order to prove physical resemblance to the putative father, but a growing majority of courts refuse to permit exhibition of the child.

4. Exhibition of Injuries

The exhibition of juries in a personal injury or criminal case is generally permitted, but the court has discretion to exclude this evidence if the exhibition would result in unfair prejudice.

5. Demonstrations

(1) Demonstrations showing effect of bodily injury.

(2) Demonstrations showing sole control of witness are excluded.

(3) Scientific experiments.

---

① 解剖,分析

Chapter 4

Documentary Evidence

Ⅰ. In General

Documentary evidence, like other kinds of evidence, must be relevant in order to be admissible. In the case of writing, the authenticity of the document is one aspect of its relevancy. Of course, documentary evidence, even if fully authenticated and relevant, may be excluded if it violates a rule of competency such as the best evidence or hearsay rule. Whenever any problem or question concerns a document, you should consider three separate and distinct possible barriers to admissibility (authentication, best evidence, and hearsay).

Ⅱ. Authentication

Before a writing or any secondary evidence of its content may be received in evidence, the writing must be authenticated by proof showing that the writing is what the proponent claims it is. The writing is usually not self-authenticating. It needs a testimonial sponsor or shepherding angel to prove that the writing was made, signed, or adopted by the particular relevant person.

Evidence of Authenticity

In general, a writing may be authenticated by any evidence that serves to establish its authenticity. The Federal Rules do not limit the methods of authentication, but rather list several examples of proper authentication.

(1) Admissions
(2) Testimony of Eyewitness
(3) Handwriting Verifications

(4) Ancient Documents

Under the Federal Rules, a document may be authenticated by evidence:

a. Is at least 20 years old;

b. Is in such condition as to be free from suspicion concerning its authenticity; and

c. Was found in a place where such writing, if authentic, would likely be kept.

(5) Reply Letter Doctrine

A writing may be authenticated by evidence that is written in response to a communication sent to the claimed author.

(6) Circumstantial Evidence in General

The Rules for ancient documents and reply letters, above, involve authentication by circumstantial evidence. A complete list of ways to authenticate by circumstantial evidence would be impossible. Any proof tending in reason to establish genuineness is sufficient.

(7) Photographs

As a general rule, photographs are admissible only if identified by a witness as a portrayal of certain facts relevant to the issue and verified by the witness as a correct representation of those facts. It suffices if the witness who identifies the photograph is familiar with the scene or object that is depicted. In general, it is not necessary to call the photographer to authenticate the photograph.

III. Best Evidence Rule

The best evidence rule is more accurately called the "original document rule." It may be stated as follows: in proving the terms of a writing (recording, photograph, or X-ray), where the terms are material, the original writing must be produced. Secondary evidence of the writing, such as oral testimony regarding the writing's contents, is permitted only after it has been shown that the original is unavailable for some reason other than the serious misconduct of the proponent.

Nonapplicability of the Rule

(1) Fact to Be Proved Exists Independently of Any Writing

Where the fact to be proved has an existence independent of any writing, the best evidence rule does not apply. Therefore, the rule does not apply to all events that happen to have been memorialized by documents. There are many writings that the substantive law does not regard as essential repositories of the facts recorded. These writings happen to record details of essentially nonwritten transactions. As to these, oral testimony may be given without production of, or explanation for the absence of, the original writings.

(2) Writing Is Collateral to Litigated Issue

Any narration by a witness is likely to include references to transactions consisting partly of written communications. The best evidence rule does not apply to writings of minor importance (i. e., ones that are collateral) to the matter in controversy.

(3) Summaries of Voluminous Records

When it would be inconvenient to examine a voluminous collection of writings, recordings, or photographs in court, the proponent may present their contents in the form of a chart, summary, or calculation. However, the originals or duplicates must be made available for examination and copying, and the judge may order them to be protected in court.

(4) Public Records

The best evidence rule is modified so that a proponent may offer into evidence a copy of an official record or a copy of a document that has been recorded and filed. Such a copy must be certified as correct by the custodian of the document or other person authorized to do so, or testified to be correct by a person who compared it to the original. The purpose of this exception is to prevent the loss or absence of public documents due to litigation.

Ⅳ. Parol Evidence Rule

The essence of the parol evidence rue is as follows: if an agreement is reduced to writing, that writing is the agreement and hence constitutes the only evidence of it. All prior or contemporaneous negotiation or agreements are merged into the written agreement. Parol (extrinsic) evidence is not admissible to add to, detract from, or alter the agreement as written.

1. Nonapplicability of Parol Evidence Rule

From an evidentiary standpoint, counsel invoking the rule is saying, "Here is the agreement. Its terms, having been reduced to writing by the parties, are indisputable; they cannot be put in issue. It follows that no evidence can be received in respect to those terms." This approach helps to explain why the parol evidence rule does not apply to exclude evidence of prior or contemporaneous agreements on the following issues:

(1) Completion of Incomplete or Ambiguous Contract

In some situation, the written instrument may be valid but still incomplete or ambiguous. In these cases, parol evidence is admitted not to contradict or vary the writing but to complete the entire agreement of which the writing was only part. Parol evidence will be admitted if the contract does not appear on its face to be the entire agreement between the parties and the parol evidence is consistent with, and not contradictory of, the written instrument. If there is uncertainty, ambiguity, or reasonable dispute as to the meaning of contract terms, parol evidence is admissible to explain the ambiguity.

(2) Reformation of Contract

Where a party alleges facts, such as mistake, entitling him to reformation of the written agreement, the parol evidence rule is inapplicable. This is so because the party is asserting that, despite the apparently unambiguous contract, its terms do not in fact constitute the agreement intended.

(3) Challenge to Validity of Contract

The parol evidence rule does not bar admission of parol evidence to show that what appears to be a contractual obligation is, in fact, no obligation at all. Thus, evidence is admissible to show that the contract was void or voidable and has been avoided, or was made subject to a valid condition precedent that has not been satisfied.

2. Subsequent Modifications of Written Contract

The rule applies only to negotiations or agreements made prior to, or at the time of, the execution of the written contract. Parol evidence is admissible to show subsequent modification or discharge of the written contract.

Chapter 5

Testimonial Evidence

Ⅰ. Competency of Witnesses

Witnesses are not "authenticated" in the same sense as real or documentary evidence. However, they too must pass tests of basic reliability to establish their competence to give testimony. Unlike the authentication situation pertaining to real or documentary proof, witnesses are generally presumed to be competent until the contrary is demonstrated.

1. Basic Testimonial Qualifications

There are four basic testimonial attributes that every witness must have to some degree. These are the capacity to observe, to recollect, to communicate, and to appreciate the obligation to speak truthfully. These, along with sincerity, are the qualities at which the cross-examiner directs his skill.

A **diminution**① of any of these capacities usually goes only to the weight of the testimony and serves to make the witness less persuasive. However, a witness can be so deficient in one or more of these basic qualifications that she will be deemed incompetent to testify at all. The problem of infancy is a good example for all aspects of the basic qualifications. A witness may be too young at the time of the event to be able to accurately perceive what happened or to be able to remember at the time of the trial. The witness may also be too young at the time of the trial to effectively relate or communicate or appreciate the obligation to tell the truth.

---

① 减少,缩小

Chapter 5
Testimonial Evidence

2. Federal Rules of Competency

Federal Rule 601 provides that "Every person is competent to be a witness unless these rules provide otherwise." The rules do not specify any mental or moral qualifications for witness testimony beyond these two limitations.

(1) The witness must have personal knowledge of the matter he is to testify about.

(2) The witness must declare he will testify truthfully, by oath or affirmation.

3. Modern Modifications If Common Law Disqualifications

At common law there were several grounds upon which a person could be disqualified from giving testimony. Persons were incompetent to testify if they had a financial interest in the suit, if they were the spouse of a party, if they lacked religious belief, if they had been convicted of a crime, or if they lacked mental capacity. These common law disqualifications have been almost entirely removed under the Federal Rules and in the vast majority of American jurisdictions.

4. Dead Man Acts

The last remaining vestige of true incompetency of a witness appears in Dead Acts. These statutes exist in most jurisdictions and their provisions vary from state to state. Although there is no Dead Man Acts in the Federal Rules of Evidence, state Dead Man Acts operate to disqualify witnesses in federal cases where state law provides the rule of decision (most diversity cases).

II. Form of Examination of Witness

The judge may exercise reasonable control over the examination of witness in order to aid the effective ascertainment of truth, to avoid wasting time, and to protect witnesses from harassment or undue embarrassment. Questions that frequently arise concerning the form of examination of witness are: when may leading questions be used, what other types of questions are objectionable, and when and how may a witness use memoranda.

1. Leading Questions

(1) Generally Objectionable

A question is leading and generally objectionable on direct examination when it suggests to the witness the fact that the examiner expects and wants to have confirmed. Questions calling for "yes" or "no" answers and question framed to suggest the answer desired are usually leading.

(2) When Permitted

Leading questions are permitted on cross-examination. Trial judges will usually allow leading questions on direct examination in noncrucial areas if no objection is made.

2. Improper Questions

(1) Misleading

A question is misleading and thus is not permitted if it is one that cannot be answered without making an unintended admission.

(2) Compound

Questions that require a single answer to more than one question are not permitted.

(3) Argumentative

Argumentative questions, which are leading questions that reflect the examiner's interpretation of the facts, are improper.

(4) Conclusionary

A question that calls for an opinion or conclusion that the witness is not qualified or permitted to make is improper.

(5) Assuming Facts Not in Evidence

An attorney is not allowed to ask a question that assumes a disputed fact is true when it has not been established in the case.

(6) Cumulative

An attorney is generally not permitted to ask a question that has already been asked and answered. More repetition is allowed on cross-examination than on direct, but if it is apparent that the cross-examiner is not moving forward, the judge may disallow the question.

3. Use of Memoranda by Witness

A witness cannot read her testimony from a prepared memorandum. However, a memorandum may be used in certain circumstances to refresh the recollection of the witness, to substitute for the witness's forgotten testimony upon authentication of the memorandum, or in cross-examination of the witness.

Ⅲ. Opinion Testimony

The word opinion used in this context includes all opinions, inferences, conclusions, and other subjective statements made by a witness. A basic premise of our legal system is that, in general, witnesses should testify as to facts within their personal knowledge and that the trier of fact should draw any conclusions therefrom. Therefore, the general policy of the law is to restrict the admissibility of opinion evidence, expect in cases where the courts are sure that it will be necessary or at least helpful. Of course, the difference between "fact" and "opinion" is matter of degree. Therefore, there cannot be any clear-cut opinion rule.

1. Opinion Testimony by Lay Witnesses

(1) Opinion by lay witnesses is generally inadmissible. However, there are many cases where, from the nature of the subject matter, no better evidence can be obtained. In these cases, where the event is likely to be perceived as a whole impression (e.g., intoxication, speed) rather than as more specific components, opinions by lay witnesses are generally admitted.

(2) Situations Where Opinions of Lay Witnesses Are Admissible

a. General Appearance or Condition of Person

Testimony that a person was "elderly," "about 60 years old," "strong," "weak," or "ill" would be admissible, but testimony that a person is suffering from specific diseases or specific injuries usually requiring knowledge of an expert would not.

b. State of Emotion

A witness would be permitted to testify that a person appeared "angry" or "was joking" but probably not that two persons were "in love" or appeared to have a strong affection for each other.

c. Matters Involving Sense Recognition

A witness would be permitted to testify that an object was "heavy," "red," "bulky," or that a certain beverage tasted like whiskey.

d. Voice or Handwriting Identification

Lay opinion is permissible and often essential to identify telephone voices and handwriting. In these instances a foundation must first be aid to show familiarity with the voice or handwriting.

e. Speed of Moving Object

f. Value of Own Service

g. Rational or Irrational Nature of Another's Conduct (Sanity)

h. Intoxication

(3) Situations Where Opinions of Lay Witnesses Are Not Admissible

a. Agency or Authorization

When agency or authorization is in issue, the witness generally may not state a conclusion as to her authorization. Rather she must be asked by whom she was employed and the nature, terms, and surrounding circumstances of her employment.

b. Contract or Agreement

When the existence of an express contract is in issue, the witness generally may not state her opinion that an agreement was made. Rather she must be asked about the facts, the existence or nonexistence of which establish whether a contract existed.

2. Opinion Testimony by Expert Witnesses

(1) Requirements of Expert Testimony

The expert may state an opinion or conclusion, provided the following conditions are satisfied:

a. Subject Matter Must Be Appropriate for Expert Testimony

Under Federal Rule 702, expert opinion testimony is admissible if the subject matter is one where scientific, technical, or other specialized knowledge would assist the trier of fact in understanding the evidence or determining a fact in issue. This test of assistance to the trier of fact subdivides into two requirements:

(a) The opinion must be relevant (i. e., it must "fit" the facts of the case); and

(b) The methodology underlying the opinion must be reliable (i. e., the proponent of the expert testimony must satisfy the trial judge by a preponderance of the evidence that (i) the opinion is based on sufficient facts or data; (ii) the opinion is the product of reliable principles and methods; and (iii) the expert has reliably applied the principles and methods to the facts of the case).

b. The Witness Must Be Qualified as an Expert

To testify as an expert, a person must have special knowledge, skill, experience, training, or education sufficient to qualify him as an expert on the subject to which his testimony relates.

c. The Expert Must Possess Reasonable Probability Regarding His Opinion

The expert must possess reasonable certainty or probability regarding his opinion. If the opinion of the expert is a mere guess or speculation, it is inadmissible.

Example: It would be error to permit plaintiff's medical expert to testify that plaintiff's symptoms "suggested" diabetes and "indicated" that the disease was caused by the accident.

d. The Expert's Opinion Must Be Supported by Proper Factual Basis

The expert's opinion may be based upon one or more of these three possible sources of information: (i) facts that the expert knows from his own observation; (ii) facts presented in evidence at the trial and submitted to the expert, usually by hypothetical question; or (iii) facts not in evidence that were supplied to the expert out of court, and which are of a type reasonably relied upon by experts in the particular field in forming opinions on the subject. Note that the expert may give opinion testimony on direct examination without disclosing the basis of the opinion, unless the court orders otherwise. however, the expert may be required to disclose such information on cross-examination.

(2) Opinion May Embrace Ultimate Issue

Federal Rule 704 (a) and the modern trend repudiate the traditional prohibition on opinions embracing the ultimate issue in the case. The rule provides: "Testimony in the form of an opinion or inference otherwise admissible is not objectionable because it embraces the ultimate issue to be decided by the trier of fact." Note, however, that to be admissible under the Federal Rules, the expert opinion must "assist the trier of fact" to understand the evidence or determine a fact in issue. Thus, an expert's conclusion that "X had testamentary capacity" is still inadmissible because it is not helpful to the jury.

Ⅳ. Cross-Examination

1. Necessity for Cross-Examination

Cross-examination of adverse witnesses is a matter of right in every trial of a disputed issue of fact. It is recognized as the most efficacious truth-discovering device. The principal basis for excluding hearsay is that the declarant whose testimony is offered cannot be subjected to the test of cross-examination. If adequate cross-examination is prevented by the death, illness, or refusal of a witness to testify on cross-examination, the direct examination is rendered incompetent and will be stricken.

2. Scope of Cross-Examination

Although a party is entitled as of right to some cross-examination, the extent or scope of cross-examination, like the order of calling witness, is frequently a matter of judicial discretion. Cross-examination is hedged about by far fewer rules than is direct examination. On cross-examination, leading questions are permissible, as are, obviously, efforts at impeachment. The most significant restriction is that the scope of cross-examination cannot range beyond the subject matter of the direct examination. This restriction does not apply to inquiries directed toward impeachment of the witness.

Ⅴ. Credibility—Impeachment

Impeachment means the casting of an adverse reflection on the veracity of the witness. The primary method of impeachment is by cross-examination of the witness under attack, although witnesses are often impeached by extrinsic proof that casts doubt on credibility. In terms of relevance, any matter that tends to prove or disprove the credibility of the witness should be admitted here.

Chapter 5
Testimonial Evidence

Impeachment on Collateral Matter

Where a witness makes a statement not directly relevant to the issues in the case, the rule against impeachment (other than by cross-examination) on a **collateral matter**[①] applies to bar the opponent from proving the statement untrue either by extrinsic contradictory facts or by a prior inconsistent statement. The purpose of the rule is to avoid the possibility of unfair surprise, confusion of issues, and undue consumption of time resulting from the attempt to prove and disprove facts that are not directly relevant.

Ⅵ. Objections, Exceptions, Offers of Proof

1. Objections

Unless an objection is made by opposing counsel, almost any kind of evidence will be admitted. Failure to object is deemed a waiver of any ground for objection. The trial judge need not raise grounds for objection on his own, but may take notice of plain errors affecting substantial rights (e.g., admission of coerced confession not objected to by defense).

(1) Objections to Trial Testimony

Objections should be made after the question, but before the answer, if it is apparent that the question calls for inadmissible matter (e.g., hearsay) or that the question is in improper form (e.g., leading). Otherwise, a motion to strike must be made as soon as the witness's answer emerges as inadmissible.

(2) Objections to Deposition Testimony

Objections to the form of question (e.g., leading) are waived unless made during the deposition, thereby affording counsel an opportunity to correct the form of his question. An objection based on a testimonial privilege should also be made then, lest it be deemed waived. However, objection going to the substance of a question or answer (e.g., relevance, hearsay) can be postponed until the deposition is offered in evidence.

(3) Specificity of Objections

An objection may be either general ("I object") or specific ("Object, hearsay").

---

① （与争议问题无直接关系的）间接问题，间接事实

(4) "Opening the Door"

One who introduces evidence on a particular subject thereby asserts its relevance and cannot complain, expects on grounds other than relevance, if his adversary thereafter offers evidence on the same subject. And counsel need not "stand" on his overruled relevance objection; he can offer counterevidence without thereby abandoning his relevance objection.

2. Exceptions

The common law rule requiring a party to "except" from an adverse trial court ruling in order to preserve the issue for appeal has been abolished in most jurisdictions. In some states, however, a writing motion for new trial, specifying the grounds, may be required.

3. Offers of Proof

On some occasions, error cannot be based on exclusion of evidence unless there has been an "offer of proof" that discloses the nature, purpose, and admissibility of the rejected evidence.

VII. Testimonial Privileges

Testimonial privileges, which permit one to refuse to disclose and prohibit others from disclosing certain sorts of confidential information in judicial proceedings, have two basic reasons for their existence: (i) practicality, and (ii) society's desire to encourage certain relationships by ensuring their confidentiality, even at the high price of losing valuable information.

Some of the testimonial privileges are frankly grounded on hardheaded practicality. The particular kind of disclosure could not be obtained, as a practical matter, even if there were no privilege. Many priests, even when confronted by a contempt of court citation, would breach the priest-penitent confidential nature even at the expense of the loss of information relevant to the issues of a law suit. These relationships will be encouraged if confidentiality, when desired, is assured. To put it more concretely, persons might forgo needed medical attention or be less than candid with legal counsel were there no guarantee that communications made during the physician-patient and attorney-client relationships would be accorded confidential status in legal proceedings.

Chapter 5
Testimonial Evidence

1. Attorney-Client Privilege

The first testimonial privilege ever established was the attorney-client privilege. It is a common law privilege, although in some jurisdictions it has now been codified by statute. It carries with its fewer exceptions than any other privilege.

Essentially, communications between an attorney and client, made during professional consultation, are privileged from disclosure. In other words, a client has a privilege to refuse to disclose, and to prevent others from disclosing confidential communications between herself (or her representative) and her attorney (or her attorney's representative). Objects and preexisting documents are not protected.

a. Attorney-Client Relationship

The attorney-client privilege required that the attorney-client relationship exists at the time of the communications. The client, or his representative, must be seeking the professional services of the attorney at the crucial time. Retainer negotiations, involving disclosures made before the attorney has decided to accept or decline the case, are covered if the other requirements of the privilege are present.

b. Confidential Communication

A communication is "confidential" if it was not intended to be disclosed to third persons, other than those to whom disclosure would be in furtherance of the rendition of legal services to the client or those who are necessary for the transmission of the communication. Communications made in the known presence and hearing of a stranger are not privileged.

c. Duration of Privilege

The attorney-client privilege applies indefinitely. Termination of the attorney-client relationship does not terminate the privilege. The privilege even continues to apply after the client's death. Rationale: Knowing that communications will remain confidential ever after death encourages the clients to communicate fully and frankly with her attorney.

2. Physician-Patient Privilege

The physician-patient privilege is a statutory privilege, which has not been adopted in all jurisdictions. However, in a substantial number of jurisdictions, a physician (and, in some jurisdictions, a dentist or nurse) is foreclosed from divulging in judicial proceedings information that he acquired while attending a patient in a professional capacity, which information was necessary to enable the physician to act in his professional capacity.

(1) Elements of Physician-Patient Privilege

 a. Professional member of relationship must be present;

 b. Information must be acquired while attending patient;

 c. Information must be necessary for treatment.

(2) Nonapplicability of the Privilege

 a. Patient puts physical condition in issue;

 b. In aid of wrongdoing;

 c. Agreement to waive the privilege;

 d. Federal cases applying federal law of privilege.

3. Psychotherapist/Social Worker-Client Privilege

The United States Supreme Court recognizes a federal privilege for communications between a psychotherapist (psychiatrist or psychologist) or licensed social worker and his client. Thus, the federal courts and virtually all of the states recognize a privilege for this type of confidential attorney-client privilege.

Jaffee v. Redmond
518 U.S. 1(1996)

Issue

Whether a psychotherapist-patient privilege was recognized under Rule 501 of the Federal Rules of Evidence. The U.S. Supreme Court granted certiorari to review a decision of the Seventh Circuit that recognized the existence of a psychotherapist-patient privilege and held that confidential communications of a police officer with a licensed social worker were protected from compelled disclosure.

Chapter 5
Testimonial Evidence

Index Topic

Confidentiality/Psychotherapist-Patient Privilege

Facts

The defendant police officer shot and killed an individual to prevent the stabbing of another person. The decedent's family brought suit against the officer alleging constitutional violations and seeking damages for wrongful death. After the shooting, the officer sought counseling from a licensed clinical social worker. Plaintiffs sought to obtain information regarding the contents of the counseling sessions. The defendant refused, citing psychotherapist-patient privilege. The trial court found that the Federal Rules of Evidence did not provide for a psychotherapist-patient privilege. When the defendant continued to refuse to comply, the trial court instructed the jury that it could draw an adverse inference from this refusal and could presume that the contents of these communications would be unfavorable to the defendant. The jury awarded the plaintiffs $545,000 in damages. The Seventh Circuit reversed, finding that the Federal Rules of Evidence did, indirectly, recognize a psychotherapist-patient privilege because all fifty states recognized some sort of psychotherapist-patient privilege. The court reasoned that recognition of the privilege would serve to encourage troubled individuals as well as those who witness, participate in, and are intimately affected by acts of violence in today's stressful, crime ridden environment, to seek the necessary professional counseling and to assist mental health professionals to succeed in their endeavors. The plaintiffs sought review in the U.S. Supreme Court.

APA's Position

APA submitted an amicus brief arguing that: (1) Federal Rule of Evidence 501 authorizes the federal courts to recognize a psychotherapist-patient privilege; (2) common law principles, applied in the light of reason and experience, strongly support recognition of a psychotherapist-patient privilege in that (a) psychot herapeutic clients have a strong expectation of confidentiality, (b) confidentiality is essential to the success of psychotherapy, (c) society has a strong interest in fostering the psychotherapeutic relationship and in protecting client privacy, and (d) the benefits of the psychotherapist-patient privilege outweigh its costs; and (3) applying the psychotherapist-patient privilege using a case-by-case balancing approach would substantially undermine the value of the privilege.

Results

The U. S. Supreme Court affirmed the Seventh Circuit decision. The Court decision supported the arguments presented in the APA brief.

4. Husband-Wife Privilege

Under the early rule, spouses were absolutely incompetent to testify for or against each other during the period of marriage, and this incompetency had the same effect as the Dead Man Acts—neither spouse could speak out in court if the other spouse was a party. The prohibition against spousal testimony in favor of the party-spouse has been abandoned. However, there remains in many states a rule that permits an accused in a criminal case to prevent his spouse from testifying against him. Apart from this rule of spousal immunity, a modern separate privilege exists in most jurisdictions that protects confidential communications during marriage. Thus, there are two separate privileges as follows: (i) the privilege not to testify against a spouse in a criminal case—inter-spousal immunity, and (ii) the privilege for confidential marital communications.

Trammel v. United States
445 U.S. 40, 100 S.Ct. 906, 62 L.Ed.2d 186 (1980)

Trammel and two other guys were arrested and charged with drug smuggling. Trammel's wife was listed among the unindicted co-conspirators. Trammel's wife had also been arrested in possession of drugs, but had agreed to testify in exchange for immunity.

At trial, when his wife took the stand to testify, Trammel objected on the grounds that her testimony was not admissible because it was protected by spousal privilege. The Trial Judge allowed her to testify to any act she observed during the marriage and to any communications made in the presence of a third person. However, confidential communications between Trammel and his wife were inadmissible because of spousal privilege.

Historically, there were two different types of spousal privilege: Spousal

Testimonial Privilege said that a spouse could never testify against the other spouse on any issue, as long as they were married. Once the marriage was over, this bar was lifted. Spousal Communications Privilege said that a spouse could never testify about communications between the two made during the marriage, even after they got divorced.

The Trial Court convicted Trammel of drug smuggling. He appealed.

The Appellate Court affirmed. Trammel appealed. The Appellate Court found that the spousal testimonial privilege did not prohibit voluntary testimony of a spouse who appears as an unindicted co-conspirator under a grant of immunity. The US Supreme Court affirmed.

The Court noted that the leading case was *Hawkins v. United States* (358 U.S. 74 (1958)), which followed the tradition that one spouse cannot testify against the other unless both consent. Under Hawkins, all testimony by the spouse was inadmissible. This was much broader than other privileges (like lawyer-client), which only applied to confidential communications. However, the Court noted that under FRE 501, the courts have the authority to continue the evolutionary development of privilege rules.

The Court found that the spousal testimonial privilege rule should be similar to other privileges. The spouse is not barred from testifying if they chose to do so. However, they cannot be compelled to do so. Basically, the testifying spouse is the only one who can raise the issue of privilege. If they want to waive it, the accused spouse can't stop the testimony.

The spousal communications privilege may be asserted by either spouse in both civil and criminal proceedings; the spousal testimonial privilege may only be claimed by the testifying spouse, and is only recognized in criminal proceedings.

5. Privilege Against Self-Incrimination

Under the Fifth Amendment of the United States Constitution, a witness cannot be compelled to testify against himself. Thus, any witness may refuse to answer any question whose answer might incriminate him, and a criminal defendant may use the privilege to refuse to take the witness's behalf.

6. Clergy-Penitent Privilege

A person has a privilege to refuse to disclose, and to prevent others from disclosing a confidential communication by the person to a member of the clergy in the clergy member's capacity as a spiritual adviser. A member of the clergy can be a minister, priest, rabbi, or other similar functionary of religious organization, or reasonably believed to be so by the person consulting him. This privilege is very similar in its operation to the attorney-client privilege.

7. Professional Journalist Privilege

Whether a journalist may be forced to divulge his source of information has been a much litigated question and the subject of a trend of statutory authority. The Supreme Court has held that there is no constitutional protection for a journalist's source of information, so the existence of the privilege is limited to individual state statutes which have been recently growing in number.

8. Governmental Privileges

(1) Identity of Informer

The federal government, or a state, generally has a privilege to refuse to disclose the identity of a person who has furnished a law enforcement officer with information purporting to reveal the commission of a crime.

(2) Official Information

This is a general catch-all privilege that attaches to certain communication made by or to public officials. Official information has been defined as information not open to the public, relating to the internal affairs of the government or its subdivisions. It applies to some fairly low-level communications made by or to officials (e.g., a judge's communications to his law clerk).

VIII. Exclusion and Sequestration[①] of Witnesses

Upon a party's request, the trial judge will order witnesses to be excluded from the courtroom so they cannot listen to the testimony of witnesses. The

---

① 隔离,扣押,查封

Chapter 5
Testimonial Evidence

trial judge may also do this on his own motion. However, Federal Rule 615 prohibits the exclusion of: (i) a party or a designated officer or employee of a party, (ii) a person whose presence is essential to the presentation of a party's case, or (iii) a person statutorily authorized to be present.

Chapter 6

The Hearsay Rule

I. Statement of the Rule

The Federal Rules define hearsay as "a statement, other than one made by the declarant while testifying at the trial or hearing, offered in evidence to prove the truth of the matter asserted." [Fed. R. Evid. 801(c)] The rule against hearsay is probably the most important exclusionary rule of evidence. If a statement is hearsay, and no exception to the rule is applicable, the evidence must be excluded upon appropriate objection to its admission. [Fed. R. Evid. 802] An out-of-court statement that incorporates other hearsay is known as "hearsay." This type of statement is admissible only if each part of the statement falls within an exception to the hearsay rule. If one part of the statement is inadmissible, the entire statement is inadmissible.

1. Reason for Excluding Hearsay

The reason for excluding hearsay is that the adverse party was denied the opportunity to cross-examine the declarant; i.e., the party had no chance to test the declarant's perception (how well did he observe the event he purported to describe), his memory (did he really remember the details he related), his sincerity (was he deliberately falsifying), and his ability to relate (did he really mean to say what now appears to be thrust of his statement).

2. "Statement"

For purpose of the hearsay rule, "statement" is (i) an oral or written assertion, or (ii) nonverbal conduct intended as an assertion. [Fed. R. Evid. 801(a)]

(1) Oral Statements

"Statement" includes oral statement (i.e., where the witness testifies that somebody said "...").

(2) Writings

Any written document that is offered in evidence constitutes a "statement" for hearsay purposes.

(3) Assertive Conduct

Conduct intended by the actor to be a substitute for words (e.g., the nod of the declarant's head indicating yes) is a "statement" within the meaning.

(4) Nonassertive Conduct

3. "Offered to Prove the Truth of the Matter"

This is the most crucial component of the hearsay rule. The basic reason for rejecting hearsay evidence is that a statement offered to prove that which it asserts is true may not be trustworthy without the guarantees of cross-examination. However, where the out-of-court statement is introduced for any purpose other than to prove the truth of the matter asserted, there is need to cross-examine the declarant, and so the statement is not hearsay.

II. Statements That Are Nonhearsay under the Federal Rules

Federal Rule 801(d) removes from the definition of hearsay certain statements that would be hearsay under the common law definition. Since the following types of statements are not hearsay, when relevant, they are admissible as substantive evidence.

1. Prior Statements by Witnesses

Certain statements by a person who testifies at the trial or hearing, and is subject to cross-examination about the statement, are not hearsay.

2. Admissions by Party-Opponent

Although traditionally an exception to the hearsay rule, an admission by a party-opponent is not hearsay at all under the Federal Rules. [Fed. R. Evid. 801 (d)(2)] An admission is a statement made or act done that amounts to prior acknowledgment by one of the parties to an action of one of the relevant facts. If the party said or did something that now turns out to be inconsistent with his contentions at trial, the law simply regards him as estopped from preventing its admission into evidence. The party who made the prior statement can hardly complain about not having had the opportunity to cross-examine himself. He said it. He is struck with it. Let him explain it if he can.

III. Hearsay Exceptions—Declarant Unavailable

Certain kinds of hearsay are considered to have special guarantees of trustworthiness and are recognized exceptions to the hearsay exclusion. The Federal Rules treat the exceptions in two groups—those that require the declarant be unavailable, and those under which the declarant's availability is immaterial. This section covers the five important exceptions requiring the declarant's unavailability: (i) former testimony, (ii) statements against interest, (iii) dying declarations, (iv) statement of personal or family history, and (v) statements offered against party procuring declarant's unavailability.

1. Former Testimony

The testimony of a now unavailable witness given at another hearing or in a deposition taken in accordance with law is admissible in a subsequent trial as long as there is a sufficient similarity of parties and issues so that the opportunity to develop testimony or cross-examine at the prior hearing was meaningful. [Fed. R. Evid. 804(b)(1)] This exception is the clearest example of hearsay with special guarantees of trustworthiness, since the former testimony was given during formal proceedings and under oath by a witness subject to cross-examination.

2. Statements Against Interest

A statement of a person, now unavailable as a witness, (may be admissible if it was) against that person's pecuniary, proprietary, or penal interest when it was made. as well as collateral facts contained in the statement, is admissible under the statement against interest exception to the hearsay rule.

3. Dying Declarations—Statements under Belief of Impending Death

In a prosecution for homicide or a civil action, a declaration made by the now unavailable declarant while believing his death was imminent that concerns the cause or circumstances of what he believed to be his impending death is

Chapter 6
The Hearsay Rule

admissible. [Fed. R. Evid. 804(b)(2)] The declarant need not actually die, but he must be unavailable at the time the declaration is offered.

4. Statements of Personal or Family History

Statements concerning birth, marriage, divorce, death, relationship, etc., are admissible under an exception to the hearsay rule. Hearsay statements concerning family history are often necessary to prove the facts of people's everyday lives. For example, most people rely on the hearsay statement of others for knowledge of where they were born, who their relatives are, etc.

5. Statements Offered Against Party Procuring Declarant's Unavailability

The statements of a person (now unavailable as a witness) are admissible when offered against a party who has engaged or acquiesced in wrongdoing that intentionally procured the declarant's unavailability. [Fed. R. Evid. 804 (b)(6)] In effect, a party forfeits his right to object on hearsay grounds to the admission of an unavailable declarant's statements when the party's deliberate wrongdoing procured the unavailability of the declarant as a witness.

IV. Hearsay Exceptions—Declarant's Availability Immaterial

1. Present State of Mind

A statement of a declarant's then-existing state of mind, emotion, sensation, or physical condition is admissible. [Fed. R. Evid. 803(3)] The exception is based on the need to obtain evidence as to the declarant's internal state of mind or emotion. It must usually be made under circumstances of apparent sincerity. The statement is often offered to establish the intent of a person, either as a fact to be proved as such (domicile, criminal intent) or as a basis for a circumstantial inference that the intent was probably carried out.

2. Excited Utterances

A declaration made by a declarant during or soon after a startling event is admissible. The declaration must be made under the stress of excitement produced by the startling event. The declaration must concern the immediate facts of the startling occurrence. [Fed. R. Evid. 803(2)] The spontaneousness of such a declaration and the consequent lack of opportunity or reflection and deliberate fabrication provide an adequate guarantee of its trustworthiness.

3. Declarations of Physical Condition

(1) Present Bodily Condition—Admissible

Generally, declarations of present bodily condition are admissible as an exception to the hearsay rule, even though they are not made to physician. They may be made to a spouse, relative, friend, or any other person. Of course, declarations made to a physician are admissible. [Fed. R. Evid. 803 (3)] Such declarations relate to symptoms, including the existence of pain. Because they are contemporaneous with the symptoms, they are more reliable than present testimony based upon recollection.

(2) Past Bodily Condition—Admissible If to Assist Diagnosis or Treatment

4. Business Records

Any writing or record, whether in the form of an entry in a book or otherwise, made as a memorandum or record of any act, transaction, occurrence, or event is admissible in evidence as proof of that act, transaction, occurrence, or event, if made in the regular courts of any business; and if it was the regular course of such business to make it at the time of the act, transaction, occurrence, or event or within a reasonable time thereafter.

5. Past Recollection Record

Witness are permitted to refresh their memories by looking at almost anything—either before or while testifying. This is called present recollection revived. However, if the witness's memory cannot be revived, a party may wish to introduce a memorandum that the witness made at or near the time of the event. Use of the writing to prove the facts contained therein raises a hearsay problem; but if a proper foundation can be laid, the contents of the memorandum may be introduced into evidence under the past recollection record exception to the hearsay rule. The rationale is that a writing made by an observer when the facts were still fresh in her mind is probably more liable than her testimony on the stand—despite the fact that cross-examination is curtailed.

6. Official Records and Other Official Writings

(1) Public Records and Reports

The exception for public records and report is necessary to avoid having public officers leave their jobs constantly to appear in court and testify to acts done in their official capacity, especially since the entrant could probably add nothing to the record. Also, such records are presumed to be trustworthy because officials are under a duty to record properly that which they do.

Beech Aircraft Corp. v. Rainey
488 U.S. 153, 109 S. Ct. 439, 102 L. Ed. 2d 445, 1988 U.S.

Brief Fact Summary

The spouses of the plaintiffs died during flight training when their plane was unable to recover from an evasive maneuver. The defendant, Beech Aircraft Corp. (the "defendant") attempted to admit an investigative report that concluded the accident was caused by pilot error.

Synopsis of Rule of Law

Federal Rules of Evidence ("F.R.E.) Rule 803(8)(c) should be construed broadly to ensure reports that contain opinions or conclusions are not automatically excluded from evidence.

Facts

The deceased spouses of the plaintiffs died during naval flight training. The cause of the accident put forth by the plaintiffs was a malfunctioning fuel control system. The defendant contended that pilot error caused the accident. To support their contention, the defendant submitted a Judge Advocate General ("JAG") investigative report that included opinions and conclusions from the investigator.

The defendant called one of the plaintiffs as an adverse witness and had the plaintiff comment on a portion of a letter that the plaintiff wrote to the naval investigators. On cross-examination, the plaintiffs were not allowed to produce additional portions of the letter on the grounds that it was an opinion.

Issue

Whether statements in the form of conclusions or opinions are by their nature excluded from F.R.E. Rule 803(8)(c)?

Whether plaintiff should be allowed to introduce further portions of evidence that were only partially admitted in order to clarify the admitted portions?

Held

The court allowed the investigation report to be admitted under F. R. E. Rule 803(8)(c) despite the presence of opinions and conclusions by the investigator. The court wanted a broad interpretation of the Rule to encompass records that may have these statements and yet have a high level of trustworthiness.

The plaintiff should be allowed to introduce other portions of a record under the "rule of completeness," a doctrine that ensures that misunderstandings or distortions of partially admitted records will be clarified.

Dissent

The dissenting judge believed that plaintiff's counsel did not properly argue for the admission of the additional portions of the record that was partially admitted, and therefore the lower court decision should stand.

Discussion

The court analyzed precedent, legislative history and treatises before concluding that "facts" as defined in the Federal Rule should include conclusions or inferences that are based on facts. The chief concern is whether the record is trustworthy, and this is why the Rule includes the "escape clause" that refuses admittance of records where circumstances lead to its unreliability.

The rule of completeness was used here to allow cross-examination by the plaintiff's own attorney in order to clarify portions of the disclosed letter. The barrier here is not the trustworthiness of the document, but rather the unfairness of allowing only selected portions of a letter to get introduced.

(2) Records of Vital Statistics

Records of births, deaths, and marriages are admissible if the report was made to a public office pursuant to requirement of law.

(3) Statement of Absence of Public Record

Evidence in the form of a certification or testimony from the custodian of public records that she has diligently searched and failed to find a record is admissible to prove that a matter was not recorded, or, inferentially, that a matter did not occur.

Chapter 6
The Hearsay Rule

(4) Prior Criminal Conviction—Felony Conviction Admissible

The Federal Rules specifically provide that judgments of felony convictions are admissible in both criminal and civil actions to prove any fact essential to the judgment. In the Rules, felony convictions are defined as crimes punishable by death or imprisonment in excess of one year. [Fed. R. Evid. 803 (22)] The convictions that may be used are limited to felonies because persons may choose not to defend misdemeanor charges.

7. Ancient Documents and Documents Affecting Property Interests

Under the Federal Rules, statements in any authenticated document 20 years old or more are admissible. [Fed. R. Evid. 803 (16)] Moreover, in contrast to the traditional view that only ancient property-disposing documents qualified for the exception, statements in a document affecting an interest in property (e. g., deed, will, etc) are admissible regardless of the age of the document.

8. Learned Treatises

Many courts do not admit statements from standard scientific treatises or authoritative works as substantive proof, limiting admissibility to use as impeachment of the qualifications of the expert witness. The Federal Rules recognize an exception to the hearsay rule for learned treatises.

9. Reputation

In addition to reputation testimony concerning a person's character [Fed. R. Evid. 803 (21)], reputation evidence concerning someone's personal or family history [Fed. R. Evid. 803 (19)] or concerning land boundaries or the community's general history [Fed. R. Evid. 803 (20)] is admissible hearsay.

10. Family Records

Statements of fact concerning personal or family history contained in family Bibles, genealogies, jewelry engraving, engravings on urns, crypts, or tombstones, or the like are admissible hearsay.

11. Market Reports

Market reports and other published compilations (lists, directories, etc.) are admissible if generally used and relied upon by the public or by persons in a particular occupation.

V. Residual "Catch-all" Exception of Federal Rules

The Federal Rules provide a general catch-all exception for hearsay statements not covered by specific exceptions. [Fed. R. Evid. 807] There are three requirements for a statement to be admitted under the catch-all exception:

1. "Trustworthiness" Factor

First of all, the statement must have "circumstantial guarantees of trustworthiness" that are equivalent to those of statements admitted under other hearsay exceptions.

2. "Necessity" Factor

The statement must be offered on a material fact, and must be more probative as to that fact than any other evidence which the proponent can reasonably produce so that the "interests of justice" will be served by its admission.

3. Notice to Adversary

Finally, the proponent must give notice in advance of trial to the adverse party as to the nature of the statement (including the name and address of the declarant) so that the adversary has an opportunity to prepare to meet it.

Chapter 7

Procedural Considerations

Ⅰ. Burdens of Proof

1. Burden of Producing or Going Forward with Evidence

(1) Produce Sufficient Evidence to Raise Fact Question for Jury

This defines the burden of one party to introduce sufficient evidence to avoid judgment against her as a matter of law. It is the burden of producing sufficient evidence to create a fact question of the issue involved, so that the issue may appropriately reach the jury. The burden of producing evidence is a critical mechanism for judicial control of the trial. Although the burden is usually cast upon the party who has pleaded the existence of the fact, the burden as to this fact may shift to the adversary when the pleader has discharged her initial duty.

(2) *Prima Facie* Case May Shift Burden of Production

Consider Plaintiff v. Defendant in a negligence action. Plaintiff offers evidence in her case-in-chief of Defendant's negligence. Defendant's motion for a nonsuit made at the conclusion of Plaintiff's case is denied. This denial reflects a judicial ruling that Plaintiff has made out a *prima facie* case of Defendant's negligence. Put it another way, it means that Plaintiff has met her burden of going forward with evidence on the negligence issue.

2. Burden of Persuasion (Proof)

(1) Determined by Jury after All Evidence Is In

This is what usually meant when the term "burden of proof" is used. This burden becomes a crucial factor only if the parties have sustained their burdens of production and only when all the evidence is in. When the time of decision comes, the jury must be instructed how to decide the issue if their minds remain in doubt. There are no tie games in the litigation process. Either the plaintiff or the defendant must win. If, after all the proof is in, the issue is equally balanced in the minds of the jury, then the party with the burden of persuasion must lose.

(2) Jury Instructed as to Which Party Has Burden of Persuasion

The burden of persuasion does not shift from party to party during the course of the trial simply because it need not be allocated until it is time for a decision by the trier of fact. The jury will be told which party has the burden of persuasion and what the quantum of proof should be. The jury is never told anything about the burden of going forward with evidence because that burden is matter for the judge alone.

II. Presumptions

A presumption is a rule that requires that a particular inference be drawn from an ascertained set of facts. It is a form of substitute proof or evidentiary shortcut, in that proof of the presumed fact is rendered unnecessary once evidence has been introduced of the basic fact that gives rise to the presumption. Presumptions are established for a wide variety of overlapping policy reasons. In some cases, the presumption serves to correct an imbalance resulting from one party's superior access to the proof on a particular issue. In others, the presumption was created as a time saver to eliminate the need for proof of a fact that is highly probable in any event. In other words, the inference from the basic fact to the presumed fact is so probable and logical that it is sensible to assume the presumed fact upon proof of the basic fact. In still other situations, the presumption serves as a social or economic policy device. It operates to favor one contention by giving it the benefit of presumption and to correspondingly handicap the disfavored adversary.

1. Effect—Shift Burden of Production

Federal Rule 301 provides that a presumption imposes on the party against whom it is directed the burden of going forward with evidence to rebut the presumption. A presumption does not, however, shift to such party the burden of proof in the sense of the risk of nonpersuasion, which remains throughout the trial upon the party on whom it was originally cast.

2. Rebutting a Presumption

A presumption is overcome or destroyed when the adversary produces some evidence contradicting the presumed fact. In other words, the presumption is of no force or effect when sufficient contrary evidence is admitted. This is federal view adopted by Federal Rule 301 except where state law provides the rule of decision.

3. Specific Presumptions

The following are common rebuttable presumptions.

(1) Presumption of Legitimacy

The law presumes that every person is legitimate. The presumption applies to all cases where legitimacy is in dispute. The mere fact of birth gives rise to the presumption. The presumption is destroyed by evidence of illegitimacy that is "clear and convincing." For example, the presumption is overcome by proof of a husband's impotency, proof of lack of access, or the negative result of a properly conducted blood grouping test.

(2) Presumption Against Suicide

When the cause of death is in dispute, a presumption arises in civil (not criminal) cases that the death was not a suicide.

(3) Presumption of Sanity

Every person is presumed same until the contrary is shown. The presumption of sanity applies in criminal as well as civil cases.

(4) Presumption of Death from Absence

A person is presumed dead in any action involving the property of such person, the contractual or property right contingent upon his death, or the administration of his estate, if:

a. The person is unexplainably absent for a continuous period of seven years (death is deemed to have occurred on the last day of the seven-year period); and

b. He has not been heard from, or of, by those with whom he would normally be expected to communicate.

(5) Presumption from Ownership of Car—Agent Driver

Proof of ownership of a motor vehicle gives rise to the presumption that the power was the driver or that the driver was the owner's agent.

(6) Presumption of Chastity

There is a presumption that every person is chaste and virtuous.

(7) Presumption of Regularity

The general presumption is that no official or person acting under an oath of office will do anything contrary to his official duty, or omit anything that his official duty requires to be done.

(8) Presumption of Continuance

Proof of the existence of a person, an object, a condition, or a tendency at a given time raises a presumption that it continued for as long as is usual with things of that nature.

(9) Presumption of Mail Delivery

A letter shown to have been properly addressed, stamped, and mailed is presumed to have been delivered in the due course of mail. The presumption is said to be based upon the probability that officers of the government will perform their duty.

(10) Presumption of Solvency

A person is presumed solvent, and every debt is presumed collectible.

(11) Presumption of Bailee's Negligence

Upon proof of delivery of goods in good condition to bailee and failure of the bailee to return the goods in the same condition, there is a presumption that the bailee was negligent.

(12) Presumption of Marriage

Upon proof that a marriage ceremony was performed, it is presumed to have been legally performed and that the marriage is valid. A presumption of marriage also arises from cohabitation.

III. Relationship of Parties, Judge, and Jury

1. Party Responsibility

Ours is an adversarial adjudicative process and so, the focus is on party responsibility or, perhaps what is more to the point, on lawyer responsibility.

Chapter 7
Procedural Considerations

Very little happens in the litigation process unless some lawyer makes it happen by filing pleadings and motions, by initiating discovery, by entering into stipulations, by calling witness and offering exhitbits at trial, or by interposing objections to the admission of evidence. In other words, the parties, through their lawyers, frame the issues in a litigation by making allegations, admissions, and denials in their pleadings, and by entering into binding stipulations. They assume the burden of proving the issues they have raised. And then, by deciding which witnesses to call to the stand and what tangible exhibits to introduce (and by deciding to what they will object), they control the flow of evidence. But the parties and their lawyer are not the only ones to be allocated important responsibilities in the adversary trial process.

2. Court-Jury Responsibility

Under our system, the trial court is more umpire than advocate. The trial judge's primary responsibility is to fairly superintend[①] the trial; the judge is not permitted to become a partisan in it. As a general rule, questions of law are for the trial court to deal with, and questions of fact determination are for the jury, although trial judges frequently encounter the necessity of making preliminary fact determinations in connection with such matter as the admission or exclusion of evidence.

3. Preliminary Determination of Admissibility

(1) Role of Judge

Before the judge allows the proffered evidence to go to the jury, she must find that the proponent of the proffered evidence has introduced evidence sufficient to sustain a finding of the existence of the preliminary fact. The court may instruct the jury to determine whether the preliminary fact exists and to disregard the proffered evidence if the jury finds that the preliminary fact does not exist. Such an instruction may be desirable if the trier of fact would otherwise be confused, but with most questions of conditional relevancy the instruction will be unnecessary, since a rational jury will disregard these types of evidence anyway unless they believe in the existence of the foundational fact. If

---

① 管理，监督

the judge allows the introduction of evidence and then subsequently determines that a jury could not reasonably find that the preliminary fact exists, she must instruct the jury to disregard that evidence.

(2) Preliminary Facts Decided by Judge

a. Facts Affecting Competency of Evidence

The question of the existence or nonexistence of all preliminary facts other than those of conditional relevance must be determined by the court. In most cases, the questions which must be decided by the judge involve the competency of the evidence or the existence of a privilege.

b. Requirements for Privilege

Preliminary facts to establish the existence of privilege must be determined by the court. This must be so, or else a privilege might be ignored merely because there was sufficient evidence (and this might not be a great deal) for a jury to find it did not exist.

c. Requirements for Hearsay Exceptions

All preliminary fact questions involving the standards of trustworthiness of alleged exceptions to the hearsay rule also are determined by the court.

(3) Testimony by Accused Does Not Waive Privilege Against Self-Incrimination

An accused may testify as to many preliminary matter (e.g., circumstances surrounding allegedly illegal search) without subjecting herself to having to testify generally at the trial. Furthermore, while testifying upon a preliminary matter, an accused is not subject to cross-examination on other issues in the case.

(4) Judicial Power to Comment upon Evidence

The trial judge is expected to marshal or summarize the evidence when necessary. However, in most state courts, the trial judge may not comment upon the weight of the evidence or the credibility of witnesses. In federal court, the trial judge has traditionally been permitted to comment on the weight of the evidence and the credibility of witness.

(5) Power to Call Witness

The judge may call witness upon her own initiative and may interrogate any witnesses who testify but may not demonstrate partisanship for one side of the controversy.

Chapter 7
Procedural Considerations

(6) Rulings

A trial judge has an obligation to rule promptly on counsel's evidentiary objections and, when requested to do so by counsel, to state the grounds for her rulings.

(7) Instructions on Limited Admissibility of Evidence

When evidence that is admissible as to one party or for one purpose, but inadmissible as to another party or for another purpose, is admitted, the trial judge, on request, shall restrict the evidence to its proper scope and instruct the jury accordingly, e. g. , "Ladies and gentlemen of the jury, the testimony that you have just heard is receivable against the defendant Bushmat only and will in no way be considered by you as bearing on the guilt or innocence of the co-defendant Lishniss."

Exercises

I. Choose the best answer to the following questions:

1. Hearsay is _____
   A. legalese for opening arguments made in court.
   B. name of a chocolate factory in Penndylvnia.
   C. holding of a belief that goes against generally accepted standards.
   D. a term of art for the type of evidence that is often excluded, unless it falls within an accepted category.

2. Preponderance of the evidence is _____
   A. the burden of proving that the existence of a fact is more probable than its nonexistence.
   B. the burden of proving a fact beyond a reasonable doubt.
   C. the burden of proving a fact with only documentary evidence.
   D. the assumption that a fact is true for purposes of appeal.

3. Peter sued Don for breach of contract. The court admitted testimony by Peter that Don and his wife quarreled frequently, a fact of no consequence to the lawsuit. Don seeks to testify in response that he and his wife never quarreled. The court _____
   A. must permit Don to answer, if he had objected to Peter's testimony.

B. may permit Don to answer, whether or not he had objected to Peter's testimony.

C. may permit Don to answer, only if he had objected to Peter's testimony.

D. cannot permit Don to answer, whether or not he had objected to Peter's testimony.

4. In a will case, Paula seeks to prove her relationship to the testator Terrence by a statement in a deed from Terrence, "I transfer to my niece Paula..." The deed was recorded pursuant to statute in the office of the county recorder and was retained there. Paula called Recorder as a witness, who authenticated an enlarged print photocopy of the deed. The photocopy was made from microfilm records kept in the Recorder's office pursuant to statute. The photocopy is _____

    A. admissible as a record of a document affecting an interest in property.

    B. admissible as recorded recollection.

    C. inadmissible as hearsay, not within any recognized exception.

    D. inadmissible under the Best Evidence Rule.

Questions 5—10 are based on the following fact situation:

Driver ran into and injured Walker, a pedestrian. With Driver in his car were two of his friends, Paul and Ralph. Passerby saw the accident and called the police department, which sent Sheriff to investigate.

All of these people are available as potential witnesses in the case of *Walker v. Driver*. Walker alleges that Driver, while drunk, struck him as he walked in a duly marked crosswalk; and that he (Walker), as a consequence, suffered physical harm to his leg and foot.

5. Counsel for Walker calls Paul to testify that just before the accident, Ralph exclaimed, "Watch out! We're going to hit that man in the crosswalk!" The trial judge should rule that this testimony is _____

    A. admissible as a spontaneous utterance reflecting Ralph's impression at the time his statement was made.

    B. admissible since it constitutes a declaration against interest as to the declarant, Ralph.

    C. inadmissible because Ralph is available as a witness.

    D. inadmissible because the statement preceded the accident.

6. Walker's counsel calls Sheriff to testify that in Driver's presence Paul said, "We hit him while he was in the crosswalk," and that Driver remained silent. The trial judge should rule this testimony _____
   A. admissible because Driver, by his silence, has made Paul his agent and would thereby be bound by any admissible Paul made.
   B. admissible because Driver's silence constitutes an admissible of a party-opponent.
   C. inadmissible as "double hearsay" in that Driver's silence is being used to prove the truth of what Sheriff said Paul had stated.
   D. inadmissible unless Driver is first called and asked to admit or deny the incident.

7. Walker's counsel seeks to introduce the testimony of Joe concerning Walker's statement three days after the accident that, "My ankle hurts so much, I'd bet almost anything that it's broken." The trial judge should rule that this testimony is _____
   A. admissible as a statement of the declarant's pain and suffering.
   B. admissible to prove that Walker's ankle was permanently injured.
   C. inadmissible as a hearsay declaration.
   D. inadmissible because proof of Walker's medical condition is a subject for expert testimony only.

8. Driver's counsel wants to introduce testimony from Sheriff concerning a discussion between Sheriff and Passerby at the police station 1/2 hour after the accident, wherein Passerby, in response to a question by Sheriff, excitedly exclaimed in a loud voice, "Walker ran out in the street and was not in the crosswalk!" Sheriff duly recorded Passerby's statement in an official police report. The trial judge should rule that Sheriff's oral testimony is _____
   A. admissible as a spontaneous utterance.
   B. admissible as based on past recollection recorded.
   C. inadmissible because of the Best Evidence Rule.
   D. inadmissible as hearsay, not within any exception.

9. Walker's counsel wants to have Sheriff testify to the following statement made to him by Ralph, out of the presence of Driver: "We were returning

from a party at which we had all downed at least four beers." The trial judge should rule this testimony _____

A. admissible as an admission of a party.

B. admissible as a declaration against interest.

C. inadmissible as hearsay, not within any exception.

D. inadmissible as opinion.

10. On the evening of the day of the accident, Ralph wrote a letter to his sister in which he described the accident. After Ralph testified that he could not remember some details of the accident, Walker's counsel seeks to show him the letter to assist Ralph in his testimony on direct examination. The trial judge should rule that this is _____

A. permissible under the doctrine of present recollection refreshed.

B. permissible under the doctrine of past recollection recorded.

C. objectionable, if Driver's counsel was not shown the letter prior to the time it was shown to Ralph.

D. objectionable, unless the letter is read into evidence.

II. Essay Questions:

Question 1

Payne sued Don alleging an oral contract to paint Don's portrait for $4,000. Don denied making the contract. The following evidence was offered by the plaintiff:

(A) Witt testified that on May 1 he heard Payne offer to paint Don's portrait for $4,000 and heard Don say he'd let Payne know within a few days.

(B) Maida, Don's maid, testified that Don's wife was a lawyer, and that while eavesdropping at Don's bedroom door on the evening of May 2, she heard Don tell his wife: "Since oral agreements are valid, I'm going to call Payne and tell him to go ahead with the portrait."

(C) Belle testified that she personally operated an answering service which handled phone calls for several artists, including Payne, and remembered receiving a call for Payne on May 3. She testified that she did not recognize the voice and could not now remember the name of the caller or the message, but remembered that she had accurately recorded the caller's name and message immediately in her Telephone Log. After she identified the Log, an entry in it

Chapter 7
Procedural Considerations

("May 3, Mr. Don called Payne, said he accepted Payne's offer to paint Don's portrait for $4,000") was admitted into evidence.

(D) Belle abruptly died of a heart attack before cross-examination. The judge refused to strike her testimony and denied a defense motion to exclude the Telephone Log from evidence.

Assume that all appropriate objections to the foregoing evidence were made by Don. Discuss the admissibility of the evidence in (A), (B) and (C), and the ruling in (D).

Question 2

P received injuries in an automobile accident involving two vehicles driven by D and X. The cars collided at an intersection, causing the vehicle driven by D to strike P, a pedestrian. P brings suit against D for $15,000.

1. At the trial, P called Dr. Jones, who testified that P was brought to his office by D shortly after the accident, and that D said: "I'll pay this man's bill."

2. P testified that prior to trial there had been extensive settlement negotiations between the parties and that D had offered to pay $5,000 in full settlement of P's claim. P also testified that during these negotiations, D had said to him on one occasion: "I might have gone through the light a little late."

3. Mrs. D, D's wife, was called as a witness by P. She testified that one evening during dinner, and while the butler was present, D said to her: "I'm afraid that I'm at fault in that collision with X."

4. Bystander is called as a witness for D. Bystander testifies that, shortly after the accident, he heard X say: "I'm dying, I'm dying. The accident was all my fault. I'm glad I have insurance." Other evidence disclosed that X, although injured, was not in serious condition. However, X died shortly thereafter en route to the hospital when the ambulance into which he had been placed struck a tree.

Discuss the admissibility of the above items of evidence, assuming that all appropriate objections have been made.

Criminal Law

> 导 读 <<
>
> 美国的刑法和其他法律一样分为联邦和州两个系统,在这其中又以各个州的立法为基础。刑法的内容一般包括犯罪行为描述,犯罪构成和刑罚。
>
> **一、犯罪构成**
>
> 刑法使用"行为"(acts)和行为人的主观意图(the actor's intent)来界定犯罪,这就是犯罪"要件"(elements)。如果行为人的主观意图就是从事州立法或者国会界定为犯罪的行为,并且实际做了,那么这一行为就构成了犯罪。这种主观意图在拉丁语中称为 *mens rea*,为"犯罪意图"(guilty mind)之意。
>
> 在主观方面的普通粗心大意(ordinary carelessness)不是犯罪,但是非普通的粗心大意,即疏忽或者刑事性过失("recklessness" or "criminal negligence")可能构成犯罪。一般而言,如果行为人对某一重大且不合理(substantial and unjustifiable)的风险疏于注意,这种粗心大意就可能称为犯罪。
>
> 没有主观故意而从事了违法行为的,在道德上是清白的,这种情况叫做"事实认识错误"("mistake of fact"),可以否定犯罪意图的存在,但是"法律认识错误"(mistake of law)却不能否定犯罪意图的存在。
>
> 有的犯罪要求"明知"("knowing")要件。行为人明知行为犯法仍然从事该行为的,就会受到法律惩罚,至于"明知"的内容,则取决于法律规定为犯罪的行为是什么。
>
> 也有的犯罪要求行为具有"恶意"(malicious)。所谓恶意,

是与"故意"和"明知"同义的,因此,"恶意"要求并没有给犯罪意图增加内容。

具有"特定故意"(specific intent)的犯罪。法律要求,不能仅仅证明被告的行为是"明知"即可构成犯罪,还要证明被告在从事违法行为时,头脑之中有一项具体的目的。

所谓动机,一般是指违法行为背后的原因(reason)。公诉人一般将被告的动机证据作为旁证提交法院,证明被告的行为是故意或明知的。如果陪审团和法官知道被告的违法行为是有动机的,他们就很有可能相信被告具有犯罪意图。被告可以提供证据,证明自己没有犯罪动机,然后说明合理怀疑的存在。

二、犯罪的类别

普通法经常区分三种类别的犯罪:叛国罪、重罪和轻罪。叛国罪最严重,轻罪最轻微。重罪在美国被认为是最严重的一类犯罪。不少辖区将重罪又进行了进一步的划分:一个以极其残忍的方式犯了重罪的累犯,其所受到的刑罚,要重于一个残忍程度和伤害性稍低的犯了重罪的初犯所受的刑罚。

重罪与轻罪的划分标准,是刑罚的严厉程度。法律规定处以超过1年监禁的,一般就是重罪,如果判处的监禁是一年或更短,就是轻罪。

罪名分类的意义也体现在程序法中,尤其在法院管辖问题上。例如,各州的基层法院的管辖范围仅限于轻罪。在有些司法管辖区,对重罪的控告必须经过大陪审团,对轻罪则无须通过大陪审团。审理重罪时,被告人一般应当到庭,才可以做出判决,对轻罪犯则可以缺席审判。

Chapter 1

Basics of Criminal Law

For most people, familiarity with criminal law comes in fragments—from movies, television, and books. But when we become personally involved in the criminal law system, real-life issues come into focus and the need for information and assistance can arise quickly.

I. Reading Federal Criminal Statutes

Criminal laws in the United States exist at both the state and federal level. The federal criminal laws are compiled and published in the United States Code. Section 1001 of Title 18 of the United States Code provides that:

Whoever, in any matter within the jurisdiction of any department or agency of the United States knowingly and willfully falsifies, conceals or covers up by any trick, scheme, or device a material fact, or makes any false, fictitious or fraudulent statements or representations, or makes or uses any false writing or document knowing the same to contain any false, fictitious or fraudulent statement or entry, shall be fined under this title or imprisoned not more than five years or both.

That statute is written as a single sentence. It is difficult for anyone to read. If it could be broken down, it would be much easier to understand. Consider this revision of 18U.S.C. §1001:

Whoever, in any matter within the jurisdiction of any department or agency of the United States,

(1) Knowingly and willfully falsifies, conceals or covers up by any trick, scheme, or device a material fact, or

(2) Makes any false, fictitious or fraudulent statements or representations, or

(3) Makes or uses any false writing or document knowing the same to contain any false, fictitious or fraudulent statement or entry, shall be fined under this title or imprisoned not more than five years or both.

In this revised version of the statute, it is easy to see that there are three ways to violate the statute. It also becomes evident that some terms may be redundant. For example, is there really a difference between "conceals" and "covers up"? Or between "false" and "fictitious"? If it were within our power to amend the statue, we might make it clearer by breaking the statute into sections and eliminating the redundant language.

II. Interpretation of Criminal Statutes

Knowing how to read the law will help you determine whether it's been broken.

All criminal statutes define crimes in terms of required acts and a required state of mind, usually described as the actor's "intent." These requirements are known as the "elements" of the offense. A prosecutor must convince a judge or jury that the person charged with the crime (the defendant) did the acts and had the intent described in the law. For example, commercial burglary is commonly defined as entering a structure (such as a store) belonging to another person, with the intent to commit petty or grand theft (that is, to steal) or any felony. To convict a person of this offense, the prosecutor would have to prove three elements:

(1) The defendant entered the structure;

(2) The structure belonged to another person;

(3) At the time the defendant entered the structure, he intended to commit petty or grand theft or any felony.

Example: Steve was stopped by a security guard as he left a department store. His oversized backpack contained three pairs of expensive running shoes and nothing else. After interviewing the guard, who described seeing Steve take the shoes and leave without paying for them, the prosecuting attorney decided to charge Steve with burglary.

At the trial, the prosecutor was able to prove the following three elements:

(1) Steve entered a structure listed in the burglary statute. (The state statute included the term "store");

(2) The structure belonged to another person. It was easy to show that Steve did not own the store;

(3) Steve entered with the intent to commit theft. The prosecutor convinced the jury that Steve's use of an oversized, empty backpack was evidence that, at the time he entered the store, he was planning to stash stolen goods. The jury didn't buy Steve's claim that he only decided to steal the shoes (and therefore formed the intent to steal) after he had entered the store.

III. Criminal Laws and Their Sources

When a society and its government decide that certain conduct is dangerous to citizens, or damaging to the society as a whole, such conduct is labeled as "crime" and is made punishable by sanctions such as fines and imprisonment. Most crimes are identified in statutes that have been enacted by federal, state, and local government legislatures, in response to issues that affect the jurisdiction. For example, a city may determine that it is a crime to be drunk in public, while the federal government decides bank robbery is a federal crime, since most banks are federally insured.

Criminal statutes describe the type of conduct that has been deemed a crime, the mindset or intent required, and in some instances, the proper punishment. For example, the following "Burglary" statutes are from the California Penal Code:

Section 459. Every person who enters any house, room, apartment, tenement, shop, warehouse, store, mill, barn, stable, outhouse or other building, tent, vessel, etc.... with intent to commit grand or petit larceny or any felony is guilty of burglary.

Section 461. Burglary is punishable as follows:

(1) Burglary in the first degree: by imprisonment in the state prison for two, four, or six years.

(2) Burglary in the second degree: by imprisonment in the county jail not exceeding one year or in the state prison.

People who are found to have violated a criminal law—whether through their own admission by a "guilty" plea, or as a result of a jury trial—can be punished through imposition of fines, imprisonment, probation, and community service, among other penalties.

IV. The Criminal Law System: Players and Procedure

The criminal law "system" encompasses the entire criminal process itself—from investigation and arrest, to conviction and sentencing—and the people who play a role in that process: the accused, police officers, prosecuting attorneys, bail bondsmen, criminal defense attorneys, judges, witnesses, probation officers, and corrections officers.

At all stages of the criminal process, a person suspected of or charged with a crime is entitled to certain fundamental rights that derive from the U. S. Constitution and key court decisions. These include the right to an attorney and the right to a speedy jury trial. These constitutional rights provide a balance between the government's interest in ensuring that criminal behavior is identified and punished, and the fundamental need to preserve and promote the individual freedoms that characterize a democratic society.

V. What Makes a Case a Criminal Case?

There are two fundamentally different types of court cases—criminal and civil. A criminal case arises when the government seeks to punish an individual for an act that has been classified as a crime by Congress or a state legislature. A civil case, on the other hand, usually has to do with a dispute over the rights and duties that individuals and organizations legally owe to each other. Among the important differences between criminal and civil cases are these:

In a criminal case a prosecutor, not the crime victim, initiates and controls the case. The prosecutor may file criminal charges even if the victim doesn't approve, or refuse to file criminal charges despite the victim's desire that criminal charges be filed. This method of beginning the case contrasts with civil cases where the injured party is the one who starts the ball rolling—although if you view the prosecutor as a stand-in for the community injured by a crime, then there's not much difference.

A person convicted of a crime may pay a fine or be incarcerated or both. People who are held responsible in civil cases may have to pay money damages or give up property, but do not go to jail or prison.

In criminal cases, government-paid lawyers represent defendants who want but can't afford an attorney. Parties in civil cases, on the other hand, usually have to represent themselves or pay for their own lawyers. (Juvenile court cases and cases involving civil contempt of court where jail is a possibility are exceptions to this general rule.)

In criminal cases, the prosecutor has to prove a defendant's guilt "beyond a reasonable doubt." In a civil case, the plaintiff has to show only by a "preponderance of the evidence" (more than 50%) that the defendant is liable for damages.

Defendants in criminal cases are almost always entitled to a jury trial. A party to a civil action is entitled to a jury trial in some types of cases, but not in others.

Defendants in civil cases may be jailed for contempt, as happened to Susan McDougal in the Whitewater case.

Sometimes the same conduct may violate both criminal and civil laws. A defendant whose actions violate both criminal and civil rules may be criminally prosecuted by the state and civilly sued by a victim for monetary damages. For instance, in 1995 O. J. Simpson was prosecuted for murder and found not guilty. In an entirely separate case, Simpson was also sued civilly for "wrongful death" by the victims' families. At the close of the civil case, in 1997, Simpson was found "liable" for (the civil equivalent to guilty meaning "responsible" for) the victims' deaths and ordered to pay millions of dollars in damages.

VI. The Outcome: How Might a Criminal Case End?

The outcome of any criminal case depends upon the crime charged, the strength of the evidence, the legal validity of law enforcement and courtroom procedure, and the goals and strategy of the government and defense. When all is said and done, there may be no legal consequence for a person charged with a crime, because the charges are dismissed, or a full-fledged jury trial might result in a criminal conviction.

Chapter 1
Basics of Criminal Law

Some potential outcomes of a criminal case are:

A criminal investigation ends with no arrest.

An arrest occurs, but the case is dismissed because the police illegally seized the only evidence of crime.

A person is arrested and charged with a crime, then enters into a plea bargain with the government, agreeing to plead "guilty" in exchange for some form of leniency, such as a lighter sentence.

A person is brought to trial and found "not guilty," or acquitted, by a jury.

A person is convicted by a jury and sentenced to a long prison term.

Chapter 2

How Defendants' Mental States Affect Their Responsibility for a Crime

What a defendant intended to do can affect whether a crime has occurred.

What makes a crime a crime? In most cases, an act is a crime because the person committing it intended to do something that the state legislature or Congress has determined is wrong. This mental state is generally referred to as *mens rea*[①], Latin for "guilty mind."

The *mens rea* concept is based on a belief that people should be punished only when they have acted in a way that makes them morally blameworthy. In the legal system's eyes, people who intentionally engage in the behavior prohibited by a law are morally blameworthy.

Ⅰ. Careless Behavior

"Ordinary" carelessness is not a crime. For example, careless ("negligent") drivers are not usually criminally prosecuted if they cause an accident, though they may have to pay civil damages to those harmed by their negligence.

However, more-than-ordinary carelessness ("recklessness" or "criminal negligence") can amount to *mens rea*. In general, carelessness can be a crime when a person "recklessly disregards a substantial and unjustifiable risk." It's up to judges and juries to evaluate a person's conduct according to community standards and decide whether the carelessness is serious enough to demonstrate *mens rea*.

---

① 犯罪意图

Chapter 2
How Defendants' Mental States Affect Their Responsibility for a Crime

Ⅱ. Unintentional vs. Intentional Conduct

People who unintentionally engage in illegal conduct may be morally innocent; this is known as making a "mistake of fact." Someone who breaks the law because he or she honestly misperceives reality lacks *mens rea* and should not be charged with or convicted of a crime. For example, if Paul Smith hits Jonas Sack because he reasonably but mistakenly thought Sack was about to hit him, Smith would not have *mens rea*.

While a "mistake of fact" can **negate**[①] *mens rea*, a "mistake of law" usually can not. Even when people don't realize what they are doing is illegal, if they intentionally commit the act, they are almost always guilty. For example, if Jo sells cocaine believing that it is sugar, Jo has made a mistake of fact and lacks *mens rea*. However, if Jo sells cocaine in the honest but mistaken belief that it is legal to do so, Jo will have *mens rea* since she intentionally committed the act. Perhaps the best explanation for the difference is that if a "mistake of law" allowed people to escape punishment, the legal system would encourage people to remain ignorant of legal rules.

Ⅲ. Crimes Requiring "Knowing" Engagement in Criminal Conduct

Some laws punish only violators who "knowingly" engage in illegal conduct. What a person has to "know" to be guilty of a crime depends on the behavior that a law makes illegal. For example:

A drug law makes it illegal for a person to "knowingly" import an illegal drug into the United States. To convict a defendant of this crime, the prosecution would have to prove that a defendant knew that what he brought into the United States was an illegal drug.

Another drug law makes it illegal to furnish drug **paraphernalia**[②] with "knowledge" that it will be used to cultivate or ingest an illegal drug. To convict a defendant of this crime, the prosecution would have to prove that a

---

① 取消,否定
② 随身用品

defendant who sold or supplied drug paraphernalia knew about the improper purposes to which the paraphernalia would be put.

IV. Crimes Requiring "Malicious" or "Willful" Behavior

In everyday usage people often use the term "malicious" to mean "spiteful" or "wicked." In most criminal statutes, however, "malicious" is synonymous with "intentional" and "knowing." As a result, the term "maliciously" usually adds nothing to the general *mens rea* requirement.

As used in murder statutes, however, the term "malice" is often interpreted as meaning the defendant had a "man-endangering" state of mind when the act was committed, which is enough to justify at least a second degree murder charge.

As with "maliciously," the term "willfully" usually adds nothing to the general *mens rea* requirement. At times, however, the term "willfully" in a statute has been interpreted to require the government to prove not only that a person acted intentionally, but also that the person intended to break the law. (This is an unusual instance in which "ignorance of the law" actually is an excuse!) For example, in one case a federal law made it illegal to willfully bring in to the country more than $10,000 in cash without declaring it to customs officials. The U.S. Supreme Court decided that to convict a person of violating this law, the government had to prove that the person knew the law's requirements. (*Ratzlaf v. U.S.*, 510 U.S. 135 (1994))

RATZLAF ET UX. v. UNITED STATES
CERTIORARI TO THE UNITED STATES COURT OF
APPEALS FOR THE NINTH CIRCUIT

No. 92-1196. Argued November 1, 1993—Decided January 11, 1994

As here relevant, federal law requires a domestic bank involved in a cash transaction exceeding $10,000 to file a report with the Secretary of the Treasury, 31 U.S.C. §5313(a), 31 CFR §103.22(a); makes it illegal to "structure" a transaction—i.e., to break up a single transaction above the reporting threshold into two or more separate transactions—"for the purpose of evading the reporting requirement," 31 U.S.C. §5324(3); and sets out

Chapter 2
How Defendants' Mental States Affect Their Responsibility for a Crime

criminal penalties for "a person willfully violating" the antistructuring provision, §5322(a). Mter the judge at petitioner Waldemar Ratzlaf's trial on charges of violating §§5322(a) and 5324(3) instructed the jury that the Government had to prove both that the defendant knew of the §5313(a) reporting obligation and that he attempted to evade that obligation, but did not have to prove that he knew the structuring in which he engaged was unlawful, Ratzlaf was convicted, fined, and sentenced to prison. In affirming, the Court of Appeals upheld the trial court's construction of the legislation.

Held: To give effect to §5322(a)'s "willfulness" requirement, the Government must prove that the defendant acted with knowledge that the structuring he or she undertook was unlawful, not simply that the defendant's purpose was to circumvent a bank's reporting obligation. Section 5324 itself forbids structuring with a "purpose of evading the [§5313(a)] reporting requirements," and the lower courts erred in treating the "willfulness" requirement essentially as words of no consequence. Viewing §§5322(a) and 5324(3) in light of the complex of provisions in which they are embedded, it is significant that the omnibus "willfulness" requirement, when applied to other provisions in the same statutory subchapter, consistently has been read by the Courts of Appeals to require both knowledge of the reporting requirement *and* a specific intent to commit the crime or to disobey the law. The "willfulness" requirement must be construed the same way each time it is called into play. Because currency structuring is not inevitably nefarious, this Court is unpersuaded by the United States' argument that structuring is so obviously "evil" or inherently "bad" that the "willfulness" requirement is satisfied irrespective of the defendant's knowledge of the illegality of structuring. The interpretation adopted in this case does not dishonor the venerable principle that ignorance of the law generally is no.

V. "Specific Intent" Crimes

"Specific intent" laws require the government to do more than show that a defendant acted "knowingly." Specific intent laws require the government to prove that a defendant had a particular purpose in mind when engaging in illegal conduct.

For example, many theft laws require the government to prove that a defendant took property "with the intent to permanently deprive a person of the property." To convict a defendant of theft, the government has to prove that a thief's plan was to forever part a victim from his or her property. For example, a culprit who drives off in another's car without permission and returns it a few hours later might be convicted only of "joyriding." However, the same culprit who drives off in another's car without permission and takes it across the country probably demonstrates a specific intent to permanently deprive the owner of the car and would be guilty of the more serious crime of car theft.

VI. The Role of "Motive" in Criminal Law

"Motive" generally refers to the reason behind an illegal act. For example, a person's need to raise money quickly to pay off a bookie may be the motive for a robbery; revenge for a personal affront may be the motive for a physical attack. Prosecutors often offer motive evidence as circumstantial evidence that a defendant acted intentionally or knowingly. Judges and jurors are more likely to believe that a defendant had *mens rea* if they know that the defendant had a motive to commit an illegal act. By the same token, defendants may offer evidence showing that they had no motive to commit a crime and then argue that the lack of a motive demonstrates reasonable doubt of guilt.

VII. Crimes That Don't Require *Mens Rea*

Laws that don't require *mens rea*—that is, laws that punish people who may be morally innocent—are called "strict liability laws." The usual justification for a strict liability law is that the social benefits of stringent enforcement outweigh the harm of punishing a person who may be morally blameless. Examples of strict liability laws include:

(1) "Statutory rape" laws, which in some states make it illegal to have sexual intercourse with a minor, even if the defendant honestly and reasonably believed that the sexual partner was old enough to consent legally to sexual intercourse.

(2) "Sale of alcohol to minors" laws, which in many states punish store

Chapter 2
How Defendants' Mental States Affect Their Responsibility for a Crime

clerks who sell alcohol to minors even if the clerks reasonably believe that the minors are old enough to buy liquor.

Strict liability laws like these punish defendants who make honest mistakes and therefore may be morally innocent.

Chapter 3
Criminal Offenses

Criminal offenses are classified according to their seriousness. For crimes against property, the gravity of a crime is generally **commensurate**① with the value of the property taken or damaged: the greater the property value, the more serious the crime. For crimes against persons, the same proportionality principle applies to bodily injury inflicted upon individuals: the greater the injury, the more serious the crime. However, a host of other factors can influence the seriousness of a criminal offense. These factors include whether the defendant had a prior criminal record; whether the defendant committed the crime with cruelty, malice, intent, or in reckless disregard of another person's safety; and whether the victim was a member of a protected class (e.g., minors, minorities, senior citizens, the handicapped, etc.). Thus, a less serious crime can be made more serious by the presence of these additional factors, and a more serious crime can be made less serious by their absence.

Three categories of criminal offenses were known at common law: treason, felony, and misdemeanor, with treason being the most serious type of crime and misdemeanor being the least serious. The common law distinction between treason and felony was particularly important in England because a traitor's lands were forfeited to the Crown. Under a doctrine known as "corruption of the blood," the traitor also lost the right to inherit property from relatives, while the relatives lost the right to inherit from the traitor. U. S. law has never endorsed corruption of the blood as a criminal penalty, and so treason was

---

① 相等的,相称的,同量的

dropped as a separate classification of crime in the colonies.

Today every U. S. jurisdiction retains the distinction between felony level criminal offenses and misdemeanor level offenses. However, most jurisdictions have added a third-tier of criminal offense, typically called an infraction or a petty offense. Although the definitions of all three classes differ from one jurisdiction to the next, they do share some common characteristics.

Felonies, Misdemeanors and Infractions

At both the federal and state levels, crimes are classified into "felonies" and "misdemeanors." A "felony" is generally a crime that is punishable by more than one year in prison. A "misdemeanor" is a less serious crime that is punishable by less than a year in prison.

1. Felonies

Felonies are deemed the most serious class of offense throughout the United States. Many jurisdictions separate felonies into their own distinct classes so that a repeat offender convicted of committing a felony in a heinous fashion receives a more severe punishment than a first-time offender convicted of committing a felony in a comparatively less hateful, cruel, or injurious fashion. Depending on the circumstances surrounding the crime, felonies are generally punishable by a fine, imprisonment for more than a year, or both. At common law felonies were crimes that typically involved moral turpitude, or offenses that violated the moral standards of the community. Today many crimes classified as felonies are still considered offensive to the moral standards in most American communities. They include terrorism, treason, arson, murder, rape, robbery, burglary, and kidnapping, among others.

In many state penal codes a felony is defined not only by the length of incarceration but also by the place of incarceration. For example, crimes that are punishable by incarceration in a state prison are deemed felonies in a number of states, while crimes that are punishable only by incarceration in a local jail are deemed misdemeanors. For crimes that may be punishable by incarceration in either a local jail or a state prison, the crime will normally be classified according to where the defendant actually serves the sentence.

2. Misdemeanors

A misdemeanor, a criminal offense that is less serious than a felony and more serious than an infraction, is generally punishable by a fine or incarceration in a local jail, or both. Many jurisdictions separate misdemeanors into three classes: high or gross misdemeanors, ordinary misdemeanors, and petty misdemeanors. Petty misdemeanors usually contemplate a jail sentence of less than six months and a fine of $500 or less. The punishment prescribed for gross misdemeanors is greater than that prescribed for ordinary misdemeanors and less than that prescribed for felonies. Some states even define a gross misdemeanor as "any crime that is not a felony or a misdemeanor". Legislatures sometimes use such broad definitions to provide prosecutors and judges with flexibility in charging and sentencing for criminal conduct that calls for a punishment combining a fine normally assessed for a misdemeanor and an **incarceration**① period normally given for a felony.

3. Infractions

An infraction, sometimes called a petty offense, is the violation of an administrative regulation, an ordinance, a municipal code, and, in some jurisdictions, a state or local traffic rule. In many states an infraction is not considered a criminal offense and thus not punishable by incarceration. Instead, such jurisdictions treat infractions as civil offenses. Even in jurisdictions that treat infractions as criminal offenses, incarceration is not usually contemplated as punishment, and when it is, confinement is limited to serving time in a local jail. Like misdemeanors, infractions are often defined in very broad language. For example, one state provides that any offense that is defined "without either designation as a felony or a misdemeanor or specification of the class or penalty is a petty offense."

4. Difference Between a Felony and a Misdemeanor

Most states break their crimes into two major groups: felonies and misdemeanors. Whether a crime falls into one category or the other depends on the potential punishment. If a law provides for imprisonment for longer than a

---

① 监禁,禁闭

year, it is usually considered a felony. If the potential punishment is for a year or less, then the crime is considered a misdemeanor.

In some states, certain crimes are described on the books as "wobblers," which means that the prosecutor may charge the crime as either a misdemeanor (carrying less than a year's jail time as punishment) or a felony (carrying a year or more).

Behaviors punishable only by fine are usually not considered crimes at all, but infractions—for example, traffic tickets. But a legislature may on occasion punish behavior only by a fine and still provide that it is a misdemeanor—such as possession of less than an ounce of marijuana for personal use in California.

Chapter 4

Implications of a Crime's Classification

The category under which a crime is classified can make a difference in both substantive and procedural criminal law. Substantive criminal law defines the elements of many crimes in reference to whether they were committed in furtherance of a felony. Burglary, for example, requires proof that the defendant broke into another person's dwelling with the intent to commit a felony. If a defendant convinces a jury that he only had the intent to steal a misdemeanor's worth of property after breaking into the victim's home, the jury cannot return a conviction for burglary.

The substantive consequences for being convicted of a felony are also more far reaching than the consequences for other types of crimes. One convicted of a felony is disqualified from holding public office in many jurisdictions. Felons may also lose their right to vote or serve on a jury. In several states attorneys convicted of a felony lose their right to practice law. Misdemeanants with no felony record rarely face such serious consequences.

Criminal procedure sets forth different rules that govern courts, defendants, and law enforcement agents depending on the level of offense charged. The Fourth Amendment to the U. S. Constitution allows police officers to make warrantless arrests of suspected felons in public areas so long as the arresting officer possesses probable cause that the suspect committed the crime. Officers may make warrantless arrests of suspected misdemeanants only if the crime is committed in the officer's presence. Police officers do not have the authority to shoot an alleged misdemeanant while attempting to make an arrest, unless the shots are fired in self-defense. Officers generally have more

Chapter 4
Implications of a Crime's Classification

authority to use deadly force when effectuating the arrest of a felon.

Most criminal courts have limited jurisdiction over the kinds of cases they can hear. A court with jurisdiction over only misdemeanors has no power to try a defendant charged with a felony. Defendants may be charged by information (i.e., a formal written instrument setting forth the criminal accusations against a defendant) when they are accused of a misdemeanor, whereas many jurisdictions require that defendants be charged by a grand jury when they are accused of a felony.

Defendants charged with capital felony offenses (i.e., offenses for which the death penalty might be imposed as a sentence) are entitled to have their cases heard by a jury of twelve persons who must unanimously agree as to the issue of guilt before returning a conviction. Defendants charged with non-capital felonies and misdemeanors may have their cases heard by as few as six jurors who, depending on the jurisdiction and the size of the jury actually impaneled, may return a conviction on a less than unanimous vote. The right to trial by jury is generally not afforded to defendants charged only with infractions or petty offenses. Defendants charged with felonies or misdemeanors that actually result in confinement to a jail or prison are entitled to the advice and representation of a court appointed counsel. Defendants charged with infractions or misdemeanors that do not result in incarceration are not entitled to court appointed counsel.

Accused felons must generally be present during their trials, while accused misdemeanants may agree to waive their right to be present. The testimony of defendants and witnesses may be impeached on the ground of a former felony conviction. But a misdemeanor is not considered sufficiently serious to be grounds for impeachment in most jurisdictions. Because of all the additional procedural safeguards afforded to defendants charged with more serious criminal offenses, defendants must usually consent to any prosecution effort to downgrade a criminal offense to a lower level at which fewer safeguards are offered.

Part Two Introduction to American Laws · Criminal Law

Exercises

I. Choose the best answer to the following questions:

1. Attorney general is _____
   A. a federal prosecutor, also known as a "district attorney."
   B. a military attorney who represents the U.S. Armed Forces.
   C. a local prosecutor who exercises powers in criminal matters.
   D. On the federal level, the attorney who is the head of the U.S. Department of Justice, and on the state level, the attorney who represents the state in court proceedings and other legal matters.

2. Misdemeanor is _____
   A. a criminal offense that is less serious than a felony and more serious than an infraction.
   B. a petty offense.
   C. the most serious class of offense throughout the United States.
   D. In many states, it is not considered a criminal offense and thus not punishable by incarceration.

3. A lawyer was livid after he was unexpectedly laid off from his longtime job with a prestigious firm. The next day, he returned to the firm and fired shotgun rounds into the air. Unfortunately, one of the bullets ricocheted off the wall and killed the lawyer's former secretary. The lawyer later testified, without contradiction, that he had not intended to kill anyone, but simply sought to exact revenge on the firm's managing partner by scaring everyone so badly that they would leave work for the day, thereby causing the firm to miss a critical deadline in a case that the partner was working on.
   The crimes below are listed in descending order of seriousness. What is the most serious crime of which the lawyer may properly be convicted?
   A. Murder. B. Voluntary manslaughter.
   C. Involuntary manslaughter. D. Assault.

4. A boyfriend stole a diamond necklace and gave it to his girlfriend as a birthday present. At the time that the boyfriend gave the necklace to his girlfriend, she did not know that it was stolen. Three weeks later, while she and her boyfriend were passionately kissing, she whispered into his ear,

Chapter 4
Implications of a Crime's Classification

"Darling, I really love the diamond necklace you gave me. It must have cost you a fortune." The boyfriend responded, "Honey, the necklace didn't cost me a dime. I stole it." Startled by her boyfriend's confession, the girlfriend broke down and started crying. However, after regaining her composure, the girlfriend decided to keep the necklace.

Which, if any, of the following crimes is the girlfriend guilty of?

A. Receiving stolen property. B. Larceny.
C. Larceny by trick. D. No crime.

5. Late one evening, a teenage boy and his 15-year-old girlfriend were leaving a public library. As they walked through the dimly lit parking lot to get to their bikes, an adult man, who was visibly intoxicated, emerged from behind a parked car and ran up to them. The man knocked the boyfriend to the ground and hit him over the head with a wrench, causing the boyfriend to lose consciousness. The man then forced the girlfriend into his car. Moments later, the boyfriend regained consciousness, and the man fled the scene. The man was subsequently charged with assault with the intent to commit rape.

Which of the following would provide the man with his best defense?

A. The man thought that the girlfriend had consented.

B. The man did not intend to rape the girlfriend.

C. The man's intoxication at the time negated the required general intent.

D. It is impossible to prove that the man was the perpetrator, because the parking lot was dimly lit.

6. In which of the following situations is a defendant most likely guilty of the offense of false pretenses?

A. A defendant falsely tells a car salesman that he is interested in buying a new car and receives permission to drive it for a short trip. The defendant drives the car to another state and does not return it.

B. A defendant falsely represents to a victim that he is a friend of the victim's boss, that he is employed by a local company, and that he has just lost his wallet. The defendant obtains a loan of $100 from the victim and falsely promises to repay the loan the next day.

C. A defendant rents a motorcycle from a dealer for one day. Later that day, a stranger asks the defendant how much he will sell the motorcycle for. The defendant sells the motorcycle to the stranger for $1,000. The defendant then falsely informs the dealer that the motorcycle was stolen.

D. A defendant fills the gas tank to his car at a self-service station and drives off without paying.

7. A defendant was wearing a grey raincoat when he entered a restaurant for dinner. He placed his raincoat on a coat rack located in the foyer of the restaurant. After his meal, the defendant picked up a similar grey raincoat, believing it to be his own. The raincoat that he took, however, belonged to another patron. The defendant left the restaurant and had walked a short distance when he realized that he had taken the wrong raincoat by mistake.

He then returned to the restaurant and placed the other patron's raincoat back on the coat rack. He found his raincoat, which had been partially hidden under a stack of other coats. The defendant was later arrested and charged with larceny of the other patron's raincoat.

Which of the following would be the strongest argument for the defendant's acquittal?

A. There was a mistake of fact.

B. The defendant returned the raincoat after discovering his mistake.

C. The defendant lacked the requisite state of mind.

D. There was no fraudulent conversion.

8. An elderly man's house was frequently the target of vandalism by local teenagers. Tired of having to repair the damage they did to his home, the man decided to lie in wait for teenagers on the night before Halloween, when they often vandalized his home. True to form, teenagers in costume appeared and began spray-painting the man's house. Wanting to scare the teenagers, the man fired a shotgun over their heads. However, some of the shotgun pellets went through the top of a tall hat one of the teenagers, who was dressed as Abraham Lincoln was wearing, though the pellets did not harm him. The man was subsequently arrested.

What crime, if any, did the man commit?

A. Mayhem.

B. Battery.

Chapter 4
Implications of a Crime's Classification

C. Attempted murder, because a shotgun is an inherently dangerous weapon.

D. No crime.

9. After he was turned down for a promotion, a man decided to murder his boss. The man purchased a gun for this purpose and then invited his boss to his house for dinner. However, the day before the boss arrived at the man's house, the man changed his mind, and left the gun under his mattress. The man was subsequently charged with attempted murder.

    Should the man be convicted or acquitted?

    A. The man should be acquitted, because the boss was unaware of the man's motives.

    B. The man should be acquitted, because his actions were not sufficient to constitute an attempt.

    C. The man should be convicted, because a person is presumed to intend the natural and probable consequences of his acts.

    D. The man should be convicted, because he purchased the gun with the intent to kill his boss.

10. As a practical joke, a defendant took a small container, filled it with gas, and placed it in the wood-burning stove in the cabin owned by his neighbor. That evening, as the temperature dropped, the neighbor decided to light a fire in his wood-burning stove. The gas exploded, causing extensive injuries to the neighbor and a great deal of damage to his cabin. The defendant was subsequently arrested and charged with arson.

    Will the defendant be convicted?

    A. No, because the defendant never intended to hurt the neighbor.

    B. No, because the cabin was unoccupied when the neighbor entered it.

    C. Yes, because the defendant's conduct was reckless.

    D. Yes, because the defendant's conduct was negligent.

Ⅱ. **Consider the following factual situation and decide whether it should be covered by 18 U.S.C. §1001. (Please refer to the text in Chapter 1.) The names of all companies are fictitious.**

The Zimmer Company of New York imports clothing from countries around the world, including China, Indonesia, Japan, Korea, Malaysia and Thailand. For several years it has purchased shirts and other articles of clothing made by the Blue Cloud Clothing Company in China. Many of these articles fall under quota levels that limit the overall number of clothing articles that may be imported from that country.

Last month, the company learned that the annual quota levels for shirts from China were already filled and that company would not be able to export its products until the quota opened up again the next year. The Zimmer Company, however, needed the shirts to sell in its stores in New York.

To avoid the quota level, a manager at the Blue Cloud Clothing Company ordered the workers to put labels on each shirt saying that they were each a "Product of Panama" instead of China. The shirts were then put in boxes and sent by ship to New York, via the Panama Canal. The manager also created commercial invoices and other shipping documents to state that the shirts were in Panama.

Questions:

1. Is it lawful to import merchandise that is falsely labeled?

2. Under what circumstances would the manager face criminal prosecution in the United States? What would happen if he never visited the U.S.?

3. What must a manager at the Zimmer Company know about the merchandise and shipping documents in order to violate the statute? What is the "mental state" required by the criminal statute?

4. To be guilty under the statue, what would they have to do with the products or with the documents? What is the "act" required by the criminal statute?

5. If the manager at the Zimmer Company told the manager of the Blue Cloud Clothing Company to create the false labels, invoices, and shipping documents, could there also be a prosecution for crimal conspiracy?

6. If the attorney for the importer gives advice on how to circumvent the law, is it possible that the attorney might be criminally prosecuted as well?

Criminal Procedure

导 读 <<

美国宪法的前八条修正案,就其内容来看,仅适用于联邦政府,但事实上,联邦最高法院已经通过第14条修正案将其中的很多权利并入正当程序的要求,因而对各州都有了约束力。

在权利法案之中,迄今尚未对各州产生约束力的规定有两点,一是公诉权(right to indictment),一是保释金畸高的禁止(prohibition against excessive bail)。

一、非法证据排除规则(Exclusionary Rule)

非法证据排除规则,是指收集证据必须依法进行,违法所得的证据不得作为定案的依据。目的是防止政府侵犯个人的宪法权利。该规则的范围,包括"毒树之果"原则(Fruit of the Poisonous Tree)及其例外。

一般而言,不仅利用非法手段获取的证据应该排除,而且从非法证据产生的证据都应该排除。"毒树之果"原则可以广泛适用,但是近来法院开始以是否能够实现制止政府的非法行为目的为标准,限制该规则的适用范围。如果不能制止政府的非法行为,该原则不予适用。所以政府非法行为和证据之间若存在微弱联系,法院可能不会排除证据。

二、第四修正案(Fourth Amendment)

第四修正案规定,不得对个人进行不合理的搜查和拘捕扣押(seizure)。搜查指政府侵入个人可以合理期待享有隐私的区域。拘捕扣押指政府对人或物施行控制。第四次修正案规定的"合理"的含义,要根据具体情况确定。

警察以提起刑事指控或者讯问为目的,违背当事人意愿而将其关押,即为逮捕。逮捕必须有合理依据(probable cause)。警察在公共场所执行逮捕无需取得逮捕令。

三、认罪陈述(Confessions)

被告的认罪陈述或者自认有罪的供述是否可以采信,需要分析宪法修正案第四、五、六条和第十四条。第四条是对搜查与拘捕扣押的限制,第五条赋予被告不予自证其罪的权利,第六条赋予被告取得律师协助的权利,第十四条保护被告不予违背自己意愿做出供述。

四、审前程序

确定拘捕合理依据的预审(preliminary hearing)。根据宪法第四修正案,如果没有合理依据,就不能拘押被告,必须立即释放,因此被告有权利要求裁判理由的合理性。预审在逮捕之后、审判之前进行,以确定是否存在合理拘捕依据为目的,是非正式、以一方申请而进行(ex parte)的非对抗性(nonadversarial)程序。

审前拘押。该程序包括几个步骤:(1) 被告人第一次在治安法官(magistrate)前露面(first appearance);(2) 保释(bail);(3) 实施审前拘押。

迅速审判(speedy trial)。第六修正案规定的迅速审判权,是社会利益与被告权益的一个巧合。确定被告的迅速审判权是否被侵犯,需要根据具体情况进行评价。

参加庭审的能力(competence to stand trial)。如果庭审时被告精神状况不佳,他就不具备参加庭审的能力,等到重新获得能力后再行庭审。

五、庭审中的问题

被告享有基本的公平审判权(basic right to a fair trial)。这些权利包括公开审判权、审判不受干扰权(right to be free of trial disruption)、获取未受不正当影响的陪审团的权利、获取陪审团审判的权利、取得律师协助的权利、与证人质证的权利等。

控方承担证明责任(burden of proof),正当程序条款要求,认定被告有罪,必须达到排除合理怀疑(beyond reasonable doubt)的程度。

六、认罪答辩(Guilt Plea)和认罪协商(Plea Bargaining)

被告做出认罪答辩,就是对第六修正案的陪审团审理权的放弃。"认罪协商"是指检察官和辩护律师在法院开庭审判之前,对被告人的定罪和量刑问题进行协商和讨价还价,检察官通过减少指控罪名或者向法官提出减轻量刑的建议来换取被告人作有罪答辩的一种活动。被告一旦进入认罪协商程序,就有权持续进行。

七、其他权利

被告在宣判阶段(sentence)和接受刑罚(punishment)时还具有相应的宪法权利。但联邦宪法没有规定被告人的上诉权,最高法院的几个判决书(opinions)中曾表达过"从宪法角度看,可以废除所有的上诉"的观点。服刑人员在接受刑罚的阶段,即在缓刑(probation)、监禁(imprisonment)、假释期间,也同样具有相应权利。根据"一事不再理原则"(double jeopardy),被告不能因为同一案由而第二次受到起诉。

Chapter 1

Exclusionary Rule

The exclusionary rule is a judge-made doctrine that prohibits the introduction, at a criminal trial, of evidence obtained in violation of a defendant's Fourth, Fifth, or Sixth Amendment rights.

Ⅰ. In General

1. Rationale

The main purpose of the exclusionary rule is to deter the government (primarily the police) from violating a person's constitutional rights: If the government cannot use evidence obtained in violation of a person's rights, it will be less likely to act in contravention of those rights. The rule also serves as one remedy for deprivation of constitutional rights (other remedies include civil suits, injunctions, etc.).

2. Scope of the Rule

(1) Fruit of the Poisonous Tree

Generally, not only must illegally obtained evidence be excluded, but also all evidence is obtained or derived from exploitation of that evidence. The courts deem such evidence the tainted fruit of the poisonous trees. For example, D was arrested without probable cause and brought to the police station. The police read D his Miranda warnings three times and permitted D to see two friends. After being at the station for six hours, D confessed. The confession must be excluded because it is the direct result of the unlawful arrest—if D had not been arrested illegally, he would not have been in custody and would not have confessed.

(2) Exception—Breaking the Causal Chain

Under the fruit of the poisonous tree doctrine, the exclusionary rule can be very broadly applied. Recently, however, the Court has begun to narrow the scope of the rule by balancing its purpose (deterrence of government misconduct). The Court generally will not apply the rule when it will not likely deter government misconduct. Thus, if there is a weak link between the government misconduct and the evidence (i. e., it is not likely that the misconduct caused the evidence to be obtained), the Court will probably not exclude the evidence.

II. Limitations on the Rule

1. Inapplicable to Grand Juries

A grand jury witness may not refuse to answer questions on the ground that they are based on evidence obtained from an unlawful search and seizure, unless the evidence was obtained in violation of the federal wiretapping statute.

2. Inapplicable to Civil Proceedings

The exclusionary rule does not forbid one sovereign from using in civil proceedings evidence that was illegally seized by the agent of another sovereign. Moreover, the Supreme Court would probably allow the sovereign that illegally obtained evidence to use it in a civil proceeding. The exclusionary rule does apply, however, to a proceeding for forfeiture of an article used in violation of the criminal law, when forfeiture is clearly a penalty for the criminal offense.

3. Inapplicable to Internal Agency Rules, Parole Revocation Proceedings

The exclusionary rule applies only if there is a violation of the Constitution or federal law; it does not apply to a violation of only internal agency rules; the rule does not apply in parole revocation proceedings.

4. Miranda Violations

The Supreme Court as suggested that fruits derived from statements obtained in violation of Miranda might be admissible despite the exclusionary rule.

III. Harmless Error Test

A conviction will not necessarily be overturned merely because improperly obtained evidence was admitted at trial; the harmless error test applies, so a conviction can be upheld if the conviction would have resulted despite the improper evidence. On appeal, the government bears the burden of showing beyond a reasonable doubt that the admission was harmless. In a *habeas corpus* proceeding, if a petitioner claims a constitutional error, the petitioner must be released if the error has substantial and injurious effect or influence in determining the jury's verdict. If the judge is in "grave doubt" as the harm (e. g., where the record is evenly balanced as to harmlessness), the petition must be granted.

Chapter 2

Fourth Amendment

The Fourth Amendment provides that people should be free in their person from unreasonable searches and seizures.

A search can be defined as a governmental intrusion into an area where a person has a reasonable and justifiable expectation of privacy.

A seizure can be defined as the exercise of control by the government over a person or thing.

What is reasonable under the Fourth Amendment depends on the circumstances. For example, certain searches and seizures are considered to be reasonable only if the government has first obtained a warrant authorizing the action, while other searches and seizures are reasonable without a warrant. The material that follows specifically outlines the requirements for searches and seizures under the Fourth Amendment.

I. Arrests and Other Detentions

Governmental detentions of persons, including arrests, certainly constitute seizures of the person, so they must be reasonable depends on the scope of the seizure.

1. Arrest

An arrest occurs when the police take a person into custody against her will for purpose of criminal prosecution or interrogation.

(1) An arrest must be based on probable cause. Probable cause to arrest is present when at the time of arrest, the officer has within the knowledge reasonably trustworthy facts and circumstances sufficient to warrant a reasonable

prudent person to believe that the suspect has committed or is committing a crime.

(2) In contrast to the rule for searches, police generally need not obtain a warrant before arresting a person in a public place, even if they have time to get a warrant.

2. Other Detentions

(1) Investigatory Detentions (Stop and Frisk)

Police have the authority to briefly detain a person for investigative purpose even if they lack probable cause to arrest. To make such a stop, police must have a reasonable suspicion supported by articulable facts of criminal activity or involvement in a completed crime. If the police also have reasonable suspicion to believe that the detainee is armed and dangerous, they may also conduct a frisk (a limited search) to ensure that the detainee has no weapons.

(2) Automobile Stops

Stopping a car is a seizure for Fourth Amendment purpose. Thus, generally, police may not stop a car unless they have at least reasonable suspicion to believe that a law has been violated. However, in certain cases where special law enforcement needs are involved, the Court allows police to set up roadblocks to stop cars without individualized suspicion that the driver has violated some law. To be valid, it appears that such roadblocks must (i) stop cars on the basis of some neutral, articulable standard; and (ii) be designed to serve purpose closely related to a particular problem related to automobiles and their mobility.

(3) Detention to Obtain a Warrant

If the police have probable cause to believe that a suspect has hidden drugs in his house, they may, for a reasonable time, prohibit him from going into the house unaccompanied so that they can prevent him from destroying the drugs while they obtain a search warrant.

(4) Occupants of Premises Being Searched May Be Detained

Pursuant to the execution of a valid warrant to search for contraband, the police may detain occupants of the premises while a proper search is conducted.

(5) Station House Detention

Police officers must have full probable cause for arrest to bring a suspect to the station for questioning or for fingerprinting. The Supreme Court has suggested that under some limited circumstances it might be permissible to require a person to go to the police station for investigatory purposes without probable cause for arrest, but the Court has never found such circumstances exist.

3. Stop and Identify Statutes

A criminal statute requiring persons who loiter or wander on the streets to provide a "credible and reliable" identification when stopped by police is unconstitutionally vague for failure to clarify what will satisfy the identification requirement.

(1) Grand Jury Appearance

For all practical purposes, seizure of a person for a grand jury appearance is not within the Fourth Amendment's protection. Even if, in addition to testifying, the person is to be asked to give handwriting or voice exemplars, there is no need for the subpoena to be based on probable cause or even objective suspicion. In other words, a person compelled to appear cannot assert that it was unreasonable to compel the appearance. However, the Supreme Court has suggested that it is conceivable that such a subpoena could be unreasonable if it was extremely broad and sweeping or if it was being used for harassment purposes.

(2) Deadly Force

There is a Fourth Amendment "seizure" when a police officer uses deadly force to apprehend a suspect. An officer may not use deadly force unless the officer has probable cause to believe that the suspect poses a significant threat of death or serious physical injury to the officer or others. On the other hand, a mere attempt to arrest those results in the death of a suspect is not necessarily a seizure governed by the Forth Amendment. For example, the Court has held that there was no seizure where an officer in a car pursued two suspects riding a motorcycle at high speeds and ran over and killed one of the suspects who had fallen.

Chapter 2
Fourth Amendment

II. Evidentiary Search and Seizure

1. Searches Conducted Pursuant to a Warrant

To be reasonable under the Fourth Amendment, most searches must be pursuant to a warrant. The warrant requirement serves as a check against unfettered police discretion by requiring police to apply to a neutral magistrate for permission to conduct a search. A search conducted without a warrant will be invalid unless it is within one of the six categories of permissible warrantless searches.

2. Exceptions to Warrant Requirement

There are six exceptions to the warrant requirement; i. e., six circumstances where a warrantless search is reasonable and therefore is valid under the Fourth Amendment. To be valid, a warrantless search must meet all the requirements of at least one exception.

(1) Search Incident to a Lawful Arrest

The police may conduct a warrantless search incident to a lawful arrest.

a. Lawful Arrest Requirement

If an arrest is unlawful, then any search incident to that arrest is also unlawful.

b. Any Arrest Sufficient

The police may conduct a search incident to arrest whenever they arrest a person. Although the rationale for the search is to protect the arresting officer and to preserve evidence, the police need not actually fear for their safety or believe that they will find evidence of a crime as long as the suspect is placed under arrest.

c. Geographic Scope

Incident to a lawful arrest, the police may search the person and areas into which he might reach to obtain weapons or destroy evidence. The arrestee's wingspan follows him as he moves. Thus, the arrestee is allowed to enter his home; police may follow and search areas within the arrestee's wingspan in the home. The police may also make a protective sweep of the area beyond the defendant's wingspan if they believe accomplices may be present.

d. Contemporaneousness Requirement

A search incident to an arrest must be contemporaneous in time and place with the arrest.

e. Search Incident to Incarceration

The police may search an arrestee's personal belongings before incarcerating him after a valid arrest. Similarly, the police may search an entire vehicle—including closed containers within the vehicle—that has been impounded.

(2) "Automobile" Exception

If the police have probable cause to believe that a vehicle such as an automobile contains contraband or fruits, instrumentalities, or evidence of a crime, they may search the vehicle without a warrant. Automobiles and similar vehicles are mobile and so will not likely be available for search by the time an officer returns with a warrant. Moreover, the Supreme Court has declared that people have a lesser expectation of privacy in their vehicles than in their homes.

(3) Plain View

The police may make a warrantless seizure when they:

a. Are legitimately on the premises;

b. Discover evidence, fruits or instrumentalities of crime, or contraband;

c. See such evidence in plain view; and

d. Have probable cause to believe (i.e., it must be immediately apparent) that the item is evidence, contraband, or a fruit or instrumentality of crime.

(4) Consent

The police may conduct a valid warrantless search if they have a voluntary and intelligent consent to do so. Knowledge of the right to withhold consent, while a factor to be considered, is not a prerequisite to establishing a voluntary and intelligent consent.

a. Authority to Consent

Any person with an apparent equal right to use or occupy the property may consent to a search, and any evidence found may be used against the other owners or occupants. The search is valid even if it turns out that the person consenting to the search did not actually have such right, as long as the police reasonably believed that the person had authority to consent.

Chapter 2
Fourth Amendment

b. Scope of Search

The scope of the search is limited by the scope of the consent. However, consent extends to all areas to which a reasonable person under the circumstances would believe it extends.

(5) Stop and Frisk

A police officer may stop a person without probable cause for arrest if he has an articulable and reasonable suspicion of criminal activity. In such circumstances, if the officer also reasonably believes that the person may be armed and presently dangerous, he may conduct a protective frisk.

(6) Hot Pursuit, Evanescent Evidence, and Other Emergencies

a. No General Emergency Exception

The Supreme Court has made clear that there is no general "emergency" exception, as the need to check occupational safety violations, the need to investigate a fire after it has been extinguished and its cause determined, and the need to search a murder scene do not justify warrantless searches.

b. Hot Pursuit Exception

Police officers in hot pursuit of a fleeing felon may make a warrantless search and seizure. The scope of the search may be as broad as reasonably necessary to prevent the suspect from resisting or escaping. When the police have probable cause and attempt to make a warrantless arrest in a "public place," they may pursue the suspect into private dwellings.

c. Evanescent Evidence Exception

The police may seize without warrant evidence likely to disappear before a warrant can be obtained, such as a blood sample containing alcohol or fingernail scrapings.

d. Other Emergencies Where Warrant Not Required

Certain other emergencies, such as contaminated food or drugs, children in trouble, and burning fires are included.

Chapter 3

Confessions

The admissibility of a defendant's **confession**① or **incriminating**② admission involves analysis under the Fourth, Fifth, Sixth, and Fourteenth Amendments. We have already discussed Fourth Amendment search and seizure limitations. The Fifth Amendment gives defendants rights against testimonial self-incrimination. The Sixth Amendment gives defendants rights regarding the assistance of counsel. The Fourteenth Amendment protects against involuntary confessions.

Ⅰ. Fourteenth Amendment—Voluntariness

For confessions to be admissible, the Due Process Clause of the Fourteenth Amendment requires that they be voluntary. Voluntariness is assessed by looking at the totality of the circumstances, including the suspect's age, education, and mental and physical condition, along with the setting, duration, and manner of police interrogation.

Ⅱ. Sixth Amendment Right to Counsel Approach

The Sixth Amendment provides that in all criminal prosecutions, the defendant has a right to the assistance of counsel. The right protects defendants from having to face a complicated legal system without competent help. It applies at all critical stages of a criminal prosecution and is violated when the police obtain a confession from a defendant without first obtaining a waiver of

---

① 认罪,悔罪
② 牵连,归罪于

the defendant's right to have counsel present. Since Miranda, below, the Sixth Amendment right has been limited to cases where adversary judicial proceedings have begun.

III. Fifth Amendment Privilege Against Compelled Self-Incrimination-Miranda

The Fifth Amendment, applicable to the states through the Fourteenth Amendment, provides that no person "shall be compelled to be a witness against himself." This has been interpreted to mean that a person shall not be compelled to give self-incriminating testimony.

1. The Warnings

In *Miranda v. Arizona*, 384 U.S. 436 (1966), the Fifth Amendment privilege against compelled self-incrimination becomes the basis for ruling upon the admissibility of a confession. The Miranda warnings and a valid waiver are prerequisite to the admissibility of any statement made by the accused during custodial interrogation. A person in custody must, prior to interrogation, be clearly informed that:

(1) He has the right to remain silent;

(2) Anything he says can be used against him in court;

(3) He has the right to be presence of an attorney; and

(4) If he cannot afford an attorney, one will be appointed for him if so desires.

Miranda v. Arizona
384 U.S. 436 (1966)

On March 13, 1963, Phoenix, Arizona, police arrested Ernesto Miranda in a lineup. The police, without advising Miranda that he had the Constitutional right to remain silent and the right to have an attorney present during questioning, took him into an interrogation room. After two hours, the police obtained a signed confession from Miranda. He also signed a waiver stating that his confession had been made voluntarily, without threats or promises of immunity, and "within full knowledge of my legal rights, understanding any statement I make may be used against me."

At his trial, Miranda's confession and waiver of his Constitutional rights were admitted into evidence against him. Found guilty, Miranda was sentenced to 20 to 30 years' imprisonment. He appealed to the Arizona Supreme Court, which affirmed his conviction and sentence.

Miranda then appealed to the United States Supreme Court. His argument was based on the inadmissibility of his confession, stating that the police would not have obtained this self-incriminating evidence or a waiver of his Constitutional rights if he had been informed of his right to remain silent and/or he had been informed of his right to have an attorney present at his questioning.

Oral arguments were heard from February 28 to March 1, 1966, the 9-0 decision of the United States Supreme Court was announced by Chief Justice Earl Warren.

2. When Required

Anyone in police custody and accused of a crime, no matter how minor a crime, must be given Miranda warnings prior to interrogation by the police.

(1) Governmental Conduct

Miranda generally applies only to interrogation by the publicly paid police. It does not apply where interrogation is by an informant who the defendant does not know is working for the police. Rationale: The warnings are intended to offset the coercive nature of police-dominated interrogation, and if the defendant does not know that he is being interrogated by the police, there is no coercive atmosphere to offset.

(2) Custody Requirement

Whether a person is in custody depends on whether the person's freedom of action is denied in a significant way. The more a setting resembles a traditional arrest, the more likely the Court will consider it to be custody. If the detention is voluntary, it does not constitute custody. If the detention is long and is involuntary, it will likely to be held to constitute custody.

(3) Interrogation Requirement

"Interrogation" refers not only to express questioning, but also to any words or actions on the part of the police that the police should know that are reasonably likely to elicit an incriminating response from the suspect. However, Miranda does not apply to spontaneous statements which is not made in response to interrogation, although officers must give the warnings before any follow-up questioning. Neither does Miranda apply to routine booking questions, even when the booking process is being taped and may be used as evidence.

(4) Waiver

A suspect may waive his Miranda rights. To be valid, the government must show, by a preponderance of the evidence, that the waiver is knowing, voluntary, and intelligent. The Court will look to the totality of the circumstances. Note that the suspect need not be informed of all subjects of all subjects of an interrogation to effect a valid waiver.

(5) Limits on Miranda

Miranda suggested that every encounter between police and citizen was inherently coercive. Hence, interrogation would result in compelled testimony for the Fifth Amendment purpose. However, the Supreme Court has been narrowing the scope of Miranda's application.

(6) Inapplicable at Grand Jury Hearing

The Miranda requirements do not apply to a witness testifying before a grand jury, even if the witness is under the compulsion of a subpoena. Such a witness who has not been charged or indicted does not have the right to have counsel present during the questioning, but he may consult with an attorney outside the grand jury room. A witness who gives false testimony before a grand jury may be convicted of perjury even though he was not given the Miranda warnings.

(7) Public Safety Exception to Miranda

If police interrogation is reasonably prompted by concern for public safety, responses to the questions may be used in court, even though the accused is in custody and Miranda warnings are not given. The scope of this exception is unclear, but may be limited to the facts of the case in which the Supreme Court announced the new rule. In that case, the suspect was handcuffed, and then asked where he has hidden his gun. The arrest and questioning were virtually contemporaneous, and police were reasonably concerned that the gun might be found and cause injury to an innocent person.

Chapter 4

Pre-Trial Procedures

The Sixth Amendment to the U. S. Constitution guarantees criminal defendants the right to a speedy trial. Consequently, prosecutors cannot wait an inordinate amount of time before filing charges or proceeding with the prosecution after filing charges. To create more precise rules for ensuring a speedy trial, Congress passed the federal Speedy Trial Act, which requires that a trial begin within 70 days of the prosecutor filing the indictment.

The Sixth Amendment also guarantees the right to a public trial by an impartial jury of one's peers. The criminal justice system provides for an impartial jury by permitting both sides to utilize peremptory challenges during jury selection. If a party exercises a peremptory challenge against a prospective juror, then the court must excuse that particular juror from the panel. These challenges occur during jury voir dire to root out bias. Neither side must explain their reasons for a challenge; however, a party may not strike a jury purely because of the juror's race or gender. *Batson v. Kentucky*, 476 U. S. 79 (1986) (prohibiting race-based challenges); *J. E. B. v. Alabama*, 511 U. S. 127 (1994) (prohibiting gender-based challenges).

Due process requires that criminal defendants receive a fair trial. In high-publicity trials, trial judges have the responsibility to minimize effects of publicity, perhaps by implementing a gag-order on the parties and to eliminate outside influences during the trial. An interesting question of outside influence went to the U. S. Supreme Court in 2007 in *Carey v. Musladin*, 549 U. S. 70 (2006). After the victim's family wore pictures of the victim on buttons during the trial, the jury convicted Musladin of murder. The Supreme Court overturned the Ninth Circuit's grant of post-conviction habeas relief for a lack of due process because no clear federal rule existed regarding spectator conduct.

Due process further commands that defendants have the right to call their own witnesses, mount their own evidence, and present their own theory of the facts. In order to properly mount a defense, the prosecution must turn over all evidence that will be presented against the defendant and have pre-trial access to depose all of the prosecution's witnesses.

Pre-trial would also be the point at which the defense might raise a defense of double jeopardy, if such a defense existed in the particular case. The Fifth Amendment, through the Double Jeopardy Clause prohibits states from charging the same defendant with substantially the same crime on the same facts.

Ⅰ. Preliminary Hearing to Determine Probable Cause to Detain ("Gerstein Hearing")

A defendant has a Fourth Amendment right to be released from detention if there is no probable cause to hold him. Thus, a defendant has a right to a determination of probable cause. A preliminary hearing is a hearing held after arrest but before trial to determine whether probable cause for detention exists. The hearing is an informal, *ex parte*, nonadversarial proceeding.

1. When Right Applies

If probable cause has already been determined (e.g., the arrest is pursuant to a grand jury indictment or an arrest warrant), a preliminary hearing need not be held. If no probable cause determination has been made, a defendant has a right to a preliminary hearing to determine probable cause if "significant pretrial constraints on the defendant's liberty" exist. Thus, the right applies is the defendant is released only upon the posting of bail or if he is held in jail in lieu of bail. It does not apply if the defendant is released merely upon the condition that he appears for trial.

2. Timing

The hearing must be held within a reasonable time, and the Court has determined that 48 hours is presumptively reasonable.

3. Remedy

There is no real remedy for the defendant for the mere denial of this hearing, because an unlawful detention, without more, has no effect on the subsequent prosecution. However, if evidence is discovered as a result of the lawful detention, it will be suppressed under the exclusionary rule.

II. Pretrial Detention

1. Initial Appearance

Soon after the defendant is arrested, he must be brought before a magistrate who will advise him of his rights, set bail, and appoint counsel if necessary. For misdemeanors, this appearance will be trial.

2. Bail

Most state constitutions or statutes create a right to be released on appropriate bail (either on personal recognizance or on a cash bond).

3. Pretrial Detention Practices

Pretrial detention practices that are reasonably related to the interest of maintaining jail security, such as double-bunking, prohibiting inmates from receiving from the outside food and personal items or books not mailed directly from the publisher, routine inspections while the detainees remain outside their rooms, and body cavity searches following contact visits, do not violate due process or the Fourth Amendment and without more do not constitute punishment.

III. Speedy Trial

1. Societal Interest

The Sixth Amendment right to a speedy trial is an unusual one in that the interests of society and the defendant coincide.

2. Constitutional Standard

A determination of whether the defendant's right to a speedy trial has been violated will be made by an evaluation of the circumstances. The following factors should be considered:

(1) Length of the delay;

(2) Reason for the delay;

(3) Whether the defendant asserted his right; and

(4) Prejudice to the defendant.

3. Remedy—Dismissal

The remedy for a violation of the constitutional right to a speedy trial is dismissal with prejudice.

4. When Right Attaches

The right to a speedy trial does not attach until the defendant has been arrested or charged. It is very difficult to get relief for a pre-arrest delay under this standard, because the defendant must show prejudice from a delay, and good faith investigative delays do not violate due process.

A defendant is not entitled to speedy trial relief for the period between the dismissals of charges and later refiling. The only limitation on pre-arrest delay seems to be the statute of limitations for the particular crime.

IV. Competency to Stand Trial

1. Competency and Insanity Distinguished

Competency to stand trial must be carefully distinguished from the insanity defense, although both rest on a defendant's abnormality. Insanity is a defense to the criminal charge; a defendant acquitted by reason of insanity may not be retried and convicted, although she may be hospitalized under some circumstances. Incompetency to stand trial depends on a defendant's mental condition at the time of trial, unlike insanity, which turns upon a defendant's mental condition at the time of the crime. Incompetency is not a defense but rather a bar to trial. A defendant who is incompetent to stand trial cannot be tried. But if he later regains his competency, he can then be tried and—unless he has a defense—convicted. Note that a defendant who is competent to stand trial is competent to plead guilty.

2. Due Process Standard

Due process of law, as well as the state law of most jurisdictions, prohibits the trial of a defendant who is incompetent to stand trial. A defendant is incompetent to stand trial under the due process standard if, because of his present mental condition, he either:

(1) Lacks a rational as well as a factual understanding of the charges and proceedings; or

(2) Lacks sufficient present ability to consult with his lawyer with a reasonable degree of understanding.

3. Burden Can Be Placed on Defendant

A state can require a criminal defendant to prove that he is not competent to stand trial by a preponderance of the evidence; this does not violate due process. However, requiring a defendant to prove incompetence by clear and convincing evidence violates due process.

Chapter 5

Trial

Once a trial begins, the U. S. Constitution affords further rights to criminal defendants. Trying to avoid convicting an innocent defendant at all costs, the law only permits the prosecution to overcome the defendant's presumption of innocence if they can show the defendant's guilt beyond a reasonable doubt. This very high burden differs drastically from a civil trial's much lower standard in which the plaintiff must only prove a claim by a preponderance of the evidence.

One such right includes the right to cross-examine the prosecution's witnesses. Defendants derive this right from the Sixth Amendment's Right to Confront Clause. The U. S. Supreme Court took up the Right to Confront Clause in *Giles v. California* (07-6053) (2008). After domestic violence resulted in a woman's murder, the Supreme Court overturned a court's admission of a murder victim's statements under a theory of forfeiture by wrongdoing. The Court reached this holding because the Framers did not recognize the forfeiture exception to the Confrontation Clause at the time of the Constitution's founding.

The Sixth Amendment guarantees a defendant the right to assistance of counsel during trial. If a defendant cannot afford an attorney, the government is required to provide the defendant an attorney. Such defendants receive legal representation from the Public Defender's Office. The Federal Rules of Criminal Procedure provide that an accused shall have access to counsel at every stage of the proceedings, beginning with the defendant's initial appearance. If a defendant demands the presence of counsel during police interrogation, police must stop the interrogation until the defendant's counsel is present.

However, if a defendant voluntarily and intelligently chooses to waive assistance of counsel and self-represent, the defendant may do so. This is called "*pro se*[①]" representation. The legal counseling received must also constitute "effective counseling." Ineffective assistance of counsel may serve as grounds for a new trial. Establishing ineffective assistance of counsel requires establishing that the prevailing professional norms at the time of trial render the actual assistance received inadequate and that the ineffective assistance caused a fundamentally unfair result.

At all times during the trial, the defendant enjoys a right of not having to provide self-incriminating testimony. Thus, the defendant can choose not to take the stand, or the defendant can choose to take the stand but not answer certain questions that would self-incriminate. The Fifth Amendment of the U.S. Constitution provides this right.

I. Basic Right to a Fair Trial

1. Right to Public Trial

The Sixth and Fourteenth Amendments guarantee the right to a public trial. However, the extent of this right varies according to the stage of the proceeding involved.

(1) Preliminary Probable Cause Hearing

Preliminary hearings to determine whether there is probable cause on which to prosecute are presumptively open to the public and the press.

(2) Suppression Hearings

The Sixth Amendment right to a public trial extends to pretrial suppression hearings. Such hearings may not be closed to the public unless:

a. The party seeking closure shows an overriding interest likely to be prejudiced by a public hearing;

b. The closure is no broader than necessary to protect such an interest;

c. Reasonable alternatives to closure have been considered; and

d. Adequate findings to support closure are entered by the trial court.

---

① 代表自己

(3) Trial

The press and the public have a right under the First Amendment to attend the trial itself, even when the defense and prosecution agree to close it. A judge may not exclude the press and the public from a criminal trial without first finding that closure is necessary for a fair trial.

2. Right to Be Free of Trial Disruption

Due process is violated if the trial is conducted in a manner or atmosphere making it unlikely that the jury gave the evidence reasonable consideration. Televising and broadcasting parts of a trial, for example, may interfere with courtroom proceedings and influence the jury by emphasizing the notoriety of the trial to such an extent that it infringes the defendant's right to a fair trial.

3. Right to Have Jury Free from Unfair Influences

If the jury is exposed to influences favorable to the prosecution, due process is violated. For example, during X's trial, two sheriffs, who were also prosecution witness, were in constant and intimate association with the jurors, eating with them, running errands for them, etc. Did the trial violate due process standard? Yes, since this association must have influenced the juror's assessment of the assessment of the credibility of the witness.

II. Right to Trial by Jury

The Sixth Amendment right to trial by jury applies to all the states. The cases after Duncan (*Duncan v. Louisiana*, 391 U. S. 145 [1968]), while zealously guarding the jury trial right, have permitted the states great latitude in the details of jury use and conduct because of (i) the view that many of the details of the jury were historical accidents, (ii) the belief that the jury will act rationally, and (iii) the cost.

1. Right to Jury Trial Only for "Serious" Offenses

There is no constitutional right to jury trial for petty offense, but only for serious offenses. Also, there is no right to jury trial in juvenile delinquency proceedings.

What constitutes a serious offense?

For purpose of the right to jury trial, an offense is serious if imprisonment for more than six months is authorized. If imprisonment of less than six months is authorized, the offense is presumptively petty, and there is no right to a jury trial. The presumption may be overcomed by showing additional penalties, but a possibility of a $5,000 fine and five year's probation is not sufficient to overcome the presumption that the crime is petty.

2. Number and Unanimity of Jurors

(1) No Right to Jury of Twelve

There is no constitutional right to a jury of 12, but there must be at least six jurors to satisfy the right to jury trial under the Sixth and Fourteenth Amendments.

(2) No Absolute Right to Unanimity

There is no right to a unanimous verdict. The Supreme Court has upheld convictions based upon 11-1, 10-2, and 9-3 votes, but probably would not approve an 8-4 vote for conviction. Six-person juries must be unanimous.

3. Right to Venire Selected from Representative Cross-Section of Community

A defendant has a right to have the **venire**① from which the jury is selected from a representative cross-section of the community. A defendant can complain of an exclusion of a significant segment of the community from the venire, even if he is not a member of that excluded segment.

4. Right to Impartial Jury

(1) Right to Questioning on Racial Bias

A defendant is entitled to questioning on *voir dire* specifically directed to racial prejudice whenever race is inextricably bound up in the case. In noncapital cases, the mere fact that the victim is white and the defendant is black is not enough to permit such questioning. However, a capital defendant accused of an interracial crime is entitled to have prospective jurors informed of the victim's race and is entitled to *voir dire* questioning regarding the issue of racial prejudice.

(2) Juror Opposition to Death Penalty

In cases involving capital punishment, a state may not automatically

---

① 陪审员召集令,到庭

exclude from all prospective jurors who express a doubt or scruple about the death penalty.

(3) Juror Favoring Death Penalty

If a jury is to decide whether a defendant in a capital case is to be sentenced to death, the defendant must be allowed to ask potential jurors at *voir dire* if they would automatically give the death penalty upon a guilty verdict. A juror who answers affirmatively should be excluded for cause because such a juror has indicated the same type of inability to follow jury instructions as a juror who has indicated an inability to impose the death penalty under any circumstances.

(4) Use of Peremptory Challenge to Maintain Impartial Jury

Peremptory challenges are not constitutionally required. Therefore, if a trial court refuses to exclude a juror for cause whom the court should have excluded, and the defendant uses a peremptory challenge to remove the juror, there is no constitutional violation.

5. Inconsistent Verdicts

Inconsistent jury verdicts (e.g., finding defendant guilty of some counts but not guilty on related counts or one defendant guilty and a co-defendant innocent on the same evidence) are not reviewable. A challenge to an inconsistent verdict would be based upon pure speculation because it is impossible to tell on which decision the jury erred.

III. Right to Counsel

A defendant has a right to counsel under the Fifth and Sixth Amendments. The Fifth Amendment right applies at all custodial interrogations. The Sixth Amendment right applies at all critical stages of a prosecution after formal proceedings have begun. If the right to counsel is denied at trial, a conviction will automatically be reversed. For nontrial denials, the harmless error test is applied.

1. Waiver of Right to Counsel and Right to Defend Oneself

A defendant has the absolute right to represent himself at trial as long as his waiver of the right to counsel is knowing and intelligent. The court must carefully scrutinize the waiver to ensure that the defendant has a rational and factual understanding of the proceeding against him. However, the defendant has a rational and factual capable of representing himself—the defendant's ability to represent himself has no bearing on his competence to choose self-representation.

2. Indigence and Recoupment of Cost

If the defendant is indigent, the state will provide an attorney. Indigence involves the present financial inability to hire counsel, but none of the right to counsel cases defines indigence precisely. In any case, judges generally are reluctant to refuse to appoint counsel because of the risk of reversal should the defendant be determined indigent. The state generally provides counsel in close cases of indigence, but it may then seek reimbursement from those convicted defendants who later become able to pay.

3. Conflicts of Interest

Joint representation (i.e., a single attorney representing co-defendants) is not *per se* invalid. However, if an attorney advises the trial court of a resulting conflict of interest at or before trial, and the court refuses to appoint separate counsel, the defendant is entitled to automatic reversal. If the defendant does not object to joint representation in a timely manner, to obtain reversal the defendant must show that the attorney actively represented conflicting interests and thereby prejudiced the defendant.

4. Right Limited While Testifying

A defendant has a general right to consult with his attorney during the course of trial; however, he has no right to consult with his attorney while he is testifying. Whether a defendant has a right to consult with his attorney during breaks in his testimony depends on the character of the break. Generally, the longer the break, the more likely the Court will find the right.

IV. Right to Confront Witnesses

The Sixth Amendment grants to the defendant in a criminal prosecution the right to confront adverse witness. This right, held applicable to the states in *Pointer v. Texas*, 380 U.S. 400 (1965), seeks to ensure that:

(1) The fact finder and the defendant observe the demeanor of the

Chapter 5
Trial

testifying witness; and

(2) The defendant has the opportunity to cross-examine any witness testifying against him.

The defendant is entitled to a face-to-face encounter with the witness, but absence of face-to-face confrontation between the defendant and the accuser does not violate the Sixth Amendment when preventing such confrontation serves an important public purpose and the reliability of the witness's testimony is otherwise assured.

1. Introduction of Co-Defendant's Confession

A right of confrontation problem develops with the introduction of a co-defendant's confession because of the inability of the nonconfessing defendant to compel the confessing co-defendant to take the stand for cross-examination at their joint trial.

If two persons are tried together and one has given a confession that implicates the other, the right of confrontation prohibits the use of that statement, even with instructions to the jury consider it only as going to the guilt of the "confessing" defendant. A co-defendant's confession is inadmissible even when it interlocks with the defendant's own confession, which is admitted.

2. Use of Prior Judicial Proceeding Hearsay

"Hearsay" (evidence of a person's statements other than those made at the trial) may be admissible despite the Confrontation Clause. However, if the hearsay consists of statements made at a prior judicial proceeding, two facts must be shown before the hearsay statement will be admitted.

(1) The prosecution has made a good faith effort to obtain the in-court testimony of the witness and has failed; and

(2) The defendant has had an opportunity to cross-examine the person as to the testimony or has otherwise had an opportunity to test its accuracy.

V. Burden of Proof and Sufficiency of Evidence

1. Proof Beyond a Reasonable Doubt

The due process clause requires in all criminal cases that the state prove guilt beyond a reasonable doubt. The prosecution must have the burden of proving the elements of the crime charged. Thus, the Supreme Court has held that if "malice aforethought" is an element of murder, the state may not require the defendant to prove that he committed the homicide in the heat of passion, on the rationale that this would require the defendant to disprove the element of malice aforethought. However, a state may impose the burden of proof upon the defendant in regard to an affirmative defense such as insanity or self-defense.

2. Sufficiency of Evidence

The requirement of proof beyond a reasonable doubt in the Due Process Clause means that the sufficiency of the evidence supporting a criminal conviction in state court is, to some extent, a federal constitutional issue. Due process is violated, viewing all the evidence in the light most favorable to the prosecution, no rational judge or jury would have found the defendant guilty of the crime of which he was convicted.

Chapter 6

Guilty Pleas and Plea Bargaining

Ⅰ. Guilty Plea Waives Right to Jury Trial

A guilty plea is a waiver of the Sixth Amendment right to jury trial. Between 70% and 95% of all criminal cases are settled by guilty pleas.

Ⅱ. Basic Trends

1. Intelligent Choice among Alternatives

The court from 1970 to the present has indicated an unwillingness to disturb a guilty plea. It is viewed as an intelligent choice among the defendant's alternatives on the advice of counsel.

2. Contract View

There is a trend toward the contract view of plea negotiation and bargaining. In this view, the plea agreement should be revealed in the record of the taking of the plea and its terms enforced against both the prosecutor and the defendant.

Ⅲ. Taking the Plea

1. Advising the Defendant of the Charge, the Potential Penalty, and His Rights

The judge must advise the defendant personally (not the defense counsel), informing him:

(1) Of the nature of the charge to which the plea is offered;

(2) Of the maximum possible penalty and of any mandatory minimum,

but the failure to explain a special parole term is not fatal; and

(3) That he has a right not to plead guilty, and that if he does, he waives his right to trial.

2. Requirement of Adequate Record

Boykin v. Alabama, 395 U.S. 238 (1969), requires that a record be made of the taking of all guilty pleas. The record must show that the above information was explained to the defendant, indicating that the plea was voluntary and intelligent.

Boykin v. Alabama
395 U.S. 238

Syllabus

Petitioner, a 27-year-old Negro, who was represented by appointed counsel, pleaded guilty to five indictments for common law robbery. The judge asked no questions of petitioner concerning his plea, and petitioner did not address the court. Under Alabama law providing for a jury trial to fix punishment on a guilty plea, the prosecution presented eyewitness testimony and petitioner's counsel cursorily cross-examined. Petitioner did not testify; no character or background testimony was presented for him, and there was nothing to indicate that he had a prior criminal record. The jury found petitioner guilty and sentenced him to death on each indictment. The Alabama Supreme Court reviewed the sentences under the State's automatic appeal statute for capital cases, which requires the reviewing court to comb the record for prejudicial error even though not raised by counsel. Petitioner did not raise the question of the voluntariness of his guilty plea, and the State Supreme Court did not pass on that question, though a majority of the court explicitly considered it in affirming his sentences of death.

Held:

1. This Court has jurisdiction to review the question of the voluntary character of the plea, since the plain error of the trial judge's acceptance of petitioner's guilty plea absent an affirmative showing that the plea was intelligent and voluntary was before the state court under the Alabama automatic

appeal statute.

2. A waiver of the privilege against compulsory self-incrimination guaranteed by the Fifth Amendment and applicable to the States by the Fourteenth; of the right to trial by jury, and the right to confront one's accusers—all of which are involved when a guilty plea is entered in a state criminal trial—cannot be presumed from a silent record.

3. Acceptance of the petitioner's guilty plea under the circumstances of this case constituted reversible error because the record does not disclose that the petitioner voluntarily and understandingly entered his plea of guilty.

Reversed.

3. Remedy

The remedy for a failure to meet the standards for taking a plea is withdrawal of the plea and pleading anew.

4. Factual Basis for Plea Not Constitutionally Required

There is no general requirement that the record contains evidence of the defendant's guilt or other factual basis for the plea.

IV. Plea Bargaining

1. Enforcement of the Bargain

A defendant who enters into a plea bargain has a right to have that bargain kept. The plea bargain will be enforced against the prosecutor and the defendant, but not against the judge, who does not have to accept the plea.

2. Power of the State to Threaten More Serious Charge

Consistent with the contract theory of plea negotiation, the state has the power to drive a hard bargain. A guilty plea is not involuntary merely because it was entered in response to the prosecution's threat to charge the defendant with a more serious crime if he does not plead guilty.

3. Power to Charge More Serious Offense

The Supreme Court has held that there is no prosecutorial vindictiveness in charging a more serious offense when defendant demands a jury trial.

4. Admission of Statements Made in Connection with Plea Bargaining

Under the Federal Rules of Evidence and of Criminal Procedure, statements made by a defendant in the course of unsuccessful plea negotiations are inadmissible at trial. However, such statements can be admitted if the defendant has knowingly and voluntarily waived such statements can be admitted if the defendant has knowingly and voluntarily waived the Federal Rules' exclusionary provisions.

5. No Right to Impeachment or Affirmative Defense Evidence

Defendants are not entitled either to impeachment evidence or to evidence relevant to affirmative defenses prior to entering a plea agreement. Failure to provide such evidence does not make a plea involuntary.

Chapter 7

Constitutional Rights in Relation to Sentence and Punishment

Sentencing usually occurs immediately for infractions and misdemeanors. For such minor infractions, penalties may include probation; fines; short-term incarceration; long-term incarceration; suspended sentence, which only takes effect if the convict fails to meet certain conditions; payment of restitution to the victim; community service; or drug and alcohol rehabilitation.

More serious crimes result in the trier of fact hearing evidence and arguments from both the prosecution and the defense regarding the appropriate sentence. Some jurisdictions allow the judge, alone, to determine the sentence; others will have a separate sentencing phase trial, complete with a new jury, to determine the sentence for certain crimes.

During a sentencing trial, the prosecution presents evidence of aggravating factors, and the defense presents evidence of mitigating factors. The U. S. Supreme Court has interpreted the U. S. Constitution to protect the right to a jury sentencing trial for all defendants facing the death penalty.

Before the judge announces the sentence, a defendant is entitled to allocution. Allocution is the right of the defendant to directly address the judge without the help of counsel. During this direct address, the defendant may offer a personal explanation of any unknown facts, may ask for mercy, or may offer an apology for the criminal behavior. This opportunity for defendants to show remorse or to offer the motivations behind their criminal acts may influence whether the judge grants some leniency.

Ⅰ. Procedural Rights in Sentence

1. Right to Counsel
Sentencing is usually a "critical stage" of a criminal proceeding, thus requiring the assistance of counsel, as substantial rights of the defendant may be affected.

2. Right to Confrontation and Cross-examination
The usual sentence may be based on hearsay and uncross-examined reports.
(1) "New" Proceeding
Where a magnified sentence is based on a statute that requires new findings of fact to be made, those facts must be found in a context that grants the right to confrontation and cross-examination.
(2) Capital Sentencing Procedures
It is clear that a defendant in a death penalty case must have more opportunity for confrontation than need not be given a defendant in other sentencing proceedings.

Ⅱ. Resentencing after Successful Appeal and Reconviction

1. General-Record Must Show Reasons for Harsher Sentence
If a judge imposes a greater punishment than at the first trial after the defendant has successfully appealed and then is reconvicted, he must be set forth in the record the reasons for the harsher sentence based on "objective information concerning identifiable conduct on the part of the defendant occurring after the time of the original sentencing proceedings." (*North Carolina v. Pearce*, 395 U.S. 711 (1969)) The purpose of this requirement is to ensure that the defendant is not vindictively penalized for exercising his right to appeal.

2. Exceptions
(1) Reconviction upon Trial *de novo*
Some jurisdictions grant the defendant the right to a trial *de novo* as a matter of course after a trial in an inferior court. A trial *de novo* involves a fresh determination of guilt or innocence without reference to the lower conviction or fact of appeal.

Chapter 7
Constitutional Rights in Relation to Sentence and Punishment

(2) Jury Sentencing

Pearce does not apply to states that use jury sentencing, unless the second jury was told of the first jury's sentence.

III. Substantive Rights in Regard to Punishment

1. Criminal Penalties Constituting "Cruel and Unusual Punishment"

The Eighth Amendment prohibition against cruel and unusual punishment places several limitations upon criminal punishments.

(1) Punishment Grossly Disproportionate to Offense

A penalty that is grossly disproportionate to the seriousness of the offense committed is cruel and unusual.

(2) Proportionality—No Right to Comparison of Penalties in Similar Cases

The Eighth Amendment does not require state appellate courts to compare the death sentence imposed in a case under appeal with other penalties imposed in similar cases.

(3) Death Penalty

a. For Murder

The death penalty is not inherently cruel and unusual punishment, but the Eighth Amendment requires that it be imposed only under a statutory scheme that gives the judge or jury reasonable discretion, full information concerning defendants, and guidance in making the decision.

b. For Rape

The Eighth Amendment prohibits imposition of the death penalty for the crime of raping an adult woman, because the penalty is disproportionate to the offense.

c. For Felony Murder

The death penalty may not be imposed for felony murder where the defendant, as an accomplice, "did not take or attempt or intend to take life, or intend that lethal force be employed." However, the death penalty may be imposed on a felony murderer who neither killed nor intended to kill where he participated in a major way in a felony that resulted in murder, and acted with reckless indifference to the value of human life.

d. Jury Responsibility for Verdict

It is unconstitutional to diminish the jury's sense of responsibility of its role in determining a death sentence.

e. Racial Discrimination

Statistical evidence that black defendants who kill white victims are more likely to receive the death penalty does not establish that the penalty was imposed as a result of unconstitutional discrimination.

f. Sanity Requirement

The Eighth Amendment prohibits states from inflicting the death penalty upon a prisoner who is insane (i. e. , one who was sane at the time the crime was committed and was properly sentenced to death, but is insane at the time of execution).

g. Mental Retardation

It is cruel and unusual punishment to impose the death penalty on a person who is mentally retarded.

h. For Minors

It is not cruel and unusual to impose the death penalty on murderers who were 16 or older at the time they committed murder because there is no national consensus forbidding such executions. However, execution of murderers who were younger than 16 at the time of their crime might be forbidden.

2. Recidivist Statutes

A mandatory life sentence imposed pursuant to a recidivist statute does not constitute cruel and unusual punishment, even though the three felonies that formed the predicate for the sentence were nonviolent, property-related offense.

3. Punishing the Exercise of Constitutional Rights

A punishment of greater length or severity cannot constitutionally be reserved by statute for those who assert their right to plead innocent and to demand trial by jury. (*United States v. Jackson*, 390 U. S. 570 (1968)—death penalty available only for federal kidnapping defendants who insist on jury trial; penalty of death in such circumstances cannot be carried out, but guilty pleas induced by such a scheme are not automatically involuntary)

Chapter 8

Constitutional Problems on Appeal and Rights During Punishment

Ⅰ. No Right to Appeal

There is apparently no federal constitutional right to an appeal. Several Supreme Court opinions suggest that all appeals could constitutionally be abolished.

Ⅱ. Equal Protection and Right to Counsel on Appeal

1. First Appeal

If an avenue of post-conviction review is provided, conditions that make the review less accessible to the poor than to the rich violate equal protection.

(1) Right to Appointed Counsel

Indigents must be given counsel at state expense during a first appeal granted to all as a matter of right. Mere failure to request appointment of counsel does not constitute waiver of the right to assistance of counsel on appeal.

(2) Attorney May Withdraw If Appeal Is Frivolous

An appellate court can permit withdrawal of counsel who concludes that appeal would be frivolous. However, before doing so, the state must take steps to ensure that the defendant's right to counsel is not being denied.

2. Discretionary Appeals

In a jurisdiction using a two-tier system of appellate courts with discretionary review by the highest court, an indigent defendant need not be provided with counsel during the second, discretionary appeal. Representation also need not be provided for an indigent seeking to invoke the United States Supreme Court's discretionary authority to review criminal convictions.

III. No Right to Self-representation

On appeal, a defendant has no right to represent himself.

IV. Retroactivity

If the Court announces a new rule of criminal procedure in a case on direct review, the rule must be applied to all other cases on direct review. Rationale: It would be unfair to allow the one defendant whose case the Supreme Court happened to choose to hear to benefit from the new rule, while denying the benefit to other similarly situated defendants simply because they were not lucky enough to have their case chosen.

V. Right to Counsel at Parole and Probation Revocations

1. Probation Revocation Involving Resentencing

If revocation of probation also involves the imposition of a new sentence, the defendant is entitled to representation by counsel in all cases in which he is entitled to counsel at trial.

2. Other Situations

If, after probation revocation, an already imposed sentence of imprisonment springs into application, or the case involves parole revocation, the right to counsel is much more limited.

There is a right to be represented by counsel only if, on the facts of the case, such representation is necessary to a fair hearing. Generally, it will be necessary if the defendant denies commission of the acts alleged or asserts an argument as to why revocation should not occur that is "complex or otherwise difficult to develop or present." In addition, each defendant must be told of his right to request appointment of counsel, and if a request is refused, the record must contain a succinct statement of the basis or the refusal.

Chapter 8
Constitutional Problems on Appeal and Rights During Punishment

VI. Prisoner's Rights

1. Due Process Rights

Prison regulations and operations may create liberty interests protected by the Due Process Clause, but due process is violated only where the regulations and operations impose "atypical and significant hardship" in relation to the ordinary incidents of prison life.

2. No Fourth Amendment Protections in Search of Cells

Prisons have no reasonable expectation of privacy in their cells, or in personal property in their cells, and hence no Fourth Amendment protection therein. Additionally, prisoners have no right to be present when prison officials search their cells.

3. Right of Access to Courts

Prison inmates must have reasonable access to courts, and no unreasonable limitations may be put upon their ability to develop and present arguments. Inmates may not be prevented from consulting with other inmates, unless a reasonable substitute is provided. No absolute bar against law students and other paraprofessionals interviewing inmates for lawyers may be imposed.

4. First Amendment Rights

Prison officials need some discretion to limit prisoners' First Amendment activities in order to run a safe and secure prison. Therefore, prison regulations reasonably related to penological interests will be upheld even though they burden First Amendment rights. For example, prison officials have broad discretion to regulate incoming mail to prevent contraband and even sexually explicit materials from entering the prison.

5. Right to Adequate Medical Care

"Deliberate indifference to serious medical needs of prisoners" constitutes cruel and unusual punishment in violation of the Eighth Amendment. However, simple negligent failure to provide care—"medical malpractice"—does not violate the amendment.

Chapter 9

Double Jeopardy

The Double Jeopardy Clause in the Fifth Amendment to the US Constitution prohibits anyone from being prosecuted twice for substantially the same crime.

I. When Jeopardy Attaches

The Fifth Amendment right to be free of double jeopardy for the same offense has been incorporated into the Fourteenth Amendment. The general rule is that once jeopardy attaches, the defendant may not be retried for the same offense.

1. Jury Trials

Jeopardy attaches in a jury trial at the empanelling and swearing of the jury.

2. Bench Trials

In bench trials, jeopardy attaches when the first witness is sworn.

3. Juvenile Proceedings

The commencement of a juvenile proceeding bars a subsequent criminal trial for the same offense.

4. Not in Civil Proceedings

Jeopardy generally does not attach in civil proceedings other than juvenile proceedings.

II. Exceptions Permitting Retrial

1. Hung Jury
The state may retry a defendant whose first trial ends in a hung jury.

2. Mistrial for Manifest Necessity
A trial may be discontinued and the defendant reprosecuted for the same offense when there is a manifest necessity to abort the original trial or when the termination occurs at the behest of the defendant on any grounds not constituting an acquittal on the merits. Thus, double jeopardy does not bar two trials but only a retrial after a determination on the merits.

3. Retrial after Successful Appeal
The state may retry a defendant who has successfully appealed a conviction, unless the ground for the reversal was insufficient evidence to support the guilty verdict. On the other hand, retrial is permitted when reversal is based on the weight, rather than sufficiency, of the evidence, or where a case is reversed because of erroneously admitted evidence.

4. Breach of Plea Bargaining
When a defendant breaches a plea bargain agreement, his plea and sentence can be vacated and the original charges can be reinstated.

III. Same Offense

1. General Rule—When Two Crimes Do Not Constitute the Same Offense
Two crimes do not constitute the same offense if each crime requires proof of an additional element that the other crime does not require, even though some of the same facts may be necessary to prove both crimes.

2. Cumulative Punishments for Offenses Constituting the Same Crime
Imposition of cumulative punishments for two or more statutorily defined offenses, specifically intended by the legislature to carry separate punishments, even though constituting the "same" crime under the Blockburge test, supra, does not violate the prohibition of multiple punishments for the same offense of the Double Jeopardy Clause, when the punishments are imposed at a single trial.

3. Conspiracy and Substantive Offense

A prosecution for conspiracy is not barred merely because some of the alleged overt acts of that conspiracy have already been prosecuted.

4. Prior Act Evidence

The introduction of evidence of a substantive offense as prior act evidence is not equivalent to prosecution for that substantive offense, and therefore subsequent prosecution for that conduct is not barred.

5. Conduct Used as a Sentence Enhancer

The Double Jeopardy Clause is not violated when a person is indicted for a crime the conduct of which was already used to enhance the defendant's sentence for another crime.

6. Civil Actions

The Double Jeopardy Clause prohibits only repetitive criminal prosecutions. Thus, a state generally is free to bring a civil action against a defendant even if the defendant has already been criminally tried for the conduct out of which the civil action arises. Similarly, the government may bring a criminal action even though the defendant has already faced civil trial for the same conduct. However, if there is clear proof from the face of the statutory scheme that its purpose of effect is to impose a criminal penalty, the Double Jeopardy Clause applies.

IV. Separate Sovereigns

The constitutional prohibition against double jeopardy does not apply to trials by separate sovereigns. Thus, a person may be tried for the same conduct by both a state and the federal government or by two states, but not by a state and its municipalities.

V. Appeals by Prosecution

Even after jeopardy has attached, the prosecution may appeal any dismissal on the defendant's motion not constituting an acquittal on the merits. Also, the Double Jeopardy Clause does not bar appeals by the prosecution if a successful appeal would not require a retrial, such as when the trial judge granted a motion to set aside the jury verdict.

VI. Collateral Estoppel

The notion of collateral estoppel is embodied in the guarantee against double jeopardy. A defendant may not be tried or convicted of a crime if a prior prosecution by that sovereignty resulted in a factual determination inconsistent with one required for conviction.

Chapter 10

Forfeiture Actions

State and federal statute often provide for the **forfeiture**[①] of property such as automobile used in the commission of a crime. Actions for forfeiture are brought directly against the property and are generally regarded as quasi-criminal in nature. Certain constitutional rights may exist for those persons whose interest in the property would be lost by forfeiture.

Ⅰ. Right to Pre-seizure Notice and Hearing

The owner of personal property is not constitutionally entitled to notice and hearing before the property is seized for purpose of a forfeiture proceeding. A hearing is, however, required before final forfeiture of the property. Where real property is seized, notice and an opportunity to be heard are required before the seizure unless the government can prove that exigent circumstances justify immediate seizure.

Ⅱ. Forfeitures May Be Subject to Eighth Amendment

The Eighth Amendment provides that excessive fines shall not be imposed. The Supreme Court has held that this Excessive Fines Clause applies only to fines imposed as punishment, i.e., penal fines. The Clause does not apply to civil fines. Thus forfeitures that are penal are subject to the Clause, but forfeitures that are civil are not.

---

① （财产等）没收

Chapter 10
Forfeiture Actions

III. Protection for "Innocent Owner" Not Required

The Due Process Clause does not require forfeiture statute to provide an "innocent owner" defense, e.g., a defendant that the owner took all reasonable steps to avoid having the property used by another for illegal purposes, at least where the innocent owner voluntarily entrusted the property to the wrongdoer. *Bennis v. Michigan*, 517 U.S. 292 (1996)—due process not violated by forfeiture of wife's car that husband used while engaging in sexual acts with a prostitute even though wife did not know of use. In justifying its holding in Bennis, the Court also noted that the statute was not absolute, since the trial judge had discretion to prevent inequitable application of the statute.

Exercises

I. Choose the best answers to the following questions:

1. Public defender is _____
   A. a person who defends public morals and notions of morality.
   B. a defense attorney who advises the trial court judge on how to rule in a particular case.
   C. an attorney who will represent the interest of the *amicus curiae*, or "friend of the court."
   D. a court-appointed attorney who will represent indigent defendants in certain criminal matters.

2. White collar crime refers to _____
   A. a crime committed in a laundry.
   B. a crime committed by "blue collar" workers.
   C. any nonviolent crime or "victimless" crime.
   D. nonviolent crimes committed by business executives, bankers, accountants, and even some lawyers.

3. Miranda warning is _____
   A. a caution against wearing large hats made of fruit, once made popular by the Hollywood actress Carmen Miranda.
   B. the right to remain silent in class.

C. the warnings that custody prior to asking them questions about a crime.

D. the warnings that police officers must give to persons who want to confess voluntarily to crimes.

4. Plea bargain is _____

   A. a meeting of the criminal minds.

   B. use of federal sentencing guidelines.

   C. a reduced court filing fee for filling pleadings.

   D. a defendant's agreement to plead guilty in exchange for a reduced charge or other special treatment.

5. "I plead (or take) the Fifth" is _____

   A. a statement made by an attorney who refuses to disclose evidence of an impending criminal act.

   B. a statement made by a special prosecutor when asked by media to explain his actions.

   C. a refusal to answer a question because the answer may lead to evidence of a crime involving that person.

   D. a statement made to a bartender when ordering, for example, a fifth of vodka.

6. *Nolo contendere* is _____

   A. a plea of guilt to a criminal offense.

   B. a plea of innocence.

   C. a plea of neither guilt nor innocence, but only that the defendant does not wish to contest the criminal charges ("no contest").

   D. a plea entered when a criminal defendant cannot be located.

Questions 7—10 are based on the following fact situation:

Informant was known to be reliable. He had given information to Officer Joe on several occasions. Informant told Officer Joe that (1) he had talked to Suspect a few minutes before, and (2) there was a bulge in the pocket of her suit, which probably indicated that Suspect was carrying an illegally concealed weapon. Officer approached Suspect (who was seated in her parked car) and asked, "May I see some ID, please?" Suspect shrugged and began to reach toward her pocket, saying, "I'll show you my license." Officer grabbed Suspect's hand and held it. Officer then patted the outside of the pocket, felt

Chapter 10
Forfeiture Actions

what he reasonably concluded was a gun, reached into Suspect's pocket, and pulled out what was indeed a gun. Officer Joe then arrested Suspect. Suspect was prosecuted for concealing an illegal weapon (a misdemeanor).

7. If Suspect moves to suppress the gun, her motion will be _____
   A. granted, because the weapon was the product of an unlawful detention.
   B. granted, because Officer Joe had failed to obtain a warrant.
   C. denied, because there was a valid detention and frisk.
   D. denied, because Officer Joe had probable cause to believe Suspect was engaged in criminal activity.

8. Suspect was convicted of the misdemeanor, which is punishable by a maximum term of three months imprisonment. Prior to her trial, Suspect asked to be tried by a jury, but her request was denied. If Suspect appeals the conviction on this basis, the trial verdict will be _____
   A. affirmed, because there is no constitutional right to a jury trial in criminal cases.
   B. affirmed, because the right to a jury trial exists only when the offense is punishable by a prison term of at least six months.
   C. reversed, because there is a right to a jury trial in all criminal case.
   D. reversed, because there is a right to a jury trial whenever a criminal defendant affirmatively requests it.

9. Assume Suspect had requested that an attorney be appointed for her, but one was not. Suspect appeals upon the ground that she was denied the right to counsel. Her appeal is based on an assumption that is _____
   A. correct, because there is a right to counsel in all criminal cases.
   B. correct, because Suspect's crime was punishable by imprisonment.
   C. correct, if Suspect was actually imprisoned.
   D. incorrect, because there is no right to counsel for crimes punishable by imprisonment of six months or less.

10. For purposes of the question only, assume that (1) Suspect was sentenced to three months imprisonment, but was immediately paroled; and (2) she filed a writ of habeas corpus with the appropriate U. S. district court, contending that the failure to appoint counsel for her constituted a Sixth Amendment violation. Suspect's appeal should be _____

A. denied, if she has not exhausted all of her state court remedies.

B. denied, because one must be in custody to assert habeas corpus.

C. denied, because there is no right to petition for habeas corpus from a state court to a federal court.

D. granted, because there is a constitutional right of habeas corpus review by a federal court with respect to all state court criminal cases.

II. Essay Questions:

QUESTION 1

State Officer Abby, an undercover agent, told her superior, Officer Sue, that Deer, a suspected dealer in stolen property, had (three hours earlier) shown Abby 12 stolen U.S. Army pistols that were stored in Deer's car trunk. Sue immediately prepared an arrest warrant affidavit alleging that "a reliable informant has reported that Deer possesses stolen property." The affidavit was presented to a magistrate, who then issued an arrest warrant. After the warrant was issued, a police bulletin was issued for Deer's arrest.

One hour later, Sue observed Deer on the public walkway outside Deer's home, watering his front lawn with a garden hose. After Sue informed Deer of the outstanding warrant, she arrested Deer, searched him, and found one of the stolen pistols in a pocket of Deer's jacket.

Concurrently with the arrest, Sue read Deer his *Miranda* warnings and then demanded that Deer reveal the location of the remaining weapons. Deer refused to say anything until he spoke with an attorney. Sue then told Deer that Deer was subject to both federal and state prosecutions, but that only the state charge would be prosecuted if he "talked immediately." In response, Deer told Sue that the other 11 pistols were in the trunk of his car parked across the street.

Sue had the car towed to a police parking lot, where the trunk was pried open and the remaining 11 pistols removed. A thorough search of the trunk also turned up a notebook, which listed the serial numbers of all the pistols, including the one Sue had taken from Deer's pocket.

Deer has been charged with receiving stolen property. He has made a motion to exclude from evidence, on federal constitutional grounds, the 12 pistols, Deer's statement to sue, and the notebook. What results on Deer's motion to exclude? Discuss.

Chapter 10
Forfeiture Actions

QUESTION 2

Dunn, a 25-year-old adult, worked as a computer programmer at Arcon Enterprises. Dunn had been seeing Sally, who was a 17-year-old minor.

Buck was jealous of Dunn. He wanted to win Sally's affections, but realized he could never do so with Dunn around. Buck knew that Sally was only 17. He decided that the best way to get rid of Dunn was to get him prosecuted for violation of a state law that provides that any adult who has sex with a person under the age of 18 has committed statutory rape. Buck began to follow Dunn and Sally around on their dates. Buck noted that on two occasions, Dunn and Sally entered Dunn's apartment at about 11:00 P.M. and did not come out until 10:00 the next morning. Buck reported his observations to the police, suggesting that they prosecute Dunn for statutory rape.

The next evening, the police began a surveillance of Dunn's apartment. Watching with the aid of high-powered binoculars from a nearby apartment building, they saw Dunn and Sally kissing. Dunn suddenly picked Sally up and carried her into what was presumably his bedroom.

The next day, after Dunn left his office to have lunch, the police were given permission by his employer to search his work area. The officers found a letter (which apparently Dunn had decided not to send) in a trash can that Dunn shared with another employee. The letter was addressed to Sally. It said that he hoped they would have "another hot night next weekend."

The next morning, the police arrested Dunn on the street as he was getting into his car to drive to work. The charge was statutory rape; the police had no arrest warrant. The arresting officers searched the vehicle and found two marijuana cigarettes under the front seat. A charge of possession of an illegal substance was then added to the charge of statutory rape.

What arguments can Dunn make to suppress the marijuana cigarettes, and what arguments is the prosecution likely to make in rebuttal?

References

1. Abedin Jamal, *An Introduction to Legal English*, 2007.

2. Barbara J. Beveridge, *Legal English—How It Development Open and Why It Is Not Appropriate for International Commercial Contracts*.

3. Debra S. Lee, Charles Hall and Marshal Hurley, *American Legal English* (University of Michigan Press 1999).

4. John C. Dernbach, Richard V. Singleton II, Cathleen S. Wharton, Joan M. Ruhtenberg, *Legal Writing & Legal Method* (2nd ed., Fred B. Rothman Publications 2000).

5. Mark E. Wojcik, *Introduction to Legal English* (2nd ed., International Law Institute 2001).

6. Nancy L. Schultz, *Legal Writing and Other Lawyering Skills* (3rd ed., Matthew Bender & Co. 1998).

7. Richard C. Wydick, *Plain English for Lawyers* (4th ed., Carolina Academic Press 1998).

8. Teresa K. Brostoff and Ann Sinsheimer, *Legal English: An Introduction to the Legal Language and Culture of the United States* (Oceana Publication, Inc., 2000).

9. 张法连. 英美法律术语辞典[Z]. 上海：上海外语教育出版社，2014。

10. 中国政法大学法律英语教学与测试研究中心课题组. 法律英语专业教学大纲[M]. 北京：高等教育出版社，2013。

11. 中国政法大学法律英语教学与测试研究中心. 法律英语综合教程[Z]. 北京：中国法制出版社，2013。